Issues and the Beast
Animals and Beasts
With Psyche Disorders,
Oh My
By Herman Franck, Esq.

Kit Media Co.
1801 7th Street, Suite 150
Sacramento, CA 95811
Tel: (916) 256-6266
Fax: (916) 447-8400
franckherman@hotmail.com

A Kit Media Co. Production

KIT MEDIA CO.

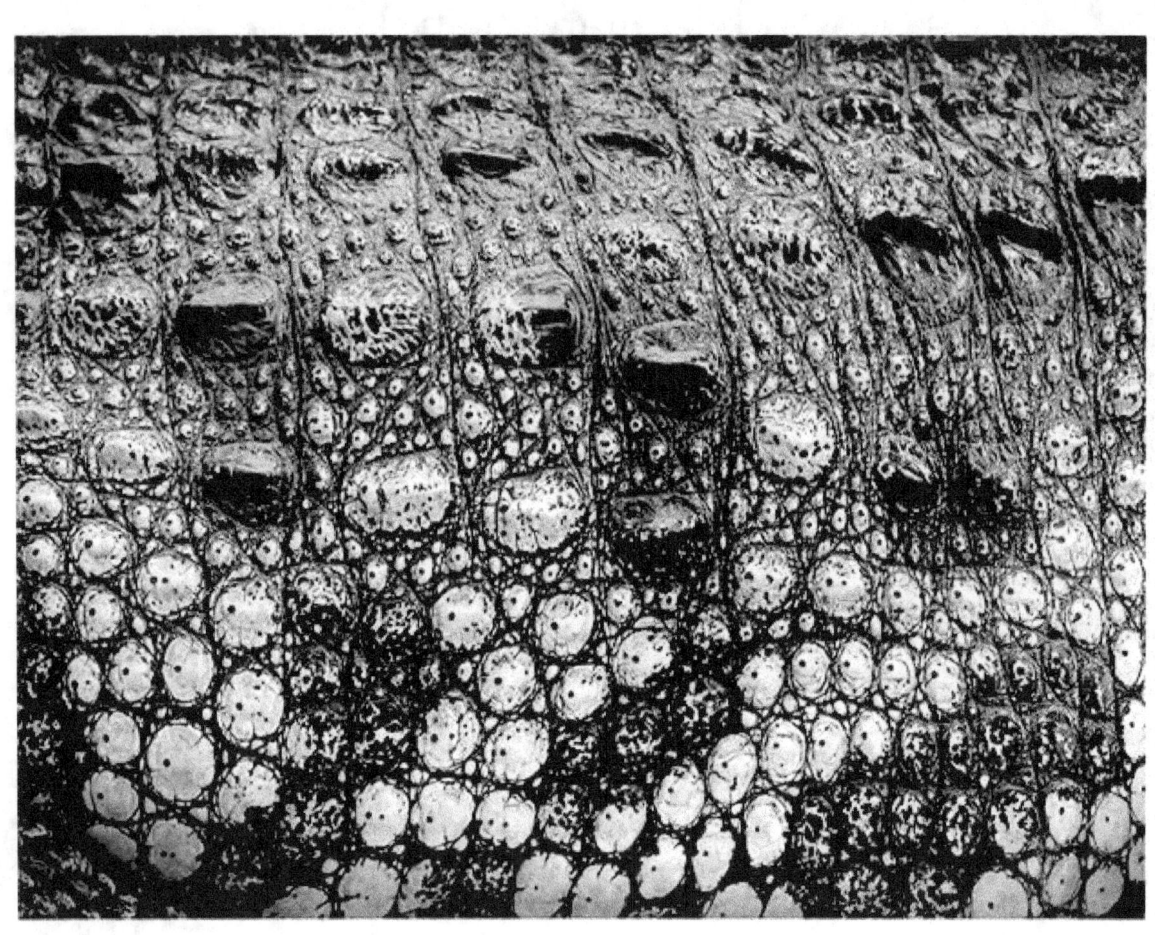

DISCLAIMER

The stories in this book are fictional. No likeness of any actual human, whale, cat, pig, ant, dog, eagle, sloth, fish, elephant or wild jungle woman is intended.

The following is from the introduction to Prof. Darwin's masterpiece, Darwin, Charles (1859) On the Origin of Species by Means of Natural Selection, or the Preservation of Favoured Races in the Struggle for Life (1st ed.). London: John Murray. ISBN 1-4353-9386-4 [page 5]

As many more individuals of each species are born than can possibly survive; and as, consequently, there is a frequently recurring struggle for existence, it follows that any being, if it vary however slightly in any manner profitable to itself, under the complex and sometimes varying conditions of life, will have a better chance of surviving, and thus be naturally selected. From the strong principle of inheritance, any selected variety will tend to propagate its new and modified form.

Charles Darwin.

DEDICATION

This book is dedicated to my sons, Adam D. Franck and Alex Q. Franck.

FURTHER DISCLAIMER AND DESCRIPTION OF APPENDICES

The author is not a medical doctor, nor a doctor of veterinarian medicine, and has had no formal training in medical science, psychology, or psychotherapy. The author's formal training was in law and economics [Juris Doctor (Georgetown), Master of Arts, Economics (Georgetown) and Bachelor of Arts (*honors*) Political Economy (Berkeley)].

The author does not intend this book to constitute any kind of medical advice, diagnosis or treatment. If you, or anyone you know, or any animal, bird, fish or insect you know is believed to suffer from any psychological disorder, please consult with an appropriate licensed medical professional to obtain any appropriate diagnosis or treatment.

ABOUT THE AUTHOR
Herman Franck, Esq.

Herman Franck, Esq. is an attorney-at-law, and practices in the field of civil trials and appeals. He is the owner of Franck and Associates, Attorneys at Law, Sacramento, California. He is a member of the State Bar of California [SBN 123476]. He has been admitted to practice before all the courts of the state of California, and is admitted to practice before the United States Supreme Court. He was previously licensed as a foreign attorney [1993] in Ukraine.

Mr. Franck received his Juris Doctor from Georgetown University Law Center [1985]. He received a Master of Arts in Economics from Georgetown University [1985]. His master's thesis was in the field of Anti-Trust Economics. He received a Bachelor of Arts [*honors*] from UC Berkeley [1981].

Mr. Franck grew up on a ranch in Scottsdale, Arizona, where he took care of animals, birds, reptiles and insects, and learned about their behavior. His step father held a Doctor degree in special education, and started a school for children with learning disabilities. His step father's interest in psychology and animals was something Mr. Franck grew up with on the ranch. Mr. Franck put two and two together to form the ideas behind *Issues and The Beast*.

Mr. Franck is an author of 25 books and 15 screenplays. Many of Mr. Franck's works are in the genre of action adventure and international crime stories. He has written a series of children's books as well.

More recently, he has endeavored into relationship books, including *Relationship Agreement* (I Universe 2003); *How to Marry and Keep a Supermodel, Lessons from a Midlife Crisis* [Createspace 2010]; *Ultimate Revenge Involuntary Transsexual* (Trafford 2011) and *East West Marriage* [Createspace 2012]. These books have brought him into the self-study of psychology. East West Marriage has been developed in a TV series.

Mr. Franck has his own publishing and media company, Kit Media Co, Sacramento, California. Kit Media develops and promotes his books, script projects, radio shows, and television programs.

Winnie and Thunderose

An autistic pony helps a special girl.

A story about friendship regained.

Based on the Illustrated book "Winnie and Thunderose"

by Herman Franck Kit Media.Co. Illustrations by Maria Byerley.

Producers: Herman Franck, Kit Media Co.; Ryan Litzinger, Hollywood Arts Society.

Screenplay by Herman Franck, Esq.

DESIDERATA BY MAX EHRMANN, 1920

Go placidly amid the noise and haste,
and remember what peace there may be in silence.

As far as possible without surrender
be on good terms with all persons.
Speak your truth quietly and clearly;
and listen to others,
even the dull and the ignorant;
they too have their story.
Avoid loud and aggressive persons,
they are vexations to the spirit.

If you compare yourself with others,
you may become vain or bitter;
for always there will be greater and lesser persons than yourself.

Enjoy your achievements as well as your plans.
Keep interested in your own career, however humble;
it is a real possession in the changing fortunes of time.
Exercise caution in your business affairs;
for the world is full of trickery.
But let this not blind you to what virtue there is;
many persons strive for high ideals;
and everywhere life is full of heroism.

Be yourself.
Especially, do not feign affection.
Neither be cynical about love;
for in the face of all aridity and disenchantment
it is as perennial as the grass.

9

Take kindly the counsel of the years,

gracefully surrendering the things of youth.

Nurture strength of spirit to shield you in sudden misfortune.

But do not distress yourself with dark imaginings.

Many fears are born of fatigue and loneliness.

Beyond a wholesome discipline,

be gentle with yourself.

You are a child of the universe,

no less than the trees and the stars;

you have a right to be here.

And whether or not it is clear to you,

no doubt the universe is unfolding as it should.

Therefore be at peace with God,

whatever you conceive Him to be,

and whatever your labors and aspirations,

in the noisy confusion of life keep peace with your soul.

With all its sham, drudgery, and broken dreams,

it is still a beautiful world.

Be cheerful.

Strive to be happy.

Acknowledgements

I thank and acknowledge the following people who helped me in the creation of this book:

Dr. John H. Hoopingarner, aka Standing Bear. My stepfather and a psychotherapist that built our family a small ranch with many animals. This is where I grew up, and where I found the seeds for this story. Thank you for that.

Michael Whelan provided excellent editing and proofreading services. Thank you for that.

Victoria M. McGlaughlin, Esq. provided excellent proofreading services. Thank you for that, counselor.

Maria Byerley provided graphics arts and cover design for the front and back covers, and for the series of black and white interior images. Thank you for that.

American Psychiatric Association, Arlington Virginia, published the Diagnostic and Statistical Manual of Mental Disorders Text Revision (4th Ed. 2000), excerpts of which are set forth in the accompanying appendices (used with permission). Thank you for letting me use these descriptions of the disorders explored in this book.

Smithsonian Institution, Washington, D.C., produced *Animal, The Definitive Visual Guide to the World's Wildlife*. (David Burnie & Don E. Wilson, Editors in Chief) (DK Publishing 2005). This wonderful book gave me all I needed to explore which animals to give what disorders to.

OTHER WORKS BY HERMAN FRANCK

Herman Franck is the author of the following other books, comic books, screenplays, radio shows, and TV shows:

Books

East West Marriage [Createspace 2011]. How an Asian woman can catch a USA man; how a USA man can catch an Asian woman. Oh my.

How to Marry and Keep a Supermodel, Lessons From a Mid Wife Crisis.(Create Space 2010) See www.midwife-crisis.com for more information.

Ultimate Revenge Involuntary Transsexual [Trafford 2011]. What he did to her was unforgivable; what they did to him/her was even worse.

Winnie & Thunderose, A Story About Friendship [Trafford 2011]. Illustrated book, story art by Maria Byerley. A special friendship between a pony and racehorse splits apart and almost find their way back.

Katie Cranberry [XLibris 2008]. Novel. Traveling fruit characters attend Katie's world university of diplomacy. Bow and Arrow recommended. Book I: Katie's Silk Road Adventure; Book II, Katie's Preview in South America; Book III, American Stonehenge

Katie Cranberry IV: Katie's North American Peace Adventure. [BookSurge 2009] Katie Cranberry and her entourage of worldly friends set out on a mission to eliminate the white man's annihilation of the Native Americans.

Supernatural CSI. Illustrated Novel, Dead People Make Excellent Witnesses. (Booksurge 2009) Trips to the otherworld reveal evidence of crimes here on earth.

Ice Dragon. [XLibris 2007] Book I. Battle of the Longheads. [Google longhead and see what you find] Kit Media produced a completed 32-page English/Spanish language color comic book based on Episode I of the book. Comic artwork, layout, lettering by Atlantis Studios, Atlanta, GA. Online comic: www.icedragon.biz

Ice Dragon [XLibris 2008] Books II and III: The Case of the Stolen Cartoons; The Case of the Missing Toys. Vincent and Ice Dragon solve the most important crimes in the history of the world.

Star Boy. [XLibris 2007] Novella. Kit Media produced a 32-page Spanish/English color comic of the first third of this novella. An ET visited earth and left a little hybrid boy for somebody to take care of. Artwork, layout, lettering of the color comic by Atlantis Studios, Atlanta, GA. [Starboy's song: I know it's true, I'm part ET, but please, don't hate me.]

Juan Bonderello Quatro Cinco Seis. Novella Book I: The Case of the Stupid Food. [XLibris 2007] Juan Bonderello is the perfect peoples' spy to save the United States from its first bout with agro terrorism.

Second Life [XLibris 2006]. Novella. Success and failure are, but two sides of the same page. A failed alcoholic doctor's soul is transferred into the body of a totally successful doctor.

Cheetah Kids [XLibris 2007]. Novel. Two infants are raised by a family of Cheetahs, and become the fastest humans on earth. A Dubai sheik with a heart of gold, as in Olympic Gold, shows them the path to glory. In the process, they find the tragedy that left them without parents. How fast can you spell revenge? See www.cheetahkids.com for more information.

The Post Debutante [iuniverse 2001] Novel. An innocent deb gets on the wrong side of a murder case. In the process, she becomes an expert on injustice and disloyalty, even among family.

The Politician [Kiwe Publishing] Novel. A new country is formed on a series of super barges and that's not treason.

The Family Business. [Createspace 2011]. Novel and screenplay. Between organized crime and corporate America, will the real criminals please stand up? Introducing Tina, Mafia spy girl, the story of Tony, who thinks he is leaving the criminal world for so called legitimate business.

The Nobel Prizener [iuniverse 2004] Novel and feature length screenplay. Rape is a hard charge to beat, especially when you're innocent.

Franck Tails. [Kiwe Publishing 2003] Collection of animal stories. Winnie and Thunderose, The Lonely Leopard, Ca Ca Boy, Wolf's Law. Also wrote a script for Winnie and Thunderose.

Relationship Agreement [Iuniverse 2003] A code of conduct for lovers. Example: you can say no, but you can't say no all the time.

Just Add Water [Kiwe Publishing 2001]. Novel. There had to be revenge for this killing.

Entrepreneur by Necessity [XLibris 2007] Booklet on how to start a business when you have to. No Ice Dragons, Starboys, or fruit characters in this one.

U.S. Grown. To Survive a Nation Must Feed Itself. The Impact of Food Imports on American Food Producers. Okay, so I wrote an economics book.

Screenplays

Reptile Man [Homo-Reptilius Criminalis] Eliminate this species and you eliminate crime. Completed 125-page feature length screenplay.

OOPS [Createspace 2011] Out of Prison Inc. has a run in with the Christian right. Completed 95-page screenplay. Where is Martha when you need her?

The Conversation. They all died and lived happily ever after. 52-page script for a poltergeist/legal drama.

The Tehachapi Militia. Ex-military turned Prison guards plus mowed over by state bureaucrats equals militia that takes over a prison. Completed 120-page feature length script.

The Debt. [Createspace 2011] It's like waking up and learning that you were Hitler in a past life. Completed 135-page feature length script. Received honorable mention in Film Makers screenplay competition, 2001.

The Shanghai Twins. [Createspace 2011] It's nighttime in Shanghai, do you know where your children are? Two part mini-series [95 pages each] based on author's grandparents' tragic experience of losing male twins in Shanghai during the 30s. We never did find them. Written in China [in English].

Mayflower. These are not the pilgrims we learned about in grade school. Completed 120-page scandalous feature length script.

Red Card, script. If you take the time to help a stranger. Geek American engineer attempts arranged marriage in Gobi Desert China. Oops, in the process he gets arrested for lying to Chinese immigration authorities. His defense never worked before, but this is a new Red China.

English for Asian Girls. Naughty Script for Asian Girls in a hurry to get married. Elements of that script are in *East West Marriage*.

The Family Business. Feature length script based on the author's novel.

The Nobel Prizener. Feature length script based on the author's novel.

Katie Cranberry. Script for a one-hour pilot for a teleseries based on the author's novel.

Winnie & Thunderose. Script for a telemovie based on the author's short story.

Ultimate Revenge Episode I of a Series of telemovies based on the author's book.

East West Marriage Script for Episodes 1-10

Wife University DVD Series Episode I Wife University is under construction. It is a school to teach women how to be good wives. A woman will have to create Husband University. Don't count on me for that.

This is USA Episodes 1 and 2 are in production. This is USA shows scenes from the USA, including Urban scenes; rural scenes; music scenes; court drama commentary; animals and natural scenes; Chinese people in USA; other scenes including grocery stores! This series is to show the USA to China. Kit Media is producing this series with Hollywood Arts Society.

Illustrated Stories

Supernatural CSI. Illustrated Novel, Dead People Make Excellent Witnesses. (Booksurge 2009) Trips to the otherworld reveal evidence of crimes here on earth.

Winnie and Thunderose [Artwork by Maria Byerley] [Trafford 2011].

The Dance of Isis [artwork by Maria Byerley].

Ice Dragon and *Starboy* [Createspace 2011] Herman Franck's two bilingual [English and Spanish] comic books based on parts of his novels

Radio Show:

Mid Life Crisis Radio Show [KABC Los Angeles] See www.midlifecrisisradioshow.com for more information.

East West Marriage Radio Show [KABC Los Angeles] [see www.eastwestmarriage.net for more information].

Television Show:

East West Marriage Show [LA 18 TV]

See www.eastwestmarriage.net for more information.   Kit Media and Hollywood Arts Society are producing a TV series based on East West Marriage.

This is USA

Books in Progress

Circle of One, by Dr. John Hoopingarner aka Standing Bear aka Johnny Sage with Herman Franck. The Story of Standing Bear. He was my stepfather.

Good Mom, Bad Wife. He was in love with her, but she wasn't in love with him.

Ultimate Revenge Book II: Relapse   Oh no not again . . .

More coming…

Table of Contents

Appendix A

Series of Diagnostic Criteria of psychiatric disorders From American Psychiatric Association: Diagnostic and Statistical Manual of Mental Disorders, Fourth Edition, Text Revision. Washington, DC, American Psychiatric Association, 2000

[DSM-IV-TR [4th Ed.]]

Table of Contents

CHAPTER 1
ISSUES AND THE BEAST

Storytellers often play around with the words "what if." *Issues and the Beast* asks, "what if animals, mammals, birds, insects, and reptiles suffer from the same psychiatric disorders that afflict human beings?"

For the psychiatrically uninitiated, prepare to be made aware of an array of psychiatric disorders, their definitions, their symptoms, and how, if untreated, they can lead to disastrous results. Each of the beasts in this book is afflicted with some kind of psyche disorder. With proper care and attention, the tragedies that could have been turn into semi-healed happy endings.

Whether we humans can learn from the experiences of these beasts is the purpose of this book.

Appendix A sets forth a series of Diagnostic Criteria of psychiatric disorders explored in these stories, from American Psychiatric Association: Diagnostic and Statistical Manual of Mental Disorders, Fourth Edition, Text Revision. Washington, DC, American Psychiatric Association, 2000 [DSM-IV-TR [4th Ed.]] [used with permission].

Appendix B sets forth a theory I developed in an article entitled Specie Enhancement Aspects of Psychiatric Disorders. Call me crazy, but I put forth the following claim:

Psychiatric disorders are part of the natural design of humans that enhance our species. They make us better, not worse.

Darla The Whale That Was Afraid of Water and her calf, Eddie
and Eddie

CHAPTER TWO

THE WHALE THAT WAS AFRAID OF WATER[1]

Of course whales do not have names, but let's give her one anyway. Her name is Darla. She swam with her calf Eddie close to her side. She was a humpback, one of the great beauties of nature. She swam in the Pacific Ocean and normally would not make her way into the San Francisco Bay. Unfortunately, today she would meet with tragedy in the Bay.

A large cruise liner, coming in from Alaska, traveled right over her back. The propellers of these cruise liners are absolutely gigantic, like being hit by a building. She was able to veer away from the boat, but the suction of the propeller brought her right to it. Her calf was on her other side. Her maternal instincts were well at work, bringing her between the propeller and her calf. She screamed. She pushed her tail fins up and down as hard as she could, trying to get away from that loud and dangerous propeller.

Unfortunately, she was unable to avoid it. She crashed right into it, colliding with her left side. Her calf on her right side would miss it entirely, but she took a major hit. It smashed down and sliced her side, leaving a substantial gap of about two and a half feet in length and about an inch wide. She screamed. Her calf screamed. The striking of the propeller onto her pushed her and turned her upside down. She flopped back right side up, went up for air and remained for several minutes unconscious.

All of the partygoers on the cruise ship and the cruise ship's operations team had no idea that they had just struck a whale. The cruise ship proceeded way, leaving the mother and her calf dangling atop the water, blood coming out in gallons. This was not a mortal injury, but the blood flow could be. She became conscious in a matter of several minutes. The pain was immense. She could feel the life leaving her body, but she also felt the power of a need to live. The life force in her, to keep her baby alive, would overwhelm the life force leaving her.

The first thing she did was to swim to the bottom of the Bay. It was not very deep in these parts. She went down to the sandy, muddy bottom and rolled into the seabed. This placed the mud, sand and yuck at the bottom of the Bay onto her wound. It worked

---

[1] For a description of Specific Phobias and Post-Traumatic Stress Disorder described in this story, See Appendix A-2 [Phobias] and A-3 [PSTD].

like a band-aid. It didn't stop the bleeding, but it slowed it down to about one-tenth of the flow. Her body was quick at work coagulating the wound, slowing the blood flow even more. The combination of her natural body process and the addition of the mud and yuck from the seabed nearly stopped the bleeding.

Cruise Ship in the San Francisco Bay

There are many boats in the San Francisco Bay. They all have propellers and they all make noise. This time the noise was a shock to her system. This was a major danger, a danger she had to escape. She could not relax with her wound healing. She had to leave. She gravitated toward the northeast portion of the Bay, to a place called San Pablo Bay. This bay is fed through a freshwater river known as the Carquinez Strait. This trail flows into the bay and connects with a series of other rivers that go up to the area known as the San Joaquin Valley, to Sacramento and beyond to the Sierra Nevada.

The cold fresh water felt wonderful flowing over her head, over her body, cleansing the wound, cleansing the mud away and addressing the coagulants. Her calf Eddie followed behind, knowing that his mother had some kind of plan even if he couldn't figure out what on Earth it was. She continued up river for miles and miles. The sight of a humpback whale in these parts was absolutely outrageous. It wasn't long until several pedestrians noticed them. It only took several phone calls and cell phone images passed along to others and before long there was a crowd of more than 5,000 people on the river banks watching her.

It took awhile for one of the pedestrians to notice it, but finally one screamed out, "She's wounded! Look."

She pointed down to a rather obvious gash coming out.

"Oh my God."

The people were amazed to see this death-defying act -- a humpback whale and calf making their way up a fresh water river, wounded, bleeding, near death.

It would take human intervention to make this right. Within 20 minutes, Doctor Laura Tannenbaum, Doctor of Veterinary Medicine at UC Davis, was dispatched to the part of the river where this whale was floating. It was an emergency. She was taken by helicopter. Rather than doing an air transport of the whale to a hospital, she brought the hospital to the humpback.

She left with a kit of items needed to suture up this wound. There were antibiotics, surgical tools, a heart monitor and a lot of penicillin. The doctor and her team of three veterinary assistants arrived at the river bank to see the beautiful humpback whale floating, shooting up spouts of water, rolling over and trying to survive.

They cordoned off the area with a group of yellow raft material, making an impromptu dam to the north and to the south of the humpback.

Darla would be dangerous if not tranquil. The helicopter had a vet tech with a rifle. He shot her with a tranquilizer dart. You know how much tranquilizer it takes to make a whale go to sleep? A lot. They figured the calf would remain at bay and would not need a tranquilizer. The calf had this sense about him, mammal to mammal, that these humans would do his mother well.

He watched as the doctors put on a series of hoops around the body of the whale. She was calm. Doctor Tannenbaum then inspected the wound. She measured it with a tape measure. It was sixteen and a half inches long and at its widest point, had a gash of four and a half inches. She examined the mud that had stuck in there. She compared it to the mud on the river floor and saw right away it was completely different. This was seabed mud, not fresh water riverbed mud.

The first project would be to take a water hose and irrigate that moss, seaweed, sand, mud and other junk out of the wound. The water flowed slowly through the crevice of the gash and made it clean.

Once fully irrigated, Doctor Tannenbaum inspected the wound. There were several chunks of skin that had to be cut out and discarded. Luckily, this first part of the whale's body is filled with blubber, which is quite expendable. She did not want any dead tissue to be left in this gash. Dead tissue will infect live tissue and will spread like a terrible wildfire. It could end up killing the whale. She removed all torn blubber, discarding it into the river piece by piece. She then poured hydrocortisone on the wound to further clean it. It was an antiseptic that would destroy any bacteria that had developed.

She then gave several shots of penicillin, to further the process of cleaning out all bacteria and other contaminants. The wound was now ready for suturing. She took an impressive needle, about seven inches long with a thread made out of a type of biodegradable wire. Since there would be no return visit to the doctor, there would be no way to remove these sutures. She sutured them carefully, like tying up a shoe -- crisscross over, crisscross back, criss-cross again and again. It had to be tight to keep it all together.

She handed the large needle back to her assistant. Her assistant handed her the last tool needed for this job, a type of vet staple gun that would apply the last solid staples to this wound. These staples were foundational and would create a solid reinforcement for the thread. The threads could tear apart with movement, particularly the type of movement a whale does when it goes to the bottom of the sea and swims up and out of the water. She put in 82 staples altogether, each one just a couple of millimeters apart.

The crowd was now gathered at about 10,000 watching the vet carefully. The vet wore a pair of surgical gloves that looked like the type you would use when you washed the dishes. When she was done, she handed the staple machine back to her assistant. She patted the whale on the back and walked out of the river to a standing ovation by the more than 10,000 people that had gathered to watch her.

Now they would wait. Several men held up the plastic material to keep her at bay. Her calf would not move from his mom. He watched her, poking her with his head. She would remain sleeping in this way under the effects of the tranquilizer for better than two hours. Not one single pedestrian would leave during this period. Nobody would walk away from this healing whale.

At last, she moved -- her tail fin first and then again and then again. Her eyes opened. The first thing she saw -- the most beautiful thing in the world: the image of her calf, staying right before her. He squealed. She squealed and made a turn to the right, a turn to the left. The calf followed. The crowd went wild and applauded, screamed and whistled.

"She's alive! She's alive!"

This whale would make it, but not without a lasting impact from what had happened to her. Her life had been threatened. Her calf had been threatened. She suffered a near-mortal blow, a slicing into her skin. She removed herself from her environment and went to a foreign environment. This was all new territory for her.

Rather than returning to the bay, she knew a safer way would be to continue upriver -- but this was not advised. This was a seawater mammal, not a freshwater mammal. The men tried to shoo her back, as though they could. It's pretty hard to stop a 30 ton mammal. They brought the plastic material up as high as they could, but it was no use. She was able to easily rise up with the water with the front of her torso and crash down on it. It made a sizeable splash. That material went right down. The men got out of the way. Her calf followed her and she proceeded upriver, along with a parallel group of watchful pedestrians who marched up the river with her. They were all on a trek, but to where?

It is perfectly natural for a humpback whale to jump out of the water. They do this to clean off barnacles that have lodged onto them. They like to jump way out of the water with a huge crashing sound onto the waves, go down again, come right back up and repeat maybe 100 times. There were no barnacles in this river. There was no reason for her to keep coming up and crashing down, but there was something about this water that she just couldn't stand. She would jump up and down and up and down. She was getting violent. There was something very wrong about this.

Her calf was trying to calm her down and got near her. In the process, she almost crushed the calf. She came down right on him, forcing him down into the riverbed. He squealed as he hit there. He had almost the whole weight of his mother on him. She bounced right back up, not even realizing she had struck him and went up and down and up and down. Her calf had become unconscious. He suffered a concussion in this process.

Doctor Tannenbaum saw this event in horror. When a mother will strike out and injure a child, anyone can quickly deduce that there's some kind of psychiatric condition in the works. Doctor Tannenbaum knew this right away. It was unintentional. She did not hurt the calf on purpose. Instead, there was a bigger problem at work here. This whale had become deathly afraid of the water that it was in. Doctor Tannenbaum went back out to the water to see a knocked out calf. Eddie was unconscious, and could drown. He went down to the bottom. A group of eight people lifted him up.

Normally, if any type of animal -- including a human -- were to touch the child of another animal, the mother would come a crashing and would destroy whatever animal had touched her child -- but not today. The mother was overtaken by another, completely different problem. The fear of water consumed her.

"I am not safe in this water. I need to get out of here." This was her recurring thought.

"Somebody must magically come and save me." Another recurring thought.

"I need to get out of here. I'm going to get out now."

The whole focus on her child, on keeping Eddie alive, on keeping herself alive so she could keep him alive, had vanished. She was preoccupied with a desire to leave the water. This was part of a reaction known as post-traumatic stress disorder. She had met with a near-death occurrence, which caused a physical injury that was now on the way to healing, but came with a psychological injury that was only just starting to take hold. The slightest noise -- a bird chirping, a fox digging, even the sound of a worm burrowing into a ground, would send this mother whale into an oblivion of self-protective measures. She would overreact; become completely hyper vigilant in every way. This was done with complete and total disregard for the safety of her child. She had turned into a selfish, phobic-centered whale, bent on disaster.

Doctor Tannenbaum cared for Eddie. Without this human intervention, this calf would not have survived. He would have floated downward to the bottom and suffocated. Instead, they carried him up. She looked for signs of fracture. She listened to his heart. It was beating very nicely. She listened to his lungs. They were breathing completely in, completely out. There were no signs of blood gushing into his lungs. She felt along his vertebrae.

She did not have an x-ray machine that would determine whether any bones had been cracked. Instead, she tried to see it by moving him. They flipped his tail up and down. They moved his body up and down. If he had had a fracture, he would have been screaming in pain with these movements. There was no screaming. Eddie would be okay. He was just conked out for awhile.

It would take awhile, but Eddie would finally come to. His mother was by this time several miles up the river. When Eddie awoke, he had no idea what was going on. He was dazed in a river and no mother in sight. There was a group of humans surrounding him, trying to calm him down.

Doctor Tannenbaum explained to him, "She's up there."

She pointed the way. Eddie seemed to understand. More instinctively, he continued up the river. These whales can move pretty quickly. A whale in search of his mother will waste no time to start. He took off, leaving Doctor Tannenbaum and her crew in the riverbed. The crowd again clapped sensationally over the quick coming-to of Eddie.

Eddie would proceed up the river after his mother. Unfortunately, as fast as Eddie was, his mother was on a crazed-filled mission going up the river, coming out of the water, back in the water, out of the water, back in the water.

She finally found that magical savior she had been searching for. On the river, there was a bend like an elbow, and in that elbow there was a significant area of sand -- a riverbed turned into a beach. As inviting as this may seem to be, it spelled a certain death for the mother. Whales do, for unknown reasons, come to a beach and beach themselves -- and when they do, the result is always the same -- a large, decomposing carcass that remains for weeks, months, even years before slowly rotting away.

The people watched in horror as she beached herself. She basked in the sun. For her, this was the perfect solution to get out of that evil water. The waterbed had brought her tragedy, the water that was more dangerous than anything imaginable. She needed to get away from the very environment that had nearly killed her. It wasn't enough to get out of the ocean. It wasn't enough to get out of the bay. It wasn't enough to go upriver. She had to get out of all water and leave all water forever.

She didn't understand she could not survive out of water. She's a whale. She has to be in water. How could anybody, including Doctor Tannenbaum, explain to her that what she needed to do was get right back into that water? One way, of course, is not to explain it at all, but just push her back in.

They caught up with her. Her child was in the water, screaming for his mom to come back. Eddie saw a terrible sight -- the sight of his mother beached. The crowd watched in horror as they saw what they knew would be a disaster. Doctor Tannenbaum walked up. She patted this beautiful whale. She squealed like a whale. This opened her mind. Doctor Tannenbaum figured if she could show the whale that the water was safe to her, maybe the whale would understand that it would be safe for her too.

There was a small problem with this comparison. She was in clothes. This would not do. She looked up and saw more than 10,000 people looking at her, wondering what she would do next. She tried it with clothes on. She walked into the water. The mother whale was not buying it. The fact that this fully clothed human could walk in and out of water had nothing to do with what the whale could or could not do.

Some men wrapped a rope around the humpback's tail. They had a Zodiac raft with a outboard motor attached. They turned the engine on. The propellor went on. Was that ever a mistake? That was the last sound this whale needed to hear. When she heard the sound of that propeller way too close to her, she just went crazy. She lifted her tail up as high as it would go and flopped it up into the air and then back down like a fly swatter. As she went up in the air, that line of rope attached to the boat flipped that boat up and out of the water. The two men went to either side. The boat did a triple twist and landed bottom side up with the engine still on and that propellor still moving.

She turned and saw that propellor and Doctor Tannenbaum figured it all out.

She screamed, "GET THAT BOAT OUT OF HERE!"

The men came back very carefully to the boat, turned the engine off, and turned the boat right side up.

Doctor Tannenbaum screamed out again, "Get it out of here!"

They walked the boat down the river, past the bend where the mother could no longer see it and hid it behind the corner.

Doctor Tannenbaum just shook her head. "Who's idea was that?"

Somebody had a stupid idea. They hadn't passed it by her and unfortunately, it turned into a disaster. Whatever progress she had made in bringing that whale back to the water -- it had all been undone by that engine going on.

She came back to Darla and patted her. Eddie remained in the water, looking at his mother, screaming for her to come back. She was not listening. Instead, she was resting, thinking she was safe.

The water plays an important role with keeping the whales' organs afloat. As the whale is swimming in the ocean, the water buoys its internal organs. Otherwise, the crushing weight of the whale comes down on the lungs and can literally suffocate the whale. A beached whale will die of asphyxiation brought about by the crushing weight of the whale onto its internal organs, and specifically, her lungs.

Doctor Tannenbaum knew all about this. The whale's breathing was getting harder and more difficult. It would not happen right away. One idea would be to prop the whale up, to make some supporters on her side. Another idea was to bring in some scuba tanks and somehow have the mother breathe out of scuba tanks. It would be very difficult to get any kind of device out there that would hold up 30 tons. The scuba tank idea had an extremely high risk of actually exploding her lungs with too much oxygen and air. There had to be some kind of way to quickly coax that whale back out into the water. It was the boat that was unsafe.

Doctor Tannenbaum had tried herself walking in the water -- then she got the idea. There were approximately 10,000 onlookers. All of these people were holding their hands out, wondering what on Earth they could possibly do to help this whale. How could they get together and convince this whale that everything would be okay?

Doctor Tannenbaum put both hands up in the air, with her palms toward her and ushered everybody down from on top of the small hill overlooking this beach.

"Come here, all of you. Come here!" she screamed at the top of her lungs.

They all walked down, slowly but surely.

She explained to them, "This is going to sound really weird, but we're all going to show an example to this mother by getting into the water. The thing is, we can't have our clothes on. It won't work. I've already tried it several times. She's not buying it. I believe if we all take off our clothes and get into this river together and start swimming around, then she will understand that the water is safe for mammals of all kind, of all color."

She looked at the polyglot of people. There were all kinds. There were people from Mexico. There were people from Asia. There were people from Africa. There were people from South America. There were people from Europe. There were people who were skinny. There were people who were chunky. There were people who were obese. People who were tall. People who were short. There were people with freckles. There were people without freckles. It was a perfect example of everything on Earth. And if everything on Earth could take off their clothes and walk into that water safely right in front of this mother -- if she could watch it, if she could see it with her own eyes -- see that the water was safe, maybe she would turn around and start the process of rolling back to the water.

Doctor Tannenbaum would lead by example. She removed her white jacket and placed it carefully down on the beach. It said in blue writing sewn into the pocket, Doctor Susan Tannenbaum, DVM. She placed it there. She took off her khaki pants, her boots, her socks. She took off her bra. She took off her panties and stood naked between the crowd and the whale.

She then turned and walked into the water. "Follow me."

A small black child removed his shirt, his pants and started to get into the water.

The doctor stopped him. "No. You must take off all your clothes."

The boy was not shy and took off his underwear and jumped into the river. Three other younger boys followed and then a couple of girls. It was the kids that lacked inhibition and were able to become completely naked in front of a crowd of 10,000.

The adults saw the example of the children and followed. Several men took off their clothes and jumped in. Several other men followed. There was a black man, a Mexican man and an Asian man. Several white guys and then more of the same. Finally the women started to take off their clothes. They naturally had more inhibitions, more to risk, more to be afraid of -- but they saw the impact on the whale. The whale was watching. It was working.

There were quite a few news reporters filming this most unusual scene. More than 10,000 people of all shapes and sizes completely naked, walking into the river and ushering the whale to start the process of turning around and coming in. They stood by her baby and petted Eddie. Eddie felt so much more comfortable with all these humans now that they were naked. He was swimming with them like a porpoise swims with people in amusement parks.

Whales don't do that, but today Eddie was making a big exception. He knew these people were trying to save his mother. He knew they were good people.

One of the things about having a psyche disorder is being able to reach out and get a little help. Trying to solve it on one's own often ends in disaster, including a slow, rotting death on a river beach -- but not today. Today the mother whale would reach out for help. Her fin raised up first. The crowd screamed in excitement.

They knew she was saying, "Help me. Help me live."

The naked people came to her aid. They all ran up to her side. They held her. They kissed her. They moved her. She squealed, a language only her son would know, but it was a good language. It was a statement. He started to squeal and jump about and swim about. They tried to push her.

Pushing a 30 ton whale is an impossible task unless you happen to have 10,000 naked people helping. It was a scene right out of a storybook, like a bunch of little tiny ants getting together like toy soldiers. In their multitude, they were able to do wondrous things. They pushed and pushed and were able to slowly get her afoot from where she was.

She flipped to the side. On her side, there was less space between her and the beach. This smaller space made for an easier fulcrum to push her. They realized that sliding her downward would be impossible, but pushing her over could cause a twisting momentum. They pushed her.

She flapped her wing, showing them the way. "Don't pull me vertically. Push me horizontally."

They followed her direction. She was signaling for help. She was telling them how to help her and they were following her guidance.

Doctor Tannenbaum pointed the way. "That way."

It didn't seem like the right way because it was a push not into the water, but to the side. What happened was perfect. As she rolled to one side, she was able to shift her entire body from being perpendicular to the water -- and in one full slide, she propelled herself in a circular manner as she rolled. The kinetic force of her body turning reduced the weight of her on the beach and it gave a moment of magic, a window of opportunity where she could twist her body like the arms of a clock going from six o'clock to a quarter of three. This brought her parallel to the water.

The crowd screamed in excitement. They realized she was helping them help her. There was recognition by this whale -- a clear recognition. She knew she needed help. She was asking for that help and she was getting that help. Eddie screamed in excitement.

So many were still in the water, ushering him forward. "Bring her to me. Bring her to me."

They pushed and they pushed again. She rolled again once and with that, caught up with some momentum and rolled two more times until her entire body splashed into the water. The crowd screamed in excitement. Everybody was in the water with this mammoth whale and her beautiful son. She knew she would be safe here and swam, her head toward back to the bay, back to the seawater where she belonged and where she would go. She swam quickly away.

Nobody was bothered by the fact that she never looked back as she and her beautiful son made their way down the river, back to the delta area, into the San Pablo Bay, back to the Bay itself and through the Golden Gate, out into the Pacific blue. She swam up and crashed down. Just like people do. And when they do, if they would just reach out their hands for a little help, they could get turned around and could find their way back to safety, back to life, back to family.

She and Eddie would survive many long years out in the gorgeous ocean.

Darla and Eddie are accompanied out to sea.

CHAPTER 3

THE SCHIZOPHRENIC CAT[2]

"What's wrong with that cat?"

---

[2] For a medical description of schizophrenia featured in this story, please refer to appendix A-3.

Maybelline The Schizophrenic Cat

Fireman Rick

Fireman Rick worked for the San Jose fire department. Today was a busy day. The auditorium of a local private high school was on fire. Fireman Rick and a group of 20 others were busy hosing down the fire. The plastic chairs in the cafeteria were melting. Melted rubber, melted plastic, burning tables--the fire poured out, thick black smoke.

The good news is that these interior items were all easily replaced. The fire on the walls and the ceilings had been put out, but the fire in the interior portion was still going. They were hosing it down when Rick noticed something flying out of the corner of his eye -- a cat, gray with darker gray stripes, green eyes, and a crazed look, had ran up the curtains of the stage to the auditorium. At first, she was self-protective and ran to the high part of the fire to avoid all danger. But, as she remained up there, seeing the fire and the odd sight of a bunch of firemen in yellow suits with their fire equipment behind them, clear plastic masks, using axes and water to put the fire out, she began to hear an inner voice.

"I am the devil. Fire is my home. I need nobody. I live alone." It was a chant repeating itself inside of her over and over again.

She was Satan. She was possessed. The fire was a place she could go for safety. Hell was her home. The fire was her home and these strange men putting the fire out were damaging the security of Hell. In her crazed space, she saw them as the enemy and the fire as her friend. She leapt off of the curtain, diving for the one part of a corner of the auditorium still in flames. She had no fear, as the place she was going to was a place that she belonged. She was sure of it. She was certain of it and jumped right into it.

Rick reacted. He didn't even think about it. He just reacted. He ran between the curtain and the cat and like a linebacker intercepting a 15 yard pass leapt forward with both hands out, and caught the cat by the neck. He brought her into his abdomen for safety and came to a sliding stop off the linoleum floor of the auditorium.

The other firemen could not believe their eyes as they saw this leap of faith by Rick. It pushed them unexpectedly right into the fire, but Rick would not be hurt. The closest fireman was about 40 feet away. He shot water in a perfect arc and was able to shoot water across the room so it would cascade like thick rain right down on Rick and the cat. Rick would not breathe in a breath of smoke. He had the gas mask on. He breathed fresh air. He kept that cat right on his abdomen.

The cat screamed and clawed. Had Rick not been wearing fire resistant material, he would have been a bloody mess, but he was not going to let go of that cat. The cat suddenly came out of a daze, realizing she was not the devil, Hell was not her home. She was soaking wet. It may have been the water that woke her up, but she became relaxed, limp like. She snuggled with Rick. She purred. She came back to her true self -- a non-possessed lovely little kitty cat that every now and then had the delusions that inside of her lived Satan himself.

There was a certain bond that developed between a person and another person or, in this case, animal that the person saves. If you save someone's life, you will naturally become bonded with them and them with you. This bond will continue even if the two of you are on opposite ends of the planet. But in this instance, Fireman Rick decided he would not remain on opposite ends of the planet with this cat. Instead, he would take the cat home.

He lived in a small apartment in downtown San Jose. It was a busy area, with thousands of cars, busses, motorcycles, bicycles, and people bustling about. He walked home with the cat in his arms. His blue shirt had the large print initials SJFD. Everyone knew that this meant he was a fireman. They smiled at him as he walked down the street. Several women also smiled at his cat and went to pet her. He was very protective of the cat that he just saved, but would allow the girls to pet her. The cat purred.

One of them asked, "What's her name?"

Rick thought about it. "As a matter of fact, I don't know."

One of the girls suggested, "She has such beautiful eyes. Look at those. They're glowing."

It was true. They were golden-greenish eyes that lit up the dark around this cat.

The girl suggested, "Why don't you name her Maybelline?"

"Maybelline?"

"Yeah, you know the cosmetic company. They make makeup for beautiful eyes. This cat has naturally beautiful eyes. So call her Maybelline."

Fireman Rick thought that was a sweet idea. "I will."

"Okay. Hello Maybelline. Do you like that name?"

The cat couldn't care less what name you gave her. In fact, this cat would never come to that name. It was just a name for the benefit of the humans. But from that day forward, this cat would go by the name of Maybelline -- at least, that's what the humans would call her.

Dr. Isabella

A very beautiful Puerto Rican woman by the name of Isabella lived two doors down from Rick's apartment. As he walked through the hallway with his cat, he saw her. She was returning from work, wearing a white coat. She was a pharmacist and knew all about medicine. Sometimes opposites attract. A super brainy dark haired Puerto Rican girl would enjoy the company of a white Irish blue eyed fireman? Oh yes! She smiled at Rick as he walked by her apartment door.

"Good afternoon, Isabella."

"Hello Rick. What do you have?"

"I got a cat."

"Oh. Can I see?"

"Why sure."

Isabella came to pet the cat. The cat looked up with those beautiful green-gold eyes.

"Wow, look at those eyes. They seem -- I don't know -- possessed."

Rick thought about it. Maybe she's right.

"What's her name?"

"Maybelline."

"Maybelline?"

"Yeah."

"Where'd you get it?"

"It's a bit of a story, but I found her in a fire."

"A fire?"

"Yes."

Rick opened his apartment door with his keychain. The clink-clink-clink of the metal on metal alerted Maybelline. She got a little nervous.

"It's okay."

Rick petted her head. Isabella loved to see how caring Rick was. It was a good sign that he could maybe be a good husband. Anybody who would care for a cat like he did could probably also care for a wife or a child in the same way.

He didn't realize that Isabella was following him down the hallway. He came in to his apartment and was about to close the door right on her face. He was pleasantly surprised that she was right there.

46

"Oh, hi."

"Oh, excuse me." She was shy and started to walk away.

"Oh no, please come in. I'm sorry. I didn't know you were there."

"I'm sorry. I shouldn't bother you. I know you're busy."

"No, I'm not busy. I'm off work -- just got home. Are you off work?"

"Yes. How was your day?"

"Busy as usual. How's the pharmacy?"

"Too busy. So many people need drugs, it's unbelievable. Seems like everybody's on drugs."

"Yeah, well, I hope somehow people stop doing that. It just seems like you should be allowed to exist without taking drugs. We don't need to solve every single problem we have with some kind of weird drug."

"I know, but it's amazing. I've got some customers in there taking nine different pills a day and they do it three times a day. It's crazy."

Rick put the cat down. The cat looked around at its new house. Her first reaction was to jump right back up into Rick's arms. She felt safe with him. She trusted him.

"Now Maybelline, you can walk around here. Don't worry."

She checked out the windowsill. It showed a busy street scene below: the busses, cars, bicycles, motorcycles and people walking by. Maybelline didn't like all that hustle and bustle. She found a couch with a blanket on it -- very nice, soft, warm blanket. She got on that blanket and quickly fell sound asleep. Isabella and Rick were as though they were looking at their new child. The cat was so peaceful -- purring, sleeping, looking so comfortable. It was hard to believe that inside this cat was the devil.

Rick did the polite thing to do. "Would you like to go out for dinner?"

Isabella tried to hide her excitement over this invitation. "Well, maybe -- I mean, if you're not busy--"

"Okay, so is that yes?"

She looked over at the cat, so comfortable sleeping. She looked up at Rick with her dark brown eyes. "Yes."

"Okay. Do you need to get ready or do you want to wear your doctor coat?"

47

She looked at herself. On her white coat, there was her name -- Doctor Isabella.

You know the saying, when the cat's away, the mice will play. Well, here's a different variant of that. While Rick and Isabella were away at dinner, Maybelline found an unlikely friend. In the kitchen area of Rick's apartment, at the floor level there was a small hole. If you look into the dark of that hole, you will see two little tiny nervous brown eyes and a little tiny nose with whiskers. It was a little mouse. The mouse peered out at the new roommate, Maybelline. Mice know that cats are dangerous and will eat them. There's no way this mouse was going to come out.

Maybelline looked at the mouse. There was a certain power that people and animals with psychiatric problems can have. They have the power to persuade, the power to magnetize, the power to make people do things that they would never ordinarily do. Maybelline looked at that mouse and convinced the mouse that she was safe.

"You can come and play with me. I am your friend."

Maybelline was not dishonest. She was a friend -- a person to trust. The mouse somehow sensed this and gently came out of his little tiny hole. Maybelline studied the mouse. He walked right in front of her, the danger zone -- looked up at her and let a little squeak. Maybelline responded with a little purr.

It was their way of saying, "Hello. What's your name?"

Except they don't ask names. For the most part, animals don't believe in names. The mouse was still a little bit nervous. Its whiskers were shaking away, twisting to the left, twisting to the right.

Maybelline would not eat this mouse and instead, would become friends. She walked over away from the mouse, back to the living room where the couch was and that super comfortable blanket. She got up there and rested. The mouse followed.

He looked up to her. "Wow. She looks so comfortable on that couch."

He climbed up the side of the couch onto the arm and went right next to Maybelline -- and there the two of them laid and went to sleep together, the mouse right by Maybelline's neck. It was so warm and furry -- so much nicer to sleep on instead of the dark, dusty area behind the kitchen. They both went into deep sleep, the mouse breathing the air that Maybelline was blowing out of her nose and mouth, breathing that in. The mouse moved away from the nose in order to get unbreathed air. This helped put the mouse into a deep sleep. He looked so comfortable, so lovely sleeping there right next to Maybelline.

They were sound asleep several hours later when Rick and Isabella returned from their dinner date. They were so fast asleep that they didn't even hear the door unlock and Rick and Isabella come in.

Isabella saw it first. "Oh my God. Look."

She pointed over to the couch.

Rick didn't know what she was referring to. "What, the cat?"

"No, look. It's the cat and a mouse."

Isabella walked over. She had never seen a mouse and a cat lie together like this. Neither had Rick.

"Oh my, will you look at that? Somehow these two animals have decided to be friends. How's that?"

Rick was so confused. Inside the cat was a devil, but also inside the cat was an angel. Somehow this cat is possessed of extreme evil and extreme good depending on its mood, depending on its environment, its hormones, its DNA, its hereditary or something. Somehow it would edge in and out of a cat possessed by a devil and a cat possessed by an angel.

Isabella studied the cat and the mouse. They sat instead of on the couch, on the rug in front of the couch. They didn't want to wake them. Rick and Isabella just sat there and watched them sleeping away, so comfortable, so seemingly in love. They saw a kind of parallel between dark and light, opposite forces coming together in comfort, in love, and in trust. They embraced -- physical, passionate, trusting, holding, hugging, peering into each other's eyes -- knowing that it was right for them to be together no matter how different they were on the outside. What mattered was the chemistry, the perfection of Mother Nature's design to bring opposites together toward an overall goal of achieving brilliance, superiority and excitement.

The next morning, the four of them awoke together. This was the first time Isabella had spent the night. They slept right there on the rug in front of that couch. She woke up a little bit embarrassed. She was still in her dress. He was still in his clothes. It was an innocent night, but still it was a night they spent together. They looked up and the cat and the mouse were gone.

"Where are they?"

They walked into the kitchen. "Oh, there they are."

They were on the kitchen floor playing together, running around. The mouse was doing twists and turns. The cat was on her back. They were having a great time.

Isabella smiled. "Can you believe that?"

It was breakfast time. Rick pulled out a blender and cracked three eggs, milk and a granola bar in there and stuck in two bananas. He blended it all up.

Something happened to that cat when Rick turned on the blender. There are triggers out there for people with problems. Certain things can be heard or seen or smelled or somehow perceived and it will cause them to go into a state -- sometimes it's a good thing, sometimes it's a bad thing. It just depends.

That blender got this cat going. The first thing she did was jump up onto the kitchen cabinet. She became transfixed to that blender. She watched in amazement as a whole banana, a group of eggs, milk and a granola bar got chomped up into liquified form.

He started it on high, pushed it onto medium, and then went to slow. Rick didn't notice the cat watching the blender in this way. Isabella did. Without warning, the cat suddenly turned on the mouse, jumped off of the kitchen cabinet onto the ground, right on top of that mouse and grabbed it.

Isabella screamed.

Rick turned around. "Wow, what's that?"

The mouse tried to get away, but the cat smacked it and grabbed it. She was about to eat it when Rick grabbed the cat by the back of the neck, pulled her off the floor, took the mouse out of the cat's mouth and quickly put him in front of his hole -- the hole to safety. The mouse scampered away into the darkness behind the wall.

He had no idea what had come over the cat. "What's wrong with that cat?"

He looked at the cat and saw that she was in the same mode as Rick first found her, when she jumped off that curtain, into the fire. Something about that blender set her off in this way. Well, for starters, how about let's not use that blender anymore? Rick poured the blender's contents into a cup.

Isabella had an idea. "Since the blender got this cat going, why don't you feed her what you made?"

Rick thought that was a good idea. He took a bowl out, poured some of the contents into the bowl and put that onto the ground. The cat went over, smelled it, licked it, licked it some more and then lapped it up -- just drank and drank and drank every molecule of what Rick had given her. He poured some more in. She lapped it up. She loved that stuff. It was amazing to watch her. Now maybe this cat hadn't eaten in awhile -- or it may be that there was just something really yummy about milk, bananas, granola bar, and eggs. Whatever it was, one thing was clear: Rick now knew what to feed the cat -- except for one problem. He couldn't use the blender. He would have to make it some other way. That blender would have to go.

It was time for work. Rick and Isabella both had busy days ahead of them. Isabella had to go back to her apartment, take a shower, get into her doctor's outfit and get down to the pharmacy to sell drugs to all kinds of people. Rick had to get into his fireman's outfit and get down to the fire station to put out fires.

He left his crazy cat and that little mouse together, hoping that either the mouse would know how to stay safe or that the cat would get back to its angel self.

Before he left, he said, "Bye Maybelline. Please be nice to the mouse."

He rolled his eyes, as though she would obey that. He closed his door, locked it, and left.

Later that day when he returned, he saw something that really bothered him. That hole where the mouse was had a bunch of scratch marks all over it. Some of them were going to the left. Some of them were going to the right. It looked like a bear had got in there and had scratched it up. The claws went into the wood. You could tell by the depth of the scratches that this cat had really tried to dig into that hole. There was paint dangling from the edges of the scratches. It was an absolutely insane attempt by that cat to somehow get that mouse. The good news for the mouse is that the wall is harder than the cat's nails.

Rick looked over to find the cat. Amazingly, she was sound asleep on the couch looking so angelic, so calm. He looked at her claws and saw they were actually bloody -- not from the mouse's blood, but from the cat's own blood. There was paint and blood mixed on it. They used to be so friendly and now she wanted to annihilate that mouse.

He wondered, "What can I do to make them friends again? Maybe nothing."

51

He sat on the couch. His weight on the couch moved the part where the cat rested and woke Maybelline up. She looked at him. She didn't smile, but she was in a smiling mood. Rick could sense that.

"Hi Maybelline." He was wondering, "Are you a devil or are you an angel?"

Right now, she was an angel -- but he knew all that could change in a manner of a second. Suddenly, she looked outside. There was a window there looking down at the street. There was something there. There was nothing there, but the cat saw something. She jumped out, screamed out in a shriek, went up to the window and smacked into it with her head.

Rick was stunned by this. "What are you doing?"

The cat stood back and ran again at the window, smashing it with her head. The window was actually pretty strong. But no matter how strong a window may be, if you pick a baseball and throw it, you can crack that window. A baseball is pretty hard, but a cat's skull is also pretty hard. A cat's head, if heaved hard enough at a window, can break it. The cat went back that third time and started running at that window.

Rick saw that the cat, if allowed, would break through that window and fly out to 10 floors below, down to the pavement. Although cats are pretty good at jumping out of windows and somehow landing on their feet and living, Rick did not want to take that chance. He intercepted the cat between its run and leap to the window, catching her right on his chest.

It was the second time he had saved the cat's life. For some reason, this death wish would be a recurring theme with this cat. The cat would see some great danger, but unlike a case of phobia, this was a case of counterphobia -- where someone is drawn to a danger that they should be afraid of. It is the opposite of a phobia. In this case, the danger was delusional. It was a pure hallucination, but rather than running from it, the cat was drawn to it. She wanted the danger. She wanted death. She was preoccupied with this suicidal image of her jumping into sharp glass, jumping into a fire, jumping off a tall building. There are a million ways to die and this cat had imagined 100,000 of them. Today was 100,001 and tomorrow would be 100,002.

Rick could save her one time, two times, three times -- but he knew right then and there that one of these times, this cat was going to see whatever monster it was seeing and jump into that monster's mouth and get gobbled up and he wouldn't be there to save her. He held her tight. The cat came back to its angelic side and purred and went to sleep in a yawn. He put her down.

Isabella came over. She was careful not to be too clingy or close to Rick. Smart girls do this. If you give too much of yourself to a man, he may shy away.

"Rick, how's that cat?"

That was an excuse. She wasn't there about the cat. She was there about Rick, but Rick was okay with that.

"Come here. I want to show you something."

He walked her over to the place by the mouse hole.

She gasped. "Oh, what happened?"

"Maybelline went off the deep end."

Isabella came over and saw what she expected to be a psychotic cat and instead found a sleeping, purring, beautiful Maybelline.

"She looks like an angel."

"This is her angel side -- but then she's got this devil side where she just goes crazy."

"What happened today?"

"I came home. She tried to smash through the window. It was like she saw something out there, something she had to have, and something she had to go to. Whatever it was, it scared her, but it invited her. It was like a scary magnet that she had to come to."

Isabella studied the cat's claws, saw the blood, and saw the paint fragments. "Look at her. I mean, she'll tear herself up. She's possessed or something. What is it?"

"I don't know. When I first found her, she was on top of the curtains and jumped into a fire -- except that I caught her. Today she tried to smash through the window and I caught her. She has some kind of death wish."

Isabella was well aware of many of her customers that had to take pills so that they would eliminate their death wish. The bigger issue that she always found unanswered is, what brought people to this point where they wanted to destroy themselves? How was it that they became possessed by some kind of being inside of them who had a control over their life force, who eliminated that life force and instead, would direct them to death? Die, die, die. Die today. Die now. Do it. Do it. Isabella looked at the cat -- so calm, so collected, so angelic -- and couldn't imagine for the life of her what it would be.

The two of them sat together on that couch and watched their patient, wondering, "How can we help her? What can we do to help this cat release its demons and become healthy and normal again?"

Do you really think there's an answer to that question? Do you really think there's something that can be done to solve this cat's problems? Or, once something gets this far gone, is it better just to let it go, and whatever defect it had, just let it be, let it run its course? That course, and make no mistake about it, is sure death.

Even with all this drama, the following morning before Rick went to work, he found, once again, the cat gently sleeping on the couch with the mouse right by its neck. The cat breathed in and out. The mouse breathed in and out. Their lungs expanded and contracted in parallel, except that the mouse's was going at a rate of about six times the cat's.

Rick smiled and shook his head in amazement, grabbed his fire coat, and left for work. On the way out of his front door, he was pleased to see Isabella in her white pharmacist coat, also going to work.

"Can I give you a ride?"

He walked downstairs where a 45 foot fire truck with a ladder awaited his arrival.

She laughed. "No thanks. I'll walk."

The crew on the fire truck laughed as they saw Isabella go in one direction and Rick get on the truck to go in another direction.

That night on the way home, he stopped by the pharmacy where Isabella worked. She was busy filling several prescriptions for some customers. It was close to 6:30 PM. The sign on the door said that the place was open until six so he was wondering why she was still serving people.

"What, I'm going to tell them to go?"

The customers looked at Rick holding his fire coat and could see right away that there was something pleasant going on between the nice pharmacist and the nice fireman. They smiled.

He guarded the door. Several others tried to walk in and he was about to usher them out when Isabella interrupted him.

"No, it's okay. Come on in."

He sat and waited another hour, until about 7:30. Isabella was at last done. She locked up the pharmacy area. There were millions of pills back there that if in the wrongs hands, could cause some pretty serious damage. There was a security area and a gate that came closed, almost like an evidence locker in a police department. She came out the front door, locked the door, and had a very pleasant walk with Rick back to the apartment.

Down the sidewalk, in front of the apartment building, they heard a very alarming sound
-- the sound of glass crashing. Rick looked up to see that crazy cat of his. She had finally smashed through the window at whatever demon was out there and was flying through the air to meet her death.

Thankfully, Rick was right there, ready to catch her and save her life again. He braced himself for the blow of the cat. The cat flew in the air, turning a few times. Glass shards were also coming down, making this a dangerous situation -- not only to the cat, but also Rick and Isabella. One shard barely missed Isabella and shattered on the ground just before her foot. She screamed and moved backwards. Rick stayed right where he was. A shard of glass came down and sliced into his shoulder, a direct hit. It didn't bounce off. It stuck in about an inch and a half. He groaned in pain, but would not move from his position.

The cat was getting closer to his open arms and was about to be caught when suddenly, out of nowhere, a bicyclist on the sidewalk smashed into Rick. It was an accident, but Rick didn't see it coming. It moved Rick right out of the way of the cat. The cat came crashing down on the sidewalk -- splat cat -- its neck broken on impact, several ribs were shattered and went right into its lungs.

The cat died in about nine different ways. The pierced lung caused asphyxiation. The broken neck severed the spinal cord and stopped the neurotransmitters from instructing the veins to pump blood to its body. The brain became oxygen-deprived and the cat went out like a light. The cat lacked blood flow to its brain, the trauma to its head during the landing caused a cranial rupture; both lungs were pierced in several places by the cat's sharp broken ribs. This cat was a goner, and was pronounced dead on landing.

Isabella and Rick studied the dead cat along with several onlookers. Rick looked way up to that window. It was hard to see the two little brown eyes. The brown eyes of the little mouse could barely be seen looking over the windowsill. No, the mouse would not be a copycat and jump off as well. Instead, he just watched and saw that his sometimes angelic friend and sometimes demon beast had passed on. It was sad for everybody.

Isabella had forgotten about the shard of glass in Rick's shoulder. He grabbed it gently.

She told him to stop. "Wait, Rick, let me do it."

She came over with her gentle hands. "Here. Come here. Sit down."

There was a bench nearby. He sat on the bench. People watched carefully. There were two big injuries. One fatal to the cat and one moderate injury to a fireman. Of course, Rick would live, but it was still a serious injury. The red blood on his white shirt looked gruesome. It was drying.

She took the shard of glass into her fingers, pinching on either side, and slowly lifted it out of his shoulder. Some blood gurgled out. She put her hand right on it to stop the blood. Rick put his hand over her hand.

A man was nearby and took a clean handkerchief out of his pocket. "Here, use this."

Isabella smiled. "Thank you."

She took the handkerchief and put it under her hand. Rick got off the bench.

Isabella didn't like this idea. "No, stay here."

Rick got up anyway. He held the handkerchief to his shoulder and walked over to the cat. He kneeled down. Maybelline's eyes were wide open. There was a terrified look in her eyes. She had seen the demon, but the demon was somehow a friend inviting her. It was one of those circumstances where the scariest thing in the world was also the most attractive thing in the world. Somehow she just had to come to it and she did. Of course, it was only a matter of time before she would succeed in her mission. No matter how many times Rick was there to save her, one of these days -- and today was that day -- she would succeed.

Isabella closed the cat's eyelids. She had not touched the cat's eyelids before, but she noticed something when she did so now. She looked at her fingers. There was some kind of weird fungal residue left on her fingers -- something from the cat's eyes.

Rick saw her examining her fingers. "What?"

She looked at him. "Some kind of fungal virus."

"Oh?"

"Yeah. It's not right -- not like anything I've ever heard of. This stuff is a very odd color and it has a kind of sandy feeling to it. There's some kind of particulates in it. It's not just fluid. It's some kind of combination of fluid and dusty material."

"Okay." Rick had no idea how this could be significant. "What do you think?"

"I don't know."

She looked at the cat. She looked at the windowsill. She looked at the broken glass.

She looked over at Rick. "We should study this cat. There's more to this than meets the eye."

There was a nearby garbage can and by that garbage, there was resting a brown paper bag filled with other paper bags. It was placed there for recycling. She took out one of those paper bags and gently picked up Maybelline and placed her in the bag. The bag had handles.

"Let's take her back to the pharmacy. I've got a refrigerator in there where we can keep her for observation."

She and Rick walked several blocks back to the pharmacy, looking like ordinary shoppers -- except Rick had a stream of blood all over his white shirt and Isabella was carrying a bag with the body of a schizoid cat. She opened the front door of the pharmacy and locked it again behind them.

The first thing she did was to deal with Rick's wound. It was easy enough. She had gauze, surgical tape and a pair of surgical scissors. She put some hydrogen peroxide on the wound and cleaned it off. She then irrigated it. Afterward she put a square gauze band-aid over it, put some tape down on that, and some more tape crisscrossing it.

"Why don't we take your shirt off?"

Rick looked down and saw all the blood and agreed. It looked a little frightening. He removed his shirt. She pretended not to look at his torso, but of course she had to sneak in a peek. He was like you would imagine him. Mmm.

"Here, wear this."

She had another white jacker with her name on it. Now Rick would go from fireman to pharmacological research assistant, all in a matter of a couple of seconds.

There was a back room where pills were brought out for mixing and placement into capsules. She cleared away a group of containers holding empty capsules. This was a stainless steel lab area, spotlessly clean. There was a microscope. She took a petri dish and a cotton swab. She applied the swab to the cat's eye, took off some of that dusty, mucousy substance, placed it onto a petri dish and closed it. She hand wrote on it, "Maybelline's eye." She took another swab and placed it onto a microscope slide. She placed the slide into the microscope and took a look.

"Oh my."

Rick was quick to wonder out loud, "What? What did you find?"

"I know what this is."

"What is it?"

"It's a kind of virus. It's called toxoplasma gondii."

"What is that?"

"It's a bacteria -- a kind of viral infection. I read about it. Hold on a second."

She went to the computer. This was a pharmacological search engine that would give you all the information about just about anything having to do with pharmaceuticals. She typed in the words "toxoplasma gondii." Up came a whole group of studies -- the first going to American Science in the year 1896.

It studied the concept that a kind of viral bacteria in cats is responsible for schizophrenia in humans. She then found an article connecting the process to mice.

"Look at this."

She pulled up the abstract from a research group in Manchester, Scotland. The mice are an intermediate carrier. They get the virus. The virus impacts their neurotransmitters. It reduces their dopamine levels. Oddly, it makes them less afraid of dangers that they should be deathly afraid of. This allows them to become friendly with predators, such as cats. The idea is that the cat then eats the mouse, which is an intermediate carrier of the virus.

The virus continues in the larger mammal and is then spread to humans. The same impact on eliminating neurotransmitters causes the cats to seek out danger and at the same time, causes miscommunications -- kind of like radio waves getting confused -- creating paranoia and fear over things that you don't need to be afraid of.

According to these studies, the humans that have schizophrenia have antibodies of toxoplasma gondii in their system. These antibodies are naturally generated pharmaceuticals in the human body that attack the toxoplasma gondii virus. The fact that these antibodies are present, according to one study, in 86% of people having schizophrenia is persuasive evidence that this virus, coming from a mouse and transmitted over to the cat, is responsible for schizophrenia.

Rick thought about that cute little mouse back at his apartment. Then he thought about something a little more practical -- Isabella. Think about it.

"She touched that stuff. The cat's been living in my house. She's been breathing in my house. Are we going to get schizophrenia? Are we going to become paranoid crazies like this cat?"

She looked at her computer screen, with all these studies connecting up toxoplasma gondii with schizophrenia. She looked at Maybelline's eyes. She looked at her fingers. She looked at the wound and the bandage on Rick's body. Some injuries are very easy to fix. Some aren't. Isabella went over to a sink. There was soap. She washed her hands and ushered Rick to come over.

"Wash your hands."

She came back over and looked at Maybelline and saw with Maybelline a problem, but also a solution.

"Rick, think about it. That mouse didn't give this to Maybelline. The way you described Maybelline, she already had this before she came to your apartment."

"Oh yeah. When I found her, she was absolutely crazed."

"So the mouse may have had it and not passed it on yet. That would explain how the mouse got friendly with the cat."

"Yeah. Who ever heard of a mouse being friendly with a cat?"

"Rarely happens, but now we may know why. It's a process of passing on this bacteria."

"For what though? What's the purpose of that?"

"Bacteria has a life desire, just like you and I do. It has a desire to exist, to grow, to become bigger, to multiply -- even though all it may do is cause damage, sickness, psychiatric disorders and huge trouble."

Rick thought about it. "Is there some good that comes out of that or is it just all bad?"

Isabella thought for a second. "I don't know, but I'll tell you what. We now have a good reason to study this. Let's try to figure it out."

Isabella continued to look into the microscope. "Here is the problem. The question is where is the solution?"

Rick, being the able if new psychopharmaceutical researcher, came up with a rather interesting concept. "How about that mouse? If that mouse didn't get it or can somehow have it and not be impacted by it -- or at least not go schizoid -- I mean, it didn't see any devils. That mouse had been in my house for quite awhile. I've never seen any kind of crazy activity by the mouse. Maybe there's something in that mouse that we should study."

Isabella smiled. "There may be something to do. Let's go get that mouse."

They put Maybelline into a large plastic Ziploc bag. She had a machine that removed 100% of all oxygen from that bag. It constricted around her. She sealed it off. She then placed the bag into a larger plastic bag and gently placed that into a refrigerator. She took the petri dish and placed that carefully into a shelf right above the bag. She locked the refrigerator. She took the microscope slide, brought it over to the sink and washed it off. That would later be sterilized, but for now she left it in the bottom of the sink. She took off her surgical gloves and threw them in the garbage.

They then left the pharmacy. She locked it up as before and they proceeded to walk back to Rick's apartment. Before they got there, they passed by a small delicatessen.

"Just a second."

Rick was wondering what was going on. Isabella walked in the deli.

He was a little bit surprised. "What, you want a sandwich? Here we are, about to make one of the greatest psychopharmacological discoveries in the world and you want some pastrami?"

She turned without another word, went into the deli and saw Lucenzo, who knew her well.

"Isabella, the most beautiful doctor in the universe. Thank you for coming again."

"Hello Lucenzo."

"What can I get you today?"

She looked at Lucenzo with her big brown eyes and smiled. "I need some cheese. The smelliest stuff you got."

Lucenzo was a man who knew his business. He put his fingers together and brought them into a circular motion above his nose as though he were already feeling the smell away from his nose. He walked back and continued to circle his hand in the air. He went to his own refrigerator, pulled out a square of saran-wrapped cheese with the ominous word "Limburger" written right on it.

"Oh yeah, that'll do."

He sliced off a couple pieces, put them on a cheese knife and put it in front of the doctor.

"Smelly enough for you?"

She took a whiff. "Whoo. Oh my God, who eats that stuff?"

"You're the one ordering it."

"That's what I want."

"Very well. How much do you need?"

"Not very much. Just a couple of slices."

"Okay, two slices it is."

He cut them off with a cheese knife, placed them into a bag, and handed them to Isabella.

"How much?"

"It's such a small amount. Today, this is on the house."

"Oh no, I can't --"

"Doctor, please. You come here so often. You buy many things from me. Allow me this chance to give you a small gift. Perhaps someday this fireman will give you a gift as well."

He smiled at Rick. Rick didn't quite get what Lucenzo was saying. It went right by him. Lucenzo laughed.

The two left the deli and were at Rick's apartment in a matter of just a few minutes. The apartment was cold because of the open window. Rick went right to it. He had his heavy fire gloves on and a brown paper bag. He picked up all the glass shards. He then swept up down below. Those little glass shards that can get stuck in your foot, never come out, and can't be seen are the trickiest to get up. After he removed the big pieces, he brought over a vacuum cleaner and sucked up hopefully all the little ones. He looked around the windowsill area, the rug area, and the wall area for signs of any blood. There was none. It was a clean crash right through that window. He looked down below 10 stories to the sidewalk below. He saw exactly how that would kill a cat.

Isabella meanwhile was on her knees in the kitchen right by that mouse hole with that super stinky Limburger cheese. The mouse had this little tiny nose with whiskers on it that first peered out that hole. She was coaxing him with the cheese. Behind her back, she had an empty glass jar. The mouse had no fear of Isabella -- the same lack of fear it had for the cat caused the mouse to figure that this human was equally unlikely to present a danger.

The mouse came out. Isabella put the piece of cheese down. The mouse started to nibble it. Rather than carry it away like most animals would do into a place of safety, the mouse just ate it right there on the kitchen floor. Isabella used this opportunity to catch the mouse by quickly placing the glass jar right over it. She then used a paper plate to slip underneath the jar. The mouse hopped up a little bit and the jar now had a floor of a paper plate. She turned it back upside down and the mouse was in the jar. She had a top, which she screwed on. She found an icepick and put it on top of the tin jar top. She hit it with the palm of her hand and the ice pick went through the top, leaving one air hole. She then did a second one, a third one and a fourth one.

The cheese was left in the jar. The mouse did not miss a beat and proceeded eating as though there were no danger to it at all. She put that jar into another bag.

She found Rick fixing his window and told him, "Let's go back to the pharmacy."

Rick was looking out his window. The good news was no one could crawl into it. The bad news was it was getting pretty cold.

Isabella had a simple idea. There was a flat screen TV across the room. It was on a table. The table had wheels. She unplugged the flat screen TV and disconnected the cable hookup. As she started to push it, Rick got the idea and helped her to push it over to the window with that facing out. It didn't make a perfect fit, but it nearly sealed off that window and created a temporary window in the form of a TV to the world.

They left and proceeded to the pharmacy. Her first order of business was to tranquilize the mouse. She did that by sprinkling some barbiturates onto some Limburger cheese, which the mouse ate. Within a matter of seconds, the mouse was out. She pulled out a new hypodermic syringe which had absolutely nothing in it. She cleaned the syringe tip with cotton gauze with isopropyl alcohol on it, stuck it into the mouse, and drew out some mouse blood -- not much, just a couple hundred milliliters.

She then asked Rick, "Rick, get me that petri dish."

Rick got the petri dish, opened it and placed it right next to the doctor. She looked at the mucous from Maybelline's eye and the syringe filled with the mouse blood. Somehow the mouse was a carrier of the virus, but it doesn't generate the psychosis. It had some psychosis. The mouse was not afraid when it should be afraid. It had a counter-paranoia disorder -- but not the heavy onslaught of schizophrenia. The answer could be in the blood.

She emptied the syringe right onto the small pile of Maybelline's eye mucous. She put the top of the petri dish back on. They placed it on the lab table and watched. I don't know what she was expecting. Maybe for it go up into flames, turn into nothing or just dissipate -- but actually, nothing happened. It remained as is. The only difference was, whatever gel that was now had blood on it.

She took a small forceps and mixed it up a little bit more. She then took some of the mixture, put it onto a microscope slide and placed it under the microscope for examination.

Rick watched anxiously. "Well?"

She pulled her head up from the microscope. She looked back over to the petri dish. She took off her gloves. She reached in with her fingers to the bloody, mucousy stuff.

Rick wanted to stop her. "No."

She proceeded and touched it. She pulled out a small amount and rubbed it between her fingers.

"That dusty particulate feel that I told you about?"

"Yes?"

"Not here anymore. That mouse blood caused that to disappear."

She looked back at her microscope. Those dust particles were part of the virus that was in a near-solid form. The mouse blood had interacted with that and broke it down into liquid form. As a liquid form under air and light, it could vaporize into gas form and be extracted and removed from the virus.

The virus, toxoplasma gondii, without these particulates was neutralized. A discovery was made that would catapult Isabella and the fireman into the journals of pharmacological discoveries.

Right then and there in this small pharmacy located in downtown San Jose, they had discovered the beginning of the cure for schizophrenia. The new drug would be called Maybelline.

Mother Oinker, The OCD Pig

CHAPTER 4
THE OCD PIG[3]

"This place is a pigsty!"

---

[3] For a medical description of obsessive-compulsive disorder featured in this story, please refer to appendix A-4.

The Pig Sty

Mother Oinker was, of course, correct. She lived in a pigsty, with about 50 other pigs. She was the grand maternal leader of this pack, and had delivered up countless litters of cute little piglets, often as many as eight at a time. She weighed more than 650 pounds, was primarily pink, and had splotches of gray on her stomach. She had nearly invisible hair throughout her body and, the last remnant of her childhood, a little curly tail.

"Look at this place! It's got mud over there. It's got crap over there. The corncobs are mixed in with all of it. The water is slopping over the water pails -- and what is this garbage over here?"

In one of the corners, there was a trough of leftover food from other animals. These pigs are considered omnivores, and live up to that name. They will absolutely eat anything you put in front of them. The trough had bits of corn, some meat, what appeared to be vegetables, and some kind of goulash -- God knows what that was, but whatever it is, the pigs at the trough ate with excitement and purpose.

Mother Oinker was absolutely repulsed by it all. "Jeez, you're mixing all your food together. Look at how it's all mixed up. You've got the corn with the meat, the meat mixing in with the vegetables and that gooey stuff -- what is it? It's disgusting."

She snorted and turned her head to the direction of the fence. "And look at this fence! Will somebody please fix it? The nails aren't right. They're crooked. This one is bent. The head is still sticking out by about a quarter inch. Look at it. Do you see what I'm talking about?

She pulled up her little paw and pointed. None of the other pigs could care less about the fact that the farmer built the pigpen in a somewhat quick and sloppy manner. It was true the boards were not perfectly level. Mother Oinker eyeballed that every single day. The slight slope, probably about a two percent grade, drove this Mother Oinker bonkers.

"Look at it. It isn't straight. This needs to be fixed!"

Her kids came over to calm her. "It's okay, mom. It doesn't need to be perfect."

Her largest child, a male Oinker, tried without success to console her.

There was a soothing element of this pig-on-pig touch. The minute her children would come over and rub their necks against her neck, she would at least temporarily forget about the crooked nails, the two percent slope of a couple of the boards, and the fact that the pig food was touching the various categories of food that was thrown into the trough. She forgot that the mud and the crap came together. She forgot that the water was pouring over the water trough -- but only for a minute. The minute her little piglets went back to sleep, her eyes would suddenly open up to all this imperfection once again.

She got up and tried to fix that fence herself. She nudged the board with her head. It looked like she was scratching her forehead, but she was trying to fix it. Unfortunately, in the process, she made it a little more crooked and created a bigger problem as the nail started to come out a little more. Instead of coming out about a sixteenth of an inch, barely perceptible, now they came out about a fourth of an inch.

There was a cycle to all this, that could be seen if you were a farmer sitting up on top of the pigpen looking down into it. The cycle went like this. This Mother Oinker would have a litter of piglets. The piglets would grow over the next three or four months and become fat little pigs. Then one day, there was a major stressor to the Mother Oinker. The farmers would come and remove those little piglets. They would take them away, never to be seen again. It was when these little piglets were taken away that Mother Oinker dove into her obsessive compulsive disorder mode. That's when she noticed most of all that there were definite, objectively identifiable imperfections in her pigpen. She would snoop around for them.

She saw that some of the vertical posts holding up the boards were also crooked. Some of them were slightly eaten away. The pigs like to gnaw at them, which gives them salt. She would sit and stare literally for hours, transfixed on a slightly gnawed wood post, wondering how it could ever get fixed, who would fix it and when it would happen.

She tried to put mud onto the eaten parts to smooth it out, but it wouldn't work. The mud would come right off. Worse yet, the mud got on her, which upset her. She ran over to the water trough and dunked her head into it, shaking her head around, getting rid of all the little mud particles -- every one of them. She would dunk her head in the trough maybe 25 times to get rid of all the mud. Then she would go back to that wood post and see again that the mud she'd placed there did not fix the problem.

She would go through this process, a ritual, for days on end -- take mud, put on the gnawed part, it didn't work, she got mud on herself, she went to the water, cleaned herself off 16 or 17 times, went over, looked at that gnawed part of the post. She would do this over and over again.

She would be pregnant with a new litter. This would calm her down, but unfortunately, the hormones that take over during a pregnancy also heightened her OCD syndrome. She became more aggressive about fixing the imperfections. She would try to fix the gnaw marks on the post. She would try to somehow hammer back in the nails that were protruding. She would use her head for this, sometimes smashing into the metal nailheads with such force that she would cause her forehead to bleed. It was a bit of a frightening sight, to see a 650 pound pregnant pig with blood coming out of her forehead.

For some reason, the mud, the corn, the goulash -- all that mixing together, as much as that would drive her crazy, the fact that she had blood coming out of her didn't seem to bother her. She didn't clean that blood off. It would come down and dry there. It was a rather frightening sight -- this crazy, starry-eyed pig filled with raging female hormones brought on by her pregnancy, needing the imperfections to be repaired -- and the farmers not heeding to her squeals and calls for repairs. The farmer couldn't care less. The other pigs didn't care at all. It's one of her biggest issues in the world -- why doesn't anybody else care about this? She did not understand that. The blood would drip from her forehead.

She wasn't going to die from loss of blood. It dried fairly quickly. She healed well, but that blood would stay there and stain her. It looked awful. It looked scary. She was like a pig horror movie.

Unfortunately, after they had taken her last litter away, there were no children of hers to soothe her through this period. That was the only calming force she could ever find. All she needed was the touch of her children -- if they would come over, put their neck on her neck, put their heads on her stomach, touch her, rub her, show her their love -- this was the only medicine that ever worked. But right now she didn't have those children. They had been taken away by the farmer.

What she had were children inside of her. She started to understand this cycle. Every time she's pregnant, she goes into this crazed mode of seeing an imperfect world.

"They're stealing my children and they're doing it every time. They won't fix the fence. They won't clean this place up, but every time I have children, they feed them this crap food, they mix it with the mud and shit and then they take them away. And where do they do? I never see them again. They're just gone."

Red Brick Farm House

She looked up, over to the farmer's house. She could see smoke coming from the chimney. She realized there was some terrible evil in that house, in the form of human beings. She looked over to that imperfect fence. The gnawing of the post had gotten bigger. One of the things that happened was when she put mud on that gnawing mark, the farmer couldn't see the full degree of its decay. It actually had gotten pretty chopped up so that the post had weakened to a point where it would creak if you pushed against it. The boards leading to that post in this corner part of her pigsty had been moved around quite a bit by her constant nudging and fiddling with them. She kept smacking them lightly with her head. She kept trying to get those nails back in, but every time she hit the boards upward, those nails would come out a little bit more. As those nails came out a little bit more, they became more dangerous and would pierce in her forehead, causing her to bleed.

She understood all this perfectly well. One day she had an epiphany. Even pigs have epiphanies.

"This is never going to be fixed. This cycle is never going to stop. My need to do these rituals is going to go on and on forever, until someday those nails are going to go through my brain and are going to kill me and then I'll never have babies again -- or worse yet, the babies I have inside me are going to die with me. I'm not going to let that happen."

She looked over and saw that smoke billowing out over the farmer's comfortable home. The bricks that made up his house were perfectly laid, all at the same level in height. The cement in between was perfect.

"I bet his boards are all straight. I bet the nails in that house are all perfectly put into the wall. I bet there's no mud in there. There's no water slopping over. How much you want to bet the vegetables and the meat that they eat doesn't touch? They're separated."

That night, the farmer's wife was cooking corn on the cob and spare ribs. She very carefully put the ribs on a separate plate and the corn on another plate and yet another plate for the bread. It was all separate and the farmer, his wife, and two kids ate in this neat manner with the help of napkins. They got to wipe their faces with the napkins. They got to clean their hands with the napkins. When all that food was gone, they got to put it all away in a garbage can. The mom would wash those dishes and put them into a dishwasher and get them all perfectly clean. Then she'd stack them all up in perfect rows -- a stack of plates, stack of bowls, the big serving trays, the silverware -- the spoons would go into the spoon container, the forks would go into the fork container. Everything was just perfect.

The pig sensed this. Mother Oinker was smart.

"Oh sure. Your world is perfect. No one ever takes your kids. All your stuff is clean. All your food is separate. You've got separate plates for everything. But when it comes time for *my world*, you're too busy to fix the fence, to fix the post, to hammer those nails in and to help us with our food and separate the food. You don't want to do any of that."

There was only one answer to any of this. She stood back. She was transfixed on that fence post. She saw the gnawed-out part. She realized it was weak. Her head had gotten pretty tough from many smashes into the nails and into the wood. She had a callused head. And this day, that callused head would turn into an awesome battering ram, fueled by 650 pounds of a pissed off, pregnant, OCD pig that had had enough.

She charged that post straight ahead and in one blow, SMASHED it. It was obliterated. It was incredible how it just flew out. That post held up the boards forming that corner in the pigsty and once that post was done, those other boards that were off by at least two degrees -- probably even three degrees. The nails were out more than a sixteenth of an inch. They all came apart.

Sometimes the best thing that can happen to you is to have your world just fall apart. For seconds, she saw the pigsty in this collapsed state. It was a thousand times more imperfect now. The post was broken. It wasn't a question of being gnawed at -- it was destroyed. All those crooked boards were now forming a jigsaw puzzle. Instead of being held up by the post, they were all on the ground. And with that, there was an opening -- an opening to her freedom, to her own process of ending this terrible cycle. The mother instinct in her saw it. She saw it as clear as the day in front of her.

She ran through that opening like her life and her children's lives depended on it. She tore through the field. It was a huge field. They grew corn out there, but right now, the corn was in the process of coming up. It was only about a foot tall. There must have been 40 acres of this corn.

She ran and ran right past that farmer's house, right past all his perfect bricks, his perfect nails, his perfect boards, his clean plates all stacked up in nice little neat ways. She looked out and saw all their clothes hanging out to dry. They were all so perfectly clean -- clean white sheets blowing in the wind, soothing her, telling her, "Go, go!"

The message was clear. A mandate was given -- get the hell off the farm. Go back to the wild where you belong.

She ran past those 40 acres, without looking back once. She continued past the square perimeter of the cornfield and got into a place that she'd never seen before. Right behind the cornfields, there was unkept land. These were untilled. This was raw land -- had never been developed since the beginning of time. In the three billion years of Earth's existence, nobody had set a plow, a building, a foundation. It had never been measured. It hadn't been surveyed. It was as Mother Earth, made by Mother Nature.

The hills went up and down and everywhere. There were rocks here, rocks there. There were little paths in and out of the bushes. Some of the bushes were big, some of them were small. They were all different sizes. Nothing was uniform. It was all perfectly imperfect.

Now somehow when the imperfection occurs in nature, this Mother Oinker saw it as pure beauty. There was a freedom in it. She knew that out here, nobody would ever take her pigs. She would live out her years in the wild. She would give birth to beautiful pigs. They would revel in the beauty of nature's imperfection, of the lack of uniformity. Big trees, small trees, trees in the middle, bushes big, bushes small. Some of them have flowers. Some of them don't have flowers. All kinds of little animals run by -- little rabbits, little mice, little rats. Some of them look disgusting. Some of them are beautiful. Some of them are dangerous.

A little lynx came by. You should see a mother pig protecting her young 'uns. She was about 100 times the size of the lynx. She got up, walked over to that lynx and squealed; the lynx went running away, scared to death and it never bothered them again.

A little rabbit ran by. That lynx would go after something its own size. The birds would chirp. Little snakes would crawl away. Lizards would run and freeze if someone saw them, as though they would become invisible. Insects burrowed away under trees. All this was shared in her new home.

She lived in a place called Mother Earth. And in that home, nobody would ever steal her children. And in that home, she would never care that everything wasn't quite perfect.

Pigs in the Wild

It's not narcissism when you really *are* the greatest.

CHAPTER 5
THE NARCISSISTIC ANT[4]

While all the other ants were busy hauling in insects weighing more than 65 times their body weight, one ant sang a song: *I AM THE HIGHWAY* [5] BY AUDIOSLAVE.

---

[4] For a medical description of narcissistic disorder featured in this story, please refer to appendix A-5.

[5] See the music video at http://www.youtube.com/watch?v=725iONdAu9Q

Sammy the Narcissistic Ant

His name was Sammy. After he finished playing the song, so many of the other ants were amazed. The beauty of his voice, his guitar playing -- it actually was quite good. Sammy would walk by them, not exactly acknowledging his fellow ants. He saw himself quite clearly as a cut above all of them. Sammy was, as could be seen, the narcissistic ant.

The queen ants scolded him about this. "You don't do any work. You don't do anything productive around here. All you do is sing and play that guitar."

Sammy looked up at the queen ant. "You know anyone else who can do that?"

"No, I don't. I realize you're the only one who can do it. But really, what good does it do? We've got work to do around here. We've got thousands of mouths to feed and   you're   off   playing   guitar."

"Oh, I'll tell you what good it does. It helps establish us as a superior species. How about that?"

"Who cares about being a superior species? I'm worried about dinner. I'm worried about feeding all those ants."

She pointed out to the interior of the ant home. There were little burrows that went on quite intricately. It was an underground highway. There were zillions of little ants in there, busy as little bees, burrowing away with moths, butterflies, beetles; carrying them into the interior chambers where all the other ants could devour them. They ate these insects and devoured every molecule of them; even the powder on the butterfly wings was eaten.

Sammy shrugged it off. "So they can catch a butterfly."

The queen interrupted him, "And carry it over 10,000 ant miles."

That would be about six yards to you and I.

"Walk it up an ant mountain."

That would be about eight inches tall, but to an ant, eight inches is pretty ominous.

"Carry it to the top of that mountain and then very carefully turn it down into the hole and drag it through these little intricate pathways, lower and lower into our chambers and down below where they share it without any question to everybody. This is what they do."

"Yeah, and look what I do. I walk up that same mountain and I sing and play this guitar and I share that without any question to everyone."

The queen was frustrated. "You know your problem? You're selfish. You're self-centered. You don't care about anyone but yourself."

"You know your problem? You don't get it. You think I'm selfish, self-centered. You think I am full of myself, don't you?"

"Oh, I know you are."

"I think the universe revolves around me."

"Oh yeah. Absolutely."

"Well, I got news for you. I *am* the greatest. I *am* the most superior ant in this entire collection of, what? One hundred million ants. I *am* number one."

The queen rolled her ant eyes. "I can't believe you're saying this. You're number one? Look at you. First of all, take a look in the mirror. Do you notice something about you? You look exactly like all those other zillions of ants. How are you different from them?"

He strummed his guitar. He played it again.

"I am not your rolling wheel. I am the highway."

The queen put up her little ant paw. "I don't want to hear it. Don't need to know it. Don't care about it."

"You just don't want to learn from what I have. You know about catching insects, about walking them up the mountain and bringing them in here and eating them. That's what you know and you're a little afraid. I got something new for you. I've got music. You know, in these songs, there's a story."

"Oh, I know. It's a story that you are the greatest in the world and you're the most wonderful and you're the most superior and let me tell you, I'm sick of it. I don't want to hear it."

"You don't want to hear the truth?"

"It isn't the truth. You're the same like the rest of us. Will you get over yourself? Geez."

Before he could respond, she continued. "I'm in command here. I am ordering you to put your guitar down and go out and find an insect, catch that insect and bring it back here. Now are you going to follow my order or do we have to get military on you?"

"Oh no, oh no. I follow all orders given by the lawful authority of the queen. It's coming right from you. I fully accept it. I will obey. When would you like me to do that?"

The queen looked up and rolled her eyes again. "How about right now?"

The ant looked around and saw the many zillions of other ants eating away at a group of butterflies. He looked down at them and noticed what they liked the most. It was the monarch butterfly. This was the prime catch. The beetles were good too, but they really were quite large. The centipedes were quite yummy because they had that long, soft part that everyone could just jam into. It was like having a big piece of French bread. But there was nothing as majestic and delicious as the monarch butterfly. That was the prime rib of all insects.

After he finished looking at the various insects, he looked up at the mother queen. "I'll do it right now."

"Take a partner."

"I don't want any partner. I'll do it on my own."

"No!" she screamed out. "Cletia!"

"No, not Cletia. No, no, no. I don't --"

"Cletia!"

Cletia was the queen's favorite female ant. She was the soldier. She won the soldier of the year award last year. There was nothing she couldn't do. She was rough. She was tough. She was combat trained. She could annihilate any kind of insect with the possible single exception of a scorpion.

Cletia came scurrying over. "Yes, ma'am. Reporting for duty."

"Cletia, you're going to go out with Sammy here --"

"Whoa, whoa, whoa. Queen, wait, wait," Sammy interrupted. He was the only ant that would ever have the nerve to interrupt a queen. "I am not going hunting with this soldier."

Cletia remained unfazed by this insult. She would do whatever the queen commanded her to do.

The queen turned to her. "This is not a debate. This is not a discussion. It's an order. You're going to go out there with Cletia and you're going to get an insect. You're going to catch that insect. You're going to kill the insect. You're going to carry that

83

insect back here and you're going to feed everybody. Is there anything about that you don't understand?"

Sammy had to comply with this direct order. He looked over at Cletia. Cletia did not budge an antenna. She was actually a very attractive ant, tough as nails, with nerves of steel. What she lacked was a little thing called emotion. Sammy, on the other hand, the music man, was filled with passion and emotion. What he lacked were nerves of steel and a thing called discipline. These two completely different ants would now be paired together to go out into the wild jungles of ant land and find themselves an insect to bring home.

The queen gave one more order. "Cletia."

"Yes, ma'am."

"You lead."

"Oh come on. What do you mean, she leads? Let me at least lead. You're putting me with this girl. You're making me do something I don't want to do. At least let me lead."

The queen responded, "Cletia leads. That's it. Now take off."

Soon enough, Cletia and Sammy were on their trek for a giant insect. Cletia rolled her eyes as Sammy played his guitar and sang at the top of his lungs,

I AM THE HIGHWAY

BY AUDIOSLAVE

"Pearls and swine bereft of me

Long and weary my road has been

I was lost in the cities

Alone in the hills

No sorrow I feel

For anything I feel yea."

Not far from their anthill, they came upon a deep green jungle with millions of gigantic green leaf trees, growing next to and on top of each other. There was hardly any space at their base to walk through. They climbed up one of the trees, and got to the top. The trees all had exactly the same height, and had a squared-off top as though someone or something had cut them. They were able to walk across these tops, until Sammy fell down one:

"Aaayyyeeeaaaooowww!   Aaayyyeeeaaaooowww!   Aaayyyeeeaaaooowww! Aaayyyeeeaaaooowww!"

Cletia watched Sammy fall down the entire length of this leaf tree. He landed on a cushy bottom. He would be fine. She traversed down the leaf tree to rescue him. He quickly got up on all sixes.

"I'm fine. Don't worry. Everything's okay."

"You sure?"

"Oh yeah."

He climbed back up to the top. Once back up there, they continued to traverse until they came upon a huge expanse of white, super hard earth. It was almost like glass, except it was porous, rough like sandpaper, and reflected the sun off of it. It was blinding.

"Aaahhh!"

Sammy, of course, was the complainer.

Cletia led the way across this huge expanse of space. It look them quite awhile, but they ended at an abrupt white cliff leading down to another huge expanse of black. The white cliff was more than five times the length of the tree leaves. It went down, seemingly for miles, and when it got to the bottom, there was a little space of white left and then it all turned back.

"Hmm."

Cletia had seen this before and knew how to traverse it. They could walk on the base of the cliff all the way down. She had been in this territory before when there was a gushing river going right through it. Today, it was dry, but some of the wet mud was still there.

When they got to the bottom, they had to step into this gooey mud stuff.

"Yuck!"

Sammy, of course was complaining again. "This stuff sucks. Why we got to walk through this?"

Cletia walked knee-deep without complaint, and trudged through what seemed like over a mile of wet, sludgy mud. After they traversed over this sludge, the next part was all black and rocky. The rocks were embedded in some kind of gooey black syrupy item. Cletia didn't really care how it was made. She just cared to cross it.

85

As she started to walk over it, Sammy asked the obvious question. "Excuse me. Why must the ant cross the road?"

Cletia refused to answer.

Sammy stopped. "Hey, I'm talking to you. Why must we cross this road? How come we can't just walk on this side of the road and find something?"

Cletia pointed with her antennae. She had sensed something. She was onto something that Sammy did not quite understand. She continued walking across and couldn't care less if he followed her or not.

Sammy took one step onto this black expanse, when suddenly out of nowhere, there was the sense of a thousand thunders, the smoke of a thousand forest fires, and the rumbling of a thousand earthquakes. It was deafening. It was asphyxiating. It was jolting. He froze in his tracks.

Cletia turned around and ordered him, "Stop!"

He obeyed; not out of a sense of obedience, but out of sheer fright. Just then, a motorized mechanical beast of some sort, more than 1,000 times Sammy's height, whizzed by. It had two circular feet, and some type of gigantic mammal sitting on it, with what appeared to be an extraterrestrial head with a fire painted on it. Luckily, this half-beast, half-machine, circular-legged, fire-spewing, thunder charged up beast did not see Sammy or Cletia, and continued to whiz right by.

Sammy shook his little head. He realized right away it might be a good idea to stay closer to Cletia. He proceeded forward across the large expanse of black boulders embedded into some type of gooey black syrupy substance.

It took forever and a day, but at last they made it across this expanse, and found themselves face-to-face with yet another white cliff.

"Oh, don't tell me we got to climb up this thing."

Cletia shook her head no.

There was an expanse of white sandy hard topped surface that abutted the cliff. This white part went on for what seemed like a couple galaxies. They proceeded down that white part. This part of it was dry, but turned wet. There was a waterfall coming over the white cliff that poured quite a bit of water onto this part.

Sammy was sure they were going to walk around it and was quite surprised to see Cletia looking for something.

86

"What are you looking for?"

She kept looking. At last, she found it. It was a huge, ready-made boat, made out of a dried up brown colored object that appeared to be a leaf in a previous life. It had a stem. She was able to swivel it so that the stem pointed downriver. She motioned with her head for Sammy to jump on. He did. She pushed it while he navigated it forward. Once it hit the water, it took off. She had to jump up and latch on to the edge of this boat. She pulled herself up and did a somersault to fly into the boat.

Wow. Now they were moving. This sped down the river at what seemed like supersonic speeds. This took them to a rectangular-shaped vortex that was sucking in all this water. It was dark. It had an iron face and an outline at its base of a gigantic fish.

"WHOA!"

Sammy looked at Cletia for guidance. "We're not going down there, are we?"

Cletia refused to comment.

Sammy got upset. "Hey, listen to me. We're not going down there. There is no way."

Unfortunately for Sammy, he was caught in a current. There was no way he would get out of it.

Cletia got up at the top of the leaf on a stem. As the leaf started to make its way into the vortex, Cletia yelled out, "Jump up!"

Sammy shook his head, no way. Then he looked down at the vortex and saw that it went downward for what appeared to be over 1,000 miles. He then saw what she was going to jump to. There was an iron vertical bar. The leaf was going through it.

She jumped from one side and latched onto that bar.

He jumped to a spot right next to her. His guitar was on his back. She had a sword on her back. The two of them traversed up this bar to the top of the vortex, and climbed out of it.

They proceeded to another white plain, this one similar to the one they had crossed before. They walked across that white plain, which opened up to a gigantic jungle the size of an entire solar system.

They proceeded into this jungle, which, like the other jungle, had extremely tall leaf trees all square cut on top. They walked on the top of the trees, and proceeded into an area that was like nothing Sammy had ever seen before.

"Wow. What is this place?"

He looked around in total bewilderment. There was some kind of device that had super large tubes going from the ground up and over, forming a frame, but without any kind of structure over the frame. Instead, a series of chains came down from the top, and held some type of soft-looking super belt.

"What the heck is that?"

Cletia had seen this place before and wasn't quite so curious. Sammy's curiosity soon got answered when one of the two-legged mammals walked over and sat on that seat. Another mammal was behind this one, and pushed him. He went forward. He went backward. He went forward -- each time getting a little bit higher up in the air. He started to scream, though the screaming sounded happy.

Sammy had never seen anything like this.

"Wow, check that out. I want one of those."

Cletia ushered him to come over to another area. In this area, there was a huge Sahara Desert of sand dunes that went on for seemingly a million miles. They climbed into it. Wow. No water, sun coming down on them, endless sand dunes. How would they ever get out of this alive?

They came upon a path that led to a gigantic castle in the sand. Again, Sammy was quite surprised. He had never seen such a castle. It was perfectly smooth, round. It had a top that was cut similar to the leaf trees. It looked as though it was made just recently. Not far from it, was another, similar castle, but it apparently had been made thousands of years ago, as it was starting to crumble. Part of its top had fallen off, part of its side had cracked apart. The ancients must have built that one.

Several mammals were found in one of the corners of this desert. They were busy constructing more of these castles. Sammy watched with great interest to see how they did it. It was simple enough. They had a gigantic red device that scooped up the sand. They then took their hands and packed it in there. Then they turned this device upside down, put it back onto the sand foundation and took the device off. What was left was yet another skyscraper building. The whole process took just a matter of a minute.

"Wow. That is pretty cool."

Two mammals, female -- one with blond hair, one with brownish hair were also building a castle. It was then that Cletia saw the insect they were looking for. She pointed to it. She drew her sword. This was the prize of all insects, the one that Cletia had been hoping to find forever, and today she found it. It was a scorpion.

Scorpion Ant Butterfly Ladybug

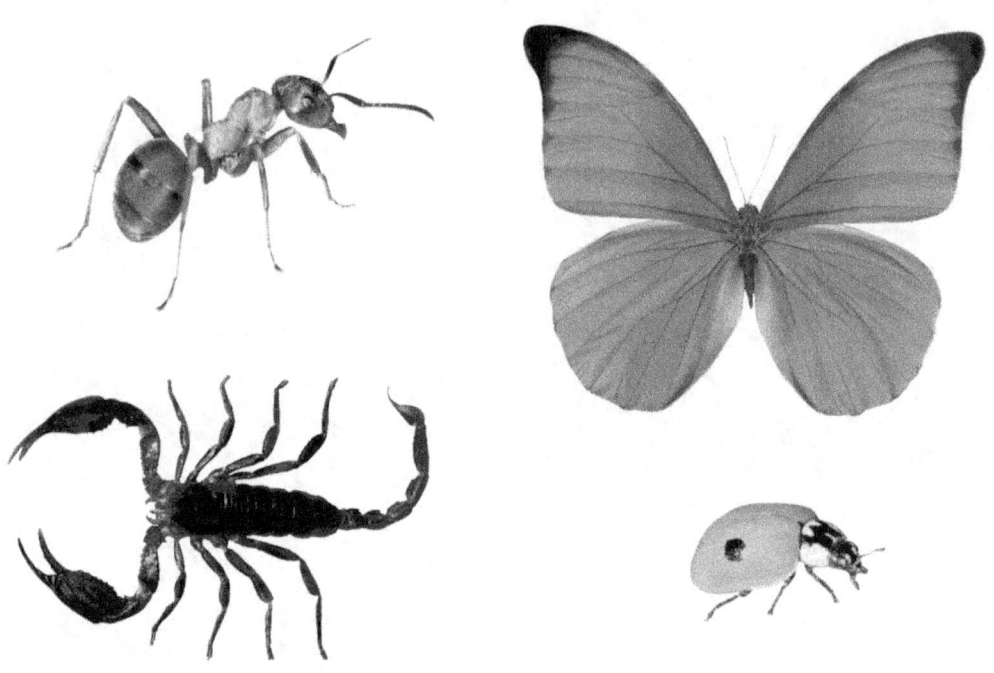

This scorpion was golden-beige in color. It had several eyes up front, two big pincers like a lobster, and a monstrous multisegmented tail, at the end of which was a large poison tail.

Sammy saw right away that Cletia wanted this beast. "Oh no. No. We don't need to chase that thing."

Cletia ushered him over. She walked up with the sword.

The thing about the scorpion was that it didn't even notice these little ants. It had its eyes on the girls. It was walking over with each of its eight legs, pod by pod. The girls had no idea that it was approaching. A larger mom mammal sat on a chair several hundred miles away and had no idea of the danger approaching.

Cletia saw the danger. She got in between the scorpion and the girls and drew her sword. The scorpion didn't even see her. As it walked right by her, she took her sword with all her might and chopped at the scorpion's exoskeleton. Her sword hit it and clanged off of it, but now she got the scorpion's attention. It quickly turned to her.

"What the hell do you think you're doing?"

Cletia responded with another whack at the pod.

Sammy couldn't believe what he was seeing. "Are you out of your mind?"

Within seconds, the scorpion lunged at Cletia with his pincer. Cletia was quite agile and did a 360 degree turn, twisting out of the way of danger. As she turned around, she chopped that pincer and was able to clip off about 10 yards of its length.

"Ow!"

The scorpion looked at what was left of its pincer and saw another part of it lying on the ground.

"Oh, it's on now. You want to chop me up, little girl? You better watch out."

This time the scorpion attacked with its other pincer. Cletia moved to the right. It missed. She moved to the left. It missed again. Then the scorpion got a little smarter. Rather than trying to put her into the pincers, it did a backhand and connected with her, full face. This threw Cletia the distance of about 100 meters. The scorpion came to her. She was near unconscious. She was panting.

Sammy saw all this and initially froze, then clicked into action. His insect instinct at last took over. At this moment, Sammy did something he had never done before. He

91

helped somebody else. He cared about somebody else. He would risk his life for somebody else.

Sammy ran over to Cletia. The scorpion was right over her, looking down on her. Sammy looked up and saw that tail, with the poison needle. It was curled, ready to strike. The scorpion with the broken pincer had no mercy. The pincer came down at the speed of 20,000 miles per hour.

Sammy had no weapon except his guitar. He turned it upside down, and swung it sideways. That needle hit right into his guitar, and got stuck in it. It made it through the outside of the guitar, through the inside of the guitar and just barely made it through the other edge of the guitar.

Sammy had the scorpion by its tail. He took the handle of the guitar and shook it as hard as he could. The scorpion swung the tail. Sammy was catapulted up into the air, but he was not going to let go of his guitar. He hung on for dear life. The scorpion swung again as Sammy went around.

Cletia saw all this and couldn't believe her own eyes. That scorpion did everything possible to get Sammy off that guitar and to remove that guitar. He swung it to the right. He swung it to the left. He swung it way up in the air, smashed it back down in the sand. There was no losing Sammy.

The scorpion made the mistake of getting close to one of those castles. Right by the castle was that device -- the castle-building machine. That device had a gigantic handle going over it. Sammy saw the handle and saw his opportunity. When the scorpion swung him again, he swung around into the device, by the handle. Sammy floated under the handle and was able to grab it. He placed the guitar right inside of the handle. It had a semi-hollow interior area. The guitar fit snugly lengthwise into this handle. When the scorpion tried to move its tail again, it now was attached to this gigantic bucket device.

Uh-oh. There goes the scorpion tail. As he moved it again, the entire back part of his tail was severed off, and came crashing down, poison and all. The scorpion now was missing its poison tail. This was one pissed off scorpion.

Sammy was down on the ground with his guitar. He looked up and saw the scorpion come over to him. The scorpion had his pincer out and was about to cut Sammy right in half. Just then, Cletia showed up and lunged her sword into the backside of the torn part of the scorpion's tail. Although his exoskeleton would protect him from the sword, this severed part was gooshy and easy to chop up. She smashed her sword into the tail. Ouch, did that ever hurt! If you're ever had a sword shoved up your tail, you would know the pain that this scorpion was suffering.

The scorpion turned around and focused on Cletia. He swung the tail, which removed her sword, and tossed her a bit. He then started to chase her. Sammy ran after the scorpion, then he stopped. He turned back. He found that severed part of the scorpion's tail. He picked it up and put it on his body. He was suddenly an ant-scorpion.

The scorpion had squared off with Cletia. Cletia defied him, sat right in front and swung away. The scorpion dodged to the right, dodged to the left, tried to backhand her again, but this time Cletia wouldn't get hit. She dove down into the jungle, down to the base of those trees where the scorpion couldn't get down. Sometimes being small has its advantage. The scorpion, though, could use his pincers to go down to the ground. It was earth-shattering as he shoved it down, smashing into the trees, smashing into the ground. He dove in once, twice, three times. Each time, Cletia would get out of the way, but he was getting closer and closer.

At last, Sammy came running to the scorpion with a new helmet on, this one having the scorpion's needle coming right out. He ran as fast as he could. The scorpion was not paying attention and was focused on lunging its pincer down into the grass. The scorpion exoskeleton has plates of armor from pincer to tail. Sammy found the soft part of the scorpion. It was the end of the tail that had been severed. It had chopped up meat from Cletia's sword. Some of that meat was dangling out. Sammy ran after that tail and hit a Bullseye. The poison tail of the scorpion had been turned inward on the scorpion. Its own weapon became its defeat.

There's a saying, those who live by the poison tail die by the poison tail -- and today, that saying would prove true. Sammy lunged that tail right into the scorpion. It suddenly jolted up with a look of shock. The poison went in the tail. A process of paralysis began. The scorpion froze up. It shook. It shook a little more. It vibrated. It went into shock. It slowly had its heart stop beating. Its lungs stopped breathing. Its eyes stopped seeing. The scorpion was dead.

Cletia had no idea what had killed the scorpion. She walked up the gigantic leaf tree and saw the rather odd sight of the scorpion's tail turned into it and at the end of that, wearing that severed part of the tail as a helmet, was none other than Sammy.

"Wow. What did you do?"

Sammy looked up with a big ant smile. "I slayed the scorpion."

Cletia walked over and saw what had happened. "You stuck it with its own tail."

"Yes."

"Oh no."

"What?"

"Oh, you ruined it."

"What do you mean, I ruined it? I killed him."

"Yeah, but you poisoned it. Now we can't eat this thing. Don't you know what you did? You see the tail? It's poisonous. When you stuck him, you released that poison into the scorpion."

"Yeah. That's what I wanted to do."

"Well, now we can't eat it."

Sammy thought about it. "Oh. I think you're right."

"Well, at least it didn't kill us."

"Yeah, but it kind of defeats the purpose. I mean, we're out here looking for food. You just spoiled the food."

Sammy shook his head. "You know, some women just can't be pleased."

Cletia looked around and then Sammy figured it out. "Wait a minute. You want to somehow deprive me of my victory, don't you?"

"No, it's not about that. It's about food for everyone back home. Don't you get it? This isn't about you."

"Yeah, but it is about me. I killed this thing and I want to bring him home."

"Oh yeah. You're going to carry this thing home, all the way back there, through all the places we just went -- how you going to do that? Have you figured that out yet? And when you finally do get it there and you feed everybody, guess what's going to happen. Everybody's going to die of scorpion poison."

"I want to bring it home to show everyone my great victory."

"You know, the problem is you're just a gigantic showoff. You don't really care about anyone but yourself. You don't care if your victory is at the cost of everybody's lives. I mean, everyone's going to start eating this thing and everyone's going to die. I don't understand why you'd want to do that."

Sammy thought about it. "You know, you're right. Of course you're right. I guess I'm just being selfish."

Cletia loved to hear Sammy acknowledge his issue. "What was that?"

"You heard me."

"Oh, I didn't quite hear it. There was something blocking my antennae. Can you say it again?"

"I guess I was being selfish."

"Oh. You -- selfish? I am the highway. I am the night. I am the lightning. Full of yourself? Gee, I guess so."

"I'm sorry, Cletia. I understand."

"You understand."

"I do."

"Are you sure?"

"Well, yeah. I'm sure."

"Well, what are you going to do about it?"

"What am I going to do about it? I'll tell you what I'm going to do about it. You see this gigantic scorpion? The greatest victory of my life ever, the one that would make me permanently famous in ant legends. You see him, dead as a doorbell?"

"Yep."

"I'm going to leave him here and I'm never going to say another word about it."

Cletia smiled. "Wow. Is that for real?"

"It's for real."

"Okay then. Let's go."

As the two of them proceeded out of this endless span of desert, Sammy looked back one more time at his kill. It was monstrous. It was majestic and it was dead, dead.

Cletia patted him on the back with her little ant arm. "Remember Sammy, I am your witness."

95

The best thing in the world was she knew it, she saw it, and she adored him for it. She knew the best solution was to feed his ego with the fact that she loved him. He didn't need the love of the entire world. He needed her love.

Sammy smiled. As he walked forward and away from this, he was prepared to make the trip home with zero evidence of his great feat, but Cletia was feeling generous. Soon enough, she came upon something that she knew was very dear to Sammy -- his guitar. It had been flung off the scorpion tail. It was still intact.

"Hey Sammy, check it out."

She picked it up. She handed it to him. He strummed it. It still worked.

"Wow."

And in that guitar, was the unmistakable proof of that day's great victory. It was a piercing hole through the top of the guitar and going through the bottom -- a hole created by the scorpion tail. A hole that would mark the point in Sammy's life where he began to understand that he was not the center of the universe, that everything did not revolve around him, that there were bigger issues and bigger concerns, that he should think of others, that he should do things for the greater good, that he shouldn't be a selfish little ant.

Cletia sensed that he was getting this important lesson. She smiled. The two of them made their way back across the great jungle, across the great white space, down the white cliff, across the large black expanse, up to the other cliff, back up the huge white expanse, up into the jungle area that led them back to their home.

Sammy Triumphs

CHAPTER 6

THE DOG WITH FALSE IDENTITY DISORDER[6]

False identity disorder is where a person believes they are somebody else. Our case study is about a dalmatian dog by the name of Spots. Spots has the following version of false identity disorder: He thinks he is a human.

Following a series of therapeutic sessions, during which Spots largely defended his "I am a human" position, it was agreed that Spots could be brought back to his true identity if he would explore his false identity in writing. As will be seen, this understandably prescribed therapeutic tool of writing it all out unfortunately backfired. Spots' paper follows.

---

[6] For a medical description of dissociative identity disorder, also known as multiple personality disorder, featured in this story, please refer to appendix A-6.

Mr. and Mrs. Spots and family

I Am Not A Dog
By Spots

My Journey Of Self Discovery

I would like to begin this essay by explaining that I have given all of this extremely serious thought. I do not come to my conclusions lightly, or flippantly. I understand the seriousness of these issues. Having gone through several therapy sessions, in which my true identity was explored, I was asked to explore it further in writing.

Having thought about this matter for days on days on end, I now write out how it is and why it is I am very certain that I am not a dog. I am a human.

I.   The Evidence Supporting My Claim to Be Human.

Let us begin by looking at the hard evidence. In this section, I will set forth a comparison of my life, my activities, what I do, when I do it, to the parallel and similar activities engaged by humans. As will be seen, my activities are EXACTLY the same as humans.

Let's start with the morning. Tell me honestly, what is the very first thing a human being does? "First, pee." Well, guess what I do first thing in the morning? I go out on the lawn and pee, exactly like a human. After that, just like a human, I will sneeze and in the process, blow my nose. I shake my head around and find a bone to gnaw on. Humans brush their teeth. I gnaw on a bone.

Next, I have breakfast. Isn't that what humans do in the morning? They have breakfast. I know this for a fact because every single morning, I look into a glass door and I see the family I live with come downstairs and have breakfast. There are three children in this family that eat out of a bowl. They pour some kind of food in it, they use a spoon and add this white liquid that I know they call milk. Well, look what I do. I've got a bowl. They pour very similar looking food into it, dry and in little balls -- only for some weird reason, probably because they just forgot, I don't get any milk in my bowl. I just get the dry food.

I'm very happy to tell you though, they put some wet food on top of it which is quite yummy. They eat breakfast out of a bowl; I eat breakfast out of a bowl. Their breakfast appears as little round hard items; so does mine. And don't let the fact that I don't have milk fool you. They just forgot to pour it in. I'm a very forgiving person, so I don't hold that against them.

I see in the morning the parents come down, one by one. They have to get dressed up to leave for their daily jobs. The kids have to get dressed up to go to school. The daughter is in high school. The two sons are in middle school. It doesn't take long for them to eat their breakfast, get all organized, and run out the door. I notice the man of the house kisses the woman before he leaves -- well, not every day, but many days he does this. Well, the same thing happens to me. Before the boys leave, they come out, they hug me, they pat me, they say goodbye. The woman gets a goodbye with a pat and a hug; I get a goodbye with a pat and a hug. So you see, it really is the same.

Now he goes off to work. She goes to work later. The three kids go to school. So everybody has this big activity. Well, guess what? So do I. What do you think I do all day in the backyard? You don't think I have anything to do? Well, let me explain how wrong that is. My goodness, I have an extremely packed day with all kinds of scheduled events.

First of all, my primary job and duty is to guard the house. You have no idea of the levels of crime out in the world. I know because I bring the paper in and I get to see the front cover. Not a day goes by when some incredible crime isn't reported -- murder this, steal that, rob them, kidnap her, torture this, beat up that -- violence, theft, murder, sex crimes -- you name it, it happens every day. So who's going to protect this house while they're gone? And let me make it very clear -- this is most certainly a world filled with evil and danger. Being a guard is no small job and that is my job. I guard the house and if you want to test me, come on by. Make my day. You try to get in that backyard and you're going to see what's going to happen to you. Check out my teeth. Check out my paws. And let me warn you -- I'm extremely fast, I'm extremely agile, I can jump up, I can run in circles, I can bite and I can bark. These are the tools of my trade.

Let's compare that to what the man of the house does. I know that he's a lawyer. So he stands up. He speaks. He uses his hands in circular motions as he explains things. He attempts to get justice for people who are wronged. He is guarding their rights in the same exact way as I guard his home.

At the end of the day, they all come back home and they know the place is safe. They show me their appreciation. The first thing I get is another bone. I love those bones. I notice in the same way, the boys get a cookie when they come home. They get a cookie; I get a bone. Okay, now tell me seriously, what is the difference between a bone and a cookie? The answer, obviously, is none.

I will agree to one difference between our activities. I do notice that when they sit down for dinner, they don't eat out of a bowl. They eat on these flat plates. I have my dinner out of a bowl. But other than that tiny difference, everything else is the same.

I should also point out -- my dinner is basically the same as my breakfast. They have a completely different meal for dinner, but here's where all gets equalized. They always give me some of it. I get a little piece of chicken, a little piece of fish, some spaghetti, some lasagna, some noodles, meatballs, pieces of steak. So on top of my regular food, they share some of their dinner with me.

After dinner, they all watch television. Well, guess who else is watching with them? That's right -- me. I think the TV is kind of funny. Sometimes it shows real life scenes. Other times it shows drawings of real life scenes. I kind of like the drawings because they're so colorful. The dramas are exciting. There's music. There's people talking. It's so comforting to lay on the floor right next to the boys as they watch television. I'm so comfortable I will go to sleep as they pet me on the head. Later, they are asleep as well. I see as the man of the house wakes them up and brings them upstairs to bed.

Now you may think just because I sleep downstairs, that I live in a completely different way. Not true. The daughter's bedroom is downstairs. So she stays downstairs; I stay downstairs. So once again, I ask you -- what is the difference?

II.   Family Dynamics.

I should point out that I took a fairly lengthy pause in the process of writing this paper. I went through a bout of depression. Why was I sad? One of the things I started to notice is that there was a huge difference between my life and the humans I live with. It was such a huge difference that I began to question whether maybe I really was not a human. Maybe it is true I am a dog. Here is what I saw.

I noticed there was a mom, a dad, and three kids. They were a family. They went out and did things together. Now they're very kind to include me as a member of their family, but let's face it. I am not their child. I am not their parent. I am not their cousin. I am not their nephew. I am not a blood relative. I can see that right away because we just don't share the same features. The biggest giveaway is they do not have spots. I have black spots all over me. I note rather plainly that not a one of them has a tail and their teeth are all very small. So let's face it. There's no way these are blood relatives of mine.

And it got me to thinking. Wow, they've got a family, they're together like this, they eat meals together, live together, work together, go to school together. There is a huge difference between my life and theirs. I don't have this family. This made me cry. I was whining, walking around dejected, despondent, depressed.

Hey, aren't those human emotions? Well, guess what? I've got all of them. How do you suppose you solve the problem of depression from loneliness that stems from not having a family? Well, duh. Get a family. And guess what?

One day, the best day in my entire life, they all left on a big trip. I could tell because they had to pack up a bunch of food, they had to put on jackets, they patted me goodbye and they took off. But I could tell in the looks of their faces, something big was going to happen that day. And you know what? It wasn't big. It was small. It was a little puppy. They brought a girl to the home. Now this girl had many of the same features I had. She had the black spots. She had a tail and she had these fangs.

I have to say, at first she wasn't very nice to me. I came up and tried to smell her, she barked and growled. What a little meanie. As we stayed together, she slowly warmed up to me. I noticed she liked to sleep right under my neck and chest. I think that's the warmest part of my body. It's where my heart beats. I think she could hear my heart beating, probably a little faster as she was laying there.

Mr. and Mrs. Spots

Well, I'm sure you know the story from here. That little puppy quickly grew up into a little girl and then a teenager and then a young woman -- and let me tell you, with all due respect to the woman of the house, this little puppy grew up into being the most beautiful woman on the planet. She is a supermodel. Her name is Diamond. Just the sound of that name gets me all excited. My tail is wagging. My hips are shaking so much that you can hear the clatter of my toenails on the hardwood floor.

Diamond does something very sexy with her mouth. When she gets excited, she smiles and pulls her lips back and shows her teeth. I love it when she does this. It shows she's thrilled to see me. I can tell by the speed of her wagging tail and the whites of her teeth that, guess what? This girl really likes me.

Not far from our house, there is a river with a levy. We go out on that levy and run. It is so much fun you can't even believe it. The boys come with us. Usually the man of the house is there, but sometimes the woman is there as well. We go on a long walk together. One of the first things I like to do is run down and jump right into the river.

I see that there are quite a few people fishing out here and they're very kind fishermen. When they catch the fish, they put it behind them. I hope I haven't misunderstood their kindness, but I see that as a gift. They are saying to me, here is a fish I caught. Please take it and eat it.

One of the reasons I think I may have misunderstood their intentions is that when I take those fish, sometimes they yell at me. I'm not sure if they're yelling at me because they're happy that I got the fish or if they're angry that I took the fish. But one thing is for sure -- those fish are sure yummy.

I'll tell you another thing they have out here on the levy -- the ultimate toy; a live jackrabbit. You may sympathize with them. They're so cute. They got those big ears, those big brown eyes. They're all furry and they got this cute little ball for a tail. And you may say, nobody should ever hurt a jackrabbit. They're just so cuuuuute. Well, don't worry because I've chased no fewer than 500 of these little cutie pies and I've yet to catch one, ever. They are so fast. They just tear away from me.

Well, one day in a big surprise, the little woman Diamond, the supermodel with spots, actually caught one. I have to tell you, I was a little bit surprised by her conduct. First of all, she got a little one -- a cute little bunny. But when Diamond got ahold of it, she suddenly switched from her suburban upbringing back into wolf mode. She just went wild on that little bunny. It may sound cruel and ugly, but let me just tell it to you truthfully. The first thing she did was bite off its head.

They say in the wild, you eat what you kill. Well, guess what? She ate that little rabbit, every bit of it. And nobody else was going to get that rabbit. I walked over just to sniff it and boy, did she ever snarl at me.

"Don't even think about it!"

I was thinking about it and she knew it and barked me away. I didn't want to take the rabbit from her. I just wanted to smell it. I'd already had a fish so I wasn't all that hungry. I sat and watched as she ate that rabbit.

Diamond was faster than me. I don't know how. She's a lot smaller. I must be about double her size, but she can sure run fast. Watching her run off that levy, down to the river chasing these rabbits -- I have to tell you, I fell in love.

And then I knew it. There's the proof, right there. Humans love and guess what? So do I.

Well, I'm sure you can figure it out. It wasn't long until Diamond and I were married, husband and wife, and right after that, we had not one, not two, not three -- well, let me just skip it. We had eight babies.

Curiously, our babies were born all white with pink skin. They look like little pigs -- no spots. Diamond didn't want me around as she had them. She barked me away. I respected her needs and let the mother do what the mother wants.

I notice that happens a lot with the man of the house. If the mother wants something, he doesn't argue. He just does it. If she needs some help, he helps. If she needs him to agree, he agrees. Well, guess what? I'm doing the same thing.

So when she told me, "Leave the room," guess what? I left the room.

And the next day, when I came back in, oh my goodness. There they all were -- eight beautiful little pink piglet-looking no-spot babies. Little tiny tails, little tiny paws, eyes closed, mouths open, hungry as can be -- and I'm just thinking, now I know what it's like to have a family.

III.   A Danger to the Family.

One of the things I noticed is that the kids like to play music. I see them playing the piano and the guitar. The mom also plays piano. The music is quite lovely. When the kids started out, they weren't so good. But as they continued to practice, they got better and better.

In the same way, my family plays music, especially when the moon is full. I can hear in the distance, off on that river, the sounds of wild coyotes yapping away in the moonlight. It's an impressive sound. They're all so busy. There must be hundreds of them out there. I never see them when I'm running out there. I don't know where they live or hide, but in the night, they come out and they sing.

Well, in the same way, I like to sing. Some say I'm not so good at it, but you know how it is. When you like to sing, you sing -- whether you're good or not. And my kids sing -- four boys, four girls. They're all yapping away. I think to every parent, their child sings in a perfect way.

But here is where a danger arose. The music to my ears, the singing of my children, apparently bothered the neighbor and it bothered him a lot. He kept coming over late at night, banging on the door. The man of the house would come over and talk to him. The man was angry and yelling. We had to be quiet.

Well, I don't know why we had to be quiet. What's wrong with that? I know that this nation was based on certain freedoms, including the freedom of speech. It's been told to me that some reasonable non-content based restrictions are allowable, but I got the idea here, the real restriction was, no more singing, ever. Just don't. Well, I'm sorry. I just don't agree with that. Who says I can't sing and who says my children can't sing? What kind of ridiculous rule is that?

So I hate to say I'm disobedient, but you know what? I'm disobedient. I sang anyway. I sang whether the moon was out or not. We sang every night. We had so much fun, all of us.

Well, this kept getting the neighbor more and more upset. Apparently he called the cops. Unbelievable.

One day the police came. They walked in, they saw us, we tried to be quiet. The woman of the house was there. The cop wrote out a little yellow ticket and gave it to her. Oh gosh. She's actually got to go to court over our singing. There's going to be a trial over our right to sing as we please. The trial would deal with the angry neighbor that wants to censor us, and our own desire to live and be free.

The stakes got a little higher when I noticed something going on with the man of the house. From time to time, he would bring over some other family. Now I don't know who these people are. They looked nice enough -- a mom, a dad, a couple little kids. But you should see what they did. It's just unbelievable, and I'm convinced it's all connected to this singing issue.

They would take one of my kids -- just take him right away. I watched as one by one, my children left the house, never to be seen again. Well, maybe it's their destiny. Maybe it's what they're supposed to do. They find their own new family, they grow up, maybe make their own families just like I did. So I'll try not to get too upset about it, but my own family went down from eight children to just two. So now there are four of us. I hope that makes the neighbor happy.

I got the idea that the more I sang, the more children I lost. So I started to cool it a little. I wanted to compromise. Hey, isn't that a very human trait? Compromise. Someone wants you to do zero something. You want to do a whole lot of something. So how about do half as much? Isn't that a nice idea? So I toned it down. We stopped the singing.

I also noticed kind of a strange thing going on. The man of the house bought this little birdhouse-looking object. Every time we started singing, there was some weird high-pitched screaming sound that came out of that bird box. I don't know what kind of bird they had in there, but I got to tell you, it really put a damper on my singing ability.

Forgiveness is also supposed to be a human trait. Well, guess what? This neighbor would not forgive. There had to be a trial on the case of whether or not I could sing, my wife could sing, my children could sing. Lucky for me, the man of the house is a lawyer and appeared in court to argue the case.

IV.   I Am Bad Like a Human.

I think it was the emotional distress and pressure of the impending trial that caused me to do something that was truly a bad thing. Like a human, I can be a bad person. Let me tell you what I did. I was a bad boy.

I was in the garage. One of the things I had noticed -- and I had never really thought about it that much -- was this white light. It's right by the door that leads into the house. I started to fixate on that light. What is it? It's not that high up. It's about at a level where if you open the door, it would be at the shoulder level of the homeowner.

So I walked up and looked at it. I jumped up on the wall, stood on my two hindfeet and with one of my paws, I struck it. Okay, I know. In retrospect, I shouldn't have done it, but I just couldn't resist. Today that bright light was just getting to me. I needed to know, what happens when you push that light?

I heard a clanging sound, the sound of a chain moving, the sound of a door opening. I looked around and what did I see? Oh my goodness. The garage door was coming open. It opened all the way up, leaving a complete opening out to total freedom.

I looked at my wife and our two sons and we all knew without saying a word what to do. We ran out of there. It was so much fun. The first thing I noticed was this big tree. It had the smell of so many of the neighbors on it. I peed all over it. My sons followed. My wife was peeing on the lawn next door.

We went to the next neighbor and we did the same thing. We had quite a time. We went across the street. I think I peed on every single yard there. My sons did as well. We were having a pee party.

One of the neighbors apparently wasn't too happy about this. They call the cops. Can you believe it? You take a pee, they call the cops. Cops show up. Oh boy, they're mad. Apparently there's another law. You can't pee or roam around loose in the neighborhood.

I don't understand who writes these laws. Obviously they've never ran around with a leash on their neck, but apparently they've written this stupid law that says I'm not allowed to run around free. I've got to be on a leash.

Cop pulls by the house and what does he see? The garage door wide open and he sees us running around. They call Animal Control.

Animal Control guy pulls up in this truck with the little prison in the back. There's no way I'm going in that prison. I'm just taking off. So we just run to the levy. We know this place very well. We've been there many times. The levy is our place.

Animal Control tries to follow us there. Now you can try to catch me in a lot of different ways, but once I get out on that levy all bets are off. I'm on raw land. It goes down to a river. I'll jump in the river and swim away. There's no way you're going to catch me.

Then a cop pulls up. This is becoming a serious police event. They are absolutely insistent on catching us. I've been a bad boy. I'm not really sure what to do here, but there's no way I'm getting inside that truck. They can just forget that. They're going to have to shoot a dart at me and tranquilize me before I'm doing that. If they lay a hand on my wife, let me just tell you, there's going to be trouble. We're all pretty fast too. We're not slow runners so we just sprint away. There's a point at which they can no longer drive and they have to stop and they walk out there and see us run away. We just keep on running.

Later that evening, the owner gets home. He's got a house filled with cops circulating around. They're not happy with him. He notices the open garage door and he explains it.

"Apparently they figured out how to open the garage door," much to his surprise.

Hah, he was not ready for that!

So he made a promise to disengage the garage door opening mechanism. It was easy enough to do -- just flick a little switch that disconnects the chain device from a little pulling device. This way when you go to open the door and pass the light, it activates the pulley system, but it's not connected to the chain and the door doesn't open. He showed that to the cops and they were satisfied.

He then came out with his two boys, with leashes. They found us. We were in the water swimming away, bothering fishermen, chasing away the fish, eating the fish that were caught and eating the bait that the fishermen wanted to use to catch more fish.

Yes, we are bad, just like humans.

113

Yolo County Superior Courthouse, Woodland, California with Adam and Alex Franck

V. The Trial of the Century.

It is no exaggeration to refer to this as a trial of the century. Look at the rights that are at stake -- whether my family can sing. Now we tried to be good about it. We tried to compromise, but oh no. Mr. Meanie next door wouldn't forgive, wouldn't compromise. For him, it was an all or nothing proposition. What a jerk.

The case was called. The first thing about the judge that I could tell immediately -- he was not a musician. Uh-oh. He didn't like any kind of singing, especially from the likes of me.

The judge spoke, "You're charged with violation of local ordinance section which makes it a crime for a local homeowner to allow their dog to bark excessively. What is your plea?"

"Your Honor, the plea is not guilty."

"Very well. Go ahead and state your case."

"Your Honor, Exhibit A to our defense is the following device that I purchased from a pet shop. It is a birdhouse that has in it an electronic device that emits a high-pitched sound, undetectable to the human ear, but detectable by the dog's ear. When the dog barks, it causes this electronic device to emit this high shrill. That high shrill stops the dog from barking. I have a duty to take reasonable steps to stop a dog from barking. This birdhouse did just that."

"Okay. Anything else?"

"Yes. We also received from the sheriff's department a brochure that talks about what you can do to keep your dog from barking. That's where I learned about this birdhouse. I bought a second one. One is for the outside. One is for inside the garage. So Exhibit B is the one I have on the inside. May I show it to the court?"

"I am very well aware of these devices, counsel."

"Very well. I installed one of these on the fence in the backyard and I installed one of these inside the garage. It had a substantial impact in reducing the frequency of barking. Generally speaking, when they bark, they bark once or twice and then they become quiet."

"Very well. Anything else?"

115

"Yes. The other pointer given to me by Animal Control was that you can interrupt your dog's barking by simply clapping your hands. This distracts them from whatever it was that was causing them to bark. I regularly practice this hand clapping, as do my sons. Whenever the dogs bark, we simply go outside, clap our hands and the dogs stop barking."

"Very well. Anything else?"

Uh-oh. I could see it in his odd look. There was something he was going to say that would blow the court away. You could tell right away that the judge was not accepting any of his defenses. The judge was unmoved by the birdhouse, unmoved by the other device, and unmoved by the hand clapping. What other defense was there? Oh gosh. Please don't. Tell me no. Oh, he's going to do it.

"Your Honor, I have one more defense."

"Very well, counsel. Proceed."

"As you know, the ordinance applies to dogs, correct?"

"Oh yes."

"It says right here a homeowner may not allow their dog to bark excessively. Well, Your Honor, I submit to the court that my dog isn't a dog at all."

"Excuse me, counsel?"

"My dog is a human being named Spots."

"Oh, come on."

"Your Honor, I have proof."

"What's the proof? This, I got to see."

"I marked as exhibit C this writing, right here, entitled, "I Am Not a Dog" by Spots."

And with that, the attorney handed the judge this very story. The judge reviewed it with great interest. I thought he might just throw it away, but he actually read it. He read it all and after he read it, he said words that we thought we would never hear.

"I find you not guilty." He slammed the gavel down. It was so ordered.

We walked out of court with a not guilty verdict, but something even bigger -- a judicial finding of something that I have known since the day I was born. I am not a dog. I am a human.

CHAPTER 7
THE EAGLE THAT WAS AFRAID OF HEIGHTS[7]

There is a place on the west side of the Grand Canyon called Eagle Point. The bald eagle soars there. Nesting on a cliff overlooking a nearby Indian reservation was the Cuscayun family of eagles. There was a father named Cuscayun, proud with white head, black body and a wingspan of about six feet. He was an accomplished hunter, a daring flyer, and soared through the face of the canyon walls.

Today we can see him soaring stomach-side toward the wall, as he proceeds in a stomach-to-cliff face trajectory. His mighty eye is focused on the pinpoint of the head of a diamondback rattler. A rattler wouldn't even have time to get into an S-shape of his neck. Cuscayun swooped by, grabbed the neck of that rattler with his talons, breaking the snake's neck immediately. His forked tongue would flop out of his mouth.

Cuscayun then proceeded up to the top of the cliff face, did a U-turn, and flew back to his family's nest. There in the nest were three young ones, Cuscayun Junior, Havasopi, and their daughter, Azure, for her blue eyes. The other eagles had golden eyes.

You should see how these young ones devour that rattlesnake. Though small, these young eagles have impressive strength in their beaks. They ripped into that snake, tore its skin off and devoured every molecule of it, even the rattler. Cuscayun and his wife Tolpe watched as their soon-to-be world class hunters received yet another taste of the wild.

---

[7] For a medical description of specific phobias featured in this story, please refer to appendix A-2A {specific phobias} and A-2B {post-traumatic stress disorder}.

Eagle Point, Grand Canyon Arizona

Grand Canyon Skywalk, Grand Canyon Arizona

Across the canyon was an interesting structure built by the local Indian tribe, the Hualapai. They made a horseshoe-shaped walkway that had clear glass underneath, and extended out from the rim of the canyon. They call it a skywalk. You can see 5,000 feet down to the Colorado River. Tourists walk on this extension, and have the fascinating view of looking straight down to the bottom of the canyon -- about a mile below. This is similar to glass bottom boats, except without the boat and the seats.

One day there was a young blond boy on the skywalk with his father. The father was named Alfred. He was a single father. The boy had a set of binoculars and found Cuscayun's eagle nest. The boy's name was Bobby.

"Daddy! Look, look. Look what I see. A bald eagle."

The boy pointed across the canyon wall in the direction of the Cuscayun family nest. The father received the binoculars from his son. He couldn't find it. He swayed back and forth. He had a super binocular set, with focus devices, near-telescopic abilities, but could not find what his son had found.

Bobby tried to help his dad. He got on his knees and pointed directly to where the eagles were. His father got directly behind him, rested the binoculars on his shoulder and in the direct line of his son's finger.

"A-ha! I see them. Wow, nice find, Bobby!"

Bobby smiled. Sons always adore the appreciation of their fathers.

His father handed him the binoculars. "They're beautiful."

Bobby looked through and sure enough, there they were -- a gorgeous family of eagles and their three young ones. His view became obstructed by a very disconcerting sight. Right in front of the skywalk, a helicopter flew by. Wow. When you look at a helicopter that close through a binocular, it is as though a building flew by. He put the binoculars down and watched as the helicopter screamed down the canyon.

Bobby looked up. "Daddy, can we go on the helicopter ride?"

"Oh, I don't know. Those helicopters are not good. Look at them. They're loud. They're noisy and they're dangerous."

Bobby looked at his father.

Bobby watched with envy as the helicopter proceeded down the canyon and continued hovering over the Colorado River, about 5,000 feet below. His father watched as he watched. Then they saw something that troubled them. The helicopter did a U-turn with the same kind of horseshoe shape as the skywalk. Now it was on a different side of the canyon, beside where the eagle's nest rested in safety.

Helicopter in Grand Canyon, Arizona

Cuscayun, the bald eagle, could hear the blades of the chopper chopping away. It was troubling to him. This kind of big bird seemed like a space monster. He knew to avoid it. This was not a bird to fight. This was also a bird that never attempted to compete for food, so its only real trouble was the vibrations, the sound and the scary sight of it. The chopper flew by the eagle's nest. The wind from the blade brushed off of him and shook him, but it was okay. Their nest was tightly nestled against the sheer face of the brim of the Grand Canyon. It wasn't going anywhere.

One of the tourists in the helicopter spied the Cuscayun family. "Oh, honey, honey, look!"

She was about 30 years old, barely attractive by her fake cowboy shirt and white cowboy boots. Her jacket, lying to the side, was white with those fake flays hanging down. She had a matching white cowboy hat. She must have been from Las Vegas or Kansas.

Her husband was more of an athletic type, a former professional athlete of some sort, most likely a football player.

His wife handed him the binoculars. "Right there, honey. Look!"

As the helicopter flew away, her husband got a glimpse at the Cuscayun eagle family.

He yelled out to the pilot, "Hey, can we turn around? Can we turn around? There's an eagle family back there I want to see."

The pilot was happy to oblige and did a U-turn. He flew back and forth several times in front of the eagle family. He was Arrowpath, a Native American from the local Hualapai tribe.

This was very upsetting to Cuscayun. He had become accustomed to these helicopters flying by once, maybe twice -- but this was the third and now fourth flyby.

The beefcake husband had a camera and started snapping some pretty decent photos of the bald eagle family. The helicopter stood in place, right in front of the bald eagle family.

Back at the skywalk, little Bobby watched all of this through his binoculars. His dad was about to walk away.

"Bobby, let's go."

123

"Dad, look."

They looked over. They saw the helicopter still in the canyon, at rim-level, appearing directly before the eagle family. Bobby noticed the eagles ducking from the force of the wind.

"Dad, they're bothering the family. Look at that."

Bobby's dad understood. He didn't know what he could do. He looked back at the administration building of the skywalk. The helicopter tour came from that same building, but there was no one there to help. He looked back.

All of a sudden, Bobby screamed, "NO!"

Cuscayun had had enough of this challenge and decided to take matters into his wings. He flew out of the nest, a huge mistake, but he did this with the full force of his paternal instinct to protect his family from any foe. Even a foe 100 times larger.

What Cuscayun did not understand was that the production of the wind that was hitting his nest came from a rapidly moving set of helicopter blades. These blades, as they turn, become invisible, even to the eagle eye. Sadly, and to the horror of his children and his wife, Cuscayun flew directly into the main helicopter blade, and was devoured by it.

He left behind a golden-eyed wife, two golden-eyed sons and a beautiful blue-eyed daughter by the name of Azure. That they should have to witness their father's death would be carried with them for the rest of their lives.

Bobby, on the other side, saw all this on the skywalk. He dropped to his knees, shook his head.

"No, no, no."

His father watched in disbelief. The helicopter returned across the way, back to a helicopter pad right over by the skywalk. Bobby ran to the helicopter. His father had to run to keep up. Bobby was getting stronger as he got older, and was able to sprint much faster than his father. He got there first.

When the helicopter door opened, he was there to greet Arrowpath, the Native American pilot. Bobby didn't mean to be so rude. The pilot smiled, thinking it was a boy interested in helicopters. Well, the helicopter pilot got that wrong. He was met by a full swing punch right in the face. The chopper pilot didn't even have a chance to block it. Arrowpath would be okay, and caught punch number two right in his hand.

"Young man, I don't know what you're so upset about, but I'm not going to let you punch me any further."

Bobby's father now caught up. "I'm so sorry. He's very upset."

Right then, as Bobby stood before the helicopter, a large black and white eagle feather flew off of one of the chopper wings and landed right before Bobby's feet. Bobby picked it up. He felt it. He touched it.

The pilot looked up and saw the blood of an eagle all over the blades and all over the roof of his chopper. The last thing anybody wants to do is to kill a bald eagle, especially if you're a Native American. They believe that birds are closer to the spirit than all other animals. Birds soar and in that soaring, are able to get close to the sun, closer to the sky, closer to the clouds and closer to the moon.

To the Native American pilot, a man named Arrowpath, it was as though he had killed an emissary to the gods.

He looked at Bobby. The two had an understanding. There was a moment of silence.

He then said what needed to be said, but he didn't say it to the boy; he said it to the Great Spirit.

Arrowpath's plea to the Great Spirit:

"Great Spirit, forgive me. I have sinned against you. I have killed your angel. I have killed your emissary. I have killed your beloved. I do not know how I can ever make up for this horrible deed. I am sorry. I am filled with regret and I ask you, please show me a sign, a path, a direction of something I can do to make up for what I have done."

As is often the case with the Great Spirit, he gave no immediate sign. Arrowpath looked around. Bobby looked around. Alfred looked around. There was nothing; no lightning bolt, no gust of wind, no snow blizzard during this beautiful autumn day. No shower of rain. It would be up to Arrowpath, with the help of Bobby, to figure out what should be done.

Arrowpath knew of one obvious process that they should bring the eagle sinner through.

He looked to Bobby's father. "I wish to invite you to a sweat lodge ceremony."

Bobby looked up with great interest. "Sweat lodge? What's that?"

Bobby's father had never heard of such a thing. "Sounds sweaty."

Arrowpath explained, "It is. We will give this feather of the great white eagle a proper blessing and ceremony to bid him farewell into the great beyond."

Bobby was ecstatic over this idea. His big blue eyes said yes all over them. His father hardly had to hear it to agree.

The three of them proceeded to Arrowpath's truck. Arrowpath was a modernized, educated Native American, skilled in aerodynamics, capable of flying a helicopter. He had adopted many of the white ways. He had not left behind his native roots. His SUV was a wood-paneled Jeep Wagoneer, dark purple in color with a curious bumper stick that read: "Get out of my sky."

He invited Bobby and his father into his truck. Bobby sat in the front seat. His dad sat in the back. Bobby looked up at the mirror and saw a dream catcher dangling from the mirror. It was a circular net with feathers hanging on it. He looked over to the sun blinder and saw photographs of what had to be Arrowpath's wife and three children, two sons and one daughter -- ages 8, 9 and 10.

Arrowpath could see Bobby's interest in his children and explained, "My family. This is my wife, Foxy, my two sons Bear and Wolf, and my daughter Sky Eyes."

Bobby was transfixed on the photo, especially the part about Sky Eyes.

The road out of Eagle Point and the skywalk is a dirt road that proceeds to the high desert of northern Arizona. There are rolling hills, some smallish mountains, trees here and there, an occasional palos verde tree.

They drove for about 20 minutes on this dirt road and turned onto another road that took them into the tribal village. Any tribe that could build the now internationally

127

famous Eagle Point Grand Canyon skywalk was no backwards tribe. This tribe had a modern administration building, which appeared like a small hotel. The residences were well-kept lovely American style suburban homes.

Arrowpath pulled into the administration building. "Please, come in."

They entered the building and met Longbow, the medicine man.

"Good afternoon, my brother. Why such a sad face?"

"Longbow, I need your help," Arrowpath explained. "This is Bobby. He is from California. Unfortunately today, I was flying the great bird and collided with a white eagle."

Longbow immediately understood the seriousness of the situation. He saw in Bobby's hand the feather from the eagle's tail.

He put his hand out. "May I?"

Bobby was at first protective.

Arrowpath explained, "Don't worry, Bobby. This is our medicine man. He is our high priest. He will return it to you after he gives it a blessing."

Bobby looked to his father. He nodded in approval. Bobby handed the feather over to the medicine man. He walked outside.

Standing outside was Arrowpath's family -- Foxy, Wolf, Bear and Sky Eyes. They smiled. They hadn't expected their father home so early from work.

"Daddy!"

Sky Eyes jumped into his arms. He caught her and swung her in a full circle and put her back down on the ground. Wolf and Bear came over and hugged him. It was as though they hadn't seen him in 100 years, even though they had seen him as recently as three hours ago.

His wife, Foxy, stood back and smiled.

"Honey, this is Bobby. He's from California. This is Bobby's father."

Bobby's father shook her hand. "Nice to meet you."

Bobby was looking over to Sky Eyes, who gave him a Grand Canyon smile. Uh-oh. There was a little thing called puppy love going on.

Arrowpath saw the connection. Foxy smiled. Bobby's dad missed all this.

The medicine man said, "We are going to the sweat lodge."

128

Arrowpath asked, "Longbow, I realize we normally don't have women in the sweat lodge. Perhaps today we can make an exception?"

Longbow looked at the eagle feather, looked over to Bobby and then to Sky Eyes. He smiled. Longbow explained.

"These are rather exceptional circumstances. So yes, we will make an exception. Sky Eyes and Foxy will be allowed."

The two families and Longbow then proceeded to walk across the tribal lands. Several other Native American children were playing a game of basketball. They stopped momentarily to watch the blond-haired, blue-eyed Bobby walk by. It wasn't the first white kid they had seen, but it was the first white kid they had seen holding an eagle feather and walking shoulder-to-hip with the medicine man. They knew right away that something important was going on. They watched solemnly as Arrowpath and Bobby's family passed by.

The sweat lodge was in the form of a tent structure, covered with wood from the nearby hills. There were pieces of greasewood, a bushy-type tree that produces an oily substance from its leaves. These leaves would provide a kind of sealant over the top of the sweat lodge. There were pieces of the ocotillo cactus, a cactus that grows in the form of long bamboo-shaped shoots, except that instead of smooth green, they are gray-white with cat claw thorns up and down.

There was an opening, like a chimney, at the top of this structure. There was a doorway to enter. The medicine man went first. Arrowpath then ushered in Bobby next, and his father. Arrowpath, his children, and his wife followed.

They sat around a fire that was cooking stones. The stones were from a riverbed, and were smooth and hot. The stones produced a heat that brought the temperature of the sweat lodge to well above 100 degrees. They don't call it a sweat lodge for nothing.

Longbow explained, "Bobby, we will each pass around the feather and we will give our individual prayer and blessing on the last passing of the great bird. Bobby, you may begin."

Bobby surprised Longbow and handed the feather to Sky Eyes sitting next to him. "If you don't mind, I would like Sky Eyes to begin."

Sky Eyes accepted the feather without hesitation and gave her prayer.

Sky Eyes' prayer:

"We have watched you so many times soar against the great canyon walls. You are the great one we call the great white bird. You are closer to the heavens than we can ever be and yet you are still here among us on the ground. We know how high and how fast you can fly, and we now know you have gone to the great beyond. We will someday all meet up again. Until that day comes, we wish you happy flying and ask that you somehow share your view of the heavens with us."

She handed the feather back to Bobby. Bobby handed it over to the boy named Wolf. Wolf took it. He held it up.

Wolf's prayer:

"The Great Spirit will take you to a place where you will live forever.
See with your wings,
Soar with your eyes,
Tell with your heart.
We are listening to all."

Wolf handed the feather back to Bobby, but Bobby did not take it. Instead, he showed his hand in the direction of Bear. Wolf handed the feather to Bear and Bear made his prayer.

Bear's prayer:

"Every eagle has a sky. Every sky has an eagle. Our sky is missing one. We will find a way to bring a new balance. What was left behind will become this new balance. Great eagle, we are watching over what you have left behind."

A tear came down Bobby's father's cheek. The prayers brought him to thinking of his own mortality, and what would happen if he should pass on and leave Bobby behind. Bobby and Alfred had already lost his mother to a terrible sickness. He felt the fragility of life, and understood that in all passings, there was a new generation of those who would make up for what was lost.

It is a biological fact that birds do not have tear ducts, and thus do not shed tears. But this is not the same as saying they do not cry.

Back at the canyon, the family of eagles left behind were all crying. The emotional impact of losing the father was scorching. For the mother eagle, she was in a depressed state, which created an emotional paralysis that made it impossible for her to go anywhere. She was in a protect mode, and huddled over her three young birds.

The two sons would see the passing of their father as a mandate for a quickened maturation process. For Azure, the loss was the hardest. Her father was her hero and savior. She could not understand the concept of life without him.

The screams of this devastated eagle family bounced off the canyon walls all the way to the river 5,000 feet below and into the white rapids. Changing life, new phases, water from green to white, turning left and right. Over rocks and boulders, the river flowed to beyond, as far as eyes, wings and hearts could see.

The eagles would find a way to make it through this tragedy.

Tolpe, the mother eagle, did something that is quite common in the wild: where a mother has young ones, and she has them in a place of danger, she will move them to a new, safer location. The problem she faced was how to move her young ones off of the side of a cliff. She stood and searched for a new location. Her eagle eye permitted her to look outward, approximately one mile.

She found what appeared to be a good location. She wanted to go check it out. She went to fly, but found to her surprise, a new part of her personality. She could no longer fly. Her children watched her, and wondered what the problem was.

"Hey mom, what's up?"

Her older son saw right away there was some kind of problem.

"You going to take off or what?"

Her little child saw the same. Azure, the youngest darling of the family, was the one who could immediately understand the problem.

135

"Oh no. Mom has a fear of flying."

Tolpe would become the eagle afraid of heights.

Back in the sweat lodge, Bobby made his prayer. He held the eagle feather above his head with both hands. Sky Eyes closed her eyes and listened to every word Bobby spoke.

Bobby's prayer:

"I saw your entire life in one second. I saw your wife. I saw your three children. I saw you and then I saw you be gone. I know I will never be the same. I know I have a mission. I have a destiny. I will live to protect your family and to make sure that they will soar as you once did."

Bobby's new mission in life, to save this broken family of eagles from whatever future challenges would lie before them, would require one important first step: he would have to find them.

Tolpe, so afraid of flying, was not afraid of walking. She brought the nest downward from the cliff to a new spot. She picked her children up one by one with her beak, and walked criss-cross style across the face of the cliff, step by step, inch by inch, and brought them around the side of an edge, to a new ledge that would face the morning sun.

The process was not an easy one. Try scaling a cliff with no hands and a baby eagle in your mouth. Her talons were extremely strong, and latched into various holes and grooves of the cliff rock. Her son, realizing the seriousness of this project, remained motionless. She got about three-fourths of the way to this new location when her son made a suggestion.

"Mom, let me take it from here. You go back and get Azure."

Her son was growing up. Tolpe agreed and latched him on to the side of the cliff. He held on firmly, spreading wings out. Though he was not ready to fly, he was ready to strike out before danger and make his way sideways on a cliff. Step by step, talon by talon -- he made it over safely to a flat ledge that would become their new home.

While he was making his way to this ledge, Tolpe returned back up and over to the nest and brought over Azure. Azure got about three-fourths of the way over and made the same suggestion.

"Mom, I can make it from here."

She put Azure on the ledge, trusting her own judgment and ability. Unfortunately, Azure was not quite as agile in her cliff-walking as her brother. A few steps into it, she missed a hole in the rock, and slipped out. She tried to hang on with one talon and couldn't. She screamed out.

Tolpe turned back in horror and watched the second worst thing she had ever seen, the sight of her precious daughter falling off the side of the cliff -- a distance of about 5,000 feet to the river below.

This blue-eyed eagle would not perish. Instead, she was caught by a greasewood tree, jutting out beneath the face of the Grand Canyon, and found herself safe within those branches.

138

But her mother and brothers didn't know this.

She was about 60 feet below. There was 5,000 feet of space below and a sheer rock faced Grand Canyon rim in between. She could not survive out there for the night.

The wind howled through the canyon walls, lifting at the trees that grew from its sides. They call the wind Mariah.

THEY CALL THE WIND MARIAH[8]

BY ALAN J. LERNER (LYRICS) AND FREDERICK LOEWE (MUSIC)

FROM PAINT YOUR WAGON (1951)

See the music video: http://www.youtube.com/user/Investools?v=-wwgkPASVwc

Way out west, they got a name

For rain and wind and fire

The rain is Tess, the fire's Joe and

They call the wind Mariah

O no, Mariah blows the stars around

And sends the clouds a-flying

Mariah makes the mountain sounds

Like folks were up there dying

Mariah, They call the wind Mariah

Now before I knew Mariah's name

And heard her wail and whining

I had a girl and she had me

And the sun was always shining

O, but then one day I left my girl

I left her far behind me

And now I'm lost, I'm oh so lost

Not even God can find me

Mariah, O, Mariah, They call the wind Mariah

I hear they got a name for rain

And wind and fire only

But when you're lost and all alone

There ain't no words but lonely

And I'm a lost and lonely man

Without a star to guide me

Mariah, blow your love to me

I need my girl beside me

140

He, Mariah, O, Mariah
I'm lonely can't you see
Mariah, O, Mariah
Please blow my love to me
Mariah, blow my love to me

The saddest thing for Azure is that her mother and brothers thought her to be dead. They were sure she'd fallen all the way down the canyon and was gone forever. She was unable to scream loud enough to be heard over the sound of the canyon winds. She screamed for quite awhile, but it was no use. Her mother couldn't hear it. Her brothers couldn't hear it.

They began the process of creating a new nest. A twig here, a twig there. It took quite a bit of time, but slowly but sure over the course of the night, a new nest was made. But Azure, she was left without anything, hung on a limb of a greasewood tree, hovering over 5,000 feet of danger.

As far as survival goes, nobody has nature beaten. The beasts that exist know survival techniques without any schooling or lessons. They just know. Little Azure knew one of the things she had to do to survive a cold, windy night was to crawl millimeter by millimeter, claw by claw, from the small limbs that she held onto, inward, toward the canyon face. She moved over ever so carefully, one foot at a time, sliding through the small branch of the greasewood tree.

Normally, an adult eagle would use its wings to balance, but Azure's were not grown yet and could not provide much help. She slipped, and turned upside down like a bat. This unnatural position would not do. She looked down below. They say you shouldn't look down, but she did and saw a great universe of distance between her and the mighty Colorado River rushing below. For a second, she wondered if perhaps she could fall, land in the river and survive. She knew that wasn't going to work.

There are times when seeing things from upside down can help. This would turn out to be one of those times. Azure could see a sign of hope. In the face below this greasewood tree, there was a small ledge. In that ledge, there was a small opening -- not large enough for a full grown eagle, but definitely large enough for an eagle chick. If she could just get over there. The hole was not directly below the greasewood tree. It was over about three feet. How could she make it over that three foot traverse? She studied the canyon face. It didn't seem passable. She looked above the tree. It didn't seem passable. As she put herself upright, she would not get to the part below the tree. She very awkwardly preceded bat-style, step by step, claw by claw, toward the underneath of this greasewood tree.

It turned out to be a better approach, as the tree was fairly clean of braches underneath. It allowed her to get to the edge of the canyon face to a small ledge. This was the daring part. There was no way for her to climb down to that ledge. It was not very far -- a distance of maybe three feet, but there was only one way to get there. She would have to release the grip on the tree and fall about three feet. If she could fall with a solid thud and not move off the ledge, she would be home free. She could then crawl into that opening and would find her way to safety.

But *Mariah* was angry that night. The wind was loud and fast. Azure swung like time's pendulum, to and fro.

She figured it out though; what she needed to do was to jump laterally, out at about three or four inches. *Mariah* would carry her to this ledge. This was the scariest thing Azure ever had to do. She jumped into the wind, about six inches over. The wind caught her. She put her little featherless wings out. It flipped her over. She ended up being jolted into the canyon face. She made a bank shot off the canyon face and went down, landing on the small ledge. She quickly dove into the cave area. Her little eagle heart was beating faster than she ever knew how.

Right after she made it inside, a huge gust of wind came that would have surely blown her away to kingdom come. She avoided it. She was safe in the cave, and would shiver there through the night.

It is well known that eagles will prey on rabbit. They search for them with their eagle eye, swoop down upon them and carry them away for food. Rabbits are well aware of this reality, and because of that, will find refuge in various holes. Including the very hole in the canyon that Azure had found.

It didn't take Azure long to figure it out. She heard the gnawing and rumbling of rabbits chomping on their teeth. Azure was at first afraid, not knowing what the rumbling was. The rabbits were also a little afraid, knowing that their new house member was none other than a bald eagle. But on this windy night, on the face of the Grand Canyon, with the wind outside, there would be no predator/prey relationship.

Instead, the mother rabbit, surrounded by her furry fat babies, would take the role of surrogate mother to Azure. The featherless eagle found her comfort in the front chest area of mother rabbit. At last, she would have the serenity to sleep through the night.

The following day, Bobby, his dad, Arrowpath and his children flew over across the canyon and landed on the flat area near where they had previously seen the eagle family. They walked about 400 meters to the edge of the canyon.

Bobby looked down and pointed. "They're gone."

The empty eagle nest told the whole story.

Arrowpath explained, "The mother knew this was a dangerous place. She moved her young ones."

The boy wondered, "But where?"

They looked at the large expanse of the Grand Canyon. There were no clues, not even a featherprint.

Arrowpath looked with his hand on his forehead. He then looked down and asked, "If I were a scared eagle, where would I go?"

It was his daughter, Sky Eyes, that had the first clue. "Look. The face of this ridge comes to a corner over there. They may have gone beyond that corner to avoid."

The father thought out loud. "Smart daughter, thinking like mother eagle."

She smiled. There's nothing a daughter enjoys more than the admiration of her father.

Bobby saw this interchange and looked to his dad. He wanted the same.

They walked over, down to the end of this ridge and saw on the other side that indeed, the eagle family had moved.

Bobby saw this first. "Look, there they are."

The mother eagle looked up and screamed out.

They wanted to show her they were friend, not foe.

She covered her two boys with her wings. They would not fight her. They were trying to help her. She came off of the nest to attack. They backed off. They showed their palms in peace. She lunged toward them.

It was then that Sky Eyes figured it out. "Hey, she's not flying."

"No, she's not," Bobby agreed. "I wonder why."

Arrowpath thought about it out loud. "I think she has a fear of flying."

"That is a disaster," said Sky Eyes.

Arrowpath agreed, "Without flying, there's no hunting. With no hunting, there's no food. With no food, they will all be dead."

144

It was then that the boy noticed, "Hey, there's one missing."

Alfred thought, "Oh no. One was lost in the process of moving the nest."

Luckily, he was wrong, but they didn't know that.

Arrowpath knew what to do. They proceeded back to the helicopter and flew it in the direction of seemingly nowhere. After about half an hour, they came upon a small shack occupied by a white bearded man who appeared to be 1,000 years old. The man had a Marine Corps tattoo on his forearm and wore a camouflage cap.

"Greetings."

He knew Arrowpath. "Hello."

"Can I see them?"

"Sure."

This man was Hal. He was a snake handler -- something you don't see a lot of nowadays. But there are those that, for whatever reason, have a kind of affinity and connection to snakes. They catch them, collect them, keep them, feed them, handle them and trade them.

Arrowpath took a look down into a plywood box. Hal opened it. Alfred pushed his eager son back.

"This looks dangerous."

Inside were a collection of more than 100 rattlesnakes. They were all on top of each other and all different kinds, all collected up from the local areas. Sidewinders, diamondbacks, you name it, they had them. They had a whole bunch of them. As dangerous as they seemed, this was exactly what the eagle family needed.

"We'll take five."

Hal packed them in a bag as though he were packing produce at a corner grocery store.

"One, two, three, four and five."

He picked them up with a snake stick -- a long, steel item that had a trigger on one end and some forceps on the other. When he pulled the trigger, the forceps became closed and clasped the snake's neck. He raised the snakes one by one from the box and gently placed them into a burlap bag. The bag had the following stenciled letters: Caution -- stand back -- live snakes inside.

He tied it with a rope and handed it to Arrowpath as though completing a transaction they had done before.

"10 bucks each."

"No problem."

Arrowpath forked over $50. This seemed like a lot of money for some snakes -- especially ones that you're going to give away. From Arrowpath's perspective, this was a problem that he had created. He recognized his own need to make it right.

They got back to the helicopter and proceeded to the area where the eagles were.

It may not seem like a very nice thing to throw a bag of rattlesnakes on a family of young eagles, but this was the perfect recipe for what they needed. The mom needed to hunt for the children. It would not be appropriate to throw them dead meat. These were not scavenger birds. They needed live meat.

They put a bag with one snake in it, opened it up and dumped it down into the canyon area. It landed with a thud not far from the newly transplanted eagle nest. The mother eagle went right into hunting mode. The snake was coiled, shaking its tail furiously. The rattle didn't echo off the canyon wall.

The two sons watched as their mother moved out of the way as the snake struck out, and caught its neck mid-strike. She whipped her body around in the process, causing the snake to whip around. The two boys had to duck to avoid it. The mom had the snake just where she wanted him -- in her talons. The snake's head was looking up, hissing, venom flowing from its fangs. The tail was shaking. The mother pierced the top of the snake's head with her beak and put it out of its misery. One piercing to his brain and the snake was dead, dead.

She tore off strips of meat up and down the snake and passed them to her children. They devoured the fresh meat without any hesitation. Mmm. Raw diamondback never tasted so good.

Arrowpath, Sky Eyes, Bobby and Alfred watched in amazement as they saw the eagles devour the snake. This was the workings of Mother Nature right before them. It was something Bobby had never seen before and would never forget.

But of course, this would not do. Arrowpath could not be expected to fly over to the snake handler, buy up snakes, fly them over, throw them down in this area and keep

146

feeding the eagles for the rest of their lives. At some point, there would have to be some kind of solution to get the mother eagle back into a mode where she could fly again and feed her own family.

Arrowpath looked at the boy's father and knew they were both searching for the same answer. What could they do to fix this problem?

Meanwhile, Azure continued in the comfort of the rabbit family. It was a warm den, they were furry and perfectly safe.

They fed her some seeds the mother rabbit had collected. Although this eagle was a meat eater, the seeds had enough protein to sustain her. The rabbits' fur was warm enough to avoid death by freezing. All in all, this was a workable solution to an otherwise harrowing set of circumstances.

Of course, there was this problem. The tunnel, though large enough for a rabbit, was certainly not large for a full grown eagle. There would come a day when Azure would have to find her way out of the rabbits' den. She would go through the tunnel that got her there and out to the canyon skies. How exactly this rabbit would train the eagle in the art of flying remained to be seen.

For now, Bobby and his father were taken back to the Indian tribal grounds for a discussion with the medicine man about what on earth to do. The medicine man had some ideas.

"In the great way of the Great Father, there are sacrifices in nature that have to be made. With the eagle clan, it is unfortunate that maybe the eagles do not make it. It is for this reason that the eagles are endangered."

The boy's father listened. "If it was just a case of nature doing her thing, I suppose we could just let it all go its course."

The boy was perplexed. "But it's not."

Arrowpath understood. "True. I intervened with a machine that is not part of nature. I caused their father's death."

The medicine man nodded. "Then you must find a way to fix the problem that you caused."

"How do we train this mother eagle to fly?"

The medicine man thought about it.

"Sometimes we must confront our fears straight on. If there is a bear in the woods and you are deathly afraid of that bear, you can walk the lands for your whole life and be afraid of all things that have fur. In the night before you sleep, you can have clenched fists and grind your teeth throughout the wee hours of the morning, living in constant fear of the bear. I have seen men who have come over these fears by coming before the bear, confronting that fear directly. They find their own way to become one with the bear, one with their fear. They understand that in the bear, there is no death. There is a sharing of earth. There is a sharing of freedom. Come before that bear, sense him, touch him, feel him, smell him. Share the earth with the bear."

The boy noticed on the medicine man's arm, there was a rather impressive scar that went from his shoulder to the elbow. It had a parallel scar right next to it. He realized the medicine man spoke a truth learned from his own experience.

Arrowpath thought, "A fear of flying. Confront the fear."

Yes. But how?

The medicine man wondered out loud. "You know, it happens that we have built a great skywalk. Perhaps we can take the eagle to the skywalk and place her on it. She can look down, just like the people do and see the space of air between her feet and the river below. Perhaps taking her there on a daily basis will bring her to a point that she can fly."

Bobby thought about it. "Yeah. That's like confronting the bear."

Alfred wondered, "Okay, and just how is it we're going to get the eagle from the canyon over to the skywalk?"

The medicine man smiled. "That's your problem."

Arrowpath had an idea.

Alfred had to ask, "We've met the snake handler. By any chance, do you know an eagle handler?"

Arrowpath knew that he would personally handle this issue. "I will do this."

The following day, they flew over across the canyon from the skywalk. They found the eagle nest. They landed purposely far away so they wouldn't shake up the eagles too much. They had a full set of climbing gear -- ropes, talons, boots and a helmet.

Arrowpath had a small hammer and hammered a stake into the ground. He tested it for strength. He tied a rope to it. It was on. He brought a large water basket with him. The basket would be placed over the mother eagle.

The boy wanted to follow, but his father would not allow it.

"No, my young explorer. You must stay above. Climbing up and down a vertical face is not something to take lightly. I have been trained in this. I know how to do it."

Arrowpath was part of the local search and rescue team and had been up and down the face of the canyon walls many times. This was his first time with an empty water basket. The basket was placed with a bandana around his head. It was light. A sudden wind could cause him to float up parachute-style, far and away, but it was a calm day. Mariah was quiet today. He put on a pair of large gloves and proceeded down the face of the canyon.

It wasn't very far down to where the eagles were. The mother eagle looked up and somehow did not see an enemy. Somehow she knew that this man was there to help.

He knew the rules of the animal kingdom. If the babies should come in contact with a human or another animal smell found upon them, for some odd reason, the mother would devour them. He would not touch them with his own hands, but instead would use his gloves. He very gently scooped up the two young boys. They looked at their mother and trusted her judgment. It was okay. He placed them into the basket. He then picked up the mother and put her in the basket. He put the lid on the basket, put the basket back on to a connection to a bandana and proceeded to climb back up the face of the canyon wall.

The basket was then secured. He brought it into the helicopter and flew back over the canyon to the area right next to the skywalk.

That day, there were about 150 visitors to the skywalk. They had no idea what was inside that basket. Arrowpath, his children, Wolf, Bear and Sky Eyes, Bobby and his father all followed with excitement as they brought the basket with the eagle family in it over to the skywalk.

They arrived and asked the onlookers, "Could you please stand back?"

They looked down. "What you got in there?"

"You'll see."

Grand Canyon Skywalk

He opened it up. The mother eagle hobbled out of the basket and onto the skywalk. The boy eagles hobbled over as well. The first thing all three of them did was to look straight down. It was about 5,000 feet. It was like they were flying. The mother eagle looked down and looked back at her sons. She screamed. She did not like where she was. She hopped forward and could see that wherever she hopped, she was still over quite a bit of air space.

It didn't help matters that just around the corner was a helicopter. She looked over there and saw what had killed her husband. One thing about eagles -- they mate for life. This machine that took her husband could never be forgiven.

Arrowpath saw that this was troubling the therapy. "I'll be right back."

He walked away, got into his chopper and flew it about half a mile away and landed it. He walked back.

By the time he'd arrived, he could see the eagle was far more comfortable sitting atop the skywalk, looking at the air space below, seeing her children standing in it as well. It was working. The two boys were not in the least bit afraid. The mother started to see -- if they weren't afraid, why should she be?

Arrowpath did something that truly amazed the tourists watching all this. He took another snake out and threw it in front of the eagle.

"Wow." The people were amazed that suddenly there was a standoff between a flightless eagle and a nasty diamondback.

The people stood back and watched as the snake neck became S-shaped, the rattle was rattling and he fired away, attempting to strike the eagle. The eagle backed away once, backed away twice and on the third time, managed to grab the snake -- this time with her beak, right around the back. The snake was strong and had jumped upward. This took the eagle upward and in a scene that no one had expected, brought her over the skywalk's railing. She went directly down 5,000 feet to the river.

Her sons looked above as their mother went into a tailspin. Arrowpath looked down. The boy looked down. His father looked down.

"Come on, fly!"

The mother just continued downward with that snake wrapped in her talons, its head in her beak. That snake was not going to get away. The question remained -- would that mother crash on the rocks below? Would she figure out that in her talons,

151

there was the key to the legacy of her once in a lifetime husband? There would be no children again for her. This was it. Either she eliminated this fear right then and there or her husband's legacy would forever dissipate into a life of starvation. This eagle family would be wiped off the earth forever. Would this mother allow that to happen?

Everyone above on the skywalk saw the eagle twisting in the wind. It was a long distance to the riverbed. They watched and prayed for that eagle.

"Fly, fly for your children."

The sons looked down and squawked loud. If they could speak, we know the words they would say.

"Fly, mom. Fly."

She got within 100 yards of a river and with all that was at stake -- the legacy of her husband, the plight of her children, the existence of her family -- for some reason, she still wasn't flying. She got within 100 feet. The airspace at this point was a matter of milliseconds before she would hit the ground. They watched from above and saw that she must be a goner. It looked like she had already hit the river below.

Down at the river, there was a large beast -- a bear. There was this short connection between the mother eagle and that bear. She caught its eyes. Eagles are never the enemy of the bear, and the bear never catches the eagle. These two coexist in nature in a friendly way. They share the earth.

This bear may have already taught lessons about fear. In a millisecond of an eyedrop, he was able to teach this eagle a thing about fear. Fear is irrational. Fear is imaginary. There is no reason to fear. Life is real. Your children are real. Your husband's legacy is real. That snake, the food you have for your children, is real. Take what is real. Use your wings to save yourself and your children. Do not let a purely imaginary fear destroy all of these wonderful things.

This communication started at an elevation of about 104 feet above the river, and was completed a millisecond later at an elevation of about 50 feet. It bolted the mother eagle into action. From up above, they thought she was already dead. They finally saw it. Her wings went out. It was majestic. She would not let go of that snake. The wings lifted her upward. All she had to do was push the wings out, tilt them upward and the air took her right up.

She then did what all eagles were born to do. She flew up and over the canyon, holding onto that snake for dear life, and came up to the level of the skywalk. To the amazement of everyone watching, she landed next to her children. As though nothing unusual had happened, she began the process of ripping that snake apart and feeding her children pieces -- piece by piece. The sons looked at their mom. If eagles had tears, they were shed that day.

Bobby watched as the mother fed her sons. He remembered how tender his mom was with him. He turned to the crowd and watched them looking in amazement. He turned to Arrowpath and nodded. They acknowledged each other.

From that day forward, the skywalk would be called Eagle's Point. There is a family of eagles that occupies it to this day.

A mother eagle that lost her fear of flying would spend her days with her eagle sons and their collective eagle eyes, searching the canyon walls for their lost daughter and lost sister. She was out there somewhere -- hopefully somewhere safe -- and they would find her some windy, sunny day.

Listai, the Bi Polar Sloth

Mylodon darwinii   **Mylodon cave, Patagonia, Chile**

CHAPTER 8
THE BIPOLAR SLOTH[8]

There is a place in Patagonia, South America, near Antarctica, called the Mylodon Cave. Archaeologists have found evidence that long ago, in the period of the Ice Age, there lived the Mylodon, a large ground sloth weighing about 600 pounds and standing about eight to ten feet high.

He had sharp hooves, like his modern day descendants, but unlike the modern day descendant, he lived primarily on the ground instead of in the trees. It is thought that the Mylodon was wiped out with other Ice Age megafauna, such as the Wooly Mammoth, the Wooly Rhinoceros, the Sabertooth Tiger, the Giant Sloth, the Giant North American Camel and the Pleistocene horses, approximately 10,000 years ago.

---

[8] For a medical description of the bipolar disorder featured in this story, please refer to appendix A-8.

Listai, the Bi Polar Sloth

Lindy the female sloth

A rather curious event occurred during 1895 when an Argentinian professor, Professor Listai, while in Patagonia, spotted a hairy beast that other paleontologists believe may very well have been a modern day Mylodon.

A hide of one was found in Patagonia, and carbon dated to approximately 5,000 years ago. This means the estimate that they were wiped off the face of the earth 10,000 years ago is apparently quite incorrect. At least one existed 5,000 years ago. And as it occurs in nature, where there is one, there are more.

Another study of the Mylodon showed that the ratio between its forearm bone and its upper arm bone indicated it was quite fast. It may have also been a meat eater. Its front claws were sharp enough to split the belly of the Ice Age giant armadillo, known as a Glyptodont.

The modern day sightings of the Mylodon by Professor Listai resulted in giving it a name in his honor, new mylodon listai. The original Mylodon was discovered by none other than Professor Charles Darwin on his trip to Patagonia. Because of that, it bears the name Mylodon darwini.

Another prehistoric fact lays the premise of our current story. There is a map, known as the Piri Reis Map, which has caused much confusion in our understanding of the history of mankind.. What is puzzling about this map is that it shows the world including parts of it, that were not discovered until well after that map was drawn. One of those parts of the world included the lower tip of South America, where there was an interesting reference in the map of a Mylodon. The map also shows the continent of Antarctica having mountains and visible areas without ice.

Whomever set sail to the southern parts of the underbelly of the earth to map out an Antarctica without ice and an area where mylodons ran would have lived many, many years ago. Whatever civilization was capable of producing a ship to go through these dangerous waters and prepare the notes for such a map back then remains as one of the great mysteries of the world.

The connection between what happened to the mylodon and the other Ice Age fauna may very well lie in a map showing a period when Antarctica had at least part of its coastal area free from ice. This created the ultimate irony; the Ice Age may have produced a polar cap free of ice. It may be that geophysical events turned the circumstances into polar caps having ice and the other continents becoming free of ice. Somewhere therein lies the explanation of the vanishing of Ice Age mammals. It was quite possibly a global catastrophe.

Professor Darwin himself noted that there was no earthly explanation for the vanishing of the species, and made the comparison to an analysis of the Ice Age horse. This horse was fast, capable, knew where to graze and reproduced itself in huge numbers. There was no reason it would just vanish and/or die out. There were too many of them to be explained away by the concept of early Ice Age hunters. There just weren't that many people back then, even hungry enough to eat a horse.

The other item of ancient lore worth mentioning here, takes us to the South American natives, whose lore talks of a mysterious hairy beast of a human, akin to North America's Bigfoot. It is understood by modern day paleontologists that this South American Bigfoot, which the local Indians called Curinquean, may very well have been a mylodon. The mylodon commonly stood on its back two feet to gain height to access the leaves of Ice Age plants and trees. An Indian coming upon such a beast may easily have mistaken it for a super huge primate with human characteristics.

The modern day tree sloth, called the giant sloth, which now occupies the Atlantic Coast of mid-South America, shows a face that could easily be mistaken for that of a super hairy human.

With these historical conundrums in mind, we turn to our present day story of a sloth that was affected with an unfortunate disorder known as bipolar disorder. If any of you have ever met a human with this problem, you will know its traits.

The first is that they are capable of going into a stage of hypomania, during which they will be unable to sleep for days, even more than a week at a time. They will be extremely active, chatty, aggressive, and will be prone toward grandiose concepts, heightened self-esteem and connections to godliness. The idea of a sloth having these traits may seem curious, but that is exactly what happened at a small Patagonian village not far from the Mylodon Cave, where a tree sloth we'll call Listai defied all characteristics of his relatives, and lived primarily on the ground.

160

Patogonia, Chile

Listai was foraging around on the ground one day when he made a rare connection with another tree sloth. For the most part, these tree sloths live a solitary life, and come in contact with one another, mainly to mate only.

On this occasion, the tree sloth spoke down to Listai, and wondered, "Why are you living on the ground?"

Listai was happy to have someone to speak with. There's nothing worse than being bipolar and not having anyone to chat it up with.
"Well, hello there."

This was a female up in the tree. Listai was very much a male. One of the other not commonly known features of the bipolar syndrome is that it evokes sexual precociousness. Whatever judgments we can place on Mother Nature for infecting about one percent of the human population with this disorder, one thing can be noted: it is handed down genetically, and has a directive to reproduce itself. This takes the form of finding itself in often super good looking and extremely talented people (think Britney Spears). Add to that an aggressiveness, and an unusually strong sexual appetite; nature has a design to make this disorder spreadable.

Such was the case that day between the tree sloth known as Lindy, and the bipolar sloth living on the ground known as Listai. He looked up to her, and as bipolar infected beasts often do, became creative.

"I can see from your image the outline of a great beauty; one that would bring peace to all of the forest, to all of the sea and one that could bring peace to my heart. I can see from your image that you have the warmth of a savior, that you have the eyes of a goddess and every bit of an angel except, alas, you are without wings. But allow me to be your wings, to carry you to a destiny, which you and I both know must include me."

The tree sloth had never heard such a thing from a fellow sloth. Most of them are lazy, unimaginative sleepers that would never think to come up with such a, whatever it was. A poem, song, set of lyrics, essay, beginning of a 500 page novel or who knows what else this ground sloth, if allowed a little time, a pen and an opposable

162

thumb, could whip up. As is often the case with those that come into contact with those with the bipolar disorder, Lindy the tree sloth was taken by him.

"What? I think I heard you say something. I don't know what it was."

He smiled. "Ooh, I have somebody interested in me."

She remained in the tree. He remained on the ground.

It is generally the case that a giant sloth will remain up in the trees about 22 hours a day, sleeping and every now and then, waking up to eat a few reeds. About the only time they come down is to defecate, and one wonders why they even bother with that. Why not just hang out and go from the tree? For whatever it's worth, they come down to the ground to defecate, forage around for a little bit, then go back up the tree for another 18 to 22 hours of sleeping.

Listai lived a completely opposite life. He was down on the ground running around, exploring caves, in and out of the rocks, the boulders, the parts of Patagonia that no tree sloth could ever imagine going. He had stories to tell; stories of adventure, stories of coming across things that you would never see way up in the trees. He would share those stories with Lindy. Lindy would listen with her big sloth eyes. They would stay open to his storytelling for hours.

He began a process of infecting her with his own bipolar syndrome. For the first time ever in her life, she stayed awake for more than nine hours straight. Before this day, this was unimaginable. She listened to him as he explained his trip down to the Mylodon Cave, where he went in and found, amazingly enough; his ancestors. They were huge beasts, capable of running across the Patagonian tundra at speeds like a horse. They could tear down what was then known as the giant armadillo. Listai explained to Lindy how his ancestors did it.

This armadillo was impervious to assault. You could shoot it with a gun and a bullet wouldn't go through it. It had a kind of shell similar to the gigantic tortoise of the Galapagos, only stronger. It was calcified. The mylodon skin had in it something known as an osteoderm. The osteoderm is a bony deposit forming scales and bone plates in the dermal layers of the skin. They are heavily vascularized, and function as both armor and as heat exchangers. If you could use it in battle today, you would be able to protect yourself, even from the smart bullets of modern day military.

Lindy listened with amazement as Listai explained how inside this cave he found the bones of his ancient ancestors. These were also Lindy's ancestors. They were powerful beasts, weighing up to 800 pounds. The size of a mid-sized elephant, but with the speed of a small horse. The claws were knife-like. They were great warriors. Nothing would take them on without receiving a severe lashing and slow, bleeding death. They prospered in this cave. It was seen firsthand by Listai that these mylodons coexisted with men.

The Mylodon Cave shows that there are the bones of the Ice Age man. They lived side by side with the mylodon. It is not known whether this was a relationship of keeper and master and slave, whether it was a relationship of farm animal and farmer, or friend and friend. They may have seen themselves as equal. There was no evidence that the Ice Age man was somehow devouring the mylodon. There was no evidence that he was killing them and using their bodies for such practical implementations, such as tools or other farming equipment. All the evidence pointed to the concept of a side-by-side existence, literally in the same cave. They shared the earth.

Lindy had never heard such tales before. All she knew was a life where there was a big tree with big leaves that she could eat for a couple hours a day and then sleep for 22 hours and then crawl down that tree, go to the bathroom and crawl back up. This had been her entire life. With Listai, it was a new window into a whole new world, a world that she had never known.

"Oh please, Listai, you must bring me there."

He looked at her. There's nothing he would rather do on this entire planet than to bring this new, lovely woman, a woman who had scarcely ever been on the ground, to walk on the ground and to go on a great adventure out of the forest. They would go into the rocky parts of the southern areas of Patagonia, a place that Lindy would never imagine going to, and to visit a place known as the Mylodon Cave.

"Of course I will bring you there. Tell me, my dearest, when would you like to leave?"

"Now!"

She wanted out of that tree. She wanted out of the life she had found. She wanted a whole new life. She was ready for adventure.

Listai knew that this was the greatest thing that had ever happened to him.

"Of course I will take you, dear."

"Which way is it?"

He pointed in a southerly direction. "It's that way."

He knew that the safest way to get there would be to walk along the coast, as the cave was not far from the southern reaches of Patagonia, an area that is not far from a place where you can see penguins.

They traveled for days. Poor Lindy was not used to this kind of exertion. She was exhausted after one day.

"Oh my God. How far away is this place?"

"Oh Lindy, my dear. May I please explain to you that we are going on an adventure to a whole another part of the world? Please don't think this is a matter of hours or days. This is a trip that will take the better part of year."

"A year? Oh my God."

She began to look back to the place she was from. It was green. It was soft. It was warm. It was familiar. It was secure. It was safe.

She looked forward to the southerly area. She saw cold rocks, boulders. Streams of icy water went in and out. She saw the beginning of a tundra, of an arctic. She saw what would truly become a kind of Ice Age in the present. It was as though they were going back in time 10,000 years. She started to wonder, "Why am I doing this?"

He then told her the fact of life that she needed to hear, right then and there.
"My dear, if you wish to return, you may. I will walk you every millimeter of the way back to where you are from. You can live in that tree where you have been living for years on end and never know the adventure that awaits you. If that is your wish, I will stand by you. Now please know, I have already done this adventure. I don't have a need for it again. I would love nothing more than to take you there. But if this is not your wish, we will return. You and I will live in the trees, eat leaves and sleep 22 hours a day."

She smiled at his statement.

"Somehow I rather doubt that. You, sleeping 22 hours a day? How about four hours a day?"

He laughed. "How about every other day?"

"Yeah, something like that."

She looked up and saw a beautiful moon. It was streaming down on them, beckoning her. There was a type of syncopation between the moon, the earth and the tides that she would feel and relate to. Just as it moves in and out, so is the movement of the heart. We come into phases. We go out of phases. It happens as this moon passes each month. Our own bodies are fixed to it and it will lead us. We must follow its path. The moon led them southerly in the direction of the Mylodon Cave.

They continued in this manner, literally for weeks. It was best to travel at night when so many beasts slept. In the daytime, they would burrow inside caves and sleep. He was excellent at finding small areas that could be dug out. They would sleep there for the entire day. This is the first time that Lindy ever slept on the ground. It was underneath a rock. He had dug out a sizable area to burrow in and the two of them laid in there. Their faces looked up at the moon. She wondered, "What the hell is the matter with this guy to make him want to travel all over the earth, sing all these crazy songs, stay up all night, travel for endless hours, miss nights of sleep, do things like he's doing and somehow find me and connect with me?"

She looked at him and smiled. "What did you do to me?"

He looked at her and laughed. "Did I put you under my spell?"

She reacted, realizing she had indeed been taken by his charm.

"Yes. You are some kind of a spellbinder. What did you do?"

"I'm sorry, my dear; but let me assure you, it's all good."

This night they came upon a deadly danger, a black jaguar. A panther appeared. This panther was way away from home. He belonged thousands of miles away. It had escaped from a local rich rancher's captivity. He got loose and was now found on the rock boulders of Patagonia. Nothing would be more delicious to this panther than a furry and slow-moving tree sloth, on the ground, vulnerable and incapable of flight. The good news for the panther, there wasn't a tree in sight.

The panther walked in his crouched position, climbing over one boulder at a time. His natural ways focused his eye pupil on Lindy first. There's a reaction between the eyesight, the brain and the gland that produces adrenaline. His heart started to pump. He went into hunt mode by stealth. Sneaky little guy, nobody saw him, even coming 100 feet away.

Lindy, however, would be protected by Listai. One of the other features of the bipolar condition is it often comes with another related condition known as attention deficit disorder. In this disorder, the affected being is incapable of focusing on a single place or concept for more than a short interval of time. This may seem like a terrible

167

deficit, if you want to be an engineer, an architect, scientist, medical doctor or in another profession that requires great periods of extreme focus.

There are many professions, however, where a scattered vision can be a good thing. For example, you would hardly want a military guard to be fixated on watching a single rock. You would want his eyes all over the terrain: up, down, around, under, to the right, to the left, to the north, to the south, to the east, to the west and all points in between. You want him to have attention deficit disorder. You want him capable of looking everywhere, anywhere all the time and the slightest little speck out in the far periphery of his vision can cause his head to swirl around and become directly focused on it.

This trait would now be invoked by Listai. He saw in the outer periphery of his eyes a slight little speck. He couldn't see the black of the jaguar, but he did see the weird yellow of his eyes. It was completely out of place. He then focused on it and indeed saw it.

"Oh my God."

Lindy wondered, "What?"

"Don't move. We got a problem."

"What's the problem?"

"Promise you won't get scared?"

"No. I make no such promise."

"Well, over there is a jaguar."

Lindy was well aware of the danger of a jaguar. She lived in a jungle that was full of them. The way to get away from a jaguar was to climb way up a tree to a place where the branches were so small that the jaguar couldn't get up there. First thing she did was look for a tree. Unfortunately, there were none. The area was rather barren.

She looked to Listai with this dreary, "you got to save me" look.

Listai understood she was counting on him.

The jaguar made its move and came crashing over the boulders, appearing on the top of one, growling, hissing. There was not a lot of space between the two sloths and the jaguar. It was getting shorter every second.

They couldn't run away. These sloths go extremely slow. To take the jaguar on, one needed some extremely creative thought. The first thing was to protect Lindy.

"You've got to get back into a burrow. Why don't you crawl in there?"

She didn't like this idea. On the one hand, it would save her. On the other hand, it would leave Listai to the jaguar.

"What about you?"

"Don't worry about me. I've got a plan."

She couldn't imagine what that plan would be. A sloth is simply no match for a jaguar. Lindy took the direction of Listai, and went into the burrow.

Listai picked up a nearby boulder and placed it in front of her. "Here, dear, this will protect you. When we're done, just move it out and you'll be safe."

Lindy was preoccupied with thoughts of what would happen in the extremely likely event that the jaguar got ahold of Listai, ripped his head off, ate him and then turned to her for its next meal. How would she possibly survive out in the Patagonia areas, an area she had no knowledge of? She knew somewhere south of there was a cave where her own ancestors once lived. Somewhere way north was the home that she had left.

She saw the day turn into night as Listai placed the boulder in front of the burrowed area. It left her in a dark way, but a safe way. Her heart was beating, pounding. She wondered what would happen next. She couldn't see the great battle between Listai and the jaguar, but she could hear it. It was an awful sound. The jaguar screamed out, hissing in a way that only a jaguar can do. The sounds were so scary that it sent Lindy into a digging mode. She was digging backwards, to wherever that burrow would send her.

As she dug into the burrow more, she found an area of super soft dirt. It was like sand. She dug into that sand. It created an opening rather easily. That opening became larger. It led her to a humungous cave. She pierced through it coming in backwards, like a turned around birth. Her toes hooked into holes on the cave all. She could not believe what she saw.

It was the most gorgeous cave imaginable. It had stalactites from the top, stalagmites from the bottom. There were ice connections. There were places where somebody held a bonfire long ago. There were paintings on the wall of hunts of some kind of mammoth creature. There were creatures drawn that appeared to be a wooly rhinoceros.

Then there was something that she had never seen before, the carcass of a mylodon. This was not a set of bones. This was a fully preserved, frozen, dead mylodon. It couldn't have been dead for thousands of years. This seemed to be a recent beast. When Listai explained it, she had a hard time believing it. She couldn't imagine that she was the descendant of some great beast like this, but now she found a connection to her past. She came from the giants.

She went over and looked at its paws. "Oh my goodness. They walked around with swords on."

These could kill anything. It was then that Lindy figured out how Listai was planning on attacking the jaguar. He was going to be a mylodon.

Here's the problem with a bipolar disorder. You can have feelings of grandiose concepts. You can have huge self-esteem. You can think you're a mylodon with swords on your hands. In reality, you're a tree sloth. Your toes are nothing other than to hang onto tree bark.

She quickly figured it out. "He thinks he's a mylodon."

She now knew what a mylodon was. She also knew that Listai was not a mylodon. He was an ordinary tree sloth with grandiose concepts that he was a giant sloth, dangerous to the point of being a killer. A meat eater, extremely fast, capable of running through the Patagonian fields, attacking great beasts, turning them over, slicing them open and devouring them with his fast-acting mouth. When in fact, this tree sloth could basically eat a leaf and that's about it.

She went into quick action. She picked up one of the claws of the mylodon. She was looking around for a tool, something to slice it off with. She could find nothing until she thought of the obvious, one of the other feet of the mylodon. She picked it up, the first time she'd ever held a weapon in her life. It made her feel powerful. Her hormones were raging. She lifted that mylodon paw up and shoved it down onto the other paw. It sliced right off and left her with a a deadly three sword weapon.

What needed to be done was to bring this back to that hole where she came from, through that tunnel that she had dug, push that boulder to the side and deliver this up to Listai before that jaguar devoured him. Well, how the heck was she going to do that?

Just then, she heard a grunt. She turned to look. To her surprise, it was a hominid. This human was a Paleolithic person, not fully formed into what we would call Homo sapiens. He stood upright, however, carried a spear, was covered with hair from head to toe. To his credit, he had with him a domesticated horse.

Lindy had never interacted with a person before, but others of her kind had. There are cases of people coming upon tree sloths, taking them into their homes and living with them.

There's a special look with the tree sloth. You can't help but to see the human in them. This Paleolithic man, when he saw Lindy, didn't see an animal. He saw a girl. He saw a friend, a friend in need.

She held out the mylodon sword set to him. He came over and smelled it. He looked over at the great beast that was lying dead. It would never have occurred to him to slice off one of the paws and to make a set of swords from it. For that ingenuity, he smiled and gave thanks to Lindy. He also sensed her distress.

She got up and waved her arms in the air. She pointed up to a direction where she knew the man that she loved was in a battle against impossible odds.

The man put her on his horse. He got on the horse. He handed the sword set back to her. She held onto it. He galloped forward. Instead of going back to the tunnel where she had come, he would take a different route. He came out the front of the cave, galloped to the left and went up a hillside.

Lindy remembered that this was exactly the direction where she had just left. The horse was a great galloper and sprinted up the rocky area, jumping over the boulders. Lindy was hanging on for dear life. If there's anything she knew how to do, it was how to hang onto things. She had been hanging onto trees her whole life. She hung onto that sword with one arm and hung onto the man with the other wrapped completely around his belly. He was an excellent horseman. He made his way quick enough to the area where the jaguar was engaged in a face-off with Listai.

Listai, unfortunately, had already been battered by this vicious jaguar. He was bleeding on his shoulder. He was bleeding on his neck. He had a severe injury to his stomach area.

The jaguar was relentless in his attack. Listai kept trying to shove his claw into him. He kept thinking he was a mylodon, he could slice them open, but his claw was nothing of the sort. It was for tree climbing and clinging, and that was about it.

For whatever reason, Mother Nature made a great beast of the mylodon, but of its descendants, she left them 100% defenseless. Their only capability was that of climbing high trees. If there were no trees, however, they are left with nothing. Against the cunning foe of a black jaguar, this was not a fair match.

The odds were now evening up, however, as the man arrived and Lindy showed up with the sword. She saw Listai in this terrible condition.

"Oh honey."

He looked up and saw the mylodon claw. "Quick, throw it to me now!"

She tossed it in the air. The jaguar had no idea what it was in for. It snarled again at Listai. It tried to grab at the sword as it was mid-flight, but it missed. It came down and stuck in the ground, just next to Listai. The jaguar took another leap at Listai. Listai took the mylodon claw out and held it in front of his stomach outward. The jaguar leapt in the air, right at Listai, and was met with a protrusion of the mylodon claw, right in its gut. It split open and through that gut. Listai took it and twisted it, one way counterclockwise and then clockwise, then took it out. With some impressive agility, he sliced the jaguar's neck left and then sliced it right. He then sliced the jaguar's body lengthwise, opening up its intestines. He reached in with that claw and dug out intestines. He was feverish and manic in his attack on the jaguar, to a point where Lindy and the man decided they needed to intervene. The jaguar was dead.

"Look, you're not going to eat it. It's dead. You're done. Relax."

Listai took note of this and did a pause. Once he saw the man, the horse and Lindy, there with her smile, so happy to be a savior, he did what any man would do under these circumstances. He fainted and went into a long sleep, a sleep that he would awaken from days later. The man placed him on the back of his horse. They traveled with him back into the mylodon cave.

They placed him by a stream of water. The man cleaned his wounds. He found some moss and placed the moss on the wounds. It worked as a cleansing bandage. Under the moss, there was a fungal bacteria that would attack any other bacteria that would create an infection. It would take awhile, but Listai would heal.

He might not ever become the mylodon that he knew or thought existed inside of him. He may never reach the stature of a 10 foot beast weighing 700 pounds. He may never run 25 miles per hour, the speed of a Pleistocene horse, catch a giant armadillo, roll it on its stomach and slice its belly and eat its insides, but he would do something equally majestic.

He found a new home in the cave. He had a beautiful wife and they had a friend, a man who would help them keep warm in the cave with fires. A man who would paint pictures and entertain them with amazing stories of things that happened many years ago; stories that had been handed down to him by his forefathers. They relaxed in the serenity of knowing they would live out their days in the Mylodon Cave, where even today, some sloths who are supposed to be living in the trees, are living on the ground.

Elwood the Flying Fish With Multiple Personality Disorder

CHAPTER 9

THE FLYING FISH WITH MULTIPLE PERSONALITY DISORDER[9]

People with multiple personality disorders believe at different times they are another person. They will give this other person a name, separate identity and a completely different set of personality traits.

A goody-two-shoes librarian can have a foul-mouthed bartender side, prone to fighting, hair-pulling and vulgar language. If you saw her at the library, you would never imagine her in this way. She may have more than one of these other personalities. Another part of her could even be a different sex, could be a different race and could be a person from a different time. She may think she's Marie Antoinette, about to be beheaded.

There is a growing psychology theory that having multiple personalities within each of us is actually a normal and common circumstance. You may have caught yourself doing something, saying something or thinking something, and then reacting viscerally with a statement along the lines of, "I don't know what came over me."

What came over you was one of your other existing personalities. Thus, a wild, long-haired, skinny hip hugger pant, heel-wearing rock star can have within him the mind and soul of a university professor of modern literature. There are times when the rock star takes off his wig, puts on a cardigan sweater, smokes a pipe and sits before a roaring fireplace with his Labrador at his feet and wonders about the lyrics of his next song.

The combination of these other personalities is what cumulatively adds up to our singular personality.

Such is the case with Elwood, the flying fish of Lake Powell, Arizona and Utah. Elwood at times thought he was a snake, at other times he thought he was a fish, and then still at other times he thought he was a bird. There were times when he thought of himself as a lizard, and in his more extreme transitional personality, he saw himself as a voyeuristic human.

---

[9] For a medical description of dissociative personality disorder, also known as multiple personality disorder that is featured in this story, please refer to appendix A-6.

In Elwood's version of this disorder, he saw himself as other beasts. As is typical in the growing theory of normalcy with multiple personality disorder, one only needs to look at Elwood to see that for the most part, having multiple personalities when you're a flying fish does indeed seem perfectly normal. He looked like a lizard snake with wings that lives in a lake.

One day Elwood was flying and swimming around his homeland, a freshwater manmade lake known as Lake Powell. A dam was placed on a portion of the Colorado River. The backup of the water created a lake in an area that was once arid.

Lake Powell, Arizona

Lake Powell Monuments

Elwood's transportation over to this lake was the result of some fortuitous events involving a fish collector that had obtained a freshwater flying fish from the Congo region of Africa. He then came to Lake Powell, and decided it would be a good idea to populate the lake with these African flying fish. Why not?

So Elwood and his band of flying fish were able to cruise around in some fairly impressive displays of flying skills, traveling as much as 200 yards at a time in mid-air, bouncing off the top of the lake, and then flying again for another 200 yards.

Elwood didn't even think twice about it; he saw what appeared to be a dragonfly and gulped it. The fake dragonfly had a hook on it, which lodged into Elwood's mouth. Ouch, that had to hurt. The hook was connected to a monofilament line that spanned about 85 feet to a nearby houseboat.

On this boat were two couples. Herman and Sabrina were from Sacramento, California and were having a short vacation with Jeremy and Karen Hatcher, friends of Herman's from his elementary and high school days. Jeremy liked to fish; Herman liked to scuba dive. Herman's wife Sabrina was a Chinese woman, in her late 30s, still looking pretty good.

Jeremy was reeling in the fish known as Elwood. As Elwood was dragged against his will across the waters into the boat, he went into one of his other personalities. This particular personality was that of a prehistoric dinosaur age flying fish that had a mouth looking similar to the mouth of a hammerhead shark, with a rather impressive array of shark-like laser sharp teeth. The wings had thorny protrusions coming out of them, which would protect it against any other fish that attempted to gobble it up. All you had to do was spread the wings, and a series of knives would poke into its predator.

Flying fish are not exactly tasty, meaty or sought-after by sports fishermen. Jeremy performed a practice politely referred to as "catch and release." He gently took the hook out of Elwood's mouth, and tossed Elwood back in.

Everyone on board was amazed to see Elwood not swim away, but rather, fly away. Elwood was, of course, convinced all the more that his prehistoric dinosaur mode scared the daylights out of this potential captor, and that once again, power and might prevailed over the weaker homo sapiens species. It was probably best to just let Elwood live on with this delusion, than trying to find a way to eliminate it.

Elwood was impressed with this victory, and decided to circle around the houseboat. He was curious to see what these homo sapiens were up to next. He watched as Herman and Sabrina put on scuba gear. They had vest wetsuits, a pair of gloves, a set of large fins with socks on, some kind of diving watch, a knife strapped to their ankle and a pair of similar, but different colored head masks. Hers was red. His was blue.

Herman spit into his head mask and wiped the glass clean. He washed it off with the lake water. Sabrina did not do the same, but instead just washed it with lake water. They put their head masks on, and sat on the edge of the houseboat, backs toward the water, flipped off in a one-quarter somersault, right on their backs. They proceeded downward, into whatever depths the lake had to offer.

Elwood circled around top to watch these humans pretend for a moment that they were fish. He began to understand a little bit about his own disorder, by watching these two humans take on the role of a fish. Sometimes it's good for a psychotic person to observe others with similar disorders. In seeing the external example of another person with a problem, they can sometimes come to terms with their own problem.

The two dove deeper and swam away. There were a series of small underwater hills to traverse up and over, without their stomachs actually touching them. They went up one, down another, up one, down another, around the corner, proceeded down a small former gulley, and then came before a clearly manmade structure from an era that had long since passed.

Sabrina saw it first and pointed up at something she recognized very well, Chinese characters. Herman looked with great interest. There was an explorer in both of them that wanted to know, what was this? You could tell by its front that it was formerly some kind of commercial structure. It had a fairly tall front area, two stories high with a group of Chinese characters in front. Then on the lower right area, where there was a double door, were the unmistakable words in English: East West Hotel. Sabrina pointed to the English and then pointed to the Chinese. Herman figured that they probably both said the same.

They opened the double door and swam inside the submerged hotel. The lobby was quite lovely. This was not a poor man's hotel. There was a chandelier still swinging with the current of the water, swaying to and fro. The glitter from the crystal glasses caught a bit of the sunlight from above and gave a color prism effect, rather like a kaleidoscope, inside the lobby. The wallpaper showed scenes from China, and gave the unmistakable hint that these people were from a noble city called Canton.

There was a period back in the early 1800s when many Chinese came from the Canton province and immigrated to the United States. It is thought that these people were primarily workers, engaged in the expansion of the United States through the construction of a railroad system. It is also true that there were many other pursuits by these Chinese people and though it is true that many of them arrived penniless; literally with the clothes on their backs and maybe a small bag of other items, not all of them were so.

It was rather obvious that whomever was the former owner of this lovely hotel, they were anything but poor. That they were rich back home was evident because of the ornate features on the wall. This was not the kind of wallpaper you bought in California back in the early 1800s. It arrived with this family from China and was carefully placed up to make this hotel seem very much like home.

Some of the pictures on the wall included black and white photos of this elegant family. They were quite lovely. The woman was fabulously beautiful, and looked extremely young, perhaps 14 or 15.

Her husband appeared in his early 30s. You could tell by his hat and beard that he was from a land-owning aristocratic family. He had knowledge of Chinese medicine. There was a photo of him with his family. His father had a large truck-type vehicle operated by horses that had Chinese characters on the side that roughly meant "pharmacy." He was a traveling doctor, going to the villages, taking care of the sick and needy, and provided them with whatever kinds of Eastern medicine could fit into that truck.

The photo showed that he was a good man. He dispatched his son and his son's beautiful wife to lands far away, in the hopes that they would bring forward something that so many of us call "the American dream."

They swam over to a bar area. Inside the bar were a group of chairs, a beautiful mahogany bar area, and a gigantic mirror. Oh, if the mirror could only show the scenes of days gone by. What was seen in this bar and lobby could fill many books of drama.

The Chinese middle class would come to this lovely hotel and bar to socialize, intermingle, marry and bring their own families forward. The next generations started in the social gatherings of this elegant hotel.

Elwood swam right above them as the two made their way from the bar area up the stairwell, into the room. The rooms, as were typical back then, were somewhat small. The rooms had basically a bed, a small mirror area and a small excuse for a toilet. The bathhouse was in a separate room, and would be shared by others. Each room had a mirror. Each room had the same Cantonese wallpaper, and still had what was now a soggy, moist bed in them. The quilts on the bed were definitely from San Francisco, very un-Chinese, but quite nice and comfortable.

Sabrina sat at the edge of one of the beds. Herman swam over and sat next to her. They both dreamt of a day long ago when some nice Chinese couple came to this room, sat on the bed just like this and began a process of regenerating their own people. All with great hope that they too would share in that concept we all know as the American dream.

Elwood, an immigrant from Africa, shared this American dream, and watched from above. His other personality, which was a bit of a dark story for him, was to occupy the persona of a human. It was perhaps fitting that he would be taking the role of two humans that were taking the role of a fish. It seemed like a fair exchange.

Elwood's human role was unfortunately subject to a further disorder. Just as a multiple personality would take on other roles, given that the other personality is premised on an existing disorder, it should perhaps not surprise us that the other personalities, would themselves be afflicted with a disorder.

In Elwood's case, his human persona was afflicted with a category of a sexual disorder, known as voyeuristic disorder. Under this disorder, the person receives self-gratification by watching others engage in sexual activity. As will be seen, Elwood's form of the disorder was extended beyond watching sexual activity. Elwood, as is the case of other people, was excited to watch another person's life, with the overall fantasy of being that person and living that person's life.

By way of counterexample, there is a common occurrence of the pin-striped suited businessman who watches in a mesmerized state as construction workers are engaged in their various construction trades. He may fantasize as being the man handling the jack-hammer, laying the brick, placing the mortar, operating the crane, pouring the cement or any of a number of trades.

After daydreaming about this completely different occupation, he will then reluctantly walk away, buy his lunch and go back to his corporate cubicle to engage in his actual trade of number-crunching.

Voyeurism, though generally assigned as a sexual disorder, can take the form of an "I want to be that person" fantasy.

In Elwood's case, it was a little bit sexual, and a whole lot of "I want to be that other person." In this case, he actually wanted to be two persons: he wanted to be both Herman and Sabrina, wanted to share their lives, live their lives, and live their adventure. It was thus with great interest that Elwood followed Herman and Sabrina as they swam through the various rooms of this sunken hotel.

They swam out of the hotel room, and continued down the hall. At the end of the hall, they could see the perimeter on the ceiling of a doorway. Herman pointed up to it. There was a small ring on the end of the door. This horizontal door easily opened. A ladder came down. They did not use the ladder.

Instead, they swam up to what was quickly understood to be an attic area. Interestingly, the roof of the hotel was apparently built watertight. The attic area inside was completely dry. It came up like a scuba diver entering into the inside underneath of a submarine. The water level remained at the ceiling level. It was starting to seep in so they closed the door behind them.

It was an eerie sight. The oxygen in this room, however much there was, was more than 150 years old. The room was dusty, and largely vacant. Normally attics are crowded with all kinds of knick-knacks and things.

Herman had a waterproof flashlight, and turned it on. As he scanned the room, there was a shiny reflection at one end. They took their fins off and held them in their hands. They walked over to that end of the room.

Elwood swam out of the hotel, and went around to the side of this attic area. There was a window he could peer into. He watched with great interest as Herman shined the flashlight on whatever created that reflection.

It was a fascinating display. There was a substantial mirror. In the mirror was an inlay of a large photo of a young boy. This was a black and white photo that had been touched up with paint, to make it appear as a color photo. The photo had somehow been inlaid into the mirror by placing a sheet of glass over the mirror and encasing it. The photo was absolutely perfectly preserved.

The mirror stood on a frame that had a leg going in the back at a 45-degree angle, rather like a typical smaller picture frame, but this mirror was no picture frame. It was about four feet high and three feet wide. The photo was placed in the inside of this mirror, and had a beautiful paper border, apparently made by the hotel owners out of the same wallpaper that adorned the hotel walls.

At the foot of the mirror, there was an array of jewelry set on some beautiful Chinese porcelain plates. These were no ordinary plates. It could be seen right away that the edges had gold on them. The interior had Chinese writing. On top of these plates was a treasure trove of jewels.

There were rubies, emeralds, diamonds, pearl necklaces, diamond rings. Most of the jewelry was loose jewelry, in the form of finished, cut stones, but not inlaid into any kind of necklace or ring. The few exceptions were a set of pearl necklaces, absolutely gorgeous in every way, and one ruby diamond tiara. By its size, it could only have belonged to a young girl, a gift from a sister.

Another plate next to these jewels had a small pyramid of silver ingots. Back in the early 1800s, there was quite a bit of silver mining going on the area of present day Nevada. Apparently, somehow this family got involved in that silver mining, and managed to collect up enough ingots to make a row of five, on which was stacked a row of four, and then a row of three, two and one. These 15 ingots had a present market value of about $2 million.

At the base of the pyramid was a much smaller four by five inch black and white photograph of what was apparently the entire family. There was a mom, a dad, a young son and a younger daughter. This photo was in a small, but beautifully ornate gold picture frame with glass in front.

The value of the ingots, the value of the tiara, the loose rubies and diamonds, the pearl necklaces must have all been well north of $5 million. The whole memorial had a value of somewhere between $6 to $7 million. Of course, all these figures were racing through Herman's mind.

Elwood, on the outside, was equally excited, but had a split attitude, which mirrored the distinction in attitudes between Herman and Sabrina. The second Herman tried to touch the memorial; Sabrina put her hand out and stopped him.

"No, we mustn't touch it."

"What are you talking about? Look at this stuff. It must be worth millions."

"It's a memorial. Can't you see that?"

"So?"

"So you can't upset a memorial. Don't you know what this is about?"

"Yeah. Some kid apparently died long ago and his rich parents built this multimillion dollar memorial in his honor."

"Yeah, and we are not going to touch it."

"Wait a minute though. Wait a minute. Let's back up a little bit."

Elwood listened in with great interest to this conversation. He could hear it in his own fish way to the vibrations of the sound waves onto the brass window that he was in front of. He put his little fish fins and ears up to that window, and received a full transmission of the words exchanged between Herman and Sabrina.

Herman explained, "Do you remember how you were telling me about our various money problems? You know, like mortgage payments, car payments. You want to buy this, you want to buy that. Remember all those discussions we've had?"

"That has nothing to do with this."

"Well, hold on. It does because if we take even half these items, all of those discussions will go away. You can buy the office building you want. You can buy the home you want. You can buy the car you want and you can take one, two, three or ten of the vacations you want."

"And we will be forever damned."

"What are you talking about?" Herman was incredulous that she would actually be thinking of passing on this once in a lifetime opportunity. "It's like winning the lottery and saying, 'I don't want to cash in the ticket.'"

Herman took out of his scuba utility belt a small wallet-looking device that had a snap button on the front. He unsnapped that button and pulled out of the satchel a largish mesh bag. As he pulled it out, he put it over the memorial area.

187

"You see? It's about the right size."

"No. A lottery is not a memorial for a dead person. Don't you get it?"

"Don't you get that this dead person is long gone, his parents are long gone. The memorial has been here for what, 150 years? I think its memorial enough."

Sabrina shook her head. "We cannot take this. You have to understand it. We just can't do it."

"What, you're just going to swim out of here and leave this here?"

"Exactly."

Just then, they heard something go, bump.

"What was that?"

"What was what?"

"I just heard something."

Elwood swam away from the window and went down to the lobby.

"Uh-oh. We got visitors."

Two other divers had arrived. One of them had an interesting tattoo of a Harley Davidson motorcycle on his forearm. The other one had a tattoo on his leg of the United States Marine Corps insignia of the globe with an anchor through it. Below that insignia was the famous call to duty of the Marines: Semper Fi.

On entering the hotel in their own scuba gear, they had opened the door, which was shut again by the current of the water. That made a bump noise that reverberated upstairs into the attic area. Water is a great conveyer of sound waves, and delivered the unmistakable sound of a new entrant into the hotel.

Any ambiguity as to whether these entrants were friendly or non-friendly was quickly dispelled by the terrifying sight out the window of the hotel. Sabrina saw it first and screamed. It was the upside down body of Herman's childhood friend Jeremy, with a spear from a scuba spear gun in his gut. His face was ashen-white and very dead.

This was Herman's dear friend from long ago. Herman was shocked to see him dead. Both hands went to his head, his mouth opened, and he let out a scream that wouldn't be heard at all. A silent scream, like screaming in a vacuum. Sabrina's scream was not so silent.

Just as the bump of the door closing downstairs was conveyed up to the attic area rather efficiently by the water, so was Sabrina's scream conveyed from the attic down to the lobby.

Herman grabbed Sabrina from the back and put his hand over her mouth. He shushed her.

Jeremy's body continued to float downward. They had put scuba belt weights on his waist. The plight of his lovely wife was not known precisely, but it doesn't take a crime scene investigation genius to figure out that one dead spouse under these circumstances probably means there are two.

Herman was so sad to see the passing of his friend. He was trying to usher up the strength to get out of this dangerous situation. He whispered to Sabrina, "Look, you can say what you want about leaving stuff here, but one thing you got to know. These men, whoever they are, are obviously killers, which means they're criminals and they're going to find this, and you know they're going to take it."

Sabrina, of course, knew Herman was right. "Maybe we can find the descendants of this family and give the memorial to them."

Herman was angry from what had happened to his dear friend, and wanted something good to come from all this.

"Great idea. Listen though, we better get out of here, like, right away."

Elwood the flying fish was busy circling the hotel, swimming by the nearby window, and watching Herman and Sabrina. He was imagining he was a fellow human helping them pack these heirlooms up. As they worked, he imagined working right beside them. His image as a hard working human flying fish may be hard to picture. For Elwood, being a human came quite naturally. It was just another of his personalities.

Herman pointed over to the very window where his friend's head just floated by as the obvious point of exit. He pointed his head in the direction of the memorial. "Shall we?"

Elwood was swimming right at this exit point, and guided them out with his wings. Yes, this was the way.

Sabrina saw Elwood's wings, and nodded her head yes. She and Elwood connected at that point, eye to eye, arm to wing.

They took the silver ingots first and put them at the bottom. They then put the plate on the side. They then took the plate of the diamonds, rubies, tiara and pearls.

Sabrina took out another bag that she had, a smaller bag. The jewels were carefully poured off the plate into that bag and sealed. The plate was then put in a larger bag. They put the smaller photo in the larger bag as well.

They looked at the mirror and wondered how could they get that out as well. It was too precious to leave behind.

Herman thought of it though. "You know, this they probably wouldn't mess with. It's the jewels they would want. We could leave that here and come back and get it later."

"Maybe we won't find this again. We better take it now."

They looked at the window. It was not big enough.

"It won't fit out of there."

Elwood was swimming in circles, wondering and wishing how he could help them. He gave them a hint by bumping his head right into the window. It didn't break. Elwood bounced back. Sabrina saw all this, and understood the basic idea of how to make a small opening larger. Bust it open.

Just then, they heard another bump. This one was quite a bit closer and louder than the first bump.

Herman shushed Sabrina. "Don't move."

He put his ear to the floorboards. What he could hear was the sound of air bubbles coming from the second floor area into the ceiling. These air bubbles were rolling along the ceiling and were climbing their way up. They found the small crack around the perimeter of the attic door and were released into the attic.

"They're getting closer," he whispered. "We got to get out of here. We're going to have to leave that here."

"No, we can't leave it here. We got to bring it. How can we bring it?"

"Here, let's go like this."

Herman took Sabrina's bag of jewelry, tied it very carefully with a string and latched it onto her belt. He made sure it was firm.

"Put your fins on."

Sabrina put her fins on.

190

Elwood got excited as the fins were put on. It was time for action. He swam around in circles, living vicariously as Sabrina.

The bag Herman had was quite heavy, as it had all the silver ingots. The bag was made of a super strong mesh material, so it could handle it. Once it got in the water, it wouldn't weigh so much, but getting it into the water was another story.

Herman pulled a small device that had a CO_2 cartridge connected to a balloon out of his utility belt. He placed the cartridge and the balloon on top of the bag. He walked the bag over to the window and placed it there. He then walked back and grabbed that large mirror item and walked it over to the window. He put it up vertically and it clearly wouldn't fit through. Horizontally, it wouldn't fit through. Diagonally, it wouldn't fit through.

Sabrina looked at the framing around the window and pointed at it. It was fairly weak. Herman understood what she was getting at. Perhaps a couple body slams into the window would take care of the situation.

Just then, the attic door opened in its downward way. Two heads with face masks appeared. Flashlights appeared. The lights went immediately onto the bag, on Sabrina's belt. They reflected the diamonds, pearls and rubies.

The man took his regulator out of his mouth. The other man came up with a spear gun and pointed it in their direction.

"Whoa, whoa, whoa. Just where do you think you guys are going?"

The spear gun was pointed right at Sabrina. Herman and Sabrina were unarmed and un-dangerous.

Herman turned to Sabrina. He put his face mask on and pointed to her regulator, which was hanging at her side. He put his in his mouth. She followed and put her mask on.

In one simple maneuver, he swung the bag of silver ingots into the window. It easily smashed open, letting in a long overdue rush of water into this formerly dry room. The water came in like a miniature tsunami.

Sabrina nodded to Elwood. Elwood smiled. They got the hint.

Herman and Sabrina dodged the strong influx of water by standing to the side like a matador does when the bull charges. The dangerous men were not so lucky. They were still in the process of coming up through that attic doorway, and got a

191

straight-on shot of a three foot by three foot square gush of water right into their heads. Their face masks were off, their regulators were out.

The spear gun went vertical. It was shot off, sending the spear into the ceiling above. This would again work against these two men. That dart into the ceiling smacked out a rafter, which was one of the supporting pieces of the roof. This opened up a fairly good sized crevice in the roof.

Elwood swam up to that opening in the roof, and looked down at the men. He roared like a dinosaur fish.

With the power of a lion's roar, several tons of water came directly down and onto their heads. This forced them back into the second floor area.

Their face masks fell off. He lost the spear gun, which floated down to the floor. They pushed down to the ground in a topsy-turvy way. They couldn't swim back up against the power of the water.

Elwood was right by the window, guiding them out with his wing.

"This way."

Sabrina again saw this, and smiled. They had a friend in Elwood.

After the attic had filled with water, it became calm. Herman then placed the bag of silver outside the window. He turned on the CO2 cartridge. The balloon was quickly filled up. He connected the bag to his belt.

The process of the water rushing in smashed through the frame of the window, and enlarged an exit hole by about two feet. This now created enough room to get that picture frame out as well.

The bag was let go, but was connected to Herman. It pulled him up. As he went to the top, Elwood swam up with him. Hermanheld onto the mirror. Unfortunately, in the process of exiting the window, the leg of the mirror got stuck and broke off.

Sabrina was going to grab it, but it escaped her grip by about two inches. It was just a wooden leg -- no big deal. She swam out the window with her bag of jewels.

Elwood looked at himself for the first time in the mirror. He saw for the first time the simple reality that he wasn't a dinosaur fish, a person, a snake, or a bird, he was flying fish. This moment saddened him.

Sabrina both looked into Elwood's eyes. Elwood was living his part as a human, vicariously through Sabrina. He was enjoying every ascending foot of it.

When they came to the surface, they saw the houseboat and the tragedy that had come to Karen. She was hanging over the houseboat with another spear in her back. It was a shocking site. Sabrina got sick and threw up, leaving some pretty disgusting contents of her stomach floating about.

Herman knew there was nothing they could do for her. He also knew that the men would come to the houseboat first.

"Over here."

Instead of going to the houseboat, they swam to shore.

Herman dragged the heavier sack onto dry land and gently placed the mirror down. They took their fins off, their scuba gear off. Both of them knew that the men that they had just pummeled with water would soon resurface. Time was short.

"We got to get out of here."

Sandstone Path

This part of the lake is adorned by reddish sandstone walls previously part of a desert region. The geological lines showed many millions of years on these walls.The sandstone straight up and down. It just stood there. There's no to climb a cliff with a bag filled with silver ingots. They walked into a crevice that had a small creek leading to the larger lake. They decided to follow that creek.

"Here, let's go like this."

They put the heavy bag gently onto the mirror. Sabrina took one end of the mirror and Herman took the other. They walked forward into this crevice, step by step. They would have to abandon their scuba gear.

Before they did that, they wanted to eliminate the rather obvious clue of where they were. So they hid it behind a couple of rocks. You would have to somehow see the rock from the shore way, park your boat, get out of your boat and look behind that rock to find these things. At some point, somebody would find them, but hopefully not today.

The high desert sun would quickly dry off the signs of water they carried with them as they walked away from this landing site. The last being to see them walk away was none other than Elwood, who cheered them on.

"Go, go, fly away!"

If Elwood could've helped them, he would've.

Sure enough, the two bad men resurfaced not far from the houseboat. They swam to the houseboat and quickly saw that Herman and Sabrina were not there. The Marine Corps guy pointed to the shore.

Elwood was nearby and saw these two bad guys. Elwood then went into one of his other personalities. The flying fish does look, in a way, like either a lizard or snake with wings. They are long and thin. This one was emerald blue in color. Elwood has a personality within him in which he is a King Cobra.

He slithered over to the men. He tried to make his head go flat and spoon shaped, but of course, it wouldn't work. The men looked at Elwood and tried to shoo him away. As one of them pushed his hand in his direction, he bit them like a poisonous snake would bite a person.

The man quickly flung Elwood away. "Ow!"

Elwood's teeth were sharp, little, but alas, not poisonous.

195

The other man tried to smash Elwood, but was surprised when Elwood went back into his true self, by far his most capable self, and flew away.

"Whoa, flying fish!"

Neither had expected to see a flying fish from the African Congo flying around in a manmade lake in Arizona. They proceeded to shore. They walked inland. The bad guys always figure out what the good guys are up to. They went behind the rock and saw the scuba gear that Herman and Sabrina had left behind. They piled theirs right next to it.

There weren't that many possible paths to embark on. There was a sandstone cliff; clearly nobody could walk up that. Then there was an inland creek with two cliff face walls on either side. That had to be the path.

They followed it. They could travel quite a bit faster than Herman and Sabrina. They were just on foot and had to carry only a spear gun, their hunting knives were strapped to their ankles. Their attitudes were particularly rotten and angry. They were both in perfect shape and could easily outrun, outsprint and overtake the two fleeing spouses, especially when they were burdened with the Chinese memorial.

As Herman and Sabrina were proceeding through this crevice, it came to a point where there was a fork; one to the right, one to the left. Which way should they go?

Herman thought about it. They stopped before it. They heard a bird fly by. He looked up in the air. To the left, he saw quite a few birds. Somehow, these birds gave him the feeling of safety. He decided to go left. As he was just about to take that turn, he heard a very unsettling sound. Crunch, the sound of someone walking on a branch. He put his ear down, Native American style, to the ground. He heard another crunch.

"They're getting close. We got to go."

They took that left turn and continued down a canyon. The canyon wiggled left and wiggled right. They snaked through the canyon walls, following a path next to a small creek. It was an amazing sight.

The sandstone had withstood the desert sun, the night winds and all that came with it for millions of years. The question, though, was whether these two humans could withstand the same elements for the next five hours.

Although Elwood could not see what they were doing, he could imagine it. He saw them walking, near horizontal and parallel to the earth, Sabrina in the back,

196

Herman in the front. They proceeded down the small creek in a fairly slow, but steady manner.

Their pursuers were running after them. It's hard to run when you're carrying multiple ingots of silver, a bag of rubies, diamonds and pearls and a large mirror. Especially when you're in the desert, and wearing nothing but neoprene socks that were quickly getting worn out.

If you were to put this in the words of an elementary school math equation, how long would it take two people, running eight miles an hour and carrying nothing, but knives and a spear gun to catch two people without weapons walking at about two miles an hour while carrying a large mirror laden with silver ingots, diamonds and rubies? The answer is, not very long. Something would have to happen, or else the adventure would meet with tragedy.

They came upon an opening between the sheer sandstone cliff walls coming down on either side of this creek. The opening was a tributary leading upwards. It was just wide enough to fit the width of the mirror.

Herman took this left hand turn, and as though they didn't have enough obstacles, began a process of walking up an elevated path. It took him from a speed of perhaps two and a half miles per hour to a new low of one mile per hour. It's tricky walking up a gully inside a hill with such a load.

Not long after they embarked on this tributary, they came upon some ancient Indian ruins. These may have been undiscovered ruins. They were from a tribe that had long ago vanished from the face of the earth, and left a red brick type pueblo structure that was still about half standing. This pueblo remained as a sanctuary to Herman and Sabrina. They entered it.

It was a former fortress, having about nine rooms, leading into the body of a cliff. The front of the structures appeared flush with the cliff, and were made of the same reddish-pinkish limestone rock.

They had managed to chisel these into thin bricks, which were carefully laid, probably about 10,000 years ago. As a testament to their bricklaying skills, the bricks remained in place.

Sabrina was pleased to see this point of safety. She had an idea.

"Perhaps we can hide these here and get out of here alive."

Herman agreed.

They searched around for a good hiding spot. They walked further and further into the cave. Unfortunately, it was all fairly open space. There were no smaller holes to walk into. It became completely dark inside. They proceeded with less fear of the dark than the fear of what was on the outside.

Meanwhile, the dangerous duo had managed to come upon the same tributary. They could see bits of the neoprene rubber shoes caught against some of the limestone.

"They went up here, probably searching for a road. Let's go."

The men proceeded at about four times the speed up the same elevation, and soon found themselves at the opening of the Anasazi Indian structure.

Of course they went in there. They figured it out immediately. They proceeded into the same cave.

Herman and Sabrina were well into the cave and heard the men stumble through the front parts.

"Shh." He stopped. "Listen."

They could hear the muffled echoing of the men's voices. "That way," were the only two words that were clearly discernible.

The good news was that it was pitch black in this inner sanctum. They decided it would be best to carefully place the mirror on the ground to the side of the cave and to remain perfectly motionless.

Unfortunately, this plan would not work out so well. They hadn't counted on the idea that the men would also have flashlights. These underwater flashlights come in handy when one is found inside the inner sanctum of an ancient cave.

The flashlights created a disturbance in the cave that the men had not predicted. These places had remained dark for so long. Every kind of environment is teeming with impossible forms of life. The same was true for this cave in the desert lands of Arizona.

Once the light came into this ecosystem, the disturbance reverberated from top to bottom, side to side, depth to height. The beings inside there, used to being blind, were guided to the light. It is somewhat natural for bugs to come to a light. It's not just bugs that are guided to lights. Wild pigs, the javelina, are allured as well. These pigs, about the size of a German shepherd, are smaller, but akin to the wild boars of Africa.

Alone, they might not present much of a danger to a human, but they are rarely alone. They travel in packs, usually more than 50.

The rumblings of their hooves could be heard. The snorting of their mouths could be heard. The chomping of their teeth could be heard. They groaned. If they were dogs, they would bark, but they were pigs so they grunted. It was not an oink grunt. It was a lower-sounded, belly-sourced moan of a grunt from an animal that had not seen such a large beast to eat.

These pigs would normally not attack a human, but there was something about this invasion of their sanctuary that bothered them. The two humans had caused an intrusion, the impact of which was to trigger a near-psychotic level of anger.

The sight that these men had to see was best described as a furry river. These javelinas have the colorings of a German shepherd, with the thickness of their hair more akin to a porcupine without needles. The cave tunnel was wide enough to fit about eight across. It must have been about 10 deep, so the total was in the realm of 80 angry, psychotically wired wild pigs.

That the two dangerous men were trained by the United States Marine Corps was the only salvation they could hope for. The spear gun was fired into the lead pig and took it out. One down, 79 to go. This bloodshed did what blood does to shark, and sent the remaining pigs into a frenzy. One of the pigs jumped one of the men, but he had his knife out. He cut its throat.

You can just keep on cutting up pigs and throwing them back at each other, but at some point, one of them is going to get you and indeed, one did. It bit the man right on the arm.

"Ow!" he screamed.

This pig had pretty impressive tusks that found their mark.

There was one thing these men could do that the pigs could not do. They could climb. They climbed to the side of this tunnel, which thankfully had places for them to grab and pull themselves up. They continued up for better than 15 feet.

The pigs jumped up against the wall, and bit a few of their toes on the way up. This little toe went to the mouth. This man would suffer many losses during his life. Today, he would lose a toe. His scream was harrowing and echoed down the tunnel.

199

Herman and Sabrina were on the safe side of this furry river. They saw their opportunity to continue their path into the inside of this cave. They hoped that somewhere it would lead to an outside, a beyond where there was daylight and hopefully a paved road.

They proceeded for several hours. It's not easy walking in the dark. After hearing those pigs and their impressive numbers, it made Herman and Sabrina wonder what other wild dangers lurked in the depths of this darkness.

These kinds of dangers can occupy a mind. It doesn't fit the definition of paranoia, which is an irrational fear. This was a wholly rational fear. Just as those men were viciously attacked by a pack of pigs, a similar danger could easily befall these two. There was no choice other than to go forward, and so go forward they did.

They didn't come upon a paved road, but they did come upon something that would be nearly as good. The cave led to a mineshaft. The shaft had a rail track in it. This was not some ancient mine. This was a current mine. There was a rail cart sitting right there, motionless. Too bad it didn't have an engine or it would've been the ultimate find, but it did push forward easily enough.

They placed the mirror and the jewels into the rail cart. This cart had hauled out quite a bit of ore from these parts and a little tiny bit of gold. Today, it would haul out a bunch of diamonds, a bunch of rubies, some pearls, silver ingots and a very interesting photo encased in glass. They pushed that cart forward on its tracks for what must've been at least a mile.

There was a light at the end of the tunnel, normally a cliché. Today's announcement was quite real. It was about a half a mile down the tracks. They proceeded to the opening.

There could've been any of a number of dangers awaiting them outside the entry into this mine shaft. The most obvious type of danger would be modern day miners. Though they may use different equipment, their attitudes and "take what you dig" approach to life has not changed much over the centuries.

They proceeded through the opening. They were faced with a non-human danger: that of endless open desert space, no water, no car, no transportation and not a road in sight.

Herman scanned the horizon. It must've been 103 degrees out. The sun was at three o'clock and pounded on them. The sun's reflection off the mirror was blinding and increased the temperature by a couple of degrees.

Herman had an idea. "Let's climb up to the top. Maybe we can find something." Sabrina didn't want to be left alone at the opening of the mine shaft. They scooted the cart back into the mine, where it would not stick out like a bright thumb.

The opening to the mine shaft was at the face of a mountain about 600 feet high. There wasn't a single tree on it. It was all brown, jagged rock, which had plenty of grooves and crevices to stick your hands and feet in.

Sabrina was surprisingly fast up the face of the mountain, and got to the top with Herman behind her at about 40 yards. Soon after he caught up with her, he was huffing and puffing and sweating profusely. She was sitting on the ledge enjoying the scenic view of the dry desert expanse and the complete absence of any humans. The desert was big.

There was a grace in all this, pure nature; harsh, stark and very real. But there was also a problem with this. How on earth could they ever get out of there alive, and with their cart of jewels and a large mirror?

Herman looked over to one side and noticed the sight of a group of circling birds. It wasn't that far from the mine shaft opening, maybe a distance of half a mile. On the ground below the birds, there was some kind of shiny object. It glittered in the sunlight.

This also caught Sabrina's eye. "Let's go check it out."

They climbed back down the mountain. It was now much later in the day, getting close to five o'clock. It was cooling off. They walked in the direction of the buzzards circling over whatever that shiny object belonged to.

It was about a half a mile walk. Well before they got to it, they got to the stench. The smell of death will hit you like a ton of bricks.

"P-U!" Sabrina had to hold her nose as they walked closer.

Then they saw what the buzzards were flying over, it was a dead person. The shiny object was a fancy looking stainless steel briefcase attached to the hand of a man in his late 40s. He was clean-shaven, wore an Oxford shirt and brown wool pants, the kind a banker might wear on a non-casual day.

Herman removed the briefcase from the dead hand, hoping that its contents would somehow lead them out of there. He opened the briefcase. It was completely empty.

Sabrina knew right away, whatever was in there got him killed. The cause of death was obvious enough; a bullet had been shot through his forehead. He died instantaneously. There was no torture, no attempt to get information, just a need to get whatever was in that briefcase.

Herman looked around and saw some tire marks. A car of some sort had driven there, dropped this guy off, shot him and removed the contents from the briefcase and then left.

Herman did a pat-down search of the man. There was something in his pocket. He pulled it out, a perfect savior for the day, an iPhone.

"Can you hear me now?"

This iPhone would be just the tool they needed to get out of this predicament.

Herman went to the iPhone's Safari function and got online to Google. The search was easy: limousine service within 50 miles. The results showed a city called Page, Arizona, which sits on the edge of Lake Powell close to the Arizona-Utah border, there was a company called Page Limousine Service. Praise the Lord.

Herman called them up. Unfortunately, he got a voicemail. Great. He left a message.

"Please call us back. We have a need for a limousine right now."

Herman realized he didn't know the phone number he was calling from so he ended the message. He found the telephone number on the settings function, and then called the limo service back.

This time a guy answered, "Limo service."

"Oh hey, I just left you a voicemail."

"You're the guy that called and didn't leave a number."

"Sorry about that. I have my number now."

"Okay. So where are you guys?"

"I am in the desert a little bit off the beaten path by some kind of a mine. We got stranded out here. My phone has a GPS so I can give you the exact coordinates."

"Okay."

"I know this though, I am within 150 miles of you."

"Okay."

"By any chance, do you own a four wheel drive truck?"

"I'm in Page. Everyone out here has a four wheel drive truck."

"I want to suggest that you use that and not a stretch limo."

"Okay. How many are there?"

"Two -- me and my wife."

"Any luggage?"

Herman looked over to Sabrina and smiled. He looked at the empty stainless steel briefcase. He picked it up.

"Just one bag and , oh yeah, a cart of some stuff."

"Okay. Well, here's the deal. I'm $80 an hour. I take cash, Visa-"

Herman interrupted him, "I can give you my Visa card number right now."

"Okay, go ahead."

"2349-1725-6298-9995."

"Okay, just a second. I'm going to charge that in the amount of, let's see, one hour to get there and then, oh yeah, I should ask, where am I taking you guys?"

"If you don't mind, we need to go to Sacramento."

"Sacramento? That's about fifteen hours from Page."

"Alright. One hour to get here. Another fifteen hours to Sacramento. So what's that all going to cost?"

"$2,000."

"Why don't we just call it an even $2,000?"

"That's what I said."

"Can you receive a text message on this phone?"

"I can."

"Alright, let me do this. I'm going to hang up right now. I'm going to get my GPS coordinates and I'm going to text them to you. There's got to be a road around here somewhere."

"You don't see a road?"

"No, but I see car tracks nearby us so there's got to be some kind of highway."

"Hey, just send me the GPS coordinates. I'll figure it out."

203

Herman hung up, brought up the GPS system on the iPhone, and found the exact coordinates of his location. He then texted those coordinates to Page Limo Service.

The man received it, pulled it up on his computer and did a Google map. The location was about five miles from not quite a highway, but still a paved road. There was a dirt road on the grid leading to an area close by.

The man called back. "Hey, tell me something."

"Yeah?"

"What kind of terrain you got out there?"

"Flat, empty, no trees. Probably some occasional ditches and dried up river beds."

"Okay. I found a road to get fairly close to you. We'll keep in touch. When I get there, I'll call you."

"Thank you."

It was not polite to steal from a dead man, but the fact remained, they needed that iPhone to get out of there alive. They took his iPhone and took his empty briefcase. Herman looked up to the buzzards.

"He's all yours."

They walked away from this unknown man, who was about to understand the phrase "ashes to ashes, dust to dust." It would be one bird bite at a time.

They came back to the mine shaft. First thing was to check the rail cart and make sure everything was there. It checked out. There was still no human in sight. They took the mirror off the cart and gently set it down. They grabbed the bag at had all of the rubies and diamonds. They opened the briefcase and gently placed the bag inside the briefcase. It fit. They closed it. They still had the other bag with the plates and the ingots.

It wasn't exactly the safest thing to wait out here until the limo driver appeared, but they had few choices.

The limo was in the form of a Humvee, slate gray.

The limo driver had the look of a gold prospector, but was polite.

"Good afternoon."

"Boy, are we glad to meet you."

204

He didn't notice the buzzards eating a man.

He didn't ask a single question about the mirror, or the bags of silver ingots, or the contents of the briefcase.

They left the mine shaft opening just in time.

As they pulled away, the two criminals, one with nine toes, hobbled out of the mine shaft, too late to get a fix on the license plate.

It took them a full day to get home. They carefully brought the memorial into their home. After a few weeks, Sabrina decided she wanted to set it up.

"Oh. Why are we doing that?'

"It just seems a shame to have this in the closet."

"Okay, but how about we hide the gems?"

It was agreed. They would put the gems into a safe deposit box at the local bank, but the mirror and inlaid photo of the long-deceased boy would be set up as a shrine next to the door and piano in their living room. The plates were without the silver ingots and gems. Instead, mandarin oranges, grapes and pomegranates were placed on them.

One day Herman came home from work and found her over the memorial, crying endlessly.

"What's wrong, dear?"

"I don't know. I'm just so sad."

"Well, what are you sad about?"

"The boy is just so special."

"Yes, he is special. But hon-"

"I know. I know he's not my son, but it's like I lost him."

"You are grieving for someone else's loss."

"It's my loss now."

Herman thought about that statement. One thing he knew right away, he HAD to find the rightful heirs to that memorial. Until he did, his wife would be suffering from a grief transference. The suffering of one mother had become hers.

Meanwhile, back at Lake Powell, Elwood continued to swim around the sunken hotel. He flew and swam around the decomposing body of Jeremy. Being around this body during its course of transference from earthly life to astral light imbued Elwood with a new personality identity; that of Jeremy's.

One of the connectors of the different personalities undertaken by Elwood was the placement of a separate being near Elwood. If he saw a whale, he might become a whale. In this case, he saw Jeremy, and developed a personality of Jeremy's. The fact that Jeremy was in this transitory state impacted Elwood's assumption of Jeremy's personality.

There was a similar impact on Sabrina as she carefully guarded over the memorial. She began to take on the life of this boy's mother. She wondered how it was to lose such a cherished son, what had caused his demise and the impact of that demise on the loving mother. It regularly brought her to tears. She went into the same level of depression that a mother who lost her son would descend into.

The more she descended into this depression, the more Herman was committed toward finding the true owners of this memorial. The house had become, in a way, haunted; not by a ghost, but by a psychological influence that created an unhealthy connection between a grieving mother and Herman's wife. The solution, obvious enough, was to find the rightful owner of this memorial, and to deliver it to them.

It was a similar danger for Elwood to take over the position of a dead person. When Elwood would transfer into the personality of Jeremy, he took not only Jeremy's life, but his death. Elwood would literally stop swimming, stop breathing. His heart would stop beating. He would float to the top of the water, belly up.

Elwood and Sabrina had this problem of undertaking another personality, itself afflicted with a severe disorder. Sabrina was clinically depressed . Elwood's was perhaps the worst and most extreme disorder of all, death.

In order to rid themselves of these disorders, both Sabrina and Elwood had to find a way to get away from the source of the shift into the other personalities.
For Sabrina, the memorial remained as a magnet. She couldn't leave it, and became obsessed with it.

For Elwood, there was a similar fascination with the decomposing body of Jeremy. He would swim down to it and in a repeated cycle, would go into a dead mode, and would float to the top of the water. After some time flopping about, he would awaken and go back into his fish state. He would soon swim back down to see Jeremy again and would repeat the process. There had to be a way to break this unfortunate cycle.

All of this would remain on the shoulders of Herman, who had not adopted any other personalities. He knew exactly what to do.

The research began with Google. He typed in the name of the family, typed in the location, typed in the date of death, but unfortunately came up empty-handed. As much information as Google has out there, it didn't have anything on the Henry Li family.

He went to ancestry.com. This website gives quite a bit of information on people's ancestors, especially those who have traveled from other countries and have made stops along the way that create official government entries of their travels, such as immigration points. Unfortunately, there were many Li families that came from Canton, China to the United States during the early 1800s.

The problem wasn't finding information about the Lis, the problem was limiting it to the Henry Li family that moved over to this northern part of Arizona, and owned a hotel there. As he examined the many, many entries on ancestry.com, he came to know one unfortunate bit of reality: he would not be able to find what he was looking for.

Sacramento, California

His search brought him to several Li families, located in San Francisco and six in Sacramento. On his eleventh attempt at connecting up with one of these possible suspects, he hit pay dirt. He knew it the second he walked into the Canton restaurant in Sacramento: the wallpaper unmistakably matched the wallpaper that he had seen back at the underwater hotel, pieces of which were in the smaller photo.

He had the photo with him and showed it to the restaurant owners. They were amazed to see the match.

"Great-great-grandmother brought that over from Canton."

They could see it right away. This is not the kind of wallpaper you can find anywhere other than Canton, China. This paper was obviously about 150 years old, and without a doubt, a perfect match. At long last, Herman had found the rightful heirs of the memorial of the boy whose death was way too soon.

The ancient woman who realized the match of the wallpaper must have been 92 years old. She asked in Cantonese, "Where did you get this?"

The restaurant manager translated. "She wants to know how you found this."

Herman stopped for a moment. He did not want to tell them too much. They may be imposters. They may not be part of the direct family. Who knows?

So he answered the question with a question, "Who owns this restaurant?"

The manager spoke, "I do."

"So this lady here, who is she?"

"She was the manager from the previous owner."

"I see. What was her last name?"

"Li."

"And your last name?"

"Wong."

"So the Wong family bought this restaurant from the Li family."

"Yes. My father did this transaction long ago."

"So when you bought it, the wallpaper was there?"

"Yes."

"Do you know this Li family?"

"I do. They're very interesting people."

209

"Interesting?"

"Oh yeah."

"Why?"

"They have become very successful businesspeople here in Sacramento and in Stockton."

"Oh?"

"Yes."

"Do you know where I can find them?"

"Certainly. It's easy."

"Okay, tell me."

"They own an Asian food store. It's located in the Asian district of Sacramento."

The ancient woman had no idea what they were talking about. The man realized this and stopped to translate. He spoke to her in Cantonese for a bit and she nodded. She took out her cell phone and made a phone call.

Within a matter of seconds, someone answered. A Cantonese conversation ensued. She then handed the phone to Herman.

"Hello?"

"Hi."

"Who am I speaking with?"

"Hi, my name is Herman. I'm a lawyer here in town and I have shown, I think your grandmother maybe-"

"That's my grandmother, yes."

"I've shown her some wallpaper samples I have."

"Okay."

"They are a perfect match for what's in this Golden Dragon Restaurant here."

"Yeah, that's from one of my ancestors who came from Canton long ago."

"Your grandmother explained it to me."

"How on earth did you get that wallpaper?"

"I'd like to explain that to you in person if you don't mind."

"Okay, come on by. We are located on the corner of Fruit Ridge Road and Stockton Boulevard."

"Oh, that large grocery store there?"

210

"Yeah."

"That's yours?"

"Yes."

"I see. Can I come by now?"

"Please do."

"I'll be there shortly."

On the way over, Herman called Sabrina.

"Sabrina, you won't believe it, but I found him."

"You found who?"

"I found the Li family."

"How did you find him?"

"I was at a restaurant and you won't believe it, there was a perfect match of the wallpaper. I spoke with this old lady there. She explained how her great-great-grandmother bought it over from Canton. Their family now owns that big grocery store on Fruit Ridge and Stockton Boulevard."

"The White Dragon?"

"Yes, that one."

Sabrina was a bit somber to hear this news.

Herman sensed that. "Hon, you got to let it go."

"I know I got to let it go, but I just, I can't."

"But you have to. This is where it belongs."

"I know. Can we please give…"

"Be careful. I mean, we got to make sure."

"I know. Let's not tell them anything until we know if this is the right group."

"Why don't you meet me there?"

"Okay."

"I'll see you there in about 40 minutes, okay?"

"Yes."

"I'm going to wait for you in the corner parking lot across the street. Let's meet there and then we can walk over together."

"Okay. I'll see you there."

When they arrived at the White Dragon Asian food store, they got an eyeful. There were four police officers pulled up in the front parking lot. There was a group of younger kids screaming and yelling. There was a large woman screaming and yelling, all in a language called Hakka, which Sabrina did not understand.

There was one of the males and his large wife on one side, a group of young kids and the older generation on the other. In the middle of that was an elderly woman, the mother of them all. A group of police officers were trying to keep them all from killing each other.

Into this mess, Herman came in.

"Wow, what's going on?"

The mother spoke. "Who are you?"

Herman explained. "Oh, sorry. I'm just here to meet John."

Everybody suddenly quieted down.

The mother asked, "Why do you want to see John?"

Herman responded, "I just talked to him on the phone. He told me I could come by right now."

The mother wanted more, "What's it about?"

Herman pulled out the wallpaper and showed them. "It's about this."

They all looked. They were amazed. One of the boys yelled out "Where did you get that?"

Herman explained, "Well, that's what I want to talk to you guys about."

A man asked, "Talk to us about what?"

Herman shifted the talk. "Just a minute. Where's John? That's the guy that the elderly lady told me to talk to. I'd feel better talking to him."

The mother asked, "Who did you speak with?" She spoke in Hakka.

One of the boys shouted out, "You spoke with grandmother down at the restaurant?"

Herman announced, "Yes."

Another man asked, "A-ha. How did you find her?"

Herman explained, "It wasn't really planned. I just happened to be there having lunch and I noticed the wallpaper. I compared it and it was a perfect match."

The mother asked, "So you found grandmother and she put you on the phone with John."

The kids ran into the store. Within a moment, clan leader John came out. He was a portly Chinese, unusual in that most of them are rail-thin.

"Hi, I'm John. I'm the president of this company."

Herman greeted him, "Yes, I can see that."

Herman turned around and looked at the amazing array of activities. Four police cars, six police, one canine unit, German shepherd in the back, ready to pounce if necessary, a screaming large woman, another man looking a bit docile, a mother screaming and yelling, people ready to fight, but over what?

Herman had to ask, "What's this all about?"

"We're having a problem with my brother."

"A problem? I'll say."

John explained, "Yeah, he's crazy."

"Well, okay. So this is the Li family?"

John smiled, "Yes, welcome."

Herman laughed, "Oh yeah, welcome indeed."

He looked at the cops. "I feel safe already."

John asked, "So tell me what you have."

Herman showed him the wallpaper.

"Amazing. I want to show you something."

Herman and Sabrina walked into the store with John. Everybody was going to follow, but John turned around.

"Whoa, whoa, whoa, whoa. I'll take them in. You guys just stay right out there."

It was impressive, the command John had over everyone. They all obeyed him. They remained silent. The police, however, were not under his spell.

"Just a minute, People. We're trying to break up this ruckus.

"Oh officer, I'm sorry." John explained, "That's my brother over there. He's suing us for all kinds of crazy stuff and he's trying to get documents and paperwork. We're just not going to let him do it, so now he's trying to force himself upon us and he needs to just go."

Herman looked at this brother.

213

The brother's wife, a large Chinese woman, yelled out, "You stole!"

John brushed her off. "Can you take this woman away? I'm so tired of her."

"You stole our money."

John said, "First of all, it's not your money. You don't belong in this family."

The lady responded, "This is my husband."

"Just butt out. Let him do his own speaking."

"I want to know what you did with the money."

"The money from this business? Look around."

The parking lot was full with customers. The store had all kinds of people going in and out, buying all kinds of different Asian foods: vegetables, meats, fish, tofu, rice, pots, pans, bowls, you name it, they sold it.

"Check it out. Did you notice there's a new paving of the entire parking lot? Check out the fence over there. You see the beautiful fence? Look at the new roof. Look at the new paint job on the whole place. We built a new wall here to make it look nicer. The whole front of the store has changed. Look inside. We've got centralized air conditioning. We've got full length freezer boxes. We've got full length refrigerators. So what do you mean, where'd the money go? Check the place out."

"No. You didn't spend this kind of money on it. We're not talking about half a million of refrigerators, a million dollars in pavement. I'm looking for $15 million of stolen money."

That was a number that caught Herman's attention.

"$15 million? Who?"

He looked over at John.

"It's bullshit. Utter and complete bullshit."

The brother shouted, "Yeah, and there's a whole tax fraud."

"Sounds like fighting words."

"There was no tax fraud. We're working it out with the IRS."

"Working what out?"

"Well, there was a situation, don't worry, it's all under control."

The other owners, five brothers, one sister, listened intently as John explained.

"The IRS is on it. We're redoing our tax filings. All problems will be solved. So why don't you just butt out, let me run the business. Everything is fine. You'll get your dividend check. Smile, be happy."

John turned around and ushered Herman and Sabrina in. They followed him.

"I want to show you something."

They walked into the entryway of the supermarket. It was a gigantic store. must have been 150,000 square feet. Tall ceilings, beautiful artwork of Chinese landscapes, cranes, mountains, and seaside villages were all over the walls. Customers were in every single aisle, picking products up, putting it into their shopping carts. Herman was the only white guy in the entire place.

They took an abrupt left and did not enter the main store area. Instead, they walked down a hallway where there was a business office. Inside the business office, the first thing Herman noticed was the same wallpaper.

"A-ha."

They took the wallpaper up there. There was no question it was a perfect match.

"So tell me, did you find it?"

Herman was taken aback by John's probing question. "Find what?"

"It's a legend. It's a mystery, but I've always thought it was true. My ancestors left some kind of monument worth probably $25 million. I think you found it."

"What if I did?"

"If you did, first of all, you have to give it to us. We are the rightful owners. We are the heirs."

"Okay. Now I would like to know how you could ever prove that. Do you have evidence?"

"Yes."

"What's that?"

"Wallpaper match. Look at that. How could I possibly have the same exact wallpaper? Impossible. By the way, my last name, Li. What's the last name on whatever you found?"

"No comment."

"Oh, no comment. Now you're sounding like a lawyer."

"I am a lawyer."

"I see. Well, what are we going to do? There's a bunch of cops out there. I could tell them about it."

"You could tell them about what? That you know me and I got some wallpaper that matches your wallpaper? What do you think they're going to do about it?"

"They might start asking you questions."

"Questions that I will refuse to answer and they cannot compel me to answer."

"You're going to refuse to cooperate with the police?"

"I'll cooperate with them. I'll explain to them that I'm not answering any questions."

"And on what basis will you decline to answer their questions?"

Sabrina looked with great interest at this. She did not want to tell these bad people about what they had found.

"Attorney-client privilege."

"Attorney-client privilege. I'm just dying to know, who is your client?"

Herman smiled. "That's privileged."

Sabrina smiled. "Privileged, that means we don't have to tell you."

John was amazed that a female Asian would speak to him in such a rough manner. "I don't know where you get off talking to me that way, lady."

John stated, "I'll tell you what. Keep it up, you'll see there's going to be a little problem here."

Sabrina responded, "Hon, let's get out of here."

John closed the door before they could get out.

"You're not going anywhere until you tell me what you have."

Herman challenged John, "Hey, you know kung fu or something? Because you're going to have to kick my ass before you block my exit from here."

John admitted, "I don't know kung fu."

Sabrina responded, "Then move out of the way."

John refused to move. He put his arms in front of him, crossing.

Herman pulled out his cell phone and called 911. "Hello, police? There's a man-
Right then, John moved out of the way.

"Oh, never mind."

He hung up the phone, and walked out the door. They walked away from several cops, away from the whole group of people that were on a standoff. They were probably wondering, who were these people? How were they involved, why did John look so upset?

As Herman and Sabrina walked away, John ushered one of the younger generation kids to follow them. Herman turned around and walked back to John. He pulled out one of his business cards.

"Look, you don't have to follow me. Here's where I am. Call me any time."

Back at the office, they pulled the name of the case from the court's website. It was a case involving the theft of over $15 million. There were deposition transcripts submitted where John had confessed to a huge tax fraud. The tax fraud involved a two book accounting system whereby they were recording actual revenues and actual profits on one ledger, and then a different set of revenue numbers and resultant lower profit numbers on another set of books. Guess which book they showed the IRS? Of course, the lower profit one. The downward statement in income was in excess of $5 million per year.

John had confessed to the IRS that he had committed this tax fraud. Under the IRS confession program, tax evaders, believe it or not, are allowed to fess up to their crime, restate their earnings, resubmit the earnings, pay all interest and penalties, including a whopper 75% tax fraud penalty, and here's the bonus, they avoid criminal prosecution and any prison time.

The allegations of the complaint were backed up by deposition transcripts of John and the other family members fully confessing to this gigantic tax fraud. Their only defense to it was that their other lone brother was in on it from the beginning, knew all about it, was the chief architect of it, and received his due part of it. Their other defense to the tax fraud was, "We already confessed. We're good with the IRS."

The matter had not been tried yet, but was set for trial.

After printing out these documents and reviewing them, Herman and Sabrina came to one obvious conclusion. However noble this family once was, they had slid down the totem pole from nobility to scum. They'd become fraudsters of the worst kind. They defrauded the U.S. government and the California state government, their new homeland. A new homeland that was extremely good to them. They had prospered in this new land. This was in the category of biting the hand that feeds them.

Rather than taking care of their government, they stole from the government. Depending on whose side of the complaint you believed, they even stole from each other; brother against brother, brother against sister, fraud against fraud, theft against theft.

Herman and Sabrina did not need to figure out who was right and who was wrong. There was enough there in the evidence submitted to the court to know that all of these people were bad apples.

Herman noted, "They don't deserve that memorial."

Sabrina agreed, "That's for sure."

Sabrina was adamant that there was no way they would ever get the memorial. That added another trouble. One of Herman's objectives was to get rid of that memorial, to get Sabrina out of her funk.

Back at the lake, Elwood the flying fish was going through his own metamorphosis. He had begun the process of eliminating Jeremy's corpse from among his multiple personalities. The way he did it was by watching the corpse slowly degrade into lake crumbs. Other fish would come by and nibble on him; the carp, the sturgeon, the bass.

The process of the water, the oxygen in the water, the CO_2 in the water, the bacteria in the water, all the life in the water brought about nature's own process of retuning Jeremy to the earth.

Ashes to ashes, dust to dust, or in this case, sludge to sludge.

As Jeremy's body finally disappeared, at last Elwood would be rid of this very dangerous part of his multiple personalities. No longer would he undertake the personality of a dead person.

There was this kind of odd connection between Elwood's pursuits, his affliction with the multiple personality disorder, and the whole transference of the grieving process onto Sabrina.

She had adopted the personality of the mother whose child had died and in that transference; she also became aware of Elwood's darts in and out of that underwater hotel.

218

They had found the treasures of this family in the attic level, but Elwood had seen that there were other parts of that hotel that had other treasures.

Sabrina was directed to go back to that lake, back to that hotel and find those other treasures. There was a problem with this, in that John Li and his errant band of bad boy brothers and sisters, the heirs to all of these family jewels, would not let it go.

Herman could tell everywhere he drove, he had a private eye driving after him. It was an Asian guy. He would turn right, the car would turn right. He would turn left, the car would turn left. The good news is that the Asian guy couldn't track phone calls, couldn't issue a wiretap and couldn't possibly know the plan that Herman had already invoked.

He was already in litigation on a case involving the United States national parks, part of the U.S. Department of the Interior. The case involved an unfortunate incident up in the northern parts of California known as the Lava Beds National Park. One of the U.S. park rangers went off on one of Herman's clients with a taser in the wrong body parts.

Through the process of litigating that case, Herman became very well acquainted with the Department of the Interior's attorneys, and was able to get a quick line into them. About three phone calls later, he was working out a deal to create a national monument that would show the impressive history of the region, and would give tribute to the good part of the Li family.

The Department of the Interior, in a letter to Herman, took the following position:

Mr. Franck:

We agree with your analysis that the memorial you have found became property of the United States government, in trust, pursuant to the Public Trust Doctrine. Under this rule, the lakes, rivers and coastlines of the United States belong to the government, but held in trust for the benefit of its citizens.

Accordingly, we accept your proposal to create a monument in which we will display the memorial in an appropriately secure brick building. We have been contacted by the local businesses, who are very much in favor of this memorial as part of a tourist attraction.

Further documentation about this memorial will follow.

Regards,

219

Henry Molinari

Office of the United States Solicitor, United States Department of the Interior

There was the interesting goal of A) how to hand off the memorial to the U.S. government without being intercepted by the goon squad and B) whether to share with the U.S. government the added fact that under the lake there is a submerged hotel with God knows what other treasures in it. These questions would have to be answered later. For now, there was a more immediate problem.

Herman and Sabrina came home from another day of work to find their home ransacked. The couches were turned upside down, the paintings on the wall were thrown on the ground, tables were overturned. The desk drawers were sticking out. Papers were all over the floor. There were cracked plates. The place was an absolute mess.

You might think that this attack on a family's home would transform the woman into a scaredy-cat. An expected response would be something like "let's just give them the jewels and be done with this."

That's not what happened. Instead, in another example of personality transference, Sabrina adopted that prehistoric shark flying fish that Elwood thought he was when he had been caught by Jeremy's hook.

Sabrina went into battle mode. Her mouth became full of saliva. When she spoke what she was about to say, spit came spraying out.

"Call the FBI."

This was the perfect thing to do. Herman picked up his cell phone. He had the FBI on his contact list. He had called them many times before.

"Can I speak with the agent on duty?"

He was transferred to Special Agent Conklin.

"Agent Conklin here."

"Agent, we have a situation at my home here in Sacramento. A group of people, and we're pretty sure we know who they are, are aware that we are about to donate a valuable memorial to the United States government. Our home was ransacked. The people that want the memorial apparently believed we had the jewels here. We don't, but there was an attempted theft and interference with our process in bringing these matters over to the possession of the U.S. government."

"Okay, wait a minute. Slow down. Who, what, when, where, why? I don't understand what you're talking about."

"Can I have you speak with U.S. Department of the Interior, Solicitor General's office, the attorney Ms. Maxplan? I've been dealing directly with her on a project to create a memorial for a person that died, apparently during the mid-1800s."

"Okay, and what? The U.S. government wants to do a memorial for this person?"

"Well, it's not just your ordinary memorial. This person wasn't your ordinary person. It's kind of a big deal and yes, the bottom line is, the government does want to and these thugs that broke into our house. They're basically stealing U.S. government property."

"That would bring the case within FBI jurisdiction."

"Bingo."

Within half an hour, there was a swarm of FBI agents, with their Crown Victorias parked out front of Herman's house. They photographed the interior of the home, looking for clues as to the culprit.

Herman didn't need these clues.

"We know who it is. It's the Li family. I'll tell you right where they are."

Four FBI agents were quickly dispatched over to the White Dragon grocery store, to do what they call an "interview" of a "person of interest."

John denied everything.

"I have no idea who would've broken into their home, busted up everything. I know nothing about it. I deny any involvement."

Unfortunately, for all the forensic analysis done by the FBI crime scene investigation team, there was not one shred of evidence left behind proving the Li family's involvement.

The U.S. Department of the Interior attorney Ms. Maxplan, however, knew that there was some immediate action to be done.

"It looks like our time schedule needs to be accelerated a bit."

Herman agreed, "Of course. How about, like, today?"

"Shall we?"

221

Four FBI Crown Victorias followed Herman and Sabrina as they drove to the downtown Wells Fargo Bank, located in an impressive high rise on the Capitol Avenue in Sacramento.

The bankers all knew Herman and Sabrina well, but didn't expect them to be followed into the bank by a group of badge-showing, gun-toting FBI agents.

Herman walked in with Department of the Interior attorney, Ms. Maxplan. They walked back into the safety deposit area. They had a rather large safety deposit box with all the jewels carefully there, in the same stainless steel attache that they had found out in the desert.

"You know, I have an idea. Just so that these bandits can know to leave us alone, if you don't mind, I would like to publicize this handoff."

Sabrina took a series of photos off her cell phone camera. They were given over to the Sacramento Bee.

The next day, there was an article in the *Sacramento Bee* and a local *Chinese Community News:*

Local Attorney Transfers Antique Memorial of Chinese Family to U.S. Department of the Interior, Memorial to be Built at Lake Powell, Arizona.

In the midst of endless bad news about recessions, bank closures, property foreclosures, people out of work and typical array of local crimes, there was this interesting breath of fresh air about an attorney and his wife, with the help of a rather interesting flying fish, that found a treasure, tried to give it to the right family, and in realizing that sometimes the descendants of wonderful people do not turn out so wonderful, decided to give it over to the U.S. government to hold in trust for the benefit of all citizens of the United States.

Herman's motivation was quoted throughout the article. Though they would lose all those jewels, they would gain much in terms of wonderful publicity for Herman's law office. More importantly, Sabrina would be relieved of her depression brought about by the transference of the mother's grief in losing her son.

Elwood the flying fish would watch with great interest as the workmen built a miniature Fort Knox out on the side of Lake Powell. There was a moment, probably a

222

half a second or two, when Sabrina and Elwood caught eyes again. Their two personalities acknowledged each other. Elwood waved his wing at her.

Elwood turned and flew away, like the bird he was, slithered like the snake he was, and swam like the fish he was.

That hotel and whatever treasures remained in it? It remains, to this day, submerged in Lake Powell, known only to Elwood, Sabrina and Herman.

Azure, the Psychopathic Eagle

CHAPTER 10

THE PSYCHOPATHIC EAGLE[10]

You may have wondered what happened to that blue-eyed bald eagle, now grown up, by the name of Azure. The news, unfortunately, is sad. Growing up with many furry rabbits around her, you might think that she would be rabbit-friendly; not so.

Instead, and it could be due to the lack of connection to her own family, she turned into something God-awful, something we call a psychopathic eagle.

She clawed out the eyes of her rabbit siblings, all eight of them. She didn't do it for food. She didn't do it to protect herself. She didn't do it to somehow better her species. She did it just to do it. You could call it fun. You could call it anxiety. You could call it a mental breakdown.

Call it whatever you want, it doesn't change a thing for the rabbits. Their eyes were gored out by her claws.

The mother tried to stop what she was doing, but it was no use. Azure turned to the mother and in several pecks with her strong beak, ripped out the flesh around her neck. She sat and watched as the mother's life bled out of her. The mother's last vision was her own children with their eyes gored out by this vicious eagle.

She didn't even eat one of them. Instead, she flew away with an odd look on her beak. It was the look of a psychopath, a person so deranged that they don't care about violating all the norms of society and nature. The rabbit family that had so nicely protected Azure would remain in their home, forever.

Azure, flying forward, would become a study in the origin of the psychopath; where it comes from, what it does and what can be done to stop it.

The following is from J. Morrison, *DSM-IV Made Easy: The Clinician's Guide to Diagnosis* (Guilford Press 2006), Page 174:

The conduct of a psychopath can be vicious, unending, repetitive, and unremorseful. They can do what they do over and over again. They will not learn their lesson. You can send them to prison for multiple years. When they

---

[10] For a medical description of antisocial disorder, also known as psychopathic disorder featured in this story, please refer to appendix A-10 {and its related disorder, known as conduct disorder}.

are young, all forms of discipline will fail. They will just keep being bad. As they get older and sent off to juvenile homes, they will continue being bad. As they become adults and sent through a series of prison terms, not one of those prison terms will ever rehabilitate them.

In the words of the doctors who have studied it, the psychopath is untreatable. Or is he?

Consider the case of Azure. We could see that a possible candidate for the source of her psychopathic tendency would be a lack of connection growing up to her immediate family, but this argument would be defeated by the following:

First, she had a nice, warm and fuzzy surrogate family. Many humans have successfully adopted surrogate families. The same is true of animals and other beasts. So the lack of family connection, in and of itself, would not explain her psychopathic ways.

There are examples of humans having wonderful family upbringings, and turning out super bad. Many death row inmates come from loving families.

According to the psychological experts, the antisocial disorder that can afflict individuals has no proven origin or source. It could be genetic, it could be environmental, or it could be a combination of both. It could occur due to a shock or stress during a woman's pregnancy. It could occur because a woman consumes drugs during her pregnancy. It could occur because a child witnesses some terrible events. It could occur because a child is removed from his or her family and has no sense of connection, either to a family unit or expanding on that comment, to any community.

Psychopaths have a complete and total disobedience of the rules of society. That's why it's called "antisocial" disorder. It doesn't mean the people are not sociable. Indeed, just the opposite can apply. Often these people can be con artists, smooth talkers, the life of a party, filled with jokes and having what are often referred to as "Type A" extroverted, talkative personalities. They can be quite literally the life of the party, but in doing that, will steal you blind.

Psychopaths tend to have zero remorse for what they do, and tend not to accept personal responsibility for what they do. They do what they do over and over, and leave a trail of multiple victims. They can steal all their money, take their life savings, their pensions, they can kill or main their daughters, they can commit heinous crimes on others, multiple serial murders -- you name it, they'll do it -- and when they do it, they will not give a damn. They won't acknowledge even that what they did was wrong or somehow inexcusable.

It is reported that many of these people will end up in prison. After a series of county jail terms, graduating into prison, they still repeat what they've done.

A psychopath will commit a heinous crime, get caught, be in complete denial that they even did it, take zero personal responsibility for doing it, and have no remorse. Upon release, the psychopath will do the same thing all over again.

It is because of the repetitive nature of people with antisocial disorder and their complete lack of remorse, that psychologists and psychiatrists have generally agreed that the condition is untreatable. The only reason solution is to lock them up.

A bit of a digression that has not been studied by psychologists or psychiatrists will be considered here. Let's step back for a moment and ask the question, "What would Charles Darwin say about this?"

Professor Darwin, the famous biologist, wrote that species have certain traits and characteristics created by nature as a means of survival. Charles Darwin, *On the Origin of Species by Means of Natural Selection, or the Preservation of Favoured Races in the Struggle for Life* (John Murray, London, 1859)

The concept of "survival of the fittest" has been implemented into a theory of evolution that postulates the notion that species have traits as a process of making the species better.

How then, would a trait like antisocial disorder possibly make a species better? How would it help them become an evolved species, one that is fit to survive?

At first blush, the answer could be, "It doesn't." Antisocial disorder people could be seen as anomalies, outliers, which in the review of the massive data of behavior of people or beasts, simply shouldn't be considered.

There is another way of looking at this, though. Let us assume for a moment that outliers, anomalies are actually not by accident, and are actually planned. They are planned by Mother Nature within the contours of the theory of evolution, and actually do indeed make the species fitter.

How so? Here are some examples.

227

First of all, and we'll use the example of humans, there is a need in humans to protect. We need warriors to protect our house and home from invaders. The competition among human beings has always been fierce, and can itself be seen as an example of the very underpinnings of Darwin's theory of survival of the fittest. Clan A will attack clan B, and in doing so will take over the clan, and as has been seen in studies of prehistoric sites, will go so far as to decimate a village, burn down all structures, and literally eat the people they took over. They will often rape the women, as a type of "victor spoils," steal their food, and look toward an overall annihilation of that clan. All of this is done, perhaps, as part of the survival of the fittest theory of Darwin's concept of evolution.

Let's step back for a second. If we had a bunch of touchy-feely people in clan A, people who were very sensitive about the feelings of others, about the impact of one's action on another, people who live by the oft-quoted Christian rule: "Do unto others as you would have them do unto you," well, obviously then, clan A would never annihilate clan B.

Within clan A, there will be people that have that type of sensitivity. They will be, no doubt, the homemakers, often female, but even male, with sensitive personalities, personalities that care. You would not want to send these people to do battle. Instead, you want the psychopaths. You want the people with the syndrome known as antisocial disorder to pick up weapons, spears, at night sneak along a trail not made, going through the bushes in the moonlight, appearing past midnight in a village, and murdering people as they sleep. These aren't going to be the sensitive, touchy-feely people that do this job. These will be the psychopaths and Mother Nature intended them as a means toward bringing about the strongest clan possible.

When clan A replaces clan B, the resultant residue of human biological specimens is fitter and better able to survive, and it may be that Mother Nature, in her infinite wisdom, purposely made it so that this antisocial disorder was permanent and "untreatable." Mother Nature intended for it to be an unstoppable force of nature.

Which brings us back to Azure. Today she's flying in the sky and she sees her favorite kind of victim below, a water snake. It's swimming in one of the small tributaries going off the Colorado River, at the base of the Grand Canyon.

Grand Canyon Snake

She swoops down and covers it once, swoops around, finds it again and gets her claws right on its neck. The snake realizes that it is about to become food. She goes up high into the air and does something that a regular eagle would never do, she drops it. The snake goes flying down about 3,000 feet, and lands on a large rock, splat!

She flies down below, sees the splatted snake on a rock. It's in probably 40 pieces, some of them pancake-thin. It looks like a bomb went off. The snake, of course, is dead-dead.

She studies the snake. She's happy about what she did. She doesn't eat it. She flies away.

She has no remorse for that snake, and it doesn't please her or disappoint her that some other animal or insect will end up eating the snake. There will be no waste of that snake. If nothing else, a zillion ants will carry it away, piece by piece.

Azure was practicing the art of annihilating any kind of danger to her clan. She would continue to do this on a daily basis. For Azure, any kind of species that is not an eagle would need to be annihilated. If she saw a rabbit, she would claw out its cute little eyes. She would mangle its ears, chop it up into bits and fly away. If she saw another rodent, she would do the same.

Every now and then, she would be hungry and would actually eat it, but for the most part, she killed these animals left and right and left them there for others to eat.

Remember that Azure had brothers that she was separated from. One day, while flying high in the sky, she was met up by one of her brothers.

"Azure, is that you?"

She looked at him as though he were a perfect stranger. In a way, he was.

"I don't know you."

"You know me. I recognize your eye. I am your brother.

"You are not my brother. I don't have a brother. I am an only child."

"No my dear, you were born with two brothers. You must remember the great event of our father being killed by the iron bird."

She had suppressed this memory. It was deep in her, having its traumatic impact on her, but not consciously. In her deep psyche, there was a need for some kind of release from the trauma. Maybe it would be revenge, maybe it would be a loud scream, maybe it would be both.

There was even a possible analysis that her desire to go around and kill things indiscriminately was itself, her own response to this subconsciously existing memory. Seeing her brother brought it all out again.

"I do remember. Oh my God, you are my brother."

"Please come with me. You have to meet the rest of the family. We have mom, we have our other brother, and by the way, I've got a bunch of young ones myself. How about you?"

"I have no mate."

"You have nobody?"

"I have nobody, just myself."

"Well, now you have all of us."

She turned and flew away. She just couldn't handle the idea of a whole family of people connected to her by blood, that were there for her in some kind of loving way. She knew a life of loneliness, of solitude, and of dealing with the bitter beginnings of her life.

Her brother chased after her. She was a fast flyer though. She went up and down. She tried to lose him. She flew over to an area where there was some human developments. There were power lines, phone poles, some building structures. This was the area by the Native American reservation.

Azure saw something that triggered an extreme reaction to an already extreme personality. She saw the snake handler. She saw him tending to the snakes. He was feeding them. Feeding a bunch of diamondbacks is a rather gruesome task. Perhaps the snake handler had a little psychopathic tendency in him. Otherwise, how do you become such a person?

He threw a handful of mice into their wooden cage. The snakes were very pleased to receive these furry meals and devoured them.

Azure did something that psychopaths often do. They bite off more than they can chew. You can have a person who thinks they can take over one bank, two banks, three banks. They'll rob every bank in a city. They'll think they're going to get away with it forever, but of course they don't. Of course they get caught. There is always the demise of the psychopath. At some point, they go down. They get caught. They get surrounded by twenty police cars with lights flaring on, guns out and the command, "Hands on your head, get down on your knees, lay down on your face," and either the guy does it or he gets filled with enough holes to turn him into a human version of swiss cheese.

This would be the day that Azure met her swiss cheese. As she flew over the wooden cage, she couldn't resist the idea of swooping in there and grabbing not one diamondback, not two, but ten. She planned her attack. She knew that the odds were against her, but she just had to do it. How would she swoop into this box, and pick up a bunch of snakes?

To the amazement of the snake handler, Azure started her descent with a bullseye down to that box. She had her eye on the largest male diamondback. Her first swoop came into that box, grabbed that diamondback by the head and left that box before a single diamondback could strike her. Ten attempted and ten missed.

She swung out of that box and flew straight up into the sky with that diamondback. She went up to a height of over 2,000 feet and did what came naturally to her, she dropped him.

Snakes can't fly. He went straight down, turning, hissing all the way, landing on a cactus that pierced him in more than 30 ways. He didn't die right away. He suffered several broken vertebrae. The snake has the equivalent of a backbone that goes up and down his entire body.

There are tiny ribs going up and down him as well. If you'd ever opened up a salmon, you would get the idea a little bit of what the inside of a snake looks like, except that the ribs are curved in a circular way. There are many ribs. They are quite soft and easy to break. This diamondback was obliterated when he landed on top of a barrel cactus. Ker plop! He was dead.

Azure was hardly done. When she got a taste of killing one, she had to do another. She flew back over. This time the snake keeper was on high alert. He was not about to let some crazy bald eagle take all his precious snakes. He was running to the cage as Azure was swooping down to get yet another snake.

There was a top to the cage that could be put back down. Once down, Azure could not get in it. Unfortunately, it worked out that Azure got to the cage a little bit before the snake handler got there. He was just in the process of putting that top back on when Azure got into the cage.

The top was connected to a hinge and was opened by a piece of wood, similar to how you can open the hood of a car and put that metal post up and keep it up. The snake holder knocked that post over and the top came down, leaving Azure in the snake cage.

Uh-oh. This is trouble. She was surrounded by a bunch of diamondbacks.

The man did not intend this result. The bald eagle is a symbol of the United States of America. This man was a Marine Corps lieutenant (retired), and deeply patriotic. The last thing he wanted to do was to see this beautiful blue-eyed bald eagle devoured by his diamondbacks.

The snakes hissed back with their S-necks. Their tails were all rattling in unison. It was a percussion ensemble like you would hear in a park on a lovely Sunday with 40 people playing the instruments in unison, rattle, rattle, rattle, rattle, over and over again. The hissing came in as well, to make the ultimate tragic, dark music. The snakes started striking Azure.

She was quite agile and moved out of the way, but this is similar to the psychopath being surrounded by twenty police officers with guns drawn. He might dodge one bullet, two, even three, but he's not going to dodge twenty and he certainly isn't going to dodge 40.

The snakes struck her and caught her in the stomach area. They caught her on her leg area. They caught her on her wing.

The man was upset over what he had caused and took immediate steps to set her free. She flew out of that box, straight up into the sky. The poison from the snakes had already filled into her veins, however, the way the poison works, it starts a process of paralysis. It creates a stop message to the central nervous system and tells every muscle in the body to stop working.

This means the wings aren't supposed to fly. The eyes aren't supposed to see. The head is not supposed to turn. Everything that is needed to fly stopped.

There is a period of time before the onset of this paralysis. It's not much time, a matter of several minutes. As she flew up in the sky to meet her maker, she saw something. Maybe it was a hallucination; no, it was real. She saw Arrowpath in his

233

helicopter. No daughter would ever forget the giant metal bird that had killed her father right before her eyes. In any life of tragedy, there is a need for closure. There is a need for balance. You take a life, you give a life and on this day, a balance would occur.

Azure smashed through the glass windshield of the helicopter. Her head came into the cockpit area, but not close enough to bite the man that had killed her father. It was close enough, however, to hit and bite a toggle switch that controlled the back tail blade of the chopper. It sent the chopper into an oblivion of turns that became quickly out of control. It flailed left, right, up and down.

Arrowpath was stunned by the sight of Azure through his windshield, pecking at his dashboard. She started pecking at every single toggle switch she could hit. There were four of them right on. The helicopter spun in circles in the sky. It make an upward spiral at first, which quickly turned to a downward spiral.

Not far from the snake handler's pit, there was a major power line system with giant silver colored structures holding up the power lines that would feed a grid from Colorado to the bottom of Arizona.

The helicopter unfortunately came into contact with these power lines and became tied up in them. The blades cut some of the power lines down, but several were left intact. The helicopter was filled with electrical charges up and down. The electrocution process took out Arrowpath and Azure.

How many ways can you die in one day? Five diamondback strikes to the body would be enough. A collision with a helicopter would be enough. Electrocution would be enough. The final blow, however, was when the helicopter left the hold of the electrical wire system and came crashing face first into the ground. The only buffer between the helicopter and the ground was Azure's feathery body, which smashed into oblivion, pierced by a thousand pieces of windshield glass, electrocuted by tens of thousands of volts of electricity.

The one silver lining in this dark picture was that on the entire path down to the ground, she had eye contact with Arrowpath. They each connected and knew each other from a time and a tragic ending that had already happened. One tragedy met another and just as Arrowpath's killing of Azure's father left her fatherless, now Azure came back and left Arrowpath's children, Wolf, Bear and Sky Eyes, in the same condition.

234

Sky Eyes would cry a million tears for her father. She loved him more than anything on the Earth and she did something that she had never done before. She called a boy, a boy named Bobby. She missed him. She remembered him so well and she told him the tragic story of the passing of her father and the finding of Azure, buried under the mass of a shattered helicopter.

Bobby and his father were invited to come to the funeral. He had never seen a Native American funeral before. This would be his first. There was a man who would officiate. He, of course, was the medicine man. He had a feather and a type of wand that had smoke coming out of it. He put ash on Bobby's chest and forehead. He put ash on Bobby's father, Alfred's chest.

This was a mark that they were connected in the earth, in the fire, in the ashes. They were all part of the same circle, the same circle of one that we are all part of. This is the circle of life.

They burned Arrowpath into the sky. He was a man of the sky. He lived in the sky. He would die in the sky. His spirit would go up and away and would look down on Sky Eyes, Wolf, Bear and his beautiful wife for the rest of time.

It was perhaps fitting that Bobby's father had lost his wife to a tragic illness. Alfred was there before Arrowpath's wife, who had just lost her husband, and in a way, to a tragic illness, the illness of psychopathy.

Alfred noticed her and she noticed him. There was an obvious connection. It was an obvious need. He was a single father. She was now a single mother. They needed each other. They knew each other. They trusted each other. Balance meets balance. Tragedy meets tragedy and sometimes, out of that, good can come.

Bobby's father would marry Arrowpath's wife. The families would unite together on Eagle Point for the rest of their lives.

Grand Canyon Skywalk

Monument to Azure the Psychopathic Eagle

Josie and Toomka, the Elephant with Borderline Personality Disorder and Intermittant Explosive Disorder

Josie and Bobo, the Elephant Who Would be King

CHAPTER 11

THE ELEPHANT WITH BORDERLINE PERSONALITY DISORDER[11]

There was a standoff in the Congo. On one side of the river was a herd of African Elephants, gigantic, majestic. There were thirteen little ones and a group of more than 40 big ones. The largest was fourteen feet high. His name was Toomka.

On the other side of the river was a pack of hungry lionesses. In the lion clan, the female does the hunting. There was a shortage of wildebeests and small deer. Ordinarily, the lioness would not attack the elephant, but for the last week, they had not found anything else.

The elephants were at the river, sucking up water, spraying each other, swimming and having a wonderful family time. Meanwhile, the lionesses hid in the amber yellow of the savannah, and could not be seen. Only their nervous, evil eye made to pierce through the grasslands.

All of a sudden, there was an attack mode. The lionesses came crashing into the river. They swam across the river and jumped onto two of the elephants that were in the water. The elephants screamed for mercy as the claws of the lions dug in deep. They bit right into the elephant neck, their sharp teeth piercing this thick elephant hide. Blood came gushing out.

The other elephants were scared to death. Rather than protecting the two in the water, they started to run. One of them did not run. That one was Toomka.

Instead, he stood up on his back two legs and came crashing down on his front two legs, making a huge thunk. It was a communication. It was a command circle. With the circle, there would be a power. The idea was, you put the young ones in the middle of the circle, you put all the adults on the outside of the circle and nobody was going to get hurt; no one, that is, except for the two that were in the water.

Toomka had very long, sharp tusks. He came running down and impaled the lioness right into her mouth. His tusk turned inward into her and came out, toward her hind end. This lioness was dead, dead and would never scratch or hurt another elephant again.

---

[11] For a medical description of borderline personality disorder and intermittent explosive disorder, please refer to appendix A-11A and A-11B.

Unfortunately, while Toomka was busy with that lioness, three others came pounding down on the circle of adult elephants. Toomka went back up on his hind legs and smashed down again on the ground, this time causing a vibration in the earth that got the other elephants to follow. They stood up on their hind ends and came crashing down. As they did, the front of their feet came onto the lion, smashing down about a foot into the ground, their brains crushed. The blood flowing from their heads was embedded permanently into the earth.

Tens of thousands of years from now, the future archaeologists of the world will find a petrified lion head smashed into the footprint of a giant elephant.

On that day, not a single small elephant would be hurt. Other than the claws and bite to the neck of the one in the river, no injuries were sustained.

The lions ran away in fear. The herd of elephants gave respect to Toomka, their leader, their savior and the mastermind of their security.

Toomka's son was one of those in the middle of the circle of security. His name was Bobo. He was first among the children, being slightly older than the rest of them. He was the new generation and someday, like his father, would be King. Today he was thankful that once again, his father saved them.

"Dad, you make me so proud."

"Bobo, please learn from me. Someday what I do, you will do."

Bobo thought about that. Of course, Toomka was right. Bobo did listen, he did watch and he did learn. Someday, maybe not so far away, he too would save the herd.

One day Toomka did something very bad to Bobo. In the past, he had yelled and screamed in a surprisingly explosive manner over what seemed to be fairly small issues.

For example, one day Bobo was giving himself a dust bath. The elephant sucks up dust through its nose and sprays it on its back. It's a way of cleaning itself. The dust went off of Bobo's back and landed on Toomka. Now you might say, big deal. You got a little dust on you. Who cares?

For some reason, this sent Toomka into a fit of anger. He stood up on his two hind legs, smashed down on the ground, screamed out in a loud way. He scared Bobo to death. Bobo went running away to his mother. Bobo's mother's name is Josie.

241

Toomka, the Elephant with Borderline Personality Disorder; and his wife Josie

The mother looked at her husband and yelled at him, "What is your problem?" It took him about a half hour to calm down. He looked at Bobo. He walked over. He put his long nose on Bobo's back. It was a way of saying, "I'm sorry."

These kinds of incidents happened on an almost weekly basis. There was another time when Bobo was in the water. He was sucking up some water and spraying it on himself and accidentally shot Toomka with a little bit of water.

Toomka just went nuts over this and started screaming, got up on his legs again, pounding down. He actually just barely missed hitting Bobo on this occasion. His mother intervened and got between the two of them. She started to understand that her husband had some kind of issue, a disorder that we call borderline personality disorder and intermittent explosive disorder.

People with this disorder are often found screaming, yelling over just about nothing; angry, disorganized, mood behaviors changing all the time, constantly upset over small things, constantly running into all kinds of problems that their anger generates for them, constantly causing disassociations and terminations of friendships, romances, work relationships, professional relationships and the like.

One of the interesting features of this disorder is that, oddly enough, these people can pair up with a person that can handle them. The trick to survival in a long-term relationship with such a person is to make sure you are that proper match for them. If you aren't, get out because what you see is what you're going to get every day, every week, every month, and every year.

For Toomka, it was definitely a weekly issue. He would pound up in the sky with his front feet, come crashing down on the ground, making a small earthquake that would reverberate 20, 30 feet away, scaring poor little Bobo to the point where he would jump up in the air himself.

His father would scream in a high-pitched way that caused Bobo's ears to flinch. His mother would intervene all the time, but it never seemed to solve the issue. Bobo would make some little tiny mistake and his father would go off on him.

This affliction can often occur to people who are extremely bright, capable people with excellent leadership qualities and high positions in their community. This was the case with Toomka. He was the herd leader, was their number one military/security expert, and had taken it upon himself to teach others, including Bobo, the fine art and science of military defense of the herd.

This was of critical importance, as in the savannah there were many dangers, lions, tigers and bears, oh my!

It was only a matter of time before tragedy would strike and today was that day. Bobo was acting like a regular kid, running around with his other playmates. They were having a ball. They were chasing each other, running after each other's tail, trying to grab onto the tail and hang on.

It got kind of out of control when Bobo grabbed onto the tail of a larger playmate, who was about three years old. That cute little elephant, named Viva, veered to the right, veered to the left, ran up, around and was trying to get her tail loose from Bobo's nose wrapped around it.

Bobo wouldn't let go, however, and ran as fast as he could after Viva. In the process, Viva took a veer a little too close to Toomka, and Bobo didn't quite make the turn and smashed into Toomka's leg.

This didn't really hurt Toomka. You're not going to break an elephant's leg by having a little kid run into it. It really upset him. He didn't mean to do it, but he did it. He swung around quickly with his head to meet what had struck him. It was an instinctive reflex, but it was also a reflex fueled by his intermittent explosive disorder. He exploded in his brain. As he turned around, his tusk met Bobo's side and pierced into his stomach.

These tusks are quite large and can easily kill when they pierce. Especially when they pierce a young elephant. Oh my goodness, you should've seen the blood coming out of poor little Bobo. It was a gruesome sight. He got him right in the middle of his abdomen. The tusk went in several inches.

Toomka pulled it out. Unfortunately, pulling it out only caused the blood to rush out faster. Poor little Bobo fell down on the ground. His mother came over and looked at her loveliest son, the future King of this herd. She looked over at her awful husband.

"Now look what you did. Oh my God."

They didn't know what to do. One of the other members of the herd cried out to everyone. Within a matter of seconds, the whole herd was there, surrounding Bobo as he lay on the ground, looking at his father and wondering how on Earth the greatest man in the world to him, the man he respected more than anyone, the man that he would forever seek guidance from, how could this man betray and kill him?

Toomka had one thing going for him. He was an extremely smart elephant. He walked over to a nearby marsh area and used his nose to pull up a sod of grass and mud. He put that on the wound, stopping the bleeding.

Bobo's mom, Josie, was amazed with how Toomka could save her son.

"Wow, it's working."

The elephants watched as the sun dried the mud into a solid cast that sealed off the gaping wound. The bleeding stopped. Bobo went into a deep sleep, a sleep that they all prayed he would rise up from.

Toomka felt just terrible about what he had done. He cried a million elephant tears that night. He slept the entire time right next to Bobo, with one eye open, one eye closed.

Thank God, in the morning Bobo woke up. The herd cheered as Bobo slowly opened both his eyes. He wiggled his ears to get rid of some flies that were flying around them.

Toomka used his nose to swat other flies that were trying to get into the wound area. Toomka used his nose to push Bobo, try to get him to stand up.

Bobo understood. He wobbled onto his back hind legs. He wobbled onto his front legs. It took awhile, but slowly and surely, he stood up to the cheers of the entire herd. No one was happier than Josie and Toomka.

After the celebrations of Bobo's rising quieted down, there was the unfortunate business of dealing with a case of justice against Toomka. This crime had to be punished. Toomka knew the punishment, banishment.

The tribe's leaders got together and explained to him, "Toomka, you're out of control. You've been one of our greatest leaders ever. You've saved the herd many times from danger. You have helped us find the right plants to eat when we're sick. You have helped save the children from illness. You have done many wonderful things, but you know the penalty for what you did."

Toomka put his head down. It was a long ago stated law that any elephant that would kill another elephant would be banished. Though Bobo had lived, it was as though he had died and came back to life again.

245

The punishment was imposed. Toomka would have to say goodbye to the woman he loved and the son that he knew he could not live without.

Bobo had already forgiven his father. It's amazing how children can do this. You can mistreat a child endlessly. You can hit them, strike them, put them outside in the cold, make them sick, betray them, lie to them, cheat them, and they will still come back to their parents for love, compassion and attachment.

Bobo knew his father had some kind of problem, but he also knew his father was his father. There was a biological bond that would never be broken.
Josie cried as she saw the sadness in Bobo's eyes, watching his father walk away slowly from the herd.

Bobo tried to follow, but the herd would not allow it. They formed a wall around Bobo. He would not get out of this wall of elephant legs. He stood below his mother's closed legs and screamed for his father.

"Don't go. I love you. I need you. Please come back."

Toomka turned to see his son and his wife and his herd for the last time. He walked out of the jungle, out of the savannah. He kept walking in a northerly direction, to lands he had never been to. The terrain changed from a beautiful lush jungle to a dry savannah to something he had not seen before, a sandy desert.

The desert was huge. It was wide open. It was actually quite beautiful. The sand dunes went up and down. It was the kind of terrain where it would've been better to be a camel.

Toomka walked up the sand hill, down the sand hill. One of them was a little bit slippery and he slid down. This was a two ton elephant surfing down a sand hill without falling. He ended up on the lower part of it and he walked up the next one and the next one. The sun beat down on him. He was searching for water and could find none.

He went a whole day without water, without food. There was nothing, but endless sand and a bright sun that glared at about 110 degrees. The only shade Toomka had was the shade from his ears. The sun was relentless.

The next day, Toomka continued to walk, searching for water and finding none. He went up another sand dune, but this time on the way down, in his weakened state, he slipped and rolled, and rolled several times. It was quite a sound that left him at the bottom of the sand dune, hurt, delirious, dying of thirst and stuck in the grips of the unyielding desert.

The good news about this fall was it made a pretty loud sound. There was another elephant herd, a group of desert African elephants, living in the country called Namibia. This is a desert country in central West Africa where the sun is always hot. The desert can barely be touched without causing a burn. Water is scarce, but somehow people and elephants manage to live here.

Another herd was alerted to the fall of Toomka. They had no idea of his past, of what crime he'd committed, of what great things he had done. All they knew was a fellow elephant was in a time of need. There would be no question that they would come to save him.

Five elephants from this herd of forty were dispatched out to find Toomka. One of them, a female named Eva, saw him first.

"There."

She pointed with her nose to the sight of a large, gray balloon object lying sideways, still breathing.

They came to him.

The first thing he saw when his eyes opened was Eva and her eyes looking at him. It was the most beautiful sight he'd ever seen. He knew right away someone was coming to save him.

Eva pushed and the others pushed him. Just as he had coaxed Bobo into rising, they coaxed him into rising. What he didn't know, what he couldn't know, is he was just two sand dunes away from a small lake of water.

Eva explained,

"There's water just over there. Please just move. We're going to get you there. You're going to be okay."

They surrounded Toomka, one in the front, one in the back, two on the side. Eva was right behind him in the back, pushing him as he walked in tiny elephant steps, step by step, up another dune. They would make sure he would not fall down by surrounding him every inch of the way.

It took about 20 minutes, but the second sand dune had a downhill that led to the greatest sight in the world for Toomka, a small lake. In this lake, there were tens of thousands of birds, several gazelles, impalas, and a herd of 40 elephants.

This herd would take Toomka in without question. The first thing he would do is fall into the water and take a big gulp. That water tasted better than any water he had ever had in his entire life. He sucked it in through his nose, sprayed it on his back, fell into the lake, moved around to the right, swam to the left. He put it all over his head, all over his ears, all over his back, even on his little tail, wagging like a small chihuahua, a chihuahua connected to an elephant.

Eva was right by his side. After he had taken care of himself, he noticed something about Eva that he had not noticed before. She had on the top of her head a vicious looking scar in the form of four parallel lines. It was the unmistakable marking of an attack by a desert leopard.

Toomka could see the whole story right away. Some leopard had jumped up on her from behind and clawed her. The marks showed that they went backwards, up her head, to the line that the leopard would've been on her back.

Eva saw that Toomka saw her scar. She bowed her head down and showed the further marks on her back. There were six different sets of these parallel scars. That leopard had really ripped her up.

Toomka looked to the other four elephants that had accompanied him out of the sand dunes and into the water.   He noticed right away something about all of them; they all had the scar of the leopard.

They explained to him,

"These desert leopards have destroyed their main food source, the impala and the gazelle. So now they're looking to us for food."

Toomka looked over and saw twelve baby elephants. They were gorgeous. One of them reminded him so much of Bobo. He looked exactly like Bobo.

He turned to Eva.

"Any of these yours?"

Eva shook her head no. She had no mate at that time. This was good news to Toomka.

Eva could tell right away that Toomka had a son. She could see by the way he was watching the other children. Nobody other than a father missing his child would look upon children in this joyful, longing manner.

"You have a child?"

"I do. I have the most wonderful child in the world."

"Where is he?"

"He's back in the jungle."

"So far away."

"I know."

Eva knew not to ask any more questions. She knew that there was a reason he had to leave the herd. Elephants don't just up and leave a herd. They don't leave their mate for life. They don't leave their child. They don't walk away from their entire environment, the place where they grew up, a place that they knew, the place where they knew how to eat, swim and find food. They don't leave all that for just nothing. They leave because they had to leave, because there was an order to leave, a mandate, a banishment.

Whatever he had done, as far as Eva was concerned, were issues of the past. They didn't need to know. This was a new day, a new beginning. Hopefully Toomka wouldn't screw it up.

One of the elephants had a fresh wound. All the others, including Eva's wounds, were from days gone by. The scars had healed. The emotional impact would still be there, but there was no pending medical problem.

The other elephant, a large male by the name of Mamu, had open scars on his leg. It was a vicious wound. There were a zillion flies on it. Toomka knew right away that these flies were bad news. They spread bacteria, disease, other toxins. They would inflame the wound, infect it with all kinds of germs, would make it worse and could cause the skin to die, and if the skin started dying, the whole elephant could die.

Eva didn't notice at first, but Toomka had become fixated on this other male elephant's legs. There was something in Toomka that just naturally made him a healer. Nobody had asked him to help. Nobody even realized there was something they could do. This herd did not have a healer.

Toomka went over to Mamu. They acknowledged each other. Toomka looked down at his leg.

Mamu explained,

"It hurts so bad."

"I know."

Toomka showed him the scar he had. It was a pretty impressive one on his back leg, a scar from a lion. The claw mark was deeper and thicker than the leopard mark. Toomka remembered very well how much that hurt and he vowed on that day that never would a lion get him again.

He remembered sitting in the mud on that leg and the cool mud seeping into the wound, and natural nutrients from the lake would seep in. It would all work as a fine medicine to help heal.

He brought Mamu into the water. He picked up mud and grass from the lake bottom and carefully packed it onto the side of the leg. Mamu took a step and the mud fell off.

Toomka explained,

"I need you to hold still."

Mamu obeyed. The rest of the herd watched as Toomka carefully packed in mud to the gaping wound and more mud outside that wound. He made a kind of flat cast that spread over most of the front leg of Mamu.

The tribe elders came by to look. They looked over at Toomka. They saw his scar, and realized this was a man who knew how to live through things. This was a man who knew how to heal things. This was a man that could help out this herd.

"Does this work?" the elder asked.

Toomka explained, "It works. The mud has nutrients that will help heal his wound. It will also keep the flies out. It works as a seal. It will also keep it from bleeding. Each day we'll wash it off and we'll put a new one back on. We're going to do this every day, for about ten days. After that, this wound is going to look just like mine."

Toomka pointed to the back. The elders saw the wound again and realized that this system, a system of healing, was one that they needed to know about. They also began to wonder, what else did Toomka know? What else could he do? What other skills did he have?

This is the thing about the people that have borderline personality disorder and intermittent explosive disorder: they can be extremely valuable people, and extremely out of control at the same time.

For this new herd, they would see the good side, not the bad side. Make no mistake about it, there would be a day when this ugly side of Toomka would rear its head. For now, however, they saw Toomka as a healer, as a person that would help their herd, and in that, they welcomed him with open tusks. Toomka had found a new home.

One of the greatest therapeutic mechanisms to resolve borderline personality disorder is to experience a great tragedy that happens as a result of an explosion.

Toomka would never forget what he had done to Bobo. Every living day, every night, every moment he would remember the crime he had committed. He felt terrible about it. He wondered how he could ever make up for what he had done. How could he make good on the bad he did?

What he didn't know is that he had already passed on to Bobo the beginning of a skillset that Bobo would use to help his herd. Bobo also was a natural healer. He would find grasses and seeds that would help the sick elephants get better. He knew where to find the leaves from certain trees high up. He would stand on his back two legs and come up to the tree, to be almost as tall as a giraffe. He would pull down the branch and while the branch was down, he would instruct other elephants to remove a certain kind of leaf, not that one. That one right there. They would pull it down. Then he would get a little pile of those and feed it to the sick elephant. Within days, that elephant would get better.

No one was more proud of her son than Josie. She could see that he had the healer in him. Josie also missed Toomka. Even though he was a crazy, explosive, loud, scary, violent elephant, he was still the man of her life, the man she would always love.

And though Toomka wouldn't know it, she forgave him, and Bobo forgave him. The herd would not forgive him, as the crime he had committed was a crime of betrayal. There's nothing worse in the elephant herd than a betrayal, especially to one's own family. They would not ever allow him back.

One day Toomka was walking with the herd, spread out on a dirt road. A small truck drove by with four men in it. The men had something that Toomka had never seen before, a rifle.

Mamu was walking right in front of Toomka. By this time, Mamu's scar had completely healed. It was a rather impressive scar, not quite as big as Toomka's. Mamu was walking along the side of this dirt road when suddenly the men in the truck pulled out the gun, and shot it. It went bam.

Toomka had never heard such a sound before. Mamu went down. Toomka walked over and saw that there was this big wound behind Mamu's head. They shot him from behind. It was something that Toomka had just never seen before. This was a new kind of danger.

He knew how to fight off lions, leopards and hyenas. The hyenas were the worst because they came in groups of 50. This group of four, however, had something he had never seen before, never dealt with before, a rifle.

The men came over to Mamu. Mamu was still breathing. They took machetes out and did something that Toomka found unimaginable. They sliced off his tusks, one and then two. They left Mamu there, bleeding, dying, without his tusks. They got into their truck.

"Oh, you think you're just going to drive away now?"

Toomka ran to that truck. The others were amazed that he would run after it. This was something they were well aware of. They knew this danger and what they knew to do was to run away from it.

Toomka said, "No. Today we are not running away from it. We're running at it."

The men got into the truck. It took them awhile to put the tusk in the back. The tusks were quite large, four feet long. They were absolutely beautiful.

One of them saw in the rearview mirror a sight he had never seen before; fifteen elephants were running right at him with Toomka in the lead.

Toomka smashed into the truck. Following him were three others that smashed into it. The truck rolled over three times. The men had their rifles with them and pulled them out and aimed right at three of the elephants.

Toomka turned around with his tusk and, just like he had gored Bobo, he pierced into the back of one of the men. The man looked at his chest and saw the sight of a tusk rammed through it. His gun dropped and he dropped.

The other men saw what had happened to their partner. They saw quite quickly that they were surrounded by angry elephants. They tried to get a shot off, but it's hard to shoot someone with a rifle when they're breathing right down your neck. These men would die a death by stomping. Though it may have seemed cruel and excessive, they deserved every single stomp they received, especially by the one by Toomka right on the man's head. He turned that round head into a pancake.

After the men were killed, they decided it would be good to leave a clear sign that this kind of conduct would never be allowed again. They rolled the truck over a few times to get it to where the men lay dead. They put the truck on top of the men. The elephants then proceeded to attack the truck with their tusks. They smashed it on the tires, on the underneath of the chassis, on the top of the hood, on the top of the roof, and slowly, but surely dismantled the entire truck.

All the wheels were off. The steering wheel was off. The roof was off. The seats were out. The floor had about 100 holes in it.

The only thing they couldn't really undo was the engine and transmission, but they were able to take it out of the truck and leave it in the middle of the road.

They took Mamu's tusks out. Toomka picked up one with his tusks. Eva picked up the other. The two of them, without saying a word to each other, knew exactly what to do. They brought them over to Mamu's body. They gently placed them in the exact position just below his nose, the natural position of where the tusks belonged.

Though Mamu would lay dead, he would lay as a complete elephant. They prayed for him, and left the markings of a story obviously told: the men that did this to the elephant would die, and anyone else would die alongside them.

The death of Mamu was an expensive lesson, but there was a new day for this desert herd. This was the first time they had annihilated the poachers. With that, there was hope that news would get out about the gruesome sight of the dead men with their dismantled trucks. News would get out with the following obvious statement; do not mess with us.

One day, Bobo catapulted himself into the herd's leadership, where he figured out a way to defend against a pack of hyenas. These wild dogs are vicious. They travel in substantial numbers, more than 50. Although one of them would never be a match for a lion, the problem is, you don't ever get one of them. You get 50 of them.

They had the same problem the other animals had, the food sources were limited. They began to attack the elephants. They were hoping to get a small one to eat. One small elephant would feed quite a few hyenas. Two small elephants would feed many more.

The elephants could do the normal protective measures. They got into a circle. They put the children in the middle. They formed a protective wall. The problem was, the hyenas were small enough that they could get under the elephants and into the interior of that circle and attack the children.

Bobo saw this happening, and realized there must be a better way. What worked to defend against the lion would not work against the hyenas. Bobo was extremely upset to see the hyenas biting on the ears of Viva. Viva was a darling girl, a little younger than Bobo. This was the love of his life.

Bobo did something he had never done before, and in that, made a startling discovery. He screamed in a way that a child would scream, with a high pitch that would be deafening to anybody standing by. He screamed again at even higher pitches, to the point where they were barely even audible. The less you could hear the scream, the bigger the impact on the hyena.

Bobo saw it right away. This was something only the children could do. The older elephants had a lower sounding scream. The younger ones joined Bobo, and in the ultimate switch on security, it would be the children that would protect the adults from these terrible hyenas. They would scream in the highest pitch they could muster up.

When that happened, the hyenas would faint and collapse. Once they collapsed, the adult elephants could then smash their heads. In this way, more than 50 hyenas fell over and were killed. The two that were biting Viva's ears were the first to go.

Bobo was hailed as a genius in the battlefield. No one had ever known that you could use a high pitch to get rid of these terrible dogs. At last, there was a good method of defense, one that was discovered by Bobo and one that would make him forever a leader of this herd.

Nobody was prouder than Josie. If only, somehow these wonderful accomplishments of her son could be known by Toomka. Toomka was still so far away. He had no idea of what his son was capable of doing.

The elephant remains pregnant for a period of about 22 months. A lot can happen in 22 months. In the desert, they have something called a periodic encyclical drought. In some places, this cycle is every three years. In some places, every five years.

It was Eva and Toomka's bad luck that in the last twelve months of her pregnancy, the drought hit. There was no rain, no water. The lake was getting dry. The birds were flying away. The animals were leaving.

One of the older elephants died of heat exhaustion. There was nothing they could do to save him. They couldn't bring over a bucket of water. There wasn't any water and there was no bucket.

This was a new kind of enemy that Toomka had not had to deal with before. He had fought hyenas, lions, leopards and, more recently, armed poachers. The drought, however, the lack of water, something coming from nature, this was a new battle. How could he fight this? How could he make it rain?

Some of the other elephants were lying down, preparing for their death. Toomka looked at them in dismay.

"We are not going to just sit here and die."

The elephants had no idea what to do though. They don't know how to make it rain.

Toomka was a finder. He decided to go and find water. He went with a couple younger elephants as scouts. They traveled in the great heat, with the huge sun in the sky; dust all the way, hardly a tree in sight; brown, barren flatland that went on seemingly forever.

They came upon a dirt road. A couple cars passed them. They followed the direction of those cars.

Not far later was a turn off of another dirt road. They took that dirt road. They came upon an area where there were human settlements. It was a small village. There

255

was a school, a church, a couple government administration buildings, some small homes and people running around. They searched for a pond or lake, but found none.

Toomka knew right away, however, if there's a small village here, somewhere near there must be water. He searched around and saw no evidence of surface water.

He walked over to an open field area with the two scouts. They saw nothing, but Toomka saw something. He stopped. They stopped.

"What?"

He looked up into the air, looked at the sky, looked at the sun, looked at the big open space, saw how thirsty his scouts were. He had a mirage of Eva back at the herd. She was lying down. She was sleeping. Their son was sleeping inside of her. He had to find a way to get them water. He wasn't going to let Eva die, his son die and the entire herd die.

He stood up on his back hind legs and came crashing down with all of his strength, right on this spot. His front legs landed with a slam into the earth and made an indentation of about four inches. His scouts were puzzled.

What they didn't know is that Toomka was having one of his intermittent explosive disorder episodes. The heat had turned up his brain. The frustration with saving his son, the frustration of saving his wife, of feeling helpless, of not knowing what to do, of being up against odds that are all against him, of being scared, of having a fear not only for the life of his family, his family-to-be, but his very self. Everything was at risk.

There was a sixth sense that came with this disorder. Somehow his body knew to have this problem right there and right then. On his sixth crashing down on this spot, the indentation had gone from four inches to 12 inches and lo and behold, much to the amazement of his scouts, it exposed something buried in the ground. It was black, it was round, it was tubular, it was made of plastic. It was a pipe, a water pipe.[12]

Toomka curled his nose around that pipe and yanked it up. It wasn't so easy to bring up. The rest of it was buried by dirt. He pulled it again. It came up a little bit more. The other scouts saw what was going on and began doing the same thing that

---

[12] For a video of a desert elephant doing this, see http://www.youtube.com/watch?v=EfbN12sxVc8

Toomka had just done. They began pounding the earth, digging into the ground and finding other segments of the same tube.

Soon there was about four feet of the tube exposed. Toomka went absolutely wild with the sight of this tube. He could smell the water, but he couldn't taste it. It had to be brought up. It had to be severed, but how?

He brought it up some more. The four foot segment went to six feet, went to eight feet. Then he curled it and made a kink in the pipe. That caused an interesting noise to be made, the sound of water coming to a kink in a pipe. It gurgles, it bubbles, it has force and when that force is stopped, it turns around to go back. As it goes back, however, it is met by the flow of other water and it starts to fill like a balloon. Something has to give. The pipe became taut.

Toomka knew that the place to stand on that pipe was right at the kink. He stood up and landed on the pipe, direct Bullseye. That pipe split open and a geyser of water came out. You should see the look on the scouts' faces when they saw that water squirt up. They hadn't had any in days. It tasted so good. Toomka took a big gulp himself.

They laid the pipe into the now six foot long indentation in the ground. The water continued out that pipe and filled up a ground laden trough. Within a matter of ten minutes, there was a small pool of water.

Toomka turned to the scouts.

"Go. Bring the herd."

It is said that an elephant can remember everything for decades. Toomka was counting on these scouts to remember how to get back to the herd, to find the herd and to bring the herd to this water. There was no other way to save them, but to get them here.

It wasn't that far away. The village was about an hour from where the herd laid down. The scouts left to bring the herd over.

Toomka was now refreshed with water. Another problem had developed. You can't just walk into a village, uproot their water supply and expect not to get some kind of reaction.

Oh boy. There was a reaction, alright. The villagers came out with machetes and started screaming at Toomka. There were 30 of them.

These were not poachers. They were not interested in Toomka's tusks. What they wanted was their water supply.

Toomka protected himself. He got up on his hind legs again and scared the daylights out of these people. He started swishing his tusks to the left, to the right and made it pretty well known that anyone that got too close to him would be knocked in half by an ivory tusk.

He backed up a bit to avoid them. They came after him. He charged them. They backed up. There was a tug-of-war going on back and forth, back and forth.

Then Toomka noticed something out of the corner of his eye. It was about 100 meters away and it was broken. It was a water pump. This water pump had previously connected up to an underground well, but wasn't working. The problem was two-fold. First, it ran on electricity and there was none. Second, because it hadn't operated in awhile, the rains of about a year ago had caused it to rust.

Toomka had an idea to use the water pump as something to hide behind. It created an iron steel buffer between him and a group of angry machete-wielding villagers.

An unexpected result occurred. Toomka, of course, had no idea that this was a water pump that wasn't working, that the villagers had been trying to fix it. There were monies set aside for an electrical generator that was in the process of being shipped over to the village. The pipe that Toomka pulled up was a makeshift alternative water supply, pumped by a tiny portable water pump system. It wasn't enough to supply the village with their water needs, but Toomka knew none of this.

When Toomka got behind the broken water pump, the villagers froze and stopped. Toomka didn't know it, but he had created a water pump hostage situation. The villagers did not want to excite Toomka into tearing down their precious water pump system.

Toomka did not know why the villagers had stopped their attack on him. They remained in a standoff, with a group of villagers on one side of the water pump and Toomka on the other.

Within about 45 minutes, Toomka's toes felt the rumbling of a herd of elephant toes approaching. It was his herd, and it included Eva and their unborn son.

Eva screamed out,

"What are you doing? Why are these men attacking you?"

Toomka explained,

"They're angry because we're taking their water."

Eva felt bad. She did not want to be a thief.

The men all looked at the herd and looked at Toomka and understood what was going on. Sometimes there are these moments when man and beast can find a way to share the Earth.

One of the men, a village elder, approached Toomka with open hands and no machete. He walked over to where Toomka was standing. Eva watched with great interest. The man then walked down, away from Toomka.

Toomka stood, but got the idea the man wanted him to follow. The man turned and waved Toomka on.

Eva followed as well.

While the rest of the herd drank water out of the trough, Eva and Toomka walked down to the area where that other pipe had been set up. There was some kind of odd, ancient-looking wood-made device that was hooked up to an ox that looked near dead. The device was an animal-driven water pump. The ox would walk around in circles. This circular movement was connected up to a system of gears that worked a hydraulic pump that brought the water up from an underground aquifer into that small pipe and into the village.

The ox obviously needed a rest. The man unhooked the ox. There were a series of horizontal wooden poles that stuck out. Toomka understood. Without direction, he walked in front of that pole. It went over the front of his legs. All he had to do was walk in a circle and the water would be pumped.

An ox can do this, but an elephant can do it better. Toomka walked around in circles, causing the pump to bring up more water than it ever had. The water sprayed out into the small trough and the elephants rejoiced in their newfound water supply.

Toomka explained to Eva,

"Go back and get some water."

She walked back without Toomka, smiling. Toomka, with all his bad personality traits, had once again saved the herd.

There was still the problem of reuniting Toomka with his son Bobo. Toomka didn't know it, but there are studies showing that elephants that grow up without their father are inclined to commit acts of violence and other crimes.14 Lest we have a new story called the Psychopathic Elephant, there needs to be a way to reunite Toomka with his son Bobo.

The problem wasn't Bobo. He loved his father and would love nothing more than to have him back.

The problem was Bobo's mother Josie and the rest of the herd. They would never forget what Toomka did. They would never forgive him and would never allow the two of them to be together. They were all in a unified stance that Toomka could never come home.

Josie didn't know it and her herd didn't know it, but this unforgiving stance would have very unfortunate repercussions on Bobo. He had the potential of turning into a great leader, a great healer and the kind of elephant that could do just about anything he put his mind to.

If somehow, somewhere Josie could be convinced to let down her tusks and permit a father/son relationship to go forward, maybe Bobo would be spared from a lifetime as a career criminal.[13]

The answer to this path lie breathing through heartbeats inside Eva. There would come a day soon when that baby elephant would be born.

---

[13] Studies on this issue are summarized by CHARLES SIEBERT in *An Elephant Crackup?* (N.Y. Times October 8, 2006) . See http://www.nytimes.com/2006/10/08/magazine/08elephant.html?pagewanted=print

Toomka, Eva and their son Wawa.

Several years later, that elephant would be ready for a great journey, a journey led by Toomka and Eva. There would come a day when they would say goodbye to the desert and Toomka would show his new herd a great forest, a great jungle, where there was plenty of water for everyone. Though not without its dangers, it was a better home than the deserts of Namibia. His herd only knew that desert, and had no idea that there were lands and places well beyond to be explored.

You should've seen the look on Josie's face when she saw the return of Toomka, with a whole new herd of elephants, a new wife and a beautiful son named Wawa.

Wawa and Bobo met eyes and knew immediately of a blood bond, the bond of brothers.

The herd and Josie will forever have their opinions about Toomka, but they would not stop the relationship between Bobo and his younger half-brother Wawa.

Wawa walked over and wrapped his trunk around the trunk of Bobo. They saw each other. They melted before each other.

Bobo had always wanted a younger brother.

Josie looked over to her ex-husband and smiled.

"This is a good day."

Josie and Josie, mother of Bobo. [Beijing China Zoo]

Tusanne, (means "Belongs to all of us") the Wild Jungle Thai Girl

CHAPTER 12
THE WILD JUNGLE THAI GIRL[14]

SIMPLE MAN

BY LYNYRD SKYNYRD; PERFORMED BY SHINEDOWN [15]

---

[14] This is an entirely fictional tale. All references to the Thai royal family, monarchy, its institutions and the Thai government "democratic" party are purely fictional. No likeness to any current monarch, member of the royal family and/or member of the Thai government and/or military or secret services branches is intended. The author claims a right under the First Amendment to the United States Constitution to write this story, and further takes the position that he is not subject to the jurisdiction of the Thai "*legal majeste*" [king is above the law] law, prohibiting any kind of negative remarks against the King.

[15] See the music Video by Shinedown for *Simple Man*:
http://www.youtube.com/watch?v=rgFQ6WmxdMs&ob=av2e

Tusanne, the wild Thai jungle girl, was running at full speed. The forest was thick with trees, rocks, creeks, and every kind of obstacle known in the jungle. She was quite graceful and elegant in her passage over, under, above and through all these obstacles. What was she running from? About 30 meters behind her were a group of eight soldiers, running as fast as they could after her. They were no match for her jungle skills.

She was wearing hardly anything. The jungle was hot. She had managed a kind of two piece outfit, the kind that you would see in a Native American score only. The soldiers were wearing green uniforms, had boots, and were carrying rifles. They were under orders to capture her. She was under her own mandate not to be caught.

She grabbed a branch, flipped over it, came up higher into a tree, jumped off one tree to another tree, swung around back onto the ground, jumped onto a large rock by a creek, jumped off of the creek rock into a pool of water, swam across the creek over to the other side, got back out of the water and continued running deep into the lush of the jungle.

The men attempted to follow, but it was not easy. They were not living in the wild as she was. They were trying to keep up, but it's not easy when the person you're chasing grew up in the jungle and you did not.

She stopped by the creek and crouched down. Her body was overheating from the lengthy run. It was well over two miles. She was huffing and puffing. She knew her body well. She knew it would be wise to just stop and rest. She gathered her strength. She gathered her heartbeat. She gathered the flow of blood through every single vein, pumping and driving oxygen into her. Her nose had seemed to modify itself to permit the flow of greater volumes of oxygen to allow her to run longer distances, to jump farther, to have stronger arms, stronger legs, and to be able to literally leap over tall rocks and high trees.

She had a kind of humanly way about her approach to the jungle. You could tell that wherever she was from, whatever her mysterious story was, one thing it included was some kind of Olympic level training in gymnastics. It was amazing to watch her flip around trees like uneven parallel bars or leap over a rock as though it were the gymnast's horse. She could flip. She could put both hands on a rock, mount that rock, catapult herself upward in the air, do a somersault and land down below on a flat area perfectly on both feet.

Tusanne thinks she is a wild dog. There is no psychological term for this disorder.
The biological term is feral child.

She would stop just for a second, come to a complete still shot, turn to the right, turn to the left, look behind her, see that it was safe to proceed and then sprint forward. There would be a branch she would jump over as though it was a 440 meter hurdle. She could jump over one, then two, and then three. She would not touch a leaf. She would clear it completely.

She came to a sheer wall. It was made of gray rock. On one side, there was a waterfall. On the other side was an endless mountain. The rock had a crack right in the middle of it. She put her fingers in between that crack, and slowly and surely was able to walk up it. It took her about 30 minutes.

Just as she was to the top, the soldiers found their way to her. Their bullets would go about 2,000 feet a second, and could travel up that mountain much quicker than she could with her fingers and toes pressing in between that crack. They did not want to kill her. They were under orders to take her alive.

The captain put his arm out. "Don't shoot."

The men obeyed. They watched in amazement as she scampered up that crack, got to the top of that cliff, and turned and saw her would-be captors. She looked at them and did something that sent chills down their spines. She hissed at them. It was a cat-like hiss, like a cougar, a puma, a tiger -- some kind of big wildcat. She was ready to fight, but knew against those odds, it was better to run.

Then in an unexpected reversal, she barked and howled. A cat dog wild jungle woman then escaped from their vision. She turned and, as they watched up in amazement, left them forever. There's no way they could make it up that hill. Once again, the jungle girl had escaped the soldiers, and had run away into the depths of a place that she called home.

Back at the military camp, the captain had a hard time explaining his failure. The gray/black-haired colonel wore sunglasses. He was not pleased.

"You let her go again?"

"We didn't exactly let her go. She escaped."

"I can't believe eight well-trained men cannot catch one girl."

"This is no ordinary girl."

"And you are no ordinary men. I've selected you from my elite team. You're the royal guards, training at the highest level in the art of capture -- and you're telling me you can't catch this girl?"

They shook their heads. It was embarrassing but true. Try as they might, for months they'd been out in this jungle and they just couldn't catch her.

The colonel shook his head. "Well, gentlemen, we have the newest weapon."

He pointed out to a truck. It was a transport truck, six-wheeler, green, military markings. In the back was a nonmilitary guy, a member of what was the equivalent of the Thai CIA. He was wearing a suit, sunglasses and looked as though he may have starred in a Hong Kong action flick, except he was darker, swarthier and quieter. Still waters run deep. His name was Special Agent Ko -- not shaken, not stirred. He was blended.

The colonel walked over. They shook hands. Inside the truck was an answer to how to catch a wild jungle woman. The truck had a canvas backing that rolled up with the simple tug of a rope, kind of like opening up a curtain in a window. Inside exposed not the weapons of mass destruction -- there were no missiles, there were no machine guns, nothing of the sort. Instead, there were a pile of nets -- nets with cable systems attached to spring-loaded devices that would hoist up if someone set off the trap.

The truck proceeded into the jungle with the eight soldiers. It was a simple matter of digging around a path where they believed the jungle girl might traverse and putting a net flat on that path with a trigger device. If weight came on it, the spring device would shoot upward and lift the net straight up into a tree. It would close and the girl would be captured. They had 64 of these nets, and spent the next week placing them in various spots in the jungle. Each of these nets had a radio device that would beep when caught.

Agent Ko explained it all. "Once she's in the net, the alarm goes off, we get a beep, it tells us where the net is, and we go and we catch her." He turned to the eight men that were busy with shovels. "No more running for you."

They smiled. "Good, because it's not working."

As the men were busy digging and placing the nets into the ground, Ko looked up into the surroundings.

He wondered, "Where are you? I know you're out there."

Her name was Tusanne. This was a girl that was believed to belong to the entire Thai nation. And rather than just let her go and run free, as she had for all of her 19 years, there was this odd decision made at the highest levels of the Thai government, coming from the King himself, that this girl should be caught and brought back into civilization. The goal, seemingly impossible, was to take the wild out of her and reformulate her as a civilized human, capable of existence in a modern city such as Bangkok.

There are some examples of attempts like this in the past. A wild jungle woman comes in and finds a small village; probably she was unable to find food and came to the village as a last resort. The village takes her and tries to teach her in the ways of civilized humanity. In every example like this, they are never able to teach the wild person to eliminate the wild and come back to civilized humans. There may be a way to do it, but mankind has not yet figured it out.

The King, for some strange reason, decided that he would be the one to figure it out. He would capture this girl, bring her into the King's castle near Bangkok, and hire the best of behavioral psychologists to somehow eliminate the wild in her and to bring her back into society.

The simplest answer to this quest is, as a New Yorker would say, "Fuggedaboutit." But the Thai King had his own agenda, his own reasons, his own desires. It wasn't really clear what he was up to, but he was fixated on this notion that this woman had to be caught.

He ordered the placement of all these nets throughout the jungle, which were carefully placed by his elite team, overseen by his CIA operative Agent Ko. Now, looking around the jungle, they would wait and hope that one day the beeper would go off and show that the jungle girl had been at last caught.

Two days later, they got the first beep. The colonel heard it. It went off right in his hand. He looked at the number. He looked at the computer program showing a GPS grid where all the nets had been placed. He could see where it was. The beep also set off a flare. The flare went up and marked the spot. The men were quickly dispatched. Eight of them went with Ko, with great excitement over the idea that they would at last catch this jungle girl.

It was not an easy place to get to. These jungle paths go into an area that's quite lush, filled with rocks, streams, and thick trees. They can only be traveled to by foot. It would help if you could fly.

The colonel and Ko decided to speed things up and took a helicopter in. The helicopter had the royal emblem on the side. When they arrived, they saw something majestic and beautiful, but it was not the jungle woman. It was a striped tiger, caught in a net, lifted about 12 feet off the ground. This was a female, probably three years old. On closer approach, there was seen something around the tiger's neck. It was some kind of red collar with a brass bell.

Ko looked at the bell and saw right away. "It's from the monastery."

The colonel knew about this. The local monks, for some reason, had managed to tame tigers and live with them. This tiger should be safe.

The colonel laughed. "I don't believe it."

Of course if you lift someone up into a net, you can't expect them to be in a good mood when you put them down. So there was the practical question of how to let this tiger loose.

The colonel had an idea. "Why don't we take a walk back to the helicopter? Here's what you'll do."

Ko figured it out right away. "You don't need to say another word."

From a distance of about 45 feet, the colonel took out his rifle. He pointed at the net. He was not going to shoot the tiger. Instead, he shot the connection point between the cable connecting the net to the tree, and hit a Bullseye. When the connection point flew apart by a single shot, the net fell to the ground.

The tiger landed on all four feet. And you might think that tiger would just thank his lucky stars that it had been let free and would run loose back into the jungle and disappear from sight. Not so. Instead, angered by the helicopter, the shooting, the fact that he had been tied up for however long he was in there, the tiger reacted like a wild animal. He came running full speed at the helicopter.

The colonel quickly tried to lift off, but there was some kind of compression problem in the helicopter that caused it to momentarily shut off. Ko looked in fascination as the tiger came running up. The door was closed. The tiger hit the helicopter door at full speed. His talons went into the door.

Ko moved over, closer to the driver's side. "Get us out of here!"

The colonel restarted the helicopter, then lifted up. The tiger had his 10 talons in the door. He was carried up, dangling in the air at about 10 or 15 feet off the ground.

Ko was trying to get rid of the tiger. He was hanging in the sky. Tiger in the sky, talon in the chopper, helicopter flying, something's going to happen.

"How do you get rid of this thing?"

"Try opening the door."

Ko was comforted by the fact that the door was closed. It shielded him off from obvious danger.

"No way."

"There is no other way. We can't go flying away. We don't want to kill this beautiful tiger."

The tigers were protected by the Thai law. They were an endangered species. This tiger was just absolutely gorgeous and there was no reason or desire to kill it.

Ko did as the colonel suggested. He opened the door. It swung backwards. The door made it so that the tiger collided with the body of the helicopter. He slammed the tiger a couple times. The tiger let loose and fell about 15 feet to the lush jungle ground, on all fours.

The tiger got up onto a ledge and jumped up at the helicopter. The colonel and Ko flew safely away.

Ko then remarked on the obvious, "Those monks somehow get the wild out of the tiger, but once the tiger gets away from the monks --"

"I know," said the colonel. "They go right back to being wild."

"What do the monks do to do that?"

"Chant."

"They chant?"

"Yeah, they chant the wild out of the tiger -- something like that."

Just then, another blinking red light went off on the colonel's control board. Another net had gone up. A flare went up. It was about a mile away. They took the chopper up and over. They had great hope that once again, they would find the jungle woman.

273

They found a wild dog, known as the dhole (*cuon alpinus*) -- brown, bushy tail, raised fox-type ears, a cute, foxy wild dog. This dog is a bit of a unique mammal. He's not quite dog, not quite wolf. Scientists have made the following distinction. The dholes have an extra set of tits, and an extra molar. But they differ from wolves as well. So they've created their own taxonomy, cuon alpinus, and are known in Thailand as a dhole.

The colonel knew this well. "We've got a dhole. Great."

The dog has an interesting yelp that is a cry out for help. He had been severed from a pack. These are pack animals. They are socially inclined, and when removed from their family, will scream out in haltingly sorrowful tones, begging to be reunited.

The colonel and Mr. Ko were not the least bit interested in hurting this dog. They cut down the net and noticed not far from the horizon, there were more than 30 others, panting and waiting. When the dhole hit the ground, he went running forward to his pack. You could see how happy he was to rejoin his family.

Then he did something which surprised the colonel and Ko. They'd never seen a dhole do anything like this. He got up on his front two legs and did a handstand, head down, tail up. While he was in this vertical position, for some reason the dhole peed. It was some kind of welcome home process.

The men shook their heads, got into the helicopter and left the dhole to be back with his family.

Not long later, another buzzer went off. It was a busy jungle. This one shot up a flare about two miles away. Within a matter of minutes, they were there. The net appeared empty. There was nothing in it. Sometimes are animals are fast to click off a trap, and get out before the trap closes. They decided to reset the trap. In the process of opening it, they noticed that indeed there was something in there -- an Asian forest leopard cat.

This is a small cat that looks like a leopard. She had leopard spots up and down, big green eyes, and was frozen in fear. She had no idea if these men taking her down were going to eat her, kill her, use her as bait, or what. The last thing she thought they would do is let her free. But this, of course, is exactly what they would do.

These Asian forest leopard cats are indigenous to Thailand, and run free in the jungle. They are often bred with domestic cats to create an interesting housecat known as a Bengal cat. Bengal cats are a popular high end cat that has a look of a wild leopard, but the behavior of a mellow housecat. This requires about four to seven generations of interbreeding, which will finally get the wild out. By breeding a wildcat with a domestic cat, the wild parent remains wild, but at some point its offspring will become domestic. Interestingly, the wild parents' genes seem to be dominant, as the domestic kitty cat still looks like a leopard.

Ko opened up the net and had to smile when he saw that leopard cat tear out of that area, run up a tree, and disappear in a matter of seconds.

"That's the last we'll see of her."

Just then, another alarm went off.

"Oh, we got another one. Let's see."

They looked at the map showing the matrix of nets and saw that this one was about two miles away.

"Probably a monkey? Maybe a baboon? Maybe a snake, some kind of viper? Or something bigger? Another forest cat, wild dog?" They speculated as they flew over to the area.

When they landed, they saw something very peculiar. The net was like a pendulum, to and fro. It was going back and forth quite rapidly, and had some force within it. That force, as could be quickly seen, was none other than Tusanne.

Ko looked at the colonel. "We got her!"

She was wearing her jungle outfit, a rather skimpy bikini, and had a weapon -- a straight spear with a sharpened edge. She had sharpened it on the jungle rocks. She saw them approach and went into a fight mode. She stood inside the net with her spear at her side. They approached her with open palms, as friends. She sat frozen inside. Her heart was going a million miles a second. Her adrenaline was flowing, but she remained still. Her eyes beaded on them. She scanned them up and down, figuring out their size, learning exactly where their heartbeat was, studying their necks and their hearts, and their most vulnerable parts. She was looking for a kill shot.

As they approached, they initially did not understand she had this spear. She did a good job of keeping it on her side. The colonel found out the hard way. As soon as he approached, she figured out through her ability to measure distances that he was within striking distance.

Before you could say boo, she took that spear and lunged it at the colonel. It went right into his neck. He gasped for air. He couldn't even scream. Ko looked in amazement as the colonel fell to his knees, holding his neck, his mouth open, coughing up his last gasp. He collapsed backwards and died with this terrified expression.

Before Ko could sympathize with the colonel, he had to deal with the bigger danger. Tusanne was now attacking him. Ko was trained in martial arts. He swerved to the right. She lunged again. He swerved to the left. He used his hands to block the spear one time, two times, three times. She could see that her lunging at him would not work. She had to try another method to kill her captor.

She looked around. This worried Ko. He could see this jungle woman was looking for another way to kill him. Within a second, she found her other weapon. In the tree was a green viper. This viper was extremely poisonous. He was close enough that she could scoop up its body at about a midpoint. With a simple flick of the wrist, that viper was thrown into the air and landed right on Ko's shoulder.

Ko was an able fighter, and had his own animal instincts that came into play. That viper went to strike him, and Ko caught its neck with his hands. He wouldn't kill the viper. Instead, he threw it about 25 feet. Then he faced off with the girl. Tusanne, wild jungle Asian girl and Special Agent Ko, special royal forces, Thai military, trained since a child in martial arts.

The fight, of course, was not fair. Tusanne was in a net. Ko was not. He decided to use a kind of psychological weapon rather than beat her, tie her, assault her. Instead, he just looked at her and she looked at him. The two of them met eyes. In the jungle, it is an act of danger and aggression for an animal to look another animal in the eyes. In human relations, it is not the same. Eye to eye contact can be a prelude to romantic love. Indeed, if there was such a thing as a law of attraction, law number one would be about eye to eye contact. They stared each other down.

Ko had to admit to himself that this girl had gotten to him. He was weakened by her beauty and by the primal force of nature within her. The pendulum action had stopped. The snake was gone. The spear was gone. The colonel lay dead, and Ko was wondering, 'What do I do with this girl?'

He went to the branch holding the rope, holding the net piece that Tusanne was caught in. He cut it down. He did not let it drop to the floor of the jungle. Instead, he caught it. He gently laid it down.

Once she was on the ground, she was going to run. Although in a net, she could still run. She made her way through the forest. Ko took off after her. Ko was an extremely fast runner and had no problem catching up. If this girl were free and not in a net, she could easily outrun him. Ko was a near-Olympian in running and was able to catch her. He was the fastest man to ever chase her.

He tackled her and brought her down. She kicked him. He blocked her kick. She punched him. He blocked her punch. She hissed at him. He moved his face away. She bit him in the neck. She bit him in the shoulder. She scratched him in the face. Ko was getting some pretty impressive wounds. At last he grabbed her wrist and was able to put it behind her. Then he grabbed her other wrist and was able to put that behind her.

Ko had a pair of handcuffs. He cuffed her. Having her hands behind her in this way was a huge help. He went to her feet and took the rope that was used to dangle the net from the tree and tied it around her ankles.

Tusanne was caught. She squirmed and wiggled, screaming out a yelping sound that sounded eerily similar to that dhole, the wild dog. The screaming continued. It was ear-piercing. He found a way to fix this problem. He took his shirt off and wrapped it around her head, gagging her by placing the mass of his shirt inside her mouth. He used another piece of rope from the net to tie that to her head.

Now he had her gagged, handcuffed and ankles tied. She looked at his impressive torso. He was a live statue. She snorted, grunted, and hissed.

He propped her up over his shoulder and walked her back to the helicopter. On the entire walk back, she continued to thump him with gyrations in her hips. She went to the left and the right, moved her head up like a butterfly stroke and came crashing down onto his back. At one point she struck him to the ground. He got back up. He decided to hold her in a different direction so her body was in front of him. She managed to do an Olympic-style one and a half twist, and ended up using the fulcrum effect of her weight, to whip around and snap her head right into his head. That was one head shot that Ko wasn't quick enough to block.

277

It separated them for a second. He fell backwards and down. She wiggled and tried to get up, but it's not easy when you're in a net, ankles tied, and you're handcuffed. She did one of these maneuvers where through a strong arch of the back and an upward thrust of her hips, she was able to get up on her feet and stand. But she couldn't run. She could only hop. But still, she hopped. She hopped one foot, two feet, three feet.

Ko got up, shook off his daze, and went to her. He figured out a new way to get her. He took the rope that was attached to the tree and used that as a kind of leash. He would drag her the rest of the way.

The jungle floor was moist. There were no heavy rocks or other dangers. This would not injure her, but it would humiliate her. He dragged her on her back, kicking all the way, to the helicopter. He put her in the passenger seat. He then used a set of seatbelts to wrap her into that seat. She was belted at the shoulder, at the waist, tied at the ankles, gagged at the mouth, still inside a net with her wrists handcuffed behind her. Ko could now take off and make his way back to the military camp.

He started the helicopter engine. The sound of that helicopter put Tusanne into a new state of rage. She knew that sound. It was something from her past. It was a terrible sound, the sound of military power, the sound of people that will kill. The minute she heard those blades start, she just went crazy in that seat. She began to jump vertically, up and down in that seat. She moaned, groaned, grunted and frothed at the mouth. Spit came down, tears poured from her eyes of terror beaming out.

What Ko didn't know was that the seat had a kind of hydraulic system to lift up and down. That hydraulic system was a little bit weakened. She was able to loosen it significantly with about seven major jumps. In the process, the seat became dislodged from the passenger side and went on its edge. She then bounced through the closed door, the same door with the tiger claws still on it. The door was severed open.

She went out of the helicopter, still stuck in the seat, and ended up on the ground. She was flailing back and forth in that seat, trying to get out of it. But the seatbelts were too tight. They had locked her in.

Ko got out of the pilot's seat, walked around the back of the helicopter and saw that he really had his hands full with this girl. She was there, all strapped in the seat, wiggling, flailing, screaming in a muffled way, spit and foam coming from her mouth, all barely audible through Ko's wrapped up shirt.

Ko went back to the helicopter and turned off the engine. The blades came to a stop. When that occurred, she finally relaxed. He put his hand on her neck. Her jugular vein was pounding. She jolted away. She couldn't turn too far away. He felt her pulse. As the blades were turned off, her pulse slowed significantly.

Ko figured it out. He could not get her out of there in his helicopter. She would just go crazy in there. She'd probably rip apart the whole dashboard, crash the thing and they would both be dead. So he radioed in for help.

"Ko to base camp. Pick up."

"Base camp."

"I need you to send some men out."

"You got her?"

"Affirmative. Let me give you my GPS coordinates." He rattled off the GPS coordinates.

"That's about six miles up here."

"Yes."

"Is there a road?"

"Not exactly. Bring some machetes. You'll need them."

The base commander brought forward a group of Jeep trucks, four wheel drive, with submachine guns mounted. Each one would have four men, each wielding a machete. They drove one after another into the jungle. There was a road that got about halfway to where Ko was, but after that it was pure jungle. They had to basically mow down trees to get there. In several parts, the men had to get out and chop through the brush. Some of the trees were simply too heavy. They had to back around and drive backwards, take another path and go forwards.

There were a couple of rivers they had to get over. One of them was simply too large to traverse. The men stopped at the riverside. No way would they get over that.

The commander radioed Ko, "Okay, look. Here's the deal. We're stuck here across the river. It's pretty large. We can't get over it. I don't know how we're going to get to you."

Ko thought about it. "Send your men by foot. They can wade over the river."

"Are you kidding? This river's flowing quickly."

"Oh, come on. You can get over it."

The commander shook his head. "Okay men, proceed on foot."

The men looked at the water. Now these were soldiers in full military outfits. For some reason, they were scared of that water.

"Come on, guys."

The commander showed his leadership skills by getting in first. He walked into the river. The rush of the water pushed him downriver in a matter of moments. He composed himself against the current, taking it in the chest. It came up to about his shoulders. He continued swimming. He got to the other side.

"Let's go."

The men followed, each coming in slowly but surely into the water, swimming over, wondering if some big river monster would bite their foot and carry them under forever. No river monsters here.

They all got to the other side safely. Soaking wet, boots wet, they walked out the other side of the river and continued into the jungle, slashing their machetes left and right to make a path.

The next 700 yards were the longest 700 yards of their lives. Slowly but surely, they made their way in. They found the helicopter, Ko, and inside a net, no longer attached to a helicopter seat, was Tusanne, the Thai jungle woman.

The men looked in astonishment. They'd never seen such a woman. They looked over at Ko and saw he had taken a couple of head butts, had a scratch on the face and several bite marks. He was missing his shirt. They saw the shirt wrapped around her head.

The commander looked at him with his hands up in the air. "What happened here?"

"It's a long story. This girl is dangerous."

"Okay, we got to get her out of here now."

"Yeah, it's going to take all of us to carry her."

The commander looked around and found something that could be useful. It was a fallen branch. A couple of the soldiers took that branch out and used their machetes to knock off the smaller branches. They then made a fairly solid three inch diameter log

280

out of that branch. They took Tusanne's arms. They right away noticed she was still handcuffed.

"Why don't we just lock her up on this log and we'll carry her pig-style?"

They took one end of the net and tied it very firmly on the log, then took the other end of the net and tied it very firmly on the log. They took Tusanne hanging there. Two men were on one end of the log, two men on the other. She could squirm all she wanted, but it didn't matter. She couldn't hit anybody. She couldn't scratch anybody. She couldn't head butt anybody. She couldn't really do anything but move around.

The entire path back to the river showed four men with the log and Tusanne shoving back and forth, trying to get at them the entire time. Even though she couldn't touch them, she would still try.

They got to the river and realized they were in for a challenging situation. All men got involved in the process. They all held the ends of the log above the water and carefully walked across the water. They weren't able to keep Tusanne out of the water, and kept her body submerged, except they were very careful to make sure her face was above water. They didn't know it, but while she was in the water making this traverse, she peed.

They successfully got to the other side of the river. They brought her out of the water. The commander checked her out. She was fine. They put her into a Jeep and drove her back to the camp. The whole time, she was staring at a machine gun, wishing she could somehow use it. She had her own little fantasy of having someone drive her. She was on the Jeep standing up, with a soldier's helmet on, and shooting away at soldiers left and right, causing hundreds of deaths.

Soon enough, she got sleepy. She finally slept in such an amazingly tranquil way, dead to the world. When they arrived at the command center, she was sound asleep.

Ko had flown the helicopter back, and had already arrived. He was right in front of the gate of the camp and saw the four Jeeps return, one of which had Tusanne in it. He was surprised to see her asleep.

"What happened?"

"She went to sleep."

He studied her for injuries. She had none. It appeared that she was indeed asleep.

They had a small jail cell that they would put her in. They carefully picked her up. In the process, she woke back up. She hissed and tried to bark. They put her in the cell. They laid her down and removed her from the log. Ko unlocked her handcuffs. She was so happy to have those off. She rubbed her wrists. It was terrible having those on. He then untied her ankles.

The first thing she did was try to kick him. He backed out of the way, closed the jail cell behind him and watched her, with the safety of a jail between him and her.

He again looked at her in the eye. She looked at him in the eye. Each trying to control the other, each a little bit mesmerized by the other. Ko had certainly never seen anything quite like her. And she had been in the wild so long that she had forgotten how to interact with humans. She was more comfortable with a pack of wild dogs. His gaze upon her calmed her. She watched him comfortably.

He brought her some water. She drank like an animal. She wouldn't hold the cup. Instead, she put it on the ground, got on all fours and licked it up.

Ko shook his head. "No, no, no, no."

She looked at him like, 'Who are you to tell me how to drink water?'

She wouldn't listen to him, and continued to drink like a lapdog. It was then that Ko understood that the beasts that had taken care of her in the jungle must have been the wild dog, the dhole.

He was sure she would like some food. He went and got a bowl of noodles. Noodles don't exactly grow in the jungle. This was a kind of food that she'd never had before. He handed her the bowl. She put it on the ground. She smelled it. She didn't like the smell. She looked back up at him.

He thought, 'Great, she's rejecting the food.' He wondered, 'A female. She needs something that's she's used to eating. If she's been running around with a pack of dogs, I wonder what they eat.'

Of course -- rabbits. It happened that the camp kept rabbits to feed soldiers. They had a whole bunch of them. He told a soldier to go get one. The soldier brought it back. It was the cutest little bunny you ever did see. It was one of those that has the ears that go downward. It was black, with these nice eyes. It was probably four months old -- small, fuzzy, warm.

When he held it, she was transfixed. She wouldn't take her eyes off it. He then handed it to her. Nature is often cruel. The second she got that bunny, the first thing she did was crack its neck and rip its head off. She then used her sharp teeth to grab its fur and make a tear. She then tore the entire skin off the bunny. She turned the bunny upsidedown and disemboweled it of all of its intestines, its stomach, its kidneys and organs. She was left with pure muscle and bone. She then devoured all of the muscle. She would not eat the bone. Within a matter of 12 minutes, that bunny was gone. Ko watched in amazement as this jungle woman tore that rabbit apart.

He brought her a pillow. She smelled the pillow. She had no idea what it was for. He put it on the ground in front of him and laid down with his head on it, and then threw the pillow into the jail cell. She got the idea pretty quickly and rather liked it. She had never slept on anything as soft as that pillow. She put her head down and went to sleep.

When she awakened several hours later, she was in the back of a transport truck. There were four uniformed soldiers in the truck with her. Ko was up front in the passenger seat. The base commander was driving. Destination: the royal guard headquarters near Bangkok, Thailand.

There was a convoy of four trucks. The one having Tusanne was number two. Behind that was a truck of soldiers, just in case she escaped or tried to pull a fast one. Do you think?

They had Tusanne cuffed with her hands behind her back. Her feet were tied at the ankles. She was no longer screaming at this point so the gag wasn't required.

The trip was more or less uneventful out of the jungle, onto some dirt roads, then onto a big road, a drive down a river. It continued on for endless miles, and then they got into the outskirts of the area where the jungle stopped and Bangkok began.

There were beautiful rice fields on both sides of the road. There were lakes. There were palm trees. It was sunny. The sky was blue. There were major clouds in the sky. Tusanne was happy to see all this beauty.

They pulled into Bangkok, and ended up initially parking in a region known as Ratchatrasong. The entourage did not mean to stop there, but was blocked by a political demonstration by a group known in Thailand as the red-shirts. These red-shirt people come from the rural areas, and claim that the current government is in the category of a dictatorship.

Their chantings and signs included, "Fair value for rice. Raise minimum wage. Give us a living."

Their concern was shown by the signs they showed, the weariness in their eyes and the powerfulness of their numbers. The existing so-called democratic government, headed up by a prime minister, had previously murdered 92 people at this very crossroads in Ratchatrasong during bloodshed on the infamous day of May 19, 2001.

Unfortunately, it looked like today would become a repeat. Tusanne saw in horror as the soldiers guarding her emptied out of the caravan truck, set up a blockage, pulled out their machine guns and aimed on literally thousands of people wearing the red shirts and carrying political signs about their issues.

In this momentary lapse of reason, the Thai military made the mistake of leaving only two guards for Tusanne. Ko had also left the truck and was watching the red-shirts. He had been assigned the critical duty of assisting the military in eliminating this group. This came from a new decree right from the prime minister, and was approved to the Thai military.

Tusanne had small, flexible wrists. She was able to wiggle free from her handcuffs, one by one. She untied her ankle ropes, and in a fleeting second, flew by her two captors, went out the back open door of the caravan truck, and was quickly found in the middle of a melee.

This melee was being well-covered by all international press. The prime minister had been talking about allowing the red-shirts to exist, but at the same time contradicting himself by lining up military units whenever they did speak. It's hard to exercise freedom of speech when you've got a bunch of machine guns aimed on your head.

This time things got really out of hand. There were probably 10,000 protestors in the street. There were more than 100 military caravans and over 1,000 soldiers, all heavily armed with machine guns, ready to fire at will. The only buffer to any of this was the international press.

One of the cameras caught a most unusual and unexpected sight of Tusanne sprinting out of the truck.

"Whoa, what was that?"

They followed her. She ran into the crowd. The soldiers took notice. Without any further command, they ran after her. In the process they had to mow over quite a few people. They started up one of the trucks and just drove after her. Never mind that there were about 2,000 people right in the middle of the road. It was either my way or the highway, literally. Several people got smashed underneath the truck. Tusanne watched in horror as the large truck wheels crushed several skulls.

The red-shirts had no idea what was going on here until one of them noticed, "It's her, the jungle woman! She does exist."

There were reports of her existence, but it was kind of like the Bigfoot reports in the United States. Everyone had heard of it, and had talked about it. There were doctored up photos of her, but nobody really saw her for real. Today, in the melee of a pro-democracy movement, with hundreds being shot down by a dictatorial elite, Tunsande had her debut.

The press was amazed to see how she ran. She was like a gazelle and an Olympic gymnast. Somewhere in her background, she obviously had had some training. She could jump over the backs of people, do half-somersaults, land on her feet. She ran over to the small stores at the side of the main road. She scaled up the wall as though her feet had suction cups. She sprinted at the wall, ran right up the vertical side of it and ended up on the top, running over an overhang that gives shade to the small stores below.

Unfortunately these overhangs were not so strong, even for her light 92 pounds. One of them gave way, and she fell through it. She landed right on a small restaurant below, and managed to hit a handle of a cooking wok. This wok had cooking oil in it, which unfortunately spread onto an open flame and started a small fire. The small fire became a large fire and within a matter of one minute, set an entire area ablaze.

Tusanne was followed by a group of 15 soldiers, and another group in a truck that continued down the packed roadway, crushing skulls in the process without care.

The red-shirts screamed out to help her. "Help her! Protect her!"

They didn't know quite how to do it. One of them tried to grab her, but she didn't know who was friend or foe here. She smashed them right in the face and pushed away. She continued through a series of restaurants. She went into a restaurant, into the back area, and out to an alleyway. Unfortunately, there she was greeted by a group of soldiers.

"Hold it!"

They held up a gun. They were about to shoot when Ko appeared and kicked one gun out of a soldier's hand, and chopped the other with his hands right out. Two guns went flying, hit the ground and shot off. The bullets just went into the wall and didn't hurt anyone.

Tusanne smiled, turned and ran. Ko was her captor and protector.

Tusanne ran away, to the watchful eye of Ko. Ko had to figure out a way to catch her. She continued down the alleyway, ran back up to the rooftop, and proceeded until she came to a stop, where the roof was separated by about 20 feet of road space. Could she jump the 20 feet? Without even thinking of it, she made a gazelle-like leap, cleared the entire roadway, and landed on the other side of the building. The soldiers couldn't do this themselves, and watched her climbing down the rooftops, out of sight.

Ko requisitioned a motorcycle by clotheslining an unsuspecting red-shirt who happened to be riding in the back alley. It was a quick arm to the motorcyclist's neck. He went flying off the bike. The bike continued forward for about 20 yards, until it fell and crashed up against the building. Ko ran to the motorcycle, picked it up, visually inspected it. It was okay, still operable. He got on it and tore down the alleyway.

He was able to clock Tusanne at a speed of about 24 miles per hour, which is Olympic speed. This is the speed of a small horse. She was sprinting on the rooftop, unimpeded by any person or other obstacle, leaping over small antennas and telephone wires in the process. She came to another roadway halfway between the buildings and again, without even thinking of it, leapt high into the air, over the street, onto the other side of the building. The people in the street watched in amazement.

This was covered by helicopter news reports that were hovering over her. The helicopters began to have a psychological impact on her. She looked up and froze at this. This gave Ko his chance. Once again, she was reacting to the noise of the helicopter. There was something about that that brought forward past events. It was a window into what had brought her into the wild. Whatever it was, it was connected to a helicopter.

The news reporters decided they would get involved. They pulled a ladder down to her and invited her to climb up. There was no way Tusanne was going to climb up to a helicopter. The helicopter was the biggest enemy to her. But this one was different. First of all, it was white in color. The ones that she had experience with were military greens. The people in the white helicopters did not wear uniforms. They wore suits. These were news people, not military people.

She saw Ko get off his motorcycle and climb up the side of the building. She saw other soldiers carrying behind him. She saw a ladder to safety. She thought about it for about a millionth of a second, and jumped onto that ladder, and climbed up it several rungs.

The helicopter pulled her inside. She came face to face with a news reporter that would now have the greatest story and interview of her life. There was also a cameraman. The reporter was Ms. Phanatu, of the International News Network [INN]. She spoke fluent Thai and English, but neither would help here. She was trying to understand some way to get at this girl. Tusanne was shivering, shaking and sweating. She was dirty. Her ribs were bloody. Ms. Phanatu went by an adopted name of Angela.

Angela took off her newscaster blazer and put it over Tusanne's shoulder. Tusanne somehow trusted her life with her. This was animal instinct, knowing the difference between a friend and a foe. As the reporter comforted her, she saw Tusanne look at a bottle of water. She handed her the water. Tusanne gulped it as though she hadn't had water in 100 years. Her body was overheating from all of the running she had done. It was a warm day, typical high humidity, which produced quite a bit of sweat. She had lost the liquid in her body and needed to replenish herself.

The reporter watched in amazement as Tusanne sucked down every drop of water in that bottle. Her throat muscles went up and down as the water charged through her throat into her system. The cameraman got every gulp on film.

She let out a gasp. "Aaaaaaaa."

The bottle was empty.

She looked at the reporter. They each looked at one another. People's memories are long. Though Tusanne had not spoken a human language in years, there was some knowledge of language. She first yelped like a dhole. The reporter was taken aback by this. Her head flinched backwards. Tusanne yelped again.

The pilot knew what that was. "It's a dhole."

"What's a dhole?"

"A wild dog."

"She's talking like a wild dog."

The reporter figured it out. "She was raised in the jungle by a pack of wild dogs. This is the language she knows. Well, I forgot to study that one."

The cameraman filmed this entire interview.

Tusanne then showed a little more about her background by saying one word, but it wasn't in a language that the reporter knew. The pilot did.

"That's Cambodian."

"Do you speak Cambodian?"

"A little."

The reporter wanted the pilot to get involved in this. "Okay, talk. Say something to her."

"What?" he asked in his broken Cambodian.

The Thai pilot spoke Cambodian in a broken Asian to Asian way. It was a hugely incorrect Cambodian, but one that still connected with her.

He asked a simple question. "What is my name?"

Tusanne shook her head and then he figured out his mistake. "I mean, what is your name?"

She answered in a kind of voice that was halting and harrowing. It was like hearing a dog speak. She said it in a half-bark, half-yelp and at the same time, a human tone.

She said the word, "Tusanne."

"Wow, she speaks."

The reporter was mesmerized by this tone. The wild woman could speak.

"Where are you from? How did you get there? Who raised you? How were you in the jungle?"

The pilot stopped her. "Whoa, whoa, whoa. You think she's going to answer all these questions, like she's in some kind of a courtroom? Just stop for a second and realize that you literally are interviewing an animal."

The pilot put his palms out in a questioning way and shrugged his shoulder up.

He asked, "How?"

She answered quickly, "Khmer."

"Khmer? What's that?"

She said it again, "Khmer."

The journalist knew. "Oh God, I know what happened. Her family was the victim of the Khmer Rouge of Cambodia."

All of a sudden, with those words, Tusanne's eyes lit up in terror. When she heard the words Khmer Rouge, it was as though someone took a knife and tried to attack her with it. She went into attack mode. She stood up. With sweat still shining from her body, she looked like a bodybuilder at an event. She was ready to kill anyone who mentioned those words.

They both tried to calm her down. "Oh no, no, no. We're on your side. We're not part of that group. We have nothing to do with them."

The man spoke in Cambodian and said, "We are friend. We will help you."

The journalist gestured with the hand motions going downward. "Sit down, relax. It's okay."

They all knew very well the tragic history of Cambodia, where the royal family was thrown out of power. The nobles, the businessmen, the professors, anybody with any kind of intellect, education, even those just happening to wear glasses, were senselessly murdered *en masse*, and buried in agricultural fields. They were known as the Killing Fields.

They slowly and surely brought out the sad story from Tusanne, that her then-pregnant mother, a former Olympic gymnast for the country of Cambodia, and her father

Suddenly there was the ominous sight of six military helicopters hovering on all sides of them. Ko was in the passenger seat of one of them and yelled out to the INN helicopter: "Land at once or you will be arrested."

The INN helicopter pilot was many things, but he would not be a martyr. He looked at the journalist and told her, "I'm landing. There's no way I'm going to have these guys blow us out of the sky."

She agreed. "I'm sure we'll have to land down."

The helicopter landed. The INN helicopter was surrounded by military might, including multiple Jeeps with mounted machine guns, several helicopters hovering above, and more than 100 soldiers on foot.

Tusanne, of course, would try to run. She jumped out of the passenger seat and ran directly into Ko's arms. She bounced off of him, into another soldier's arms. She wiggled free from that soldier, got through that initial line into another level of soldiers. She could've easily escaped 1, 5, 10, probably even 20 of them, but not 100.

Ko screamed out, "Don't hurt her!"

They were pretty good at following that order. But better than 10 of them finally brought her down. Ko cuffed her. They lifted her and placed her into a transport van. Ko would travel with her. Before he left, he went to the journalist. He did not ask for the cameraman's camera. He just took it. He opened it up, popped the video out and gave the camera back.

"I'll take this."

"Under what authority?"

"It's evidence."

"Evidence of what?"

"A crime."

The journalist now was intrigued. "What crime?"

"The crime of murder in the first degree."

The journalist was surprised.

"You two shall not speak a word of this incident."

The journalist looked around. "Well, look around, officer. You've got international press everywhere. They're up in the sky. Do you really expect this to be held under wraps?"

"I'm ordering you to keep silent about whatever you learned during your interview."

Angela smiled. "I will of course obey you."

290

Of course she would not.

The helicopter took off. The transport van left. The Jeep with machine guns left. All the foot soldiers left.

Angela, the cameraman and the Cambodian-speaking pilot were left alone. They got into the helicopter.

Angela pulled out her iPhone and showed it to her cameraman. "He forgot to ask me for my cell phone camera."

The cameraman smiled. "Oops."

Angela had gotten it all on her iPhone. The only difference is the iPhone version would show Tusanne from the reporter's purse, which was on the ground, up, whereas the video would show her from the top of her head down. This way the international public would see Tusanne's face from the ground up, and showing the dramatic, enlarged nostrils breathing up and in and out, in a way that only an animal could.

When that video hit YouTube from "anonymous," it was hands down the most visited YouTube video ever. The number of visits weren't in the millions. It was in, for the first time in YouTube history, the billions. Everybody wanted to know about Tusanne. Who is she? Where is she from? She became a lightning rod to expose not just an animal with a psyche disorder, or a person, but the collective concept of an entire nation suffering from a psyche disorder of denial. A delusional denial of stating there is democracy when in fact they're a dictatorship. How will Tusanne show this and fix this?

The question becomes more complicated when we see that her fix to the problem will take place while she remains on death row in prison.

At the King's palace, a somber monarch listened to the mess that had been created over his very simple desire to catch and have this jungle woman.

"I just don't understand why we need a criminal trial out of this."

Ko explained, "Your majesty, she's guilty of the murder of a colonel."

The colonel's father, one of the highest ranking generals in the Thai military, explained, "This was my son. She killed him. We must have justice."

The King asked Ko, "You were there. Did the colonel do anything to provoke this murder?"

Ko answered honestly, "No, your majesty. He was just standing there."

"And how did she kill him?"

"She used a spear."

"A spear?"

"Yes."

"Sounds rather primitive."

"It was."

"Do you have this spear?"

"No. We left it in the jungle."

"Well, perhaps you should go back there and get it. If they're going to do a murder prosecution, don't you think you should have the murder weapon?"

The general agreed. "We'll go get it. We'll have it today."

Later that week, the general's son would have a high military honors funeral. Tens of thousands of officers and soldiers were there, laying down flowers for him. A procession of elephants dressed up in costume surrounded the ceremony. There were photos of the colonel. He was given a full military salute. Jet planes flew overhead. The royal guard fired shots up in the air. The general's son would be laid to rest, but he would not be forgotten.

It was understood between the King and the general that the situations going on in Thailand required absolute cooperation between the King, the Parliament, the prime minister, and the military. At stake was nothing less than the survival of the present form of government. The question was whether the current regime would stay in power or be taken over by the so-called red-shirts.

The general explained, "We cannot support a government that does not support us. And when an enemy kills one of our soldiers, justice must be done. And if there is no justice for this killing, I will tell our government that we cannot be counted on to bring justice to the government."

The prime minister understood.

"There is a condition."

"What condition?"

"The jungle girl?"

"Yes."

"You must hire for her the greatest lawyer in the country of Thailand."

292

"Done."

"Do you know who this person is?"

"I know."

"Where is he?"

"We will call him back. He is our former ambassador to the United States, a former ambassador to the United Nations. He's now a professor of international law in San Francisco. He has a doctorate in law from the University of Paris. He has a doctorate in law from the Thai Law Institute. He has a doctorate in law from Oxford University. He's an expert in Thai law, common law, and French civil law. He knows international treaty law. He is the perfect lawyer for her, and I'm absolutely sure he will take the case. His name is Ambassador Baba."

It took little doing to get Ambassador Baba to fly back to Thailand and defend Tusanne. He wore wire-rimmed glasses, had the white hair of a judge, and spoke in a soft, elegant tone. Of all the things he knew, unfortunately he did not know how to speak the language of the wild dog known as a dhole, and did not know her broken language of Cambodian.

"My first effort at defending her will be to bring aboard an animal behavioralist expert who can tell me everything about the dhole wild dog -- how they live, how they breed, how they are organized in their societies, and how they communicate through these cat-like yelps.

"The second person on my team must be Cambodian and an expert in all things regarding the Cambodian history, their fall from grace, and the ousting of the royal government by the Khmer Rouge, and the complete takeover and annihilation of their elite classes by the communist regime.

The third team member I need is an expert in Thai military law. I want to make sure we have a proper case to remove this out of the military court and get it into the civilian court."

The trial of the millennium had begun. With Ambassador Baba at the helm, Tusanne would receive the best possible criminal defense to defend her on a murder charge that she was 100% absolutely guilty of.

During all the pretrial proceedings, there would be two basic circumstances: first, Tusanne would remain in a military prison. Second, the international press would be all over it.

Back at the King's castle, just outside of Bangkok, the King wondered aloud with his son about what to do. The Prince was a handsome young man, and had three lovely sisters. The sisters were quite vocal about Tusanne.

Princess Thananata begged her father, "You must let her go. Father, don't you understand what she did was just like an animal reacting out of fear?"

The Prince remained silent.

Her father spoke, "My dear, someday when you grow older --"

"Oh father, please. I am already older. I know of the ways of the world. I know the issues that you speak of. But you can't just kill this girl. Don't you see?"

The other princess intervened. "Father, she's right. This will rile up the red-shirts even more. If you kill this girl, you will have the entire country against you."

The King was frustrated. "If I don't kill her, my military support will disappear and my kingdom will crumble overnight."

The Prince had become angry that his sisters were not supporting his father. "Enough! You three are bickering with father. This is unacceptable. All of you, leave at once."

The princesses, though equal in ranking to their brother, were still subservient to him. They bowed their heads, stood up, and walked away. The Prince watched carefully as they exited the door and left the door.

He turned to his father. "Maybe there's a way to do this where everybody can be happy."

"Oh? And what's that?"

"You give her a full trial. Of course she's convicted. And then after that, you give her a King's pardon."

"I can't pardon her. The general isn't going to have that. I've already spoken with the general about it. He's very well aware of my powers to give a pardon and he's made it very clear -- if I give that pardon, he will not support our house anymore."

It took several weeks to get all of the papers together to file a motion before the country's military tribunal. There was a motion to dismiss the criminal complaint alleging one count of murder in the first degree, based on a lack of jurisdiction over Tusanne.

That day in court, there was a three judge military panel. They were in military uniforms. Tusanne was in leg irons, wrist and waist chains, with her wrists handcuffed in front of her. She wore a purple jail pants and top. You could tell by her look that she was completely bewildered. She had no idea where she was or why she was there.

They sat her next to her able defense counsel, the ambassador. The prosecutor was a steely-nosed, silver-rimmed glass, bald guy, a colonel by the name of Van Rekeon.

The case was called to order.

"In the matter of the court martial of Tusanne, we have before us today the defendant's motion to dismiss for lack of jurisdiction."

"Good morning, Your Honor. Ambassador Baba on behalf of the defendant, who is present."

"Good morning, Ambassador. It is an honor to have you in our courtroom."

"Thank you."

"Good morning, Your Honor. Colonel Van Rekeon on behalf of the royal military service of Thailand."

"Thank you. You may sit down."

The colonel did not want to sit and remained standing for a couple more seconds. He realized it was not his turn to speak and so he sat.

The ambassador spoke, "First of all, let me say that whether this case is tried before this military tribunal or our civil justice system, the result should be the same. My client, Tusanne, should be found 100% not guilty of murder in the first degree. I want to emphasize that she does not have any kind of technical defense. She has a defense that says quite plainly, she is not guilty of the crime charged."

The packed courtroom applauded in excitement over this announcement. The press was rolling. Cameras were wheeling. Journalists were writing. The judges were not used to this kind of public and slammed down the gavel.

"Order! Order! I will not have this kind of jubilance in my courtroom. I want everyone here to understand, if you do not remain quiet I will order all of you to leave. Do you understand?"

Everybody nodded.

The ambassador continued, "This case does not belong before this military court for the simple reason that the defendant is not a member of the armed services. And I would like to cite to you a provision of the Thai Constitution, that all laws are inviolate and all citizens enjoy a right to a full due process of law before a proper civil court."

"Yes, but I'm sure as you know, she is accused of murdering a military colonel during a military operation."

"Let's see what we have here. Who is this woman they were hunting and why were they hunting her? They created basically an illegal hunt of an innocent person. They had no business chasing her down. They had no business hunting her. The whole idea that this was a military process is itself an illegal act."

There was a silence in the courtroom. The ambassador was accusing the royal Thai military of engaging in illegal conduct. This was not normal.

The prosecutor became upset. "I don't know why our ambassador, such an honorable citizen of this country, would accuse the high ranking military of engaging in illegal activities. Our military is --"

The ambassador interrupted, "Not above the law."

The audience couldn't help but to engage in more grandstanding and cheerleading. They clapped, they yelled. There was a huge issue with the military's crackdown on the red-shirts. Many had been killed and now, whether or not the military was above the law or not, had at least seen its first day in court.

The judges responded. "First of all, no person with the exception of the royal family is above the law. This is the law of Thailand."

The crowd clapped again, as at last, for the first time, there was a pronouncement of a well-needed law. The military was subject to the law and could be found to have engaged in illegal conduct.

The prosecutor rose. "I am not trying to say they're above the law. I'm saying they acted within the law."

The judges explained, "We have seen what you said in your legal brief. You have argued this for 25 pages, but what we fail to see is the legal basis for a military operation inside the country of Thailand, against a citizen of Thailand who was not engaged in any kind of armed violence or other insurrection against the government. What is your legal authority that allows for this military operation?"

"Your Honor, it was done on the King's order. It was a royal decree."

The judge smiled and noted a rather obvious fact, "If the King wants to chase down a girl in the jungle, he may do so, for the King is truly above the law in this country. But when he asked the military to do his work, then we must apply the law of Thailand to the conduct of the military. We hold today in a unanimous decision. My brothers are with me on this."

The two other judges to the panel nodded.

"We rule that the military operation, even though subject to a royal decree, was still a military operation and is governed by the law of the Thai Constitution. Under the Constitution, it is illegal for the military to engage in the hunting down and capture of a citizen who is not engaged in any kind of insurrection or other behavior against the state. Accordingly, it is our ruling that though she may be guilty of murdering a Thai military colonel, she does not come within the jurisdiction of our military system of justice, and this tribunal hereby dismisses the case against her."

The judge slammed down the gavel. He could not calm the cheers of the gallery, filled with journalists, red-shirts, poor people, and one royal attache that would have some bad news for the King.

The following day, the headlines in the world papers read quite simply, "Case Dismissed." The people of the world joined in jubilation with the idea that the military case against Tusanne had gone away. The one person that did not cheer in this jubilation was her able attorney, the ambassador.

"Look," as he explained in the press interview. "It's not over. All we're doing is transferring the venue. Instead of having this trial before the military court, we will now proceed in our country's civil court. She hasn't been found not guilty. She's just gotten out of one court. I expect her to be charged with murder, probably before the end of the day."

Indeed, at four PM the same day, royal guards visited Tusanne in her military prison cell and served her with a civil arrest warrant, charging her with one count of murder in the first degree. A courtesy copy was delivered to the ambassador. She

297

would be transferred over to the Thai civil justice system, criminal department, for proceedings to set a file date on her murder charge.

The Thai government was not pleased with the international press coverage of this event. The Thai government came under a microscope. The red-shirts were gathering in numbers now. They were coming out of the hills and out of the rural areas, all coming into Bangkok to support Tusanne. She became a lightning rod for their own network. It was the effort of the jungle people, of the people living way out in the rural areas, who had never had a voice before. Now that they had found one of their own being charged with a heinous crime.

They came into the city in tens of thousands, all wearing their emblematic red shirts, carrying posters saying, "Free Tusanne, free Tusanne." The King looked out his window at the crowd and shook his head.

"We can't be shooting these people. There's just too many of them."

Helicopters with international press were flying over, filming every inch of it. If the Thai government did anything to annihilate this group, the entire country would face a worldwide international indictment. Thailand would become a pariah of the world. This could not be. The legitimacy of the Thai monarchy hung in the balance. The King looked out.

The Prince, the heir to this estate, saw the worried look on his father. Would the Prince lose his kingdom? The King saw the son's worried look and tried to allay his fears.

"Son, we will find a solution."

The process of the initial arrest of Tusanne, bringing her into the military prison, having a motion filed for dismissal of the military charges, reissuing a new civil complaint for murder, and bringing her to a civilian prison took about 45 days.

During this period, Tusanne did not really understand what was going on, why there was all this excitement about her, why she was in a cage and why so many people had taken an extreme interest in her.

The ambassador had a top-rated animal behavioralist attempt to interview her. Dr. Peter Theroux was French. He tried to apply western psychology and methodology to train a human raised by wild dogs to speak in a regular way. He showed her the Thai language, the letters, the words, the vowels. He went through them one by one. She just stared at him. Every now and then she would bark. She would whistle and give out a bird-like chirping sound.

Finally the doctor just gave up. "It's no use. We're not teaching this woman today."

A nurse accompanied him. There was a rule that female prisoners could never be alone with a male so the nurse was always present.

On the way out, the nurse had an interesting discussion with the doctor. She was a lovely Thai woman wearing all white, against white white. White stockings, white shoes, white dress, and a white hat.

"Doctor, may I inform you of something?"

"Yes. What information do you have, nurse?"

"Well, how shall I say this? She has been under my care now for close to 65 days. I have watched her every day. I have fed her. I have bathed her."

"Okay."

"Well, there's something that hasn't happened."

"Oh. What hasn't happened?"

"She hasn't had a period."

"No period?"

"No period."

"For how long?"

"60 days."

Dr. Theroux looked at her. She was still very taut, very muscular; she did not have the slightest physical look of being pregnant. He hadn't seen her throw up. She was a strong animal woman. Tusanne somehow had managed to get herself pregnant.

The doctor asked, "Now wait a minute. You're with her at all times, right?"

"Yes."

"I mean, there's never been a situation where a male has been in the jail with her and you have not been there."

"Right."

"Has anybody overpowered you?"

"No."

"Has there been any misconduct that you can tell me about?"

"None, doctor. We run a very professional prison here."

"So this must've happened before she was brought in."

"Yes, I think so."

"But who?'

The nurse didn't know. She shrugged her shoulders. "I don't know who did it, but somebody made her pregnant."

"This has to be top secret. Do not tell anybody. Do you understand?"

The nurse nodded. "I understand."

"If the press gets ahold of this -- oh my God."

The doctor felt duty-bound to inform the King of this. He approached the royal appointment secretary and asked for an appointment.

The secretary declined to the good doctor. "I'm sorry. The King will not see you."

"Oh, he ought to see me. I've got some news for him."

"I'm sorry, but he has too many things going on to see you right now."

"Okay. Why don't we go like this? Why don't you tell him I'm a doctor, I've been visiting with Tusanne and I have some news that is unfortunately going to ruin his day. And let me tell you, if it comes out later that you didn't tell him about this news and he learns about through the press -- when he finds out that you blocked this information, I guarantee it, you will be fired."

The secretary took his round glasses off and put them on the desk. He was silent. "Just a moment. Stay right here."

He walked on the marbled floors. His leathered shoes made this little tippy-tap noise as he left the room. A royal guard watched the good doctor. The guard did not smile.

It took about eight minutes. All of a sudden, the guard got uptight. The door opened and there was the King. He was with the appointment secretary.

The doctor bowed before the King.

"My good doctor, my appointment secretary tells me you've got some news about Tusanne. It sounds like bad news. Can you please explain?"

"Your Excellency, may I suggest that we talk in private?"

The King looked at the guard and the appointment secretary. They both left the room.

"Okay, doctor. You wanted a private audience, you have a private audience. Tell me the news."

"Your Excellency, Tusanne is pregnant."

The King looked at his son with great despair. "Oh shit."

They both realized that there were many things in life and on this world that a person cannot do, even a King. And one of them, rather obviously at the top of the list, is to execute a pregnant woman. The second is to execute a woman who had just had a baby.

The first thing he had to tell the Prince was rather obvious. "Do not tell your sisters about this."

The Prince laughed. "Oh yeah."

They realized if the sisters knew, they would do something drastic to make sure that Tusanne would have her baby and that her baby would have Tusanne.

The King knew the rather obvious thing to do here. He had a meeting with the prosecutor. The prosecutor was an elderly gentleman. He had seen many things in his life -- many ugly, unpleasant things. Nothing was quite as unpleasant and ugly as the idea of putting this beautiful woman to death for a crime that was committed under circumstances that began with an already judicially pronounced illegal military operation.

The King did not want to explain to the prosecutor why he wanted a speedy trial. He just wanted to make it happen.

"By royal decree, I am creating a new law in Thailand. It is called the Speedy Trial Act."

"The Speedy Trial Act?"

"Yes. From now on, all criminal trials will occur within 60 days of the arrest. This way if somebody is innocent, they will not have a prolonged period in jail."

"Oh, I see. That's a great idea. Here's the only problem. We don't have enough judges. We don't have enough courtrooms. There is no way we can have trials in 60 days. We have backlogs going back for years. You realize we have people in jail right now for two years who haven't had their trial? How are we supposed to get all of them to justice?"

"By my next decree. I am tripling the number of judges and courthouses in Bangkok."

"Okay, now that's a great idea. I completely support that, but let's understand something. How long does it take to build a courthouse?"

The King knew, of course, it would take a long time to build another courthouse, but he also had a simple solution. "You know what? I have a summer house not far out of Bangkok."

"Yes, I'm very well aware of the estate, Your Excellency."

"I am going to turn that palace into a new courthouse. We have enough rooms in there for 25 new courts. It is in that palace that Tusanne's trial will take place."

And with that, the King issued a decree for the creation of 25 new judgeships and 25 new courthouses in the royal summer palace.

Thai Courthouse at King's Royal Summer Palace

This was a gorgeous estate outside the city limits. It was pastoral, it was green, it was gorgeous. Inside these walls, many ugly things would happen -- the first of which was a quick criminal trial of Tusanne.

The ambassador was immediately suspicious. "Since when does the King find an interest in speedy trials?"

He looked at his client up and down, and wondered and speculated, "What could it be?"

It was a good thing because after all, people do rot away in jail waiting their charges. It was very common for a person to be in jail for two years before their trial date. Often that was used as a way to get plea bargains out of people. The best way to get out of jail in Thailand was to plead guilty, take your prison sentence, do the sentence and get out. Often the pretrial sentence was longer than the prison sentence from the trial.

The ambassador had a practical problem though. His client wouldn't be able to speak, except to chirp, bark and an occasional haunting tone, a hard, husky voice, sounding part dog, part cat. It was raspy, it was odd and it really didn't say anything other than "return me home."

The ambassador prepared a motion seeking a jury trial. This was his idea to arrange the proper form of justice, and it was one that there was absolutely zero legal support for. Thailand did not have a jury trial right in their constitution.

But this was a concept that the King thought could be the ultimate solution. If there was to be a jury of citizens to judge the guilt or innocence of Tusanne -- well, the result would be rather obvious. There were not 12 people in the entire country that would find her guilty. But the civil judges would apply the facts to the law. In an unemotional application of that law, they would only have one recourse but to find her guilty.

Jury nullification is, strictly speaking, an illegal act. It's where a jury listens to a judge instruct them as to the applicable law, but rather than applying that law to the fact, the jury comes up with an emotional, human reaction and pronounces the defendant not guilty. In western justice systems, when the jury says not guilty, no matter how completely wrong that verdict may be, it will stand.

When the King learned of the ambassador's motion to require a jury trial, he was overjoyed. "At last, a solution. The judges will grant this motion. She will be given a jury trial of 12 citizens, and I'm sure those citizens will find her not guilty."

The Prince smiled and had just one question for his father. "Why would the judges grant such a motion? He will be taking away a lot of power from them, number one. Number two, there's nothing in our constitution allowing for such a jury trial. And number three, the judges are not allowed to created such a thing. Father, I don't even think you have the right to create that by decree."

The hearing on this unprecedented motion was placed before the world court of international journalists. They took down every word that was stated.

Before the ambassador could even speak, the three judge panel had a whole ruling for him.

"On the motion by the defendant to require this court to afford Tusanne a jury trial, we state as follows. We have reviewed the papers submitted by the able ambassador, and we thank you for bringing to our attention the international precedents supporting a natural right for a jury trial. That such a right does not come out of constitutional pronouncement, judicial decree or statute, but is rather a matter of natural law, of God-given law, in the category of an inalienable right.

"We have reviewed those authorities, and we must announce, however artfully and wonderful they sound, we are unable to accept them. We should state at the outset that we would like to accept them because we are people of justice, and we believe that a people's justice, a justice where the people decide guilt or innocence, and take that ultimate power of a conviction and a death sentence away from government actors, that such a system is definitely a preferred system of justice.

"But we are still a nation of laws. I am not a King. I am not a member of parliament. I do not have the legislative power. I do not have the power of judicial decree. Ours is a power to enforce the laws that others make. And in our system, nobody has made this law that you have declared to be an inalienable right.

"Unfortunately, until either the King acts or until parliament acts, we are duty-bound to deny the motion for a jury trial and do hereby deny the motion."

He slammed the gavel down. The prosecutor smiled. The ambassador frowned.

Tusanne yelped and chirped in a highly audible fashion. The press wrote it down.

The judge continued, "We also are now subject to the newly created Speedy Trial Act and we hereby order that this trial commence in 25 days, on September 15th at nine AM. Counsel, will you be ready for trial at that time?"

The ambassador nodded. "I will be ready."

"Very well then. It is so ordered."

The judge slammed the gavel and thereby paved the way for the trial of the millennium, to occur at the King's summer palace on September 15th before a world court. The matter would be decided by three judges, all of whom were former members of the Thai royal military, had been Thai prosecutors, and now had become Thai judges. Any concept that Tusanne would get a fair trial was absolutely out of the question.

The King met with the Supreme Commander of the military, the general whose son unfortunately had been murdered by Tusanne.

"Can you find it in your heart to forgive this woman for what she did?"

"No. She killed my son. How do you expect me to forgive her?"

"What if we made Tusanne your personal slave for the rest of your life?"

"Then my first act as her master would be to murder her."

"What if we paid you $10 million in gold to forgive her?"

"You cannot put a price tag on the memory of my son. Your Excellency, I support you 1,000%. I will always kiss your hand. I will always kiss your feet. But I want you to know that this woman must have proper justice. Please see to it that it is so."

The King and the Prince stood stoically. They looked back out at the throngs of people that had collected outside the summer palace. There were literally hundreds of thousands of red-shirts, crying out for justice.

"Free Tusanne! Free Tusanne!"

Helicopters flew with international press cameras rolling. Every day was a new article about Tusanne, asking, who was this woman? Where did she come from? How did she become the way she was? Where were the dogs that had raised her? Could we find them?

A search party would go out. The pack of dogs that they believed were her family were rounded up and brought before the summer palace. They kept them in the gardens of the palace.

The courtroom was in a theater room where the King had enjoyed private performances. There was a large audience area, capable of seating more than 200 people. It was packed with others standing against the wall and people on the outside dreaming to get inside.

The televised event would be shown to the world. There were cameras going in all four corners of the courtroom.

That day in court, the first day of her trial began with the judges asking for her plea.

"To the charge of murder in the first degree, how do you plead?"

The ambassador rose. "We plead not guilty."

The crowd went wild with the plea.

The judges banged the gavel. "Order, order."

The crowd silenced. There was this barely perceptible, extremely high pitched noise that came out. It was Tusanne giving some kind of bird-like signal to the dogs that had been collecting out front. They responded back to her with their own bird-like chirping and odd form of a yelp. These dogs barked a little bit like a cat bark. It's hard to describe, other than to say a cheetah barks like a dog so nature produced a dog that barks like a cat.

"The prosecutor will call its first witness."

It was, unfortunately, Agent Ko of the Thai royal special forces. When Agent Ko took the stand, he subconsciously noticed that the woman his testimony would put to death was also the mother of his child. He could see it in her eyes. He could see it in her own way of looking at him. There was some kind of telepathic communication. It may have been through the chirping, but Tusanne fully communicated the fact of her pregnancy to Agent Ko. He froze. They met eyes. He was transfixed on her. A tear came down his cheek, and another tear.

The prosecutor didn't understand. This was a man who had been trained to withstand torture and not give up state secrets. This was a man who was a master of martial arts. This was a high ranking spy in the royal government -- the equivalent of a Thai James Bond. And without anybody saying a word, here he was, crying like a baby.

The press was stunned. Close up photos of his tears would appear in the afternoon paper. "Why Was This Man Crying?" headlines would read.

The judges looked at him and didn't understand it. Did he cry for himself or was he crying for the defendant? Was he crying for the entire nation? The judges didn't know, but Tusanne knew and the King knew. The good doctor knew that he cried for his only son.

"Do you swear to tell the truth, the whole truth and nothing but the truth, so help you God?"

Ko wiped the tears from his eye. "I'm sorry. Could you please say that again?"

"Do you swear to tell the truth, the whole truth and nothing but the truth?"

"I do."

The judges looked at the prosecutor and nodded him forward.

"Can you tell us where you were on July 17th?"

"Yes."

"Where were you?"

"I was deep in the Thai jungle."

"Were you on a military operation?"

"I was."

"Can you describe that operation?"

"We were attempting to find the jungle girl."

"The jungle girl known as Tusanne?"

"Yes."

"The girl that is here today?"

"Yes."

"Can you tell us what you did to catch her?"

"We set up a number of nets throughout the jungle."

"Okay. And did these nets catch her?"

"One of them did."

"And when you caught her, how did you find the net that she was in?"

"The nets had a monitoring system that gave a radio signal to us."

"And who was us?"

"The deceased, the colonel."

"You were with him that day?"

"I was."

"How did you get to where she was?"

"By helicopter."

"Who operated the helicopter?"

"The colonel did."

"Did you land about where she was?"

"I did."

"But when you landed, did you see her in the net?"

"I did."

"Did you approach her?"

"Yes."

"Did you notice if she had any weapons?"

"Initially, no."

"Initially?"

"Right."

"As you got closer, did you see a weapon?"

"No."

"Did you learn later that she had a weapon?"

"Yes."

"How did you learn?"

He looked at Tusanne. He was bound to tell the truth. If he was to lie, it would be a letdown of his entire government, of his years of service to the King, of everything in his life that he stood for. But the father in him created a desire to tell a gigantic lie, that he did not know how the colonel died. He was the one and only witness to this event. If he would simply state, "I don't know what happened," there could be no conviction. Under Thai law, a murder conviction required an eyewitness account. He was that witness. He knew he held the bullet to her execution in his mouth. All he had to say is, "I don't know what happened."

The pause seemed like an hour, but was actually only about a minute. But a minute with the world court of the international press hanging over you, a three judge panel hanging over you and a prosecutor with a dangling question out there can seem like an hour.

The judges turned to the witness. "Can you answer the question?"

"Yes. Yes."

"Yes what?"

"Yes, I saw her with a weapon."

Tusanne continued to chirp in a loud fashion.

The justices finally had enough of this. "I'm sorry. We just can't have that going on. Is there any way to silence her?"

"I object." The ambassador was quick to speak. "She needs to participate in these proceedings. You cannot gag her."

"We have a right to justice and we have a right to control this process in the court. She is interfering and obstructing that process. I want you to tell your client to stop that noise now or we will gag her."

The ambassador brought over his behavioralist and attempted to have that behavioralist decree in a dog mimic that it was time to be quiet. Amazingly, in a process watched by the press with great fascination, the behavioralist gave several chirps. He communicated in the simple language of the dhole, that sometimes it was better to be quiet. She stopped the chirping, and would remain silent throughout the rest of the trial.

The justices were pleased, and waved on the prosecutor to continue with his next question.

"You said yes."

"Yes."

"You saw her with the weapon."

"Yes."

"Can you tell us when you first saw her with the weapon?"

This was a terrible truth he would have to say, but he had to say it. "Without any kind of warning, she took a spear that she had hidden behind her back and lunged it into the colonel's neck. That was the first time I saw her weapon."

The crowd of journalists wrote down every line that was said. The press was saddened by this rather obviously convicting testimony. They all knew that Tusanne had done something terribly wrong.

After he said this, the prosecutor wanted to smell the aroma of this fine testimony, savor it in his mouth, breath in its fumes, listen to it and let every little hair lining his eardrum. The justices asked him to proceed. He did.

"Before Tusanne had lunged this spear into the colonel's neck, did he do anything violent toward her?"

"No."

"Did he yell at her?"

"No."

"Did he pull a gun on her?"

"No."

"Did he attempt to hit her?"

"No."

"Did he attempt any kind of aggression toward her?"

"No."

"In fact, weren't the circumstances that she was held against her will in a net?"

"Yes."

"She was secure."

"Yes."

"Were you worried she was going to run away?"

"No, she was dangling in the air at that time."

"So there was no way she could get away?"

"Not that I could see."

"Did you see any kind of danger presented in any way, shape or form by the colonel toward her?"

"No."

"So this was an unprovoked killing of the colonel."

The ambassador stood.

"Objection; calls for a conclusion."

The judge ruled without hesitation.

"Overruled. You may answer the question."

"Could you repeat the question?"

Ko just wanted to deflect the inevitable.

The prosecutor quickly repeated it.

Ko's answer:

"Yes."

"Your Honor, I have no further questions."

The justices turned over to the defense. "Your witness."

The ambassador stood. He brought over a handkerchief to Ko and handed it to him.

Ko wiped the tears from his eye.

The ambassador would ask the question that everybody wanted to know the answer to.

"Tell me, Agent Ko, you are a trained assassin. You are part of the royal special forces. You trained for years in martial arts. You are trained to withstand torture. You are trained to be one of the coldest, toughest pro-government citizens of this nation and of this kingdom. So please tell us all, tell us all, why do you cry?"

This toughest man in Thailand broke down right then and there. He went from shedding tears in silence to bawling like a baby. It was an uncontrollable cry that went on in an embarrassing manner. He held his head down. He shook. He cried. Tusanne saw him and she cried with him. They were crying together. There was a connection. Nature's forces were at play. She would no longer squeal. She would no longer chirp. She would no longer yelp. She would cry with the man that would convict her and would cause her death. And the two of them knew exactly why they were crying.

Ko didn't know he knew. He didn't know that she'd communicated that she was pregnant with his son. He didn't know in his conscious way but subconsciously he did know. It was his subconscious knowledge that created the tears that flowed down his cheeks. His only answer was the God's honest truth.

"I don't know. I don't know."

The nurse, the doctor, the King and the Prince were the only people in the entire world that knew the answer to that question. It would remain one of the secrets, one of the mysteries, of Thailand.

The ambassador sat down. "No further questions."

There is a thinking in criminal law that cross-examination of a government witness is futile and will just be an instant replay of damning testimony.

"That was it?"

"That's it."

"Okay. Any redirect?"

"None, Your Honor."

"Very well. This witness may step down. You may call your next witness."

"Your Honor, if it may please the court, the prosecution rests its case."

"Okay. The defense may call its witness."

"Your Honor, we call animal behavioralist and psychologist Dr. Theroux to the stand."

The prosecutor stood up. "Objection. Relevance, improper expert opinion, lack of foundation, lack of a duly accepted peer reviewed scientific area of knowledge that would justify this testimony."

The judge queried, "Okay. Let's talk about that. I understand the doctor is going to talk about the fact that, psychologically speaking, this woman, the defendant, is not capable of forming the intent requisite for a charge of murder in the first degree. Is that correct?"

Ambassador Baba quickly responded, "Yes, Your Honor."

"And the reason behind that is that she was apparently raised by a pack of dogs, the dholes, in the jungles of Thailand, and lived by the animal rules and behaved herself pursuant to the law of the jungle."

"Correct."

"The objection is overruled. Dr. Theroux, you may take the stand."

Dr. Theroux walked up and was sworn in.

"Do you swear to tell the truth, the whole truth and nothing but the truth?"

"I do."

The ambassador began, "Dr. Theroux, can you begin by telling us your educational background?"

"I have a PhD in Psychology from the Sorbonne University in Paris; postdoctoral research in animal behavior at Oxford. I received a DSc in animal behavior."

"So you have a background in animal behavior and human behavior."

"I do."

"And have you worked in this field since then?"

"I have."

"What is your approach?"

"I investigate some of the raw wirings of the human psyche, and I connect human behavior back to our status as animals. Many things that we do can be connected to the basic reality that we are, in a biological way, members of the animal kingdom. We are programmed, we are wired in a certain way that creates our motivations, our emotions, our conduct."

"Very well. So though Tusanne is more of a pure animal, would you say?"

The prosecutor stood.

"Objection; leading."

"Overruled."

"I would."

"You would also say, though, that her animal behavior is perhaps not all that different than the rest of our behavior."

"I would agree with that, counselor -- with one caveat."

"What's that?"

"Her's is as pure as the driven snow. Our is polluted by culture, by peer group pressure, by opinion and by manmade law."

"Okay. Well, this brings us to the core of our defense. Now you heard the testimony of Agent Ko, that before she lunged at the colonel with a spear in the neck, that Agent Ko had not undertaken any violent act or act of aggression toward her. Did you hear that testimony?"

"I did."

"Let's say we accept all that as 100% true. We have no evidence to the contrary. He's the only eyewitness. I don't have any other witness to contradict it. Unfortunately my client can't speak -- at least, not very much. So I need to speak on her behalf, and to explain to the court how her conduct and what she did was indeed an act of self-defense."

"Objection. Leading."

314

"Sustained. Rephrase."

"Can you explain the raw wiring in her system, as far as her upbringing, as far as who she is and how it led her to this attack on the colonel?"

"I can. First of all, from what I understand, the little that she has described to us tells us that she was raised by the dholes, the wild dogs. We know these animals to be a pack animal, not that different from the wolf. We also know that they're not a wolf and that they're not a dog. They're somewhere in between. So just as she has lived in between two worlds, the world of the animal and the world of the civilized human, her family lives in a similar way. These animals are not that far from being a domestic dog and yet are more in line with being a wild wolf.

Now let's thinking about the conduct of the wolf. They'll howl at the moon. The dhole doesn't howl. They chirp, as you've heard here in court."

"Yes, and I'm glad to note that you were able to convince her to stop."

"I have some limited power of communication with her."

"Alright. So tell us, what is going on in her mind, as she is resting, captive in a net, hanging from a tree, dangling over the ground seeing a military officer and Agent Ko approach her?"

"Yes. I also know from her interview with the press that she claims to have been born of a woman that was murdered by the Khmer Rouge in Cambodia. She is Cambodian. She came to us as an escapee from the Killing Fields of Cambodia."

This was the first time that this information had been leaked out. The press people that had taken this before had been sequestered, but now it became known.

"The Khmer Rouge, as you know, murdered millions of Cambodians. All members of the royal family, anyone part of the ruling elite -- a nobleman, a noble family, an educated family, a professor. We understand that her mother was a gymnast."

As the doctor spoke of Tusanne's mother, Tusanne did something completely unexpected. She stood on her feet. Then, ever so slowly, she raised up her feet vertically and got onto her tippy-toes, ballerina-style. She stood vertically like this, perfectly still. She took one of her arms and did a perfectly 360 degree turn on her toes, came back to a full face position to the court and sat back down.

Everybody watched this in silence.

The doctor continued, "I was about to say that her mother was a world-famous gymnast and ballerina from Cambodia. We believe we know who she was."

"You do?"

"Yes."

Tusanne's Mother Performing the Peacock Dance

This was stunning information. The doctor pulled out a black and white photo of an absolutely gorgeous ballerina. The doctor pulled out a second photo of that same ballerina wearing a gymnast outfit and receiving a silver medal in the Olympics for uneven parallels.

"There aren't many people on this planet that can win a silver medal in the Olympics for uneven parallels, and also be a prima ballerina in the Cambodian Royal Ballet. There just aren't many candidates out there. We believe that this woman was Tusanne's mother."

The King was watching all this on televised circuit in his palace. The close up to the photo of Tusanne's mother was mesmerizing. This was the most gorgeous Cambodian woman ever on planet Earth. She was jaw-dropping and she was so talented. They showed videos of her doing the uneven parallels. It was incredible what she had done. In fact, one wondered how she got a silver medal and not a gold. She lost the gold by 0.01 when a young girl from Romania got a set of perfect 10s. She received perfect 10s and one 9.99.

When Tusanne saw the photos of her mother, the chirping and yelping came back in an uncontrollable manner. The dogs outside joined her in this effort. There would have to be a brief intermission. The court process had temporarily quite literally gone to the dogs. There was howling and chirping. She was screaming.

For the first time, Tusanne had seen a photo and a video of her mother. Everybody realized that there would have to be some allowance for her behavior. The justices were forgiving.

"Perhaps, doctor, you could put all of that away."

Tusanne calmed herself and cried at the photo of her mother. One of the most beautiful women ever on Earth, senselessly murdered by a communist regime that was bent on eliminating all forms of talent in the former royal kingdom in Cambodia.

It appears that during the extermination of all these people, that somehow her mother handed the newborn Tusanne off to a pack of dholes. They raised and took care of her, and brought her up as one of their own.

"So then doctor, could you tell us, in the case of Tusanne, does she conduct herself in line with being a dhole?"

318

"It is her only behavioral set of rules. She does not know any of man's rules. She does not know any of man's laws. She does not know any of the things that the rest of us live by."

The justice interrupted, "My good doctor, I must inform you that ignorance of the law is not an excuse, nor is it a defense. Mr. Ambassador, I am sure you are aware of this basic rule of criminal law."

"I am, but there's something else at stake here and it is called a lack of intent. This murder charge, murder in the first degree, requires premeditation, requires malice aforethought, requires a heart that wants to kill. Doctor, here's the question I have for you. Did Tusanne, in killing the colonel, have a desire to kill in a malicious way or in a self-protective way?"

"It is my opinion that she killed in self-defense."

"The colonel did not attack her, did not threaten her. Where is the self-defense?"

"You have to understand that this girl remembers the last sight of her mother as being murdered by military people wearing a uniform very similar to what the colonel was wearing. She saw and remembered the trauma of what her mother had been through. When she saw the colonel come to her in the same outfit of the people that killed her mother, she felt right away that they were coming for her. There was unfinished business that these soldiers didn't complete before and they were now going to complete it. She was convinced that the colonel was going to kill her.

"And let's not forget, let me tell you a definition of violence. If you take somebody and capture them, and you put them in a net, and you hold them against their will and you have them up in the air suspended, helpless and defenseless -- let me tell you that in the animal kingdom, that is an act of aggression, that is an act of violence.

"So this whole idea that there was no violence toward her, I say is false. Maybe under man's law there was no violence, but under the dhole law, under the animal law and under the memory of Tusanne in knowing what had happened to her mother, she saw this as extremely violent and she acted in accordance with self-preservation, self-defense, and is here alive today as a result."

The ambassador stopped right there. "No further questions, Your Honor."

The judges looked over to the prosecutor. "You may proceed."

"You agree that she did indeed kill the colonel, correct?"

"Correct."

"You do not have any information to the contrary, do you?"

"No, I do not. As you know, there is only one eyewitness, Agent Ko, and his testimony stands."

"Very well. In accordance with animal law, you would find that she committed an act of self-defense. True?"

"Yes."

"I want you to apply Thai law. In accordance with Thai law, did she commit an act of self-defense?"

The doctor did not like this question, for there was only one honest answer. "No, she did not."

"Thank you, doctor. I have no further questions."

So then, the case would boil down to what set of laws to apply -- the law of the jungle or the King's law, the law of Thailand.

There was silence but the ambassador decided to move things along. "We call our next witness."

"Proceed." The judge was happy to keep the trial going. That created a perfect silence in the courtroom.

"Our next witness is Tusanne."

Now this should get interesting. Calling a witness that didn't speak in a language was a curious process.

The ambassador asked for leeway on this. "If I may?"

"Yes?"

"In order to bring out the testimony, we may need a little assistance. I request leave to bring in a dhole."

"You want to bring a dog in the courtroom?"

"Don't worry. It'll be in a cage."

"Okay. Anything else?"

"Yes."

"What's that?"

He signalled over to the doctor. The doctor wheeled out a laptop.

"We have a video on this to show. It's on this computer. May we play it on the court's computer?"

"Counsel, have you shown this to the prosecutor?"

The prosecutor nodded. "Indeed, we have seen the whole thing."

"Do you have objections?"

The prosecutor stood. He was about to make a feeble excuse about how wrongful, convoluted and completely irrelevant the video was.

He suddenly decided not to, and instead pleased the entire court audience when he announced, "No objection."

Nobody was more glued to their seat than Agent Ko. He watched every move Tusanne made, every facial expression. He was transfixed and completely mesmerized. None of this was lost on anyone.

Two behaviorist assistants working for the doctor wheeled in a cage. Inside the cage was not one, but two dhole dogs. They were quiet until they saw Tusanne. They chirped and squealed like a cat. Tusanne turned around and had an ear-to-ear grin. She straightened her back and neck out, and put her face up in the air. They smelled the air around her and took her in. She smelled the air around them and took them in. There was a process of communicating that was going on through a sense of smell.

The judges, the lawyers, the doctor, and the audience all watched in silent amazement as the wild dogs and Tusanne communicated. The judges knew they had before them a true member of the animal kingdom.

The doctor connected the laptop to the courtroom television. He had his assistants move the cage of two dogs right into the middle of the court area. The cage was on a crate system with wheels underneath and was easy enough to push around.

The doctor explained to the judge, "Having the dogs present will assist the process of bringing testimony out of Tusanne."

The judge looked to the ambassador for guidance. This was a situation that they had never faced before.

The ambassador explained, "This is what I understand to be the case. If members of her peer group are present, she is more likely to give good evidence than if she's all by herself."

It was already rather obvious that Tusanne came to life when the dogs came in. She was still stretching her neck out in a somewhat provocative manner.

People looked at her and started wondering, "Wow, she's gorgeous."

They saw how the dogs were so happy to see her. Somehow they got dogs from right around where she was found in the jungle. These dogs were part of her clan.

The judge brought the circumstances forward. "Okay. The video's hooked up?"

"Yes, Your Honor," the ambassador was pleased to note.

"So how do you want to proceed, counsel?"

"First, I have some questions for Tusanne and then I'd like to play a video."

"Very well, proceed."

"Tusanne, where are you from?"

She couldn't answer. She was silent.

The ambassador asked again, "Come on, tell us. Where are you from?"

She then used a kind of half-dog, half-cat, half-human language, where she barked and chirped out in a high and coming downward voice, "I don't know."

The voice was halting. The members of the press and the rest of the audience had not heard her speak before. It was just so strange to hear it. The dogs listened to her, every single word from her.

The ambassador then made this suggestion. "Your Honor, if I may, this is why we made a video. I believe we can ask her these questions if we show her a video and ask again."

"Is that the purpose of the video?"

"Yes."

"Proceed."

The video first opened to a scene of Bangkok. The ambassador put his hand out to the video and asked again, "Are you from here?"

Tusanne studied the video very carefully. She shook her head and said in a halting way, "Nooooo."

He fast-forwarded the video of the streets of Bangkok onto the suburbs of Bangkok, and showed the place where the courthouse now was, the King's summer palace.

The ambassador showed her the King's summer palace and asked the question again, "Are you from here?"

She quickly knew the answer to this. "Nooooo."

Her voice each time went from a start of a high chirp, cat-like hiss and then continued to go down in tone and ended up in a dog-like low growl and grumble, with elements of human sounds in between. The word no was clearly perceptible in this odd exchange.

He then proceeded to show the next scene. It was a picture of downtown Phnom Penh. The pictures showed the King's palace there, a beautiful majestic place. It showed a different street with lots of little cars, motorcycles, small buildings, small businesses. It showed a gorgeous hotel with a beautiful lobby in it. It showed some monuments. It showed people running around. It showed a river with homes not so nice coming to the river. It showed a busy market square. It showed a scene with a concrete rhinoceros with a couple of boys sitting on it. It showed some scenes of dancers. It showed some scenes of a gymnastics studio. It showed a theater where a ballet was playing. It showed ballerinas. It showed the opening of the curtains for the ballet. It showed a gymnast scene in some major international competition. It showed some women winning medals. Then he stopped the video.

He turned to Tusanne. Her answer was obvious in the tears rolling down her face.

The dogs looked at her and wondered why she was crying. The court knew right away that this place, a place called Phnom Penh, was obviously her home.

The ambassador asked the obvious question anyway. "Is this your home?"

She wiped her tears. She looked up with a beautiful smile and in a high growl/hiss of a chirp, bird-like, cat-like, dog-like, said in an excited tone, "Yeeeeeeeeesssss."

That yes went from high to a rumbling low, but it was clearly yes.

Next was the photo that the doctor had before with the beautiful ballerina who was also a gymnast. It was up on the screen as a still shot. Tusanne's eyes got big. Her mouth went open. She stood up and grinned. She came over to the TV. She put her hands on the screen. She put her nose on the screen.

She put her mouth on the screen.

Without being asked, she explained, "Mama. Mama."

The journalists stopped taking notes and just watched.

The video showed a picture of a man that was known to be married to this very famous ballerina/gymnast. He was a decorated war hero in Cambodia, a member of the royal guard. The photo showed him with medals all over. The military uniform of the royal guard, a proud man.

She put her face up to her father's image and said, "Papa. Papa."

The ambassador let the situation stay right there. The next scene showed a picture of her mother and her father together. These were found in archives from Cambodian images placed up by people living outside of Cambodia. Anyone in Cambodia possessing these pictures would be arrested. They do not permit these kinds of photos from a prior time in the country's history, a time when the country had a Prince and a princess, a King and a queen, and palace guards to guard them.

The ambassador then showed a scene dated back in the year 1973. Members of a new government were shown arresting members of the Cambodian royal family. They took them away. There were lots of black and white photos, of scenes where a new government took away all kinds of people -- anybody connected to the King, anybody connected to royalty, anybody connected to the universities, anybody who was a professional, anybody who wore a pair of glasses. They were all taken away.

He showed pictures of people marching out of the city, into the fields of Cambodia.

Tusanne cried. The dogs whimpered with her. They knew that this is where they came in. Some of the people in the pictures were shown carrying babies. Some of those babies were just born. Some were a little bit older. There were some pictures of women being taken down into the rice paddies and drowned in the water.

Tusanne was crying. She put her hand against her eyes and covered them. She yelled out, "Stop!" It was a pure human stop. No cat growl, no dog meow, no bird chirping. It was a whole human stop.

The last scene showed a woman holding a baby with three armed and uniformed military officers pointing that she should go in the rice field with her baby, where she would be drowned and put to death. It was a harrowing scene too real for Tusanne.

324

The ambassador turned the TV off. The screen went blank. The courtroom was silent.

He then asked Tusanne the big question of the day. "Did you fear for your life when you killed the colonel?"

She was quiet. She wouldn't answer. Mainly, she didn't understand the question.

The doctor tried to help out, but there could be no further evidence coming from Tusanne at this point.

The best the ambassador could hope for was that the visual imagery and the impact it had on Tusanne fully answered the question.

The ambassador tried the question two more times, but he couldn't get an answer. She remained silent.

She stared, put her head down, shook her head and then said, "Why they kill my mama? Why they kill my papa?"

The ambassador knew the answer to that question but wouldn't give it. He took a handkerchief and gave it to her. She looked at it, put it in her hand. He showed her with his own hand to pat it on her cheeks, to dry up her tears. She got the idea and did that.

The ambassador said, "No further questions, Your Honor."

The judges turned to the prosecutor. "I don't know how you want to do this, but do you have any questions?"

The prosecutor stood, walked over to her. He studied her up and down. He tried to imagine a way in which he could ask a question but he couldn't. He shook his head. He came over to the dogs. They were quiet. They sniffed at his hand.

He turned to the judges. "No questions, Your Honor."

"Very well. You may step down."

The judges then realized, of course, she wouldn't understand that.

The good doctor got up and escorted her back to her seat.

"Any further witnesses?"

"None, Your Honor."

"The defense rests?"

"The defense rests."

"Any rebuttal witnesses by the prosecution?"

"None, Your Honor."

"Prosecution rests?"

"We rest."

"Very well. Court is hereby adjourned. We will be back tomorrow morning at nine o'clock to read our verdict."

With that, the judges closed the evidentiary portion of the trial, and slammed down the gavel. This made the dogs' ears perk up but they didn't bark or meow. They just watched as the three judges stood and walked out of the courtroom. They could tell that somehow the plight of their favorite human was in their hands.

The ambassador exited the courthouse after all the press. Everybody followed him. He walked out to the porch area of the King's summer palace. The first thing he could see was rather blinding. There must've been 50,000 people out there, wearing red shirts and holding signs up in support of Tusanne. "Free Tusanne. She's innocent." These signs were everywhere. There were multiple press helicopters. There were throngs of people from all over watching this trial. Probably 100 microphones awaited him.

"Mr. Ambassador, Mr. Ambassador, how do you feel about the way the trial went? Do you think she'll be convicted? Are they going to give her the death sentence? What's going to happen and what's going on with Agent Ko?"

"Ladies and gentlemen, please, please. I'm a rather emotional wreck right now, if you don't mind me saying so."

The ambassador clearly had never had any kind of trial like this. This was the kind of case that would bring even the most reserved attorney down to his knees. There was nothing this ambassador wanted more than to obtain an acquittal of his special client.

Ko walked out not long after the ambassador. The ambassador turned and looked at him, and started to piece something together.

"Agent Ko, please come here."

The press watched as the two men walked away. They followed.

The ambassador turned. "Please, may we have some privacy?"

They walked away, about 15 feet.

Ko asked, "Yes, ambassador?"

"What's going on with you and Tusanne?"

"Nothing's going on."

"Oh, come on. Something's going on. What is it?"

"I don't know."

"Are you withholding evidence in a murder trial? Are you obstructing justice?"

"No, I'm not."

The fact was, Ko didn't know. But there was something he did know. He forgot to tell the ambassador that there was a little situation out in the jungle, during the several hours of waiting time. When the colonel had been killed, Ko figured out that the helicopter could never be used because it got her too crazy and they had to wait for quite awhile for the transport teams to arrive.

How long does it take for a man to fall in love with a woman? A couple minutes?

During that time Ko had her calmed down, he looked at her. She had looked at him. He did something he shouldn't have done but he couldn't help it. He uncuffed her. He took her rope off.

And there was something that happened to her as well. You see, Ko, being a special agent, was not wearing a military outfit. He was in a suit. He was a very handsome man.

There was an animal magnetism, literally, between the two of them, and there was a situation that happened, that shouldn't have happened. But it did happen and it happened with an unstoppable force.

All the King's men and all the King's horses could never have separated them. How long does it take for a woman to fall in love with a man? The answer is the same exact time for a man to fall in love with a woman.

Inside the heat of the jungle, where nothing was there to stop the thrill of passion, two unlikely people fell in love and made a baby that, as events would show, would change the course of history for all of Thailand.

Dr. Theroux had overseen this discussion. Although he couldn't hear a word, he could tell by the seriousness of the ambassador's face what the subject matter was. It was highly unusual for a member of the defense team to be holding a gigantic secret, but the doctor was sworn to secrecy by the King himself. He would live up to that

327

promise. He knew that the best thing for Thailand was to keep this secret from the public, maybe.

That evening's press was preoccupied by speculation and commentary on the trial. All over Thailand, southeast Asia, China, Japan, the entire Asian continent was abuzz with analysis of the trial, of Tusanne's amazing testimony and the ultimate speculation -- what would happen to her? What would the court do?

The next morning, they moved Tusanne from the makeshift jail inside the King's palace into the courtroom. They brought her in at 8:30, just to make sure the press didn't interrupt the process.

The ambassador was there with her. They sat silently at the table.

At 8:50, they opened the courtroom doors. The press swept in to take every available seat.

By nine o'clock, all seats were filled. The ambassador and Dr. Theroux sat at the defense table with Tusanne. Three guards sat behind them. The prosecutor walked in with a briefcase. He nodded to the ambassador. The ambassador nodded back. The cameras were rolling.

At 9:05, the longest five minutes of Tusanne's life, the three judges came out and took their chairs. They would not look at her in the eye but she looked into theirs.

Just as the judge was about to speak, something unexpected happened. Tusanne looked at the ambassador with this terrified face, looked behind at the audience, turned to her left and proceeded to throw up a bunch of liquid, all over the courtroom floor.

She was so upset at having done this and so filled with misunderstanding about what caused it that she proceeded to cry and cry and cry.

The press, of course, was all over this.

The doctor stood up. He felt so guilty because of course he knew what had caused this.

The court clerk, a nice Thai woman, picked up the phone and within about one minute a janitor had arrived with a mop. Everybody had to wait while that janitor mopped up the liquid mess on the floor.

Tusanne continued to cry. Ko was in the front row. He watched as amazement as the woman of his dreams was showing to him their permanent connection.

Once the janitor wheeled out his mop and bucket set, the court resumed.

"Ambassador, may we proceed?"

"Yes, of course, Your Honor. I'm very sorry."

"No need to apologize. Let's just go forward."

"Very well."

The chief justice spoke. "We are, of course, mindful that the entire world watches. We wish to be seen as a fully developed nation, as a fair country, as a country where all people are afforded due process of law and the right to a fair trial. We are proud of this trial because we believe that we have done that and we have openly shown it to the world.

"We congratulate the defendant's attorney on doing an excellent job on an extremely impossible case and we wish to give this as an example of the friendliness and modernness of our country. We gave her the best lawyer this country has.

"But this case began with an unfortunate reality. It's a stone cold fact that the defendant committed an act of murder. We are certain that the world and others --"

The judges gazed down at Ko.

"Have fallen in love with the defendant. We are not cold reptiles ourselves, and have been impacted by her -- her presence, her grace, her story, her history -- all her wonderful beginnings, her tragic separation from her wonderful parents, leading to her life in the jungle and her having been brought up apparently by wild forest dogs. These are all amazing events, and events that have impacted our hearts and our emotion, not only as human beings but as judges and government servants.

"But we are servants of the law. It is not our prerogative to disregard the law. It is not within our power to nullify the law. It is our duty, pursuant to an oath of justice that the three of us took. Many years ago when we became justices, we took an oath to uphold the law, to interpret the law and to make decisions in accordance with the law.

"I remind everyone that even the defendant's expert, a man that we respect, a man whose opinion remains uncontradicted, even he was of a view that the self-defense asserted by the defense team applies only in the realm of the law of the jungle, and not in the realm of the law of man, of the law of Thailand.

"It is with regret that we must inform the world community, the press, this courtroom, and the defendant that we are bound to apply man's law, the law of

329

Thailand, not the law of the jungle. There are many laws out there to apply. There is God's law, there is natural law, and there is man's law. But we are here today in a court built by men applying law created by man, and the law that we have says that no person may take the life of another without having a particular justification or privilege."

"The privilege asserted in this circumstance is that of self-defense. It is a defense recognized in natural law, in God's law. It is a defense about self-preservation and it says that we do have a God-given right to defend ourselves."

"The problem in this case is that, there was no right to self-defense. The colonel, when he approached Tusanne on this day, as we all know, did nothing aggressive, did nothing violent, and did nothing to give the defendant the right to kill him. We accordingly find the defendant guilty of murder in the first degree."

With that pronouncement, the courtroom went crazy. People screamed and shouted. Outside, there was a roar of anger. This roar would be heard around the world.

The justices banged the gavel and ordered everyone back to composure, to permit the remainder of the court's judgment.

"The court has two roles here. The first was to make a pronouncement -- a finding of guilt or innocence, and we have done that and we find the defendant guilty.

"The second is to pass a sentence onto the defendant. This is where we have the worst day of our lives. Under our system of government, there is only one sentence for a finding of guilt for murder in the first degree -- and that is the death sentence. With coldness and shivering in our heart, on a day that we will look upon forever as the worst day of our lives, it is with great regret that we do collectively impose the sentence of death on the defendant, and order that she be taken out and killed by firing squad, this sentence to be carried out immediately."

The justices knew that the nation would need healing, that there would have to be a quick death.

"Your Honor, I request a stay of execution pending appeal to the Thai Supreme Court."

The justices looked at each other and knew there could only be one answer. "Granted, on conditions that your appeal be filed by the end of tomorrow."

"It will be done."

And with that, the court slammed down its gavel and completed the sentence that would tear Thailand apart at the seams.

Tusanne did not understand a word that the judges had said. Instead, she received a full report of what had happened from the look into Ko's eye. The tear said it all. Ko had witnessed the murder. He had given testimony of the murder and had unfortunately, intractably, given the very evidence that would send Tusanne to the firing squad. The worst day of the judge's life was nothing in comparison to the worst day of Ko's life.

ONE DROP OF TEARS FOR YOU
BY HERMAN FRANCK

Seems that nature always wants to renew

Twisters fires then skies of blue

But I've still got one drop of tears for you

Rolling down my cheeks, nothing I can do

One drop

One drop

Of tears for you

I've got one drop

One drop

Of tears for you

Of course I know our end is forever;

You will never again be here.

But I've still got One drop of tears for you

Rolling down my cheeks,

Nothing I can do.

One drop of tears for you.

One drop of tears for you

331

The appeal process would take about a month. Justice can happen quickly when the government is attempting to kill you. They kept Tusanne under a secret prison. As the months passed, she went into her third month of pregnancy. She was showing a little, but not enough for anyone to notice.

Predictably, the Supreme Court affirmed the death sentence and the finding of guilt, agreeing with the trial justices that the law of Thailand could only give one result to this case. The court ruled there was only one sentence -- a sentence of death.

During the time waiting for the Supreme Court decision, Tusanne had two regular visitors. One was Princess Lara, the King's youngest daughter. She was a beautiful, caring person, and had taken a keen interest in the plight of Tusanne. She begged her father to pardon this sweet girl, but her father was bound by a political problem, a problem that he explained over and over to deaf ears.

His daughter refused to listen. "Father, you cannot possibly execute this girl. It is obscene, it is inhuman."

"My darling daughter, you must understand --"

"Stop, father. I've heard your argument. I understand. The general says he won't protect you, but father, I have a different question for you to consider."

"Okay."

"Who is going to protect you from me?"

The father was taken aback by this direct challenge from his youngest daughter. She stood before him and did something quite un-princessly.

She pointed at him. "Hear my words, father. Hear my words. If you do not pardon this girl, you will lose your family."

The other princesses stood and stared down their father. The Prince did not share in this unity.

It came time for Tusanne to have her last and final appeal of her case. This was a pardon procedure. Under Thai law, all criminal defendants are granted the opportunity to present a case for a pardon. The conditions are the defendant MUST confess. Without a confession, Thai law prohibits a pardon. Here is where there was a problem with Tusanne. Getting her to confess to this crime was a little bit complicated.

The able ambassador appeared on her behalf before the summer palace. This was not a public event, so the press was not invited. But the press knew already what the result would be, and so did the ambassador. Outside the summer palace, there were more than 50,000 red-shirts, angrily waving flags of Thailand, and posters talking about the need for the King to pardon Tusanne.

One of the ironies of the jungle rural support of Tusanne was that it spearheaded an unexpected and extremely thorough investigation of the murder of Tusanne's parents. Their photos were put out on posters decrying the regime known as the Khmer Rouge, led by the now-dead leader Pol Pot. The United Nations and Cambodian extraordinary court proceedings by genocide charges were quoted in these posters.

There was no question that the regime had senselessly murdered somewhere up to 1.7 million of the former elites of the Cambodian nation. The United Nations and Cambodian government were cooperating in bringing four of the former leaders to trial in Cambodia. This caused a stir of examination into which of the 1.7 million victims should become the victims with a face. The appearance had been a collection of skeletal remains, a collection of skulls, and a Halloween-looking archive of literally millions of dead.

The answer, of course, was Tusanne's parents. They would become the face of that genocide trial and would become the lightning rod for justice in Cambodia for what had happened to them. As this message came out, the idea that Tusanne had acted in self-defense came out all again. She was literally reacting to a senseless genocide, torture, and mass murder committed by an outrageous regime that took hold in Cambodia.

The King looked out his window and saw the red-shirts angrily holding the evidence of genocide up, screaming to the King, "You must pardon her! You must pardon her!"

There were signs saying, "We will never forgive. We will never forget." There were letters to the King from literally every ambassador of the world, even the Saudi Arabian ambassador. The collection of letters was on the King's desk. He was reading the most recent one, from the President of the United States.

"Your Excellency, I urge you to please grant Tusanne a pardon. We all know what happened in Cambodia. It will all come to light in the upcoming genocide trial. Please see that she is not a victim again. Regards, the President of the United States of America."

333

It's pretty hard to turn down all these world leaders, but the King also knew that he had to have the support of the general. The general was present at the pardon. He didn't have to say a word. The King was well aware that the general could easily snap his fingers and cause the military to stand down, and that if this did occur, the red-shirts would take over. And high on the red-shirts' list was a desire to eliminate the royal family. Not by a senseless murder, but by a constitutional amendment that would end the millennia of royal authority in Thailand. The royal family would be no more.

The King was well aware of this, and was duty-bound to his own ancestors to decline this pardon. But of course, he couldn't explain it that way. He had to explain it a different way.

When Tusanne was brought into the royal chambers, she was greeted by the ambassador, the doctor, her nurse and the entire royal family. Also present was Ko. Ko had accompanied Lara on her visits to the jail. During these visits, Ko and Lara had struck up a bond, a friendship. Lara could see the love in Ko's face and could see rather obviously that he had a bond with Tusanne.

As they walked out of the jail, she told him very clearly, "Do not worry, Ko. I am going to save her."

Ko smiled. He adored the princess. He had known her since he was just a child. He was proud of how she'd become a young woman, how she had stood up to her father, how she had taken a mission to save a girl named Tusanne, a girl that meant everything in the world to Ko.

Princess Lara smiled at Tusanne and glanced over to Ko. He saw her smile at her as well. Lara had seen Tusanne many times at the jail. But today, there was something different about her. Today she was not wearing the baggy clothes. There may have been some issue about the laundry at the jail. Today she was wearing tighter clothes. There was something that made Lara gasp for air. She could tell. Tusanne was pregnant.

She turned to her father with big eyes, and without saying a word she could see the guilt, that her father had known during the entire time.

Tusanne was now a little over six months pregnant. Lara walked over to Tusanne and hugged her. Tusanne hugged her back. When Lara did this, she brought her hands down to Tusanne's stomach. Tusanne trusted her. Lara felt the baby kick.

She turned to her father and shook her head. "You knew."

She turned back to Tusanne and lifted up her shirt about halfway up her abdomen, showing a clearly pregnant woman.

The Prince knew as well. He put his head down. The other princesses did not know, and put their hands to their mouths.

Ko finally knew the answer to the question, why did he cry? He stood. He walked over to Tusanne. He put his hand on her stomach. Lara had her hand on her stomach. Tusanne smiled at the only two people that she would ever let touch her in this way.

Ko turned to the King. "Your Majesty, surely you are not going to execute a pregnant woman."

The King knew that his job became a thousand times harder. He looked at Tusanne with tears in his eyes. He knew his daughter would never in a million years forgive him. He looked out the window and saw 50,000 red-shirts. When word got out to them that Tusanne was pregnant, oh my. There would be hell to pay. For a King to execute this pregnant hero would be so unforgiveable that he might as well pack his bags and fly off to Cambodia, and live the rest of his life in the jungle.

He turned and looked at the general. The general was stone-faced. The King knew the whole position of the general. It didn't matter that Tusanne was pregnant. She took a life. She must give a life. It is a question of balance. The justice of Thailand required it. The law required it, and if it wasn't done right, the general would see that the King's days would be numbered.

It was almost like whatever he did would result in the same outcome. Either he would deny the pardon and see Tusanne executed, in which case he would lose his daughters or the daughters would go over to the red-shirts and would see to it that the royal family toppled. All of the King's mens and all of the King's horses would never put him back together again.

On the other hand, if he pardoned her, the general would withdraw the military from his support and would allow the red-shirts to take over.

This is where it's good to have a wise ambassador in the room. The wise Ambassador Baba came to the King and had a suggestion. He whispered it into the King's ear. The King smiled. The King brought the pardon proceedings to order.

335

"Princess Lara, you will remain by the side of Tusanne. Agent Ko, you will remain by the side of Tusanne. Mr. Ambassador, do you have a request of the king?"

"I do, Your Royal Highness."

"Please state the request."

"I request the full pardon of Tusanne."

"Does she admit her guilt?"

He turned to Tusanne.

She spoke in a way that a mother speaks to save her child. No barking, no chirping. It was pure human language.

"My King, I admit my guilt."

These were the words that would set her free.

"By the power vested in the Constitution of the nation of Thailand, I hereby decree that Tusanne be granted a full pardon under the following conditions. Condition number one, Tusanne is hereby adopted into the royal family as my daughter. Condition number two, Agent Ko, I request that you marry her."

Agent Ko stood. "It would be a dream of all dreams for me to marry the love of all loves."

"Agent Ko, I request that you marry her RIGHT NOW."

Ko turned to Tusanne. He got on his knees. He looked around for a ring. Of course he didn't have one. He was not expecting this to occur.

Lara had a beautiful ring on her finger. It was 300 years old, and bore the royal crest. She removed it. It had emeralds and diamonds that sparkled gorgeously. She handed it to Ko.

Ko looked up at the pregnant abdomen of the most beautiful woman in the world and asked her, "Would you make me the happiest man on Earth and agree to marry me?"

Tusanne gave out a primal yelp. It went at a high pitch and came down to a rumbling roar of a wolf-like, dog-like, bird-like, cat-like, human-like, "Yes, I will."

"The marriage of Agent Ko and Tusanne is hereby solemnized. You two are now declared by royal decree to be husband and wife. Ko, you may now kiss the bride."

He kissed her in a way that made everybody blush. It's supposed to be just a simple peck, but this was a kiss of a lifetime. This was a kiss of rather than dying tomorrow, you are going to live forever.

The King interrupted, "I'm not done."

The ambassador smiled. He knew the next part was the best of all.

The King looked at his son and put his hand on his shoulder. He knew his son had many expectations in life, and that what he was about to say would be a huge disappointment. He walked over to Tusanne, got down before her and put his cheek on her stomach and listened to the heartbeat of his son. He stood. He put his hand on her shoulder. He put his hand on Ko's shoulder.

"I hereby decree that I will make a rare exception to the law of primogenitor. The man who will become King will be the unborn child in Tusanne."

He turned to the general and said, "Please join me in this event. Please join me."

He then turned back to his family and smiled. "Welcome to the royal family."

Tusanne smiled. She cried. The King stood back. His able servant had written all of these conditions down on a parchment paper and handed them to the King. The King took out his pen and wrote down the words that would make it all so: It is so decreed. He signed it.

The able servant took that decree, made a copy of it, scanned it into a PDF and sent it off to more than 100 international newspapers, including Angela's. They would immediately report that Tusanne would forever be known as Princess Tusanne, and her son would become King of all of Thailand, and nobody but nobody could do a damn thing about it. It was so decreed by the King of Thailand.

It was a solution to an impossible problem. With Tusanne as princess, her son as stated heir to the throne, the red shirts would now at last accep the royal family as a partner for the people that lived in the jungles of Thailand.

As Tusanne lived and breathed, the Royal Family would live and breathe.

APPENDICES

Appendix A

Series of Diagnostic Criteria of psychiatric disorders From American Psychiatric Association: Diagnostic and Statistical Manual of Mental Disorders,Fourth Edition, Text Revision. Washington, DC, American Psychiatric Association, 2000

[DSM-IV-TR [4th Ed.]]

Table of Contents

Appendix A

Appendix A-2A: Specific phobia

From American Psychiatric Association: Diagnostic and Statistical Manual of Mental Disorders,Fourth Edition, Text Revision. Washington, DC, American Psyychiatric Association, 2000

[DSM-IV-TR [4th Ed.]]

300.29 Specific Phobia (formerly Simple Phobia)

Diagnostic criteria for

300.29

Specific Phobia

Marked and persistent fear that is excessive or unreasonable, cued by the presence or anticipation of a specific object or situation (e.g., flying, heights, animals, receiving an injection, seeing blood).Exposure to the phobic stimulus almost invariably provokes an immediate anxiety response, which may take the form of a situationally bound or situationally predisposed Panic Attack. Note: In children, the anxiety may be expressed by crying, tantrums, freezing, or clinging.The person recognizes that the fear is excessive or unreasonable. Note: In children, this feature may be absent.The phobic situation(s) is avoided or else is endured with intense anxiety or distress.The avoidance, anxious anticipation, or distress in the feared situation(s) interferes significantly with the person's normal routine, occupational (or academic) functioning, or social activities or relationships, or there is marked distress about having the phobia.In individuals under age 18 years, the duration is at least 6 months.The anxiety, Panic Attacks, or phobic avoidance associated with the specific object or situation are not better accounted for by another mental disorder, such as Obsessive-Compulsive Disorder (e.g., fear of dirt in someone with an obsession about contamination), Posttraumatic Stress Disorder (e.g., avoidance of stimuli associated with a severe stressor), Separation Anxiety Disorder (e.g., avoidance of school), Social Phobia (e.g., avoidance of social situations because of fear of embarrassment), Panic Disorder With Agoraphobia, or Agoraphobia Without History of Panic Disorder.

Specify type:

Animal Type Natural Environment Type (e.g., heights, storms, water)Blood-Injection-Injury Type Situational Type (e.g., airplanes, elevators, enclosed places)Other Type (e.g., fear of choking, vomiting, or contracting an illness; in children, fear of loud sounds or costumed characters)

Diagnostic Features

The essential feature of Specific Phobia is marked and persistent fear of clearly discernible, circumscribed objects or situations (Criterion A). Exposure to the phobic stimulus almost invariably provokes an immediate anxiety response (Criterion B). This response may take the form of a situationally bound or situationally predisposed Panic Attack (see Features). Although adolescents and adults with this disorder recognize that their fear is excessive or unreasonable (Criterion C), this may not be the case with children. Most often, the phobic stimulus is avoided, although it is sometimes endured with dread (Criterion D). The diagnosis is appropriate only if the avoidance, fear, or anxious anticipation of encountering the phobic stimulus interferes significantly with the person's daily routine, occupational functioning, or social life, or if the person is markedly distressed about having the phobia (Criterion E). In individuals under age 18 years, symptoms must have persisted for at least 6 months before Specific Phobia is diagnosed (Criterion F). The anxiety, Panic Attacks, or phobic avoidance are not better accounted for by another mental disorder (e.g., Obsessive-Compulsive Disorder, Posttraumatic Stress Disorder, Separation Anxiety Disorder, Social Phobia, Panic Disorder With Agoraphobia, or Agoraphobia Without History of Panic Disorder) (Criterion G).

The individual experiences a marked, persistent, and excessive or unreasonable fear when in the presence of, or when anticipating an encounter with, a specific object or situation. The focus of the fear may be anticipated harm from some aspect of the object or situation (e.g., an individual may fear air travel because of a concern about crashing, may fear dogs because of concerns about being bitten, or may fear driving because of concerns about being hit by other vehicles on the road). Specific Phobias may also involve concerns about losing control, panicking, somatic manifestations of anxiety and fear (such as increased heart rate or shortness of breath), and fainting that might occur on exposure to the feared object. For example, individuals afraid of blood and injury may also worry about the possibility of fainting; people afraid of heights may also worry about dizziness; and people afraid of closed-in situations may also worry about losing control and screaming. These concerns may be particularly strong in the Situational Type of Specific Phobia.

Anxiety is almost invariably felt immediately on confronting the phobic stimulus (e.g., a person with a Specific Phobia of cats will almost invariably have an immediate anxiety response when forced to confront a cat). The level of anxiety or fear usually varies as a function of both the degree of proximity to the phobic stimulus (e.g., fear intensifies as the cat approaches and decreases as the cat withdraws) and the degree to which escape from the phobic stimulus is limited (e.g., fear intensifies as the elevator approaches the midway point between floors and decreases as the doors open at the next floor). However, the intensity of the fear may not always relate predictably to the phobic stimulus (e.g., a person afraid of heights may experience variable amounts of fear when crossing the same bridge on different occasions). Sometimes full-blown Panic Attacks are experienced in response to the phobic stimulus, especially when the person must remain in the situation or believes that escape will be impossible. Occasionally, the Panic Attacks are delayed and do not occur immediately upon confronting the phobic stimulus. This delay is more likely in the Situational Type. Because marked anticipatory anxiety occurs if the person is confronted with the necessity of entering into the phobic situation, such situations are usually avoided. Less commonly, the person forces himself or herself to endure the phobic situation, but it is experienced with intense anxiety.

Adults with this disorder recognize that the phobia is excessive or unreasonable. The diagnosis would be Delusional Disorder instead of Specific Phobia for an individual who avoids an elevator because of a conviction that it has been sabotaged and who does not recognize that this fear is excessive and unreasonable. Moreover, the diagnosis should not be given if the fear is reasonable given the context of the stimuli (e.g., fear of being shot in a hunting area or a dangerous neighborhood). Insight into the excessive or unreasonable nature of the fear tends to increase with age and is not required to make the diagnosis in children.

Fears of circumscribed objects or situations are very common, especially in children, but in many cases the degree of impairment is insufficient to warrant a diagnosis. If the phobia does not significantly interfere with the individual's functioning or cause marked distress, the diagnosis is not made. For example, a person who is afraid of snakes to the point of expressing intense fear in the presence of snakes would not receive a diagnosis of Specific Phobia if he or she lives in an area devoid of snakes, is not restricted in activities by the fear of snakes, and is not distressed about having a fear of snakes.

Subtypes

The following subtypes may be specified to indicate the focus of fear or avoidance in Specific Phobia (e.g., Specific Phobia, Animal Type).

Animal Type. This subtype should be specified if the fear is cued by animals or insects. This subtype generally has a childhood onset.Natural Environment Type. This subtype should be specified if the fear is cued by objects in the natural environment, such as storms, heights, or water. This subtype generally has a childhood onset.Blood-Injection-Injury Type. This subtype should be specified if the fear is cued by seeing blood or an injury or by receiving an injection or other invasive medical procedure. This subtype is highly familial and is often characterized by a strong vasovagal response.Situational Type. This subtype should be specified if the fear is cued by a specific situation such as public transportation, tunnels, bridges, elevators, flying, driving, or enclosed places. This subtype has a bimodal age-at-onset distribution, with one peak in childhood and another peak in the mid-20s. This subtype appears to be similar to Panic Disorder With Agoraphobia in its characteristic sex ratios, familial aggregation pattern, and age at onset.Other Type. This subtype should be specified if the fear is cued by other stimuli. These stimuli might include the fear of choking, vomiting, or contracting an illness; "space" phobia (i.e., the individual is afraid of falling down if away from walls or other means of physical support); and children's fears of loud sounds or costumed characters.

The frequency of the subtypes in adult clinical settings, from most to least frequent, is Situational; Natural Environment; Blood-Injection-Injury; and Animal. Studies of community samples show a slightly different pattern, with phobias of heights and of spiders, mice, and insects most common, and phobias of other animals and other elements of the natural environment, such as storms, thunder, and lightning, least common. Phobias of closed-in situations (a Situational Type of phobia) may be more common in the elderly. In many cases, more than one subtype of Specific Phobia is present. Having one phobia of a specific subtype tends to increase the likelihood of having another phobia from within the same subtype (e.g., fear of cats and snakes).

346

When more than one subtype applies, they should all be noted (e.g., Specific Phobia, Animal and Natural Environment Types).

Associated Features and Disorders

Associated descriptive features and mental disorders.

Specific Phobia may result in a restricted lifestyle or interference with certain occupations, depending on the type of phobia. For example, job promotion may be threatened by avoidance of air travel, and social activities may be restricted by fears of crowded or closed-in places. Specific Phobias frequently co-occur with other Anxiety Disorders, Mood Disorders, and Substance-Related Disorders. For example, in community samples, rates of co-occurrence with other disorders range from 50% to 80%, and these rates may be higher among individuals with early-onset Specific Phobias. In clinical settings, Specific Phobias are very common comorbid diagnoses with other disorders. However, Specific Phobias are rarely the focus of clinical attention in these situations. The Specific Phobia is usually associated with less distress or less interference with functioning than the comorbid main diagnosis. Overall, only 12%–30% are estimated to seek professional help for their Specific Phobias. In the absence of other diagnoses, help seeking for Specific Phobias is more likely with more functionally impairing phobias (e.g., phobias of objects or situations that are commonly encountered), multiple phobias, and Panic Attacks in the phobic context. In contrast, individuals with irrational fears of blood injury, medical procedures, and medical settings may be less likely to seek help for phobias.

Associated physical examination findings and general medical conditions.

A vasovagal fainting response is characteristic of Blood-Injection-Injury Type Specific Phobias; approximately 75% of such individuals report a history of fainting in these situations. The physiological response is characterized by an initial brief acceleration of heart rate and elevation in blood pressure followed by a deceleration of heart rate and a drop in blood pressure, which contrasts with the usual acceleration of heart rate and elevation in blood pressure in other Specific Phobias. Certain general medical conditions may be exacerbated as a consequence of phobic avoidance. For example, Specific Phobias, Blood-Injection-Injury Type, may have detrimental effects on dental or physical health, because the individual may avoid obtaining necessary medical care.

Similarly, fears of choking may have a detrimental effect on health when food is limited to substances that are easy to swallow or when oral medication is avoided.

Specific Culture, Age, and Gender Features

The content of phobias varies with culture and ethnicity. For example, fears of magic or spirits are present in many cultures and should be considered a Specific Phobia only if the fear is excessive in the context of that culture and causes significant impairment or distress. Specific Phobias may be more common in the lower socioeconomic strata, although the data are mixed.

In children, the anxiety may be expressed by crying, tantrums, freezing, or clinging. Children often do not recognize that the fears are excessive or unreasonable and rarely report distress about having the phobias. Fears of animals and other objects in the natural environment are particularly common and are usually transitory in childhood. A diagnosis of Specific Phobia is not warranted unless the fears lead to clinically significant impairment (e.g., unwillingness to go to school for fear of encountering a dog on the street).

Overall, the ratio of women to men with Specific Phobias is approximately 2:1, even among the elderly. However, the sex ratio varies across different types of Specific Phobias. Approximately 75%–90% of individuals with the Animal and Natural Environment Type are female (except for fear of heights, where the percentage of females is 55%–70%). Similarly, approximately 75%–90% of individuals with the Situational Type are female. Approximately 55%–70% of individuals with the Blood-Injection-Injury Type are female.

Prevalence

Although phobias are common in the general population, they rarely result in sufficient impairment or distress to warrant a diagnosis of Specific Phobia. The reported prevalence may vary depending on the threshold used to determine impairment or distress and the number of types of phobias surveyed. In community samples, current prevalence rates range from 4% to 8.8%, and lifetime prevalence rates range from 7.2% to 11.3%. Prevalence rates decline in the elderly. Also, prevalence estimates vary for different types of Specific Phobias.

Course

The first symptoms of a Specific Phobia usually occur in childhood or early adolescence and may occur at a younger age for women than for men. Also, the mean age at onset varies according to the type of Specific Phobia. Age at onset for Specific Phobia, Situational Type, tends to be bimodally distributed, with a peak in childhood and a second peak in the mid-20s. Specific Phobias, Natural Environment Type (e.g., height phobia), tend to begin primarily in childhood, although many new cases of height phobia develop in early adulthood. The ages at onset for Specific Phobias, Animal Type, and for Specific Phobias, Blood-Injection-Injury Type, are also usually in childhood. Fear of a stimulus is usually present for some time before becoming sufficiently distressing or impairing to be considered a Specific Phobia.

Predisposing factors to the onset of Specific Phobias include traumatic events (such as being attacked by an animal or trapped in a closet), unexpected Panic Attacks in the to-be-feared situation, observation of others undergoing trauma or demonstrating fearfulness (such as observing others fall from heights or become afraid in the presence of certain animals), and informational transmission (e.g., repeated parental warnings about the dangers of certain animals or media coverage of airplane crashes). Feared objects or situations tend to involve things that may actually represent a threat or have represented a threat at some point in the course of human evolution. Phobias that result from traumatic events or unexpected Panic Attacks tend to be particularly acute in their development. Phobias of traumatic origin do not have a characteristic age at onset (e.g., fear of choking, which usually follows a choking or near-choking incident, may develop at almost any age). Specific Phobias in adolescence increase the chances of either persistence of the Specific Phobia or development of additional Specific Phobias in early adulthood but do not predict the development of other disorders. Phobias that persist into adulthood remit only infrequently (around 20% of cases).

Familial Pattern

There is an increased risk for Specific Phobias in family members of those with Specific Phobias. Also, there is some evidence to suggest that there may be an aggregation within families by type of phobia (e.g., first-degree biological relatives of persons with

Specific Phobias, Animal Type, are likely to have animal phobias, although not necessarily of the same animal, and first-degree biological relatives of persons with Specific Phobias, Situational Type, are likely to have phobias of situations). Fears of blood and injury have particularly strong familial patterns.

Differential Diagnosis

Specific Phobias differ from most other Anxiety Disorders in levels of intercurrent anxiety. Typically, individuals with Specific Phobia, unlike those with Panic Disorder With Agoraphobia, do not present with pervasive anxiety, because their fear is limited to specific, circumscribed objects or situations. However, generalized anxious anticipation may emerge under conditions in which encounters with the phobic stimulus become more likely (e.g., when a person who is fearful of snakes moves to a desert area) or when life events force immediate confrontation with the phobic stimulus (e.g., when a person who is fearful of flying is forced by circumstances to fly).

Differentiation of Specific Phobia, Situational Type, from Panic Disorder With Agoraphobia may be particularly difficult because both disorders may include Panic Attacks and avoidance of similar types of situations (e.g., driving, flying, public transportation, and enclosed places). Prototypically, Panic Disorder With Agoraphobia is characterized by the initial onset of unexpected Panic Attacks and the subsequent avoidance of multiple situations thought to be likely triggers of the Panic Attacks. Prototypically, Specific Phobia, Situational Type, is characterized by situational avoidance in the absence of recurrent unexpected Panic Attacks. Some presentations fall between these prototypes and require clinical judgment in the selection of the most appropriate diagnosis. Four factors can be helpful in making this judgment: the focus of fear, the type and number of Panic Attacks, the number of situations avoided, and the level of intercurrent anxiety. For example, an individual who had not previously feared or avoided elevators has a Panic Attack in an elevator and begins to dread going to work because of the need to take the elevator to his office on the 24th floor. If this individual subsequently has Panic Attacks only in elevators (even if the focus of fear is on the Panic Attack), then a diagnosis of Specific Phobia may be appropriate. If, however, the individual experiences unexpected Panic Attacks in other situations and begins to avoid or endure with dread other situations because of fear of a Panic Attack, then a diagnosis of Panic Disorder With Agoraphobia would be warranted. Furthermore, the presence of pervasive apprehension about having a Panic Attack even when not anticipating exposure to a phobic situation also supports a diagnosis of Panic Disorder With Agoraphobia. If the individual has additional unexpected Panic Attacks in other situations but no additional avoidance or endurance with dread develops, then the appropriate diagnosis would be Panic Disorder Without Agoraphobia.

Concurrent diagnoses of Specific Phobia and Panic Disorder With Agoraphobia are sometimes warranted. In these cases, consideration of the focus of the individual's concern about the phobic situation may be helpful. For example, avoidance of being alone because of concern about having unexpected Panic Attacks warrants a diagnosis of Panic Disorder With Agoraphobia (if other criteria are met), whereas the additional phobic avoidance of air travel, if due to worries about bad weather conditions and crashing, may warrant an additional diagnosis of Specific Phobia.

Specific Phobia and Social Phobia can be differentiated on the basis of the focus of the fears. For example, avoidance of eating in a restaurant may be based on concerns about negative evaluation from others (i.e., Social Phobia) or concerns about choking (i.e., Specific Phobia). In contrast to the avoidance in Specific Phobia, the avoidance in Posttraumatic Stress Disorder follows a life-threatening stressor and is accompanied by additional features (e.g., reexperiencing the trauma and restricted affect). In Obsessive-Compulsive Disorder, the avoidance is associated with the content of the obsession (e.g., dirt, contamination). In individuals with Separation Anxiety Disorder, a diagnosis of Specific Phobia is not given if the avoidance behavior is exclusively limited to fears of separation from persons to whom the individual is attached. Moreover, children with Separation Anxiety Disorder often have associated exaggerated fears of people or events (e.g., of muggers, burglars, kidnappers, car accidents, airplane travel) that might threaten the integrity of the family. A separate diagnosis of Specific Phobia would rarely be warranted.

The differentiation between Hypochondriasis and a Specific Phobia, Other Type (i.e., avoidance of situations that may lead to contracting an illness), depends on the presence or absence of disease conviction. Individuals with Hypochondriasis are preoccupied with fears of having a disease, whereas individuals with a Specific Phobia fear contracting a disease (but do not believe it is already present). In individuals with

Anorexia Nervosa and Bulimia Nervosa, a diagnosis of Specific Phobia is not given if the avoidance behavior is exclusively limited to avoidance of food and food-related cues. An individual with Schizophrenia or another Psychotic Disorder may avoid certain activities in response to delusions, but does not recognize that the fear is excessive or unreasonable.

Fears are very common, particularly in childhood, but they do not warrant a diagnosis of Specific Phobia unless there is significant interference with social, educational, or occupational functioning or marked distress about having the phobia.

Appendix A-2B: Post traumatic stress disorder

From the DSM-IV-TR [4th Ed.] Published by the American Psychiatric Association [APA]. Copyright APA. Used with Permission

309.81 Posttraumatic Stress Disorder

Diagnostic criteria for

309.81

Posttraumatic Stress Disorder

The person has been exposed to a traumatic event in which both of the following were present:the person experienced, witnessed, or was confronted with an event or events that involved actual or threatened death or serious injury, or a threat to the physical integrity of self or othersthe person's response involved intense fear, helplessness, or horror. Note: In children, this may be expressed instead by disorganized or agitated behaviorThe traumatic event is persistently reexperienced in one (or more) of the following ways:recurrent and intrusive distressing recollections of the event, including images, thoughts, or perceptions. Note: In young children, repetitive play may occur in which themes or aspects of the trauma are expressed.recurrent distressing dreams of the event. Note: In children, there may be frightening dreams without recognizable content.acting or feeling as if the traumatic event were recurring (includes a sense of reliving the experience, illusions, hallucinations, and dissociative flashback episodes, including those that occur on awakening or when intoxicated). Note: In young children, trauma-specific reenactment may occur.intense psychological distress at exposure to internal or external cues that symbolize or resemble an aspect of the traumatic eventphysiological reactivity on exposure to internal or external cues that symbolize or resemble an aspect of the traumatic eventPersistent avoidance of stimuli associated with the trauma and numbing of general responsiveness (not present before the trauma), as indicated by three (or more) of the following:efforts to avoid thoughts, feelings, or conversations associated with the traumaefforts to avoid activities, places, or people that arouse recollections of the traumainability to recall an important aspect of the traumamarkedly diminished interest or participation in significant activitiesfeeling of detachment or estrangement from othersrestricted range of affect (e.g., unable to have loving feelings)sense of a foreshortened future (e.g., does not expect to have a career, marriage, children, or a normal life span)Persistent symptoms of increased arousal (not present before the trauma), as indicated by two (or more) of the following:difficulty

354

falling or staying a sleep irritability or outbursts of anger difficulty concentrating hypervigilance exaggerated startle responseDuration of the disturbance (symptoms in Criteria B, C, and D) is more than 1 month.The disturbance causes clinically significant distress or impairment in social, occupational, or other important areas of functioning.

Specify if:

Acute: if duration of symptoms is less than 3 monthsChronic: if duration of symptoms is 3 months or more

Specify if:

With Delayed Onset: if onset of symptoms is at least 6 months after the stressor

Diagnostic Features

The essential feature of Posttraumatic Stress Disorder is the development of characteristic symptoms following exposure to an extreme traumatic stressor involving direct personal experience of an event that involves actual or threatened death or serious injury, or other threat to one's physical integrity; or witnessing an event that involves death, injury, or a threat to the physical integrity of another person; or learning about unexpected or violent death, serious harm, or threat of death or injury experienced by a family member or other close associate (Criterion A1). The person's response to the event must involve intense fear, helplessness, or horror (or in children, the response must involve disorganized or agitated behavior) (Criterion A2). The characteristic symptoms resulting from the exposure to the extreme trauma include persistent reexperiencing of the traumatic event (Criterion B), persistent avoidance of stimuli associated with the trauma and numbing of general responsiveness (Criterion C), and persistent symptoms of increased arousal (Criterion D). The full symptom picture must be present for more than 1 month (Criterion E), and the disturbance must cause clinically significant distress or impairment in social, occupational, or other important areas of functioning (Criterion F).

Traumatic events that are experienced directly include, but are not limited to, military combat, violent personal assault (sexual assault, physical attack, robbery, mugging), being kidnapped, being taken hostage, terrorist attack, torture, incarceration as a prisoner of war or in a concentration camp, natural or manmade disasters, severe automobile accidents, or being diagnosed with a life-threatening illness. For children, sexually traumatic events may include developmentally inappropriate sexual experiences without threatened or actual violence or injury. Witnessed events include, but are not limited to, observing the serious injury or unnatural death of another person due to violent assault, accident, war, or disaster or unexpectedly witnessing a dead body or body parts. Events experienced by others that are learned about include, but are not limited to, violent personal assault, serious accident, or serious injury experienced by a family member or a close friend; learning about the sudden, unexpected death of a family member or a close friend; or learning that one's child has a life-threatening disease. The disorder may be especially severe or long lasting when the stressor is of human design (e.g., torture, rape). The likelihood of developing this disorder may increase as the intensity of and physical proximity to the stressor increase. The traumatic event can be reexperienced in various ways. Commonly the person has recurrent and intrusive recollections of the event (Criterion B1) or recurrent distressing dreams during which the event can be replayed or otherwise represented (Criterion B2). In rare instances, the person experiences dissociative states that last from a few seconds to several hours, or even days, during which components of the event are relived and the person behaves as though experiencing the event at that moment (Criterion B3). These episodes, often referred to as "flashbacks," are typically brief but can be associated with prolonged distress and heightened arousal. Intense psychological distress (Criterion B4) or physiological reactivity (Criterion B5) often occurs when the person is exposed to triggering events that resemble or symbolize an aspect of the traumatic event (e.g., anniversaries of the traumatic event; cold, snowy weather or uniformed guards for survivors of death camps in cold climates; hot, humid weather for combat veterans of the South Pacific; entering any elevator for a woman who was raped in an elevator).

Stimuli associated with the trauma are persistently avoided. The person commonly makes deliberate efforts to avoid thoughts, feelings, or conversations about the traumatic event (Criterion C1) and to avoid activities, situations, or people who arouse recollections of it (Criterion C2). This avoidance of reminders may include amnesia for an important aspect of the traumatic event (Criterion C3). Diminished responsiveness to the external world, referred to as "psychic numbing" or "emotional anesthesia," usually begins soon after the traumatic event. The individual may complain of having markedly diminished interest or participation in previously enjoyed activities (Criterion C4), of feeling detached or estranged from other people (Criterion C5), or of having markedly reduced ability to feel emotions (especially those associated with intimacy, tenderness, and sexuality) (Criterion C6). The individual may have a sense of a foreshortened future (e.g., not expecting to have a career, marriage, children, or a normal life span) (Criterion C7).

The individual has persistent symptoms of anxiety or increased arousal that were not present before the trauma. These symptoms may include difficulty falling or staying asleep that may be due to recurrent nightmares during which the traumatic event is relived (Criterion D1), hypervigilance (Criterion D4), and exaggerated startle response (Criterion D5). Some individuals report irritability or outbursts of anger (Criterion D2) or difficulty concentrating or completing tasks (Criterion D3).

Specifiers

The following specifiers may be used to specify onset and duration of the symptoms of Posttraumatic Stress Disorder:

Acute. This specifier should be used when the duration of symptoms is less than 3 months.Chronic. This specifier should be used when the symptoms last 3 months or longer.With Delayed Onset. This specifier indicates that at least 6 months have passed between the traumatic event and the onset of the symptoms.

Associated Features and Disorders

Associated descriptive features and mental disorders.

Individuals with Posttraumatic Stress Disorder may describe painful guilt feelings about surviving when others did not survive or about the things they had to do to survive. Avoidance patterns may interfere with interpersonal relationships and lead to marital conflict, divorce, or loss of job. Auditory hallucinations and paranoid ideation can be present in some severe and chronic cases. The following associated constellation of symptoms may occur and are more commonly seen in association with an interpersonal stressor (e.g., childhood sexual or physical abuse, domestic battering): impaired affect modulation; self-destructive and impulsive behavior; dissociative symptoms; somatic complaints; feelings of ineffectiveness, shame, despair, or hopelessness; feeling permanently damaged; a loss of previously sustained beliefs; hostility; social withdrawal; feeling constantly threatened; impaired relationships with others; or a change from the individual's previous personality characteristics.

Posttraumatic Stress Disorder is associated with increased rates of Major Depressive Disorder, Substance-Related Disorders, Panic Disorder, Agoraphobia, Obsessive-Compulsive Disorder, Generalized Anxiety Disorder, Social Phobia, Specific Phobia, and Bipolar Disorder. These disorders can either precede, follow, or emerge concurrently with the onset of Posttraumatic Stress Disorder.

Associated laboratory findings.

Increased arousal may be measured through studies of autonomic functioning (e.g., heart rate, electromyography, sweat gland activity).

Associated physical examination findings and general medical conditions.

Physical injuries may occur as a direct consequence of the trauma. In addition, chronic Posttraumatic Stress Disorder may be associated with increased rates of somatic complaints and, possibly, general medical conditions.

Specific Culture and Age Features

Individuals who have recently emigrated from areas of considerable social unrest and civil conflict may have elevated rates of Posttraumatic Stress Disorder. Such individuals may be especially reluctant to divulge experiences of torture and trauma due to their vulnerable political immigrant status. Specific assessments of traumatic experiences and concomitant symptoms are needed for such individuals.

In younger children, distressing dreams of the event may, within several weeks, change into generalized nightmares of monsters, of rescuing others, or of threats to self or others. Young children usually do not have the sense that they are reliving the past; rather, the reliving of the trauma may occur through repetitive play (e.g., a child who was involved in a serious automobile accident repeatedly reenacts car crashes with toy cars). Because it may be difficult for children to report diminished interest in significant activities and constriction of affect, these symptoms should be carefully evaluated with reports from parents, teachers, and other observers. In children, the sense of a foreshortened future may be evidenced by the belief that life will be too short to include becoming an adult. There may also be "omen formation"—that is, belief in an ability to foresee future untoward events. Children may also exhibit various physical symptoms, such as stomachaches and headaches.

Prevalence

Community-based studies reveal a lifetime prevalence for Posttraumatic Stress Disorder of approximately 8% of the adult population in the United States. Information is not currently available with regard to the general population prevalence in other countries. Studies of at-risk individuals (i.e., groups exposed to specific traumatic incidents) yield variable findings, with the highest rates (ranging between one-third and more than half of those exposed) found among survivors of rape, military combat and captivity, and ethnically or politically motivated internment and genocide.

Course

Posttraumatic Stress Disorder can occur at any age, including childhood. Symptoms usually begin within the first 3 months after the trauma, although there may be a delay of months, or even years, before symptoms appear. Frequently, a person's reaction to a trauma initially meets criteria for Acute Stress Disorder (see 308.3 Acute Stress Disorder) in the immediate aftermath of the trauma. The symptoms of the disorder and the relative predominance of reexperiencing, avoidance, and hyperarousal symptoms may vary over time. Duration of the symptoms varies, with complete recovery occurring within 3 months in approximately half of cases, with many others having persisting symptoms for longer than 12 months after the trauma. In some cases, the course is characterized by a waxing and waning of symptoms. Symptom reactivation may occur in response to reminders of the original trauma, life stressors, or new traumatic events.

The severity, duration, and proximity of an individual's exposure to the traumatic event are the most important factors affecting the likelihood of developing this disorder. There is some evidence that social supports, family history, childhood experiences, personality variables, and preexisting mental disorders may influence the development of

Posttraumatic Stress Disorder. This disorder can develop in individuals without any predisposing conditions, particularly if the stressor is especially extreme.

Familial Pattern

There is evidence of a heritable component to the transmission of Posttraumatic Stress Disorder. Furthermore, a history of depression in first-degree relatives has been related to an increased vulnerability to developing Postraumatic Stress Disorder.

Differential Diagnosis

In Posttraumatic Stress Disorder, the stressor must be of an extreme (i.e., life-threatening) nature. In contrast, in Adjustment Disorder, the stressor can be of any severity. The diagnosis of Adjustment Disorder is appropriate both for situations in which the response to an extreme stressor does not meet the criteria for Posttraumatic Stress Disorder (or another specific mental disorder) and for situations in which the symptom pattern of Posttraumatic Stress Disorder occurs in response to a stressor that is not extreme (e.g., spouse leaving, being fired).

Not all psychopathology that occurs in individuals exposed to an extreme stressor should necessarily be attributed to Posttraumatic Stress Disorder. Symptoms of avoidance, numbing, and increased arousal that are present before exposure to the stressor do not meet criteria for the diagnosis of Posttraumatic Stress Disorder and require consideration of other diagnoses (e.g., a Mood Disorder or another Anxiety Disorder). Moreover, if the symptom response pattern to the extreme stressor meets criteria for another mental disorder (e.g., Brief Psychotic Disorder, Conversion Disorder, Major Depressive Disorder), these diagnoses should be given instead of, or in addition to, Posttraumatic Stress Disorder.

Acute Stress Disorder is distinguished from Posttraumatic Stress Disorder because the symptom pattern in Acute Stress Disorder must occur within 4 weeks of the traumatic event and resolve within that 4-week period. If the symptoms persist for more than 1 month and meet criteria for Posttraumatic Stress Disorder, the diagnosis is changed from Acute Stress Disorder to Posttraumatic Stress Disorder.

In Obsessive-Compulsive Disorder, there are recurrent intrusive thoughts, but these are experienced as inappropriate and are not related to an experienced traumatic event.

Flashbacks in Posttraumatic Stress Disorder must be distinguished from illusions, hallucinations, and other perceptual disturbances that may occur in Schizophrenia, other Psychotic Disorders, Mood Disorder With Psychotic Features, a delirium, Substance-Induced Disorders, and Psychotic Disorders Due to a General Medical Condition.

Malingering should be ruled out in those situations in which financial remuneration, benefit eligibility, and forensic determinations play a role.

Appendix A-3: Schizophrenia

From the DSM-IV-TR [4th Ed.] Published by the American Psychiatric Association [APA]. Copyright APA. Used with Permission

Schizophrenia

Diagnostic criteria for Schizophrenia

Characteristic symptoms: Two (or more) of the following, each present for a significant portion of time during a 1-month period (or less if successfully treated):delusionshallucinationsdisorganized speech (e.g., frequent derailment or incoherence)grossly disorganized or catatonic behaviornegative symptoms, i.e., affective flattening, alogia, or avolition Note: Only one Criterion A symptom is required if delusions are bizarre or hallucinations consist of a voice keeping up a running commentary on the person's behavior or thoughts, or two or more voices conversing with each other.Social/occupational dysfunction: For a significant portion of the time since the onset of the disturbance, one or more major areas of functioning such as work, interpersonal relations, or self-care are markedly below the level achieved prior to the onset (or when the onset is in childhood or adolescence, failure to achieve expected level of interpersonal, academic, or occupational achievement).Duration: Continuous signs of the disturbance persist for at least 6 months. This 6-month period must include at least 1 month of symptoms (or less if successfully treated) that meet Criterion A (i.e., active-phase symptoms) and may include periods of prodromal or residual symptoms. During these prodromal or residual periods, the signs of the disturbance may be manifested by only negative symptoms or two or more symptoms listed in Criterion A present in an attenuated form (e.g., odd beliefs, unusual perceptual experiences).Schizoaffective and Mood Disorder exclusion: Schizoaffective Disorder and Mood Disorder With Psychotic Features have been ruled out because either (1) no Major Depressive, Manic, or Mixed Episodes have occurred concurrently with the active-phase symptoms; or (2) if mood episodes have occurred during active-phase symptoms, their total duration has been brief relative to the duration of the active and residual periods.Substance/general medical condition exclusion: The disturbance is not due to the direct physiological effects of a substance (e.g., a drug of abuse, a medication) or a general medical condition.Relationship to a Pervasive Developmental Disorder: If there is a history of Autistic Disorder or another Pervasive Developmental

Disorder, the additional diagnosis of Schizophrenia is made only if prominent delusions or hallucinations are also present for at least a month (or less if successfully treated).

Classification of longitudinal course (can be applied only after at least 1 year has elapsed since the initial onset of active-phase symptoms):

Episodic With Interepisode Residual Symptoms (episodes are defined by the reemergence of prominent psychotic symptoms); also specify if: With Prominent Negative Symptoms Episodic With No Interepisode Residual Symptoms Continuous (prominent psychotic symptoms are present throughout the period of observation); also specify if: With Prominent Negative Symptoms Single Episode In Partial Remission; also specify if: With Prominent Negative Symptoms Single Episode In Full Remission Other or Unspecified Pattern

The essential features of Schizophrenia are a mixture of characteristic signs and symptoms (both positive and negative) that have been present for a significant portion of time during a 1-month period (or for a shorter time if successfully treated), with some signs of the disorder persisting for at least 6 months (Criteria A and C). These signs and symptoms are associated with marked social or occupational dysfunction (Criterion B). The disturbance is not better accounted for by Schizoaffective Disorder or a Mood Disorder With Psychotic Features and is not due to the direct physiological effects of a substance or a general medical condition (Criteria D and E). In individuals with a previous diagnosis of Autistic Disorder (or another Pervasive Developmental Disorder), the additional diagnosis of Schizophrenia is warranted only if prominent delusions or hallucinations are present for at least a month (Criterion F). The characteristic symptoms of Schizophrenia involve a range of cognitive and emotional dysfunctions that include perception, inferential thinking, language and communication, behavioral monitoring, affect, fluency and productivity of thought and speech, hedonic capacity, volition and drive, and attention. No single symptom is pathognomonic of Schizophrenia; the diagnosis involves the recognition of a constellation of signs and symptoms associated with impaired occupational or social functioning.

Characteristic symptoms (Criterion A) may be conceptualized as falling into two broad categories: positive and negative. The positive symptoms appear to reflect an excess or distortion of normal functions, whereas the negative symptoms appear to reflect a diminution or loss of normal functions. The positive symptoms (Criteria A1–A4) include distortions in thought content (delusions), perception (hallucinations), language and thought process (disorganized speech), and self-monitoring of behavior (grossly disorganized or catatonic behavior). These positive symptoms may comprise two distinct dimensions, which may in turn be related to different underlying neural mechanisms and clinical correlates. The "psychotic dimension" includes delusions and hallucinations, whereas the "disorganization dimension" includes disorganized speech and behavior. Negative symptoms (Criterion A5) include restrictions in the range and intensity of emotional expression (affective flattening), in the fluency and productivity of thought and speech (alogia), and in the initiation of goal-directed behavior (avolition).

Delusions (Criterion A1) are erroneous beliefs that usually involve a misinterpretation of perceptions or experiences. Their content may include a variety of themes (e.g., persecutory, referential, somatic, religious, or grandiose). Persecutory delusions are most common; the person believes he or she is being tormented, followed, tricked, spied on, or ridiculed. Referential delusions are also common; the person believes that certain gestures, comments, passages from books, newspapers, song lyrics, or other environmental cues are specifically directed at him or her. The distinction between a delusion and a strongly held idea is sometimes difficult to make and depends in part on the degree of conviction with which the belief is held despite clear contradictory evidence regarding its veracity.

Although bizarre delusions are considered to be especially characteristic of Schizophrenia, "bizarreness" may be difficult to judge, especially across different cultures. Delusions are deemed bizarre if they are clearly implausible and not understandable and do not derive from ordinary life experiences. An example of a bizarre delusion is a person's belief that a stranger has removed his or her internal organs and has replaced them with someone else's organs without leaving any wounds or scars. An example of a nonbizarre delusion is a person's false belief that he or she is under surveillance by the police. Delusions that express a loss of control over mind or body are generally considered to be bizarre; these include a person's belief that his or her thoughts have been taken away by some outside force ("thought withdrawal"), that alien thoughts have been put into his or her mind ("thought insertion"), or that his or her body or actions are being acted on or manipulated by some outside force ("delusions of control"). If the delusions are judged to be bizarre, only this single symptom is needed to satisfy Criterion A for Schizophrenia.

Hallucinations (Criterion A2) may occur in any sensory modality (e.g., auditory, visual, olfactory, gustatory, and tactile), but auditory hallucinations are by far the most common. Auditory hallucinations are usually experienced as voices, whether familiar or unfamiliar, that are perceived as distinct from the person's own thoughts. The hallucinations must occur in the context of a clear sensorium; those that occur while falling asleep (hypnagogic) or waking up (hypnopompic) are considered to be within the range of normal experience. Isolated experiences of hearing one's name called or experiences that lack the quality of an external percept (e.g., a humming in one's head) should also not be considered as symptomatic of Schizophrenia or any other Psychotic Disorder. Hallucinations may be a normal part of religious experience in certain cultural contexts. Certain types of auditory hallucinations (i.e., two or more voices conversing with one another or voices maintaining a running commentary on the person's thoughts or behavior) have been considered to be particularly characteristic of Schizophrenia. If these types of hallucinations are present, then only this single symptom is needed to satisfy Criterion A.

Disorganized thinking ("formal thought disorder") has been argued by some to be the single most important feature of Schizophrenia. Because of the difficulty inherent in developing an objective definition of "thought disorder," and because in a clinical setting inferences about thought are based primarily on the individual's speech, the concept of disorganized speech (Criterion A3) has been emphasized in the definition for Schizophrenia used in this manual. The speech of individuals with Schizophrenia may be disorganized in a variety of ways. The person may "slip off the track" from one topic to another ("derailment" or "loose associations"); answers to questions may be obliquely related or completely unrelated ("tangentiality"); and, rarely, speech may be so severely disorganized that it is nearly incomprehensible and resembles receptive aphasia in its linguistic disorganization ("incoherence" or "word salad"). Because mildly disorganized speech is common and nonspecific, the symptom must be severe enough to substantially impair effective communication. Less severe disorganized thinking or

366

speech may occur during the prodromal and residual periods of Schizophrenia (see Criterion C).

Grossly disorganized behavior (Criterion A4) may manifest itself in a variety of ways, ranging from childlike silliness to unpredictable agitation. Problems may be noted in any form of goal-directed behavior, leading to difficulties in performing activities of daily living such as preparing a meal or maintaining hygiene. The person may appear markedly disheveled, may dress in an unusual manner (e.g., wearing multiple overcoats, scarves, and gloves on a hot day), or may display clearly inappropriate sexual behavior (e.g., public masturbation) or unpredictable and untriggered agitation (e.g., shouting or swearing). Care should be taken not to apply this criterion too broadly. For example, a few instances of restless, angry, or agitated behavior should not be considered to be evidence of Schizophrenia, especially if the motivation is understandable.

Catatonic motor behaviors (Criterion A4) include a marked decrease in reactivity to the environment, sometimes reaching an extreme degree of complete unawareness (catatonic stupor), maintaining a rigid posture and resisting efforts to be moved (catatonic rigidity), active resistance to instructions or attempts to be moved (catatonic negativism), the assumption of inappropriate or bizarre postures (catatonic posturing), or purposeless and unstimulated excessive motor activity (catatonic excitement). Although catatonia has historically been associated with Schizophrenia, the clinician should keep in mind that catatonic symptoms are nonspecific and may occur in other mental disorders (see Mood Disorders With Catatonic Features, Catatonic Features Specifier), in general medical conditions (see Catatonic Disorder Due to a General Medical Condition, 293.89 Catatonic Disorder Due to a General Medical Condition), and Medication-Induced Movement Disorders (see Neuroleptic-Induced Parkinsonism, 332.1 Neuroleptic-Induced Parkinsonism).

The negative symptoms of Schizophrenia (Criterion A5) account for a substantial degree of the morbidity associated with the disorder. Three negative symptoms—affective flattening, alogia, and avolition—are included in the definition of Schizophrenia; other negative symptoms (e.g., anhedonia) are noted in the "Associated Features and Disorders" section below. Affective flattening is especially common and is characterized by the person's face appearing immobile and unresponsive, with poor eye contact and reduced body language. Although a person with affective flattening may smile and warm up occasionally, his or her range of emotional expressiveness is clearly diminished most of the time. It may be useful to observe the person interacting with peers to determine whether affective flattening is sufficiently persistent to meet the criterion. Alogia (poverty of speech) is manifested by brief, laconic, empty replies. The individual with alogia appears to have a diminution of thoughts that is reflected in decreased fluency and productivity of speech. This must be differentiated from an unwillingness to speak, a clinical judgment that may require observation over time and in a variety of situations. Avolition is characterized by an inability to initiate and persist in goal-directed activities. The person may sit for long periods of time and show little interest in participating in work or social activities.

Although common in Schizophrenia, negative symptoms are difficult to evaluate because they occur on a continuum with normality, are relatively nonspecific, and may be due to a variety of other factors (including positive symptoms, medication side effects, depression, environmental understimulation, or demoralization). If a negative symptom is judged to be clearly attributable to any of these factors, then it should not be considered in making the diagnosis of Schizophrenia. For example, the behavior of an individual who has the delusional belief that he will be in danger if he leaves his room or talks to anyone may mimic social isolation, avolition, and alogia. Certain antipsychotic medications often produce extrapyramidal side effects, such as bradykinesia, that may mimic affective flattening. The distinction between true negative symptoms and medication side effects often depends on clinical judgment concerning the type of antipsychotic medication, the effects of anticholinergic medications, and dosage adjustments. The difficult distinction between negative symptoms and depressive symptoms may be informed by the other accompanying symptoms that are present and the fact that individuals with symptoms of depression typically experience an intensely painful affect, whereas those with Schizophrenia have a diminution or emptiness of affect. Finally, chronic environmental understimulation or demoralization may result in learned apathy and avolition. In establishing the presence of negative symptoms that are to be used in making the diagnosis of Schizophrenia, perhaps the best test is their persistence for a considerable period of time despite efforts directed at resolving each of the potential causes described above. It has been suggested that enduring negative symptoms that are not attributable to the secondary causes described above be referred to as "deficit" symptoms.

Criterion A for Schizophrenia requires that at least two of the five items be present concurrently for much of at least 1 month. However, if delusions are bizarre or hallucinations involve "voices commenting" or "voices conversing," then the presence of only one item is required. The presence of this relatively severe constellation of signs and symptoms is referred to as the "active phase." In those situations in which the active-phase symptoms remit within a month in response to treatment, Criterion A can still be considered to have been met if the clinician judges that the symptoms would have persisted for a month in the absence of effective treatment. In children, evaluation of the characteristic symptoms should include due consideration of the presence of other disorders or developmental difficulties. For example, the disorganized speech in a child with a Communication Disorder should not count toward a diagnosis of Schizophrenia unless the degree of disorganization is significantly greater than would be expected on the basis of the Communication Disorder alone.

Schizophrenia involves dysfunction in one or more major areas of functioning (e.g., interpersonal relations, work or education, or self-care) (Criterion B). Typically, functioning is clearly below that which had been achieved before the onset of symptoms. If the disturbance begins in childhood or adolescence, however, there may be a failure to achieve what would have been expected for the individual rather than a deterioration in functioning. Comparing the individual with unaffected siblings may be helpful in making this determination. Educational progress is frequently disrupted, and the individual may be unable to finish school. Many individuals are unable to hold a job for sustained periods of time and are employed at a lower level than their parents ("downward drift"). The majority (60%–70%) of individuals with Schizophrenia do not marry, and most have relatively limited social contacts. The dysfunction persists for a substantial period during the course of the disorder and does not appear to be a direct result of any single feature. For example, if a woman quits her job because of the circumscribed delusion that her boss is trying to kill her, this alone is not sufficient evidence for this criterion unless there is a more pervasive pattern of difficulties (usually in multiple domains of functioning).

Some signs of the disturbance must persist for a continuous period of at least 6 months (Criterion C). During that time period, there must be at least 1 month of symptoms (or less than 1 month if symptoms are successfully treated) that meet Criterion A of Schizophrenia (the active phase). Prodromal symptoms are often present prior to the active phase, and residual symptoms may follow it. Some prodromal and residual symptoms are relatively mild or subthreshold forms of the positive symptoms specified in Criterion A. Individuals may express a variety of unusual or odd beliefs that are not of delusional proportions (e.g., ideas of reference or magical thinking); they may have unusual perceptual experiences (e.g., sensing the presence of an unseen person or force in the absence of formed hallucinations); their speech may be generally understandable but digressive, vague, or overly abstract or concrete; and their behavior may be peculiar but not grossly disorganized (e.g., mumbling to themselves, collecting odd and apparently worthless objects). In addition to these positive-like symptoms, negative symptoms are particularly common in the prodromal and residual phases and can often be quite severe. Individuals who had been socially active may become withdrawn; they lose interest in previously pleasurable activities; they may become less talkative and inquisitive; and they may spend the bulk of their time in bed. Such negative symptoms are often the first sign to the family that something is wrong; family members may ultimately report that they experienced the individual as "gradually slipping away."

Subtypes and Course Specifiers
The diagnosis of a particular subtype is based on the clinical picture that occasioned the most recent evaluation or admission to clinical care and may therefore change over time. Separate text and criteria are provided for each of the following subtypes:
295.30 Paranoid Type (see 295.30 Paranoid Type)295.10 Disorganized Type (see 295.10 Disorganized Type)295.20 Catatonic Type (see 295.20 Catatonic Type)295.90 Undifferentiated Type (see 295.90 Undifferentiated Type)295.60 Residual Type (see 295.60 Residual Type)

The following specifiers may be used to indicate the characteristic course of symptoms of Schizophrenia over time. These specifiers can be applied only after at least 1 year has elapsed since the initial onset of active-phase symptoms. During this initial 1-year period, no course specifiers can be given.

Episodic With Interepisode Residual Symptoms. This specifier applies when the course is characterized by episodes in which Criterion A for Schizophrenia is met and there are clinically significant residual symptoms between the episodes. With Prominent Negative Symptoms can be added if prominent negative symptoms are present during these residual periods.Episodic With No Interepisode Residual Symptoms. This specifier applies when the course is characterized by episodes in which Criterion A for Schizophrenia is met and there are no clinically significant residual symptoms between the episodes.Continuous. This specifier applies when characteristic symptoms of Criterion A are met throughout all (or most) of the course. With Prominent Negative Symptoms can be added if prominent negative symptoms are also present.Single Episode In Partial Remission. This specifier applies when there has been a single episode in which Criterion A for Schizophrenia is met and some clinically significant residual symptoms remain. With Prominent Negative Symptoms can be added if these residual symptoms include prominent negative symptoms.Single Episode In Full Remission. This specifier applies when there has been a single episode in which Criterion A for Schizophrenia has been met and no clinically significant residual symptoms remain.Other or Unspecified Pattern. This specifier is used if another or an unspecified course pattern has been present.

Recording Procedures

The diagnostic code for Schizophrenia is selected based on the appropriate subtype: 295.30 for Paranoid Type, 295.10 for Disorganized Type, 295.20 for Catatonic Type, 295.90 for Undifferentiated Type, and 295.60 for Residual Type. There are no fifth-digit codes available for the course specifiers. In recording the name of the disorder, the course specifiers are noted after the appropriate subtype (e.g., 295.30 Schizophrenia, Paranoid Type, Episodic With Interepisode Residual Symptoms, With Prominent Negative Symptoms).

Associated Features and Disorders

Associated descriptive features and mental disorders.

The individual with Schizophrenia may display inappropriate affect (e.g., smiling, laughing, or a silly facial expression in the absence of an appropriate stimulus), which is one of the defining features of the Disorganized Type. Anhedonia is common and is manifested by a loss of interest or pleasure. Dysphoric mood may take the form of depression, anxiety, or anger. There may be disturbances in sleep pattern (e.g., sleeping during the day and nighttime activity or restlessness). The individual may show a lack of interest in eating or may refuse food as a consequence of delusional beliefs. Often there are abnormalities of psychomotor activity (e.g., pacing, rocking, or apathetic immobility). Difficulty in concentration, attention, and memory is frequently evident.

A majority of individuals with Schizophrenia have poor insight regarding the fact that they have a psychotic illness. Evidence suggests that poor insight is a manifestation of the illness itself rather than a coping strategy. It may be comparable to the lack of awareness of neurological deficits seen in stroke, termed anosognosia. This symptom predisposes the individual to noncompliance with treatment and has been found to be predictive of higher relapse rates, increased number of involuntary hospital admissions, poorer psychosocial functioning, and a poorer course of illness.

Depersonalization, derealization, and somatic concerns may occur and sometimes reach delusional proportions. Anxiety and phobias are common in Schizophrenia. Motor abnormalities (e.g., grimacing, posturing, odd mannerisms, ritualistic or stereotyped behavior) are sometimes present. The life expectancy of individuals with Schizophrenia is shorter than that of the general population for a variety of reasons. Suicide is an important factor, because approximately 10% of individuals with Schizophrenia commit suicide—and between 20% and 40% make at least one attempt over the course of the illness. Although the risk remains high over the whole lifespan, specific risk factors for suicide include male gender, being under 45 years of age, depressive symptoms, feelings of hopelessness, unemployment, and recent hospital discharge. Suicide risk is also elevated during postpsychotic periods. Males successfully complete suicide more often than females, but both groups are at increased risk relative to the general population.

Many studies have reported that subgroups of individuals diagnosed with Schizophrenia have a higher incidence of assaultive and violent behavior. The major predictors of violent behavior are male gender, younger age, past history of violence, noncompliance with antipsychotic medication, and excessive substance use. However, it should be noted that most individuals with Schizophrenia are not more dangerous to others than those in the general population.

Rates of comorbidity with Substance-Related Disorders are high. Nicotine Dependence is especially high, with estimates ranging from 80% to 90% of individuals with Schizophrenia being regular cigarette smokers. Furthermore, these individuals tend to smoke heavily and to choose cigarettes with high nicotine content. Comorbidity with Anxiety Disorders has also been increasingly recognized in Schizophrenia. In particular, rates of Obsessive-Compulsive Disorder and Panic Disorder are elevated in individuals with Schizophrenia relative to the general population. Schizotypal, Schizoid, or Paranoid Personality Disorder may sometimes precede the onset of Schizophrenia. Whether these Personality Disorders are simply prodromal to Schizophrenia or whether they constitute a separate earlier disorder is not clear.

An increased risk of Schizophrenia has been found in association with prenatal and childhood factors (e.g., prenatal exposure to flu, prenatal exposure to famine, obstetric complications, central nervous system infection in early childhood).

Associated laboratory findings.

No laboratory findings have been identified that are diagnostic of Schizophrenia. However, a variety of measures from neuroimaging, neuropsychological, and neurophysiological studies have shown differences between groups of individuals with Schizophrenia and appropriately matched control subjects. In the structural neuroimaging literature, the most widely studied and most consistently replicated finding continues to be enlargement of the lateral ventricles. Many studies have also demonstrated decreased brain tissue as evidenced by widened cortical sulci and decreased volumes of gray and white matter. However, there is ongoing controversy as to whether the apparent decrease in brain tissue is a focal as opposed to a more diffuse process. When examined by region, the temporal lobe has most consistently been found to be decreased in volume, while the frontal lobe is implicated less often. Within the temporal lobe, there is evidence of focal abnormalities, with medial temporal structures (hippocampus, amygdala, and entorhinal cortex), as well as the superior temporal gyrus and planum temporale, most consistently found to be smaller in volume.

Decreased thalamic volume has also been observed in both individuals with Schizophrenia and their unaffected first-degree relatives, but fewer studies have looked at this. Another finding that has been consistently replicated is that of increased basal ganglia size, but there is increasing evidence that this may be an epiphenomenon of treatment with typical neuroleptic medication. An increased incidence of large cavum septum pellucidi has also been demonstrated in individuals with Schizophrenia. This may have important pathophysiological implications, because it is suggestive of an early (i.e., prenatal) midline developmental brain abnormality, at least in a subgroup of individuals with Schizophrenia.

In terms of functional brain imaging studies, hypofrontality (i.e., a relative decrease in cerebral blood flow, metabolism, or some other proxy for neural activity) continues to be the most consistently replicated finding. However, there is increasing recognition that functional abnormalities are unlikely to be limited to any one brain region, and most of the more recent studies suggest more widespread abnormalities involving cortical-subcortical circuitry.

Neuropsychological deficits are a consistent finding in groups of individuals with Schizophrenia. Deficits are evident across a range of cognitive abilities, including memory, psychomotor abilities, attention, and difficulty in changing response set. In addition to the presence of these deficits among chronically ill individuals with Schizophrenia, there is increasing evidence that many of these deficits are found among individuals during their first psychotic episode and prior to treatment with antipsychotic medication, in individuals with Schizophrenia who are in clinical remission, as well as in unaffected first-degree relatives. For these reasons, some of the neuropsychological deficits are thought to reflect more fundamental features of the illness and, perhaps, to reveal vulnerability factors for Schizophrenia. These deficits are clinically meaningful in that they are related to the degree of difficulty that some individuals with Schizophrenia have with activities of daily living as well as the ability to acquire skills in psychosocial rehabilitation. Accordingly, the severity of neuropsychological deficits is a relatively strong predictor of social and vocational outcome.

Several neurophysiological abnormalities have been demonstrated in groups of individuals with Schizophrenia. Among the most common are deficits in the perception

374

and processing of sensory stimuli (e.g., impairment in sensory gating), abnormal smooth pursuit and saccadic eye movements, slowed reaction time, alterations in brain laterality, and abnormalities in evoked potential electroencephalograms.

Abnormal laboratory findings may also be noted as a complication either of Schizophrenia or of its treatment. Some individuals with Schizophrenia drink excessive amounts of fluid ("water intoxication") and develop abnormalities in urine specific gravity or electrolyte imbalances. Elevated creatine phosphokinase (CPK) levels may result from Neuroleptic Malignant Syndrome (see 333.92 Neuroleptic Malignant Syndrome). Associated physical examination findings and general medical conditions.

Individuals with Schizophrenia are sometimes physically awkward and may display neurological "soft signs," such as left/right confusion, poor coordination, or mirroring. Some minor physical anomalies (e.g., highly arched palate, narrow- or wide-set eyes or subtle malformations of the ears) may be more common among individuals with Schizophrenia. Perhaps the most common associated physical findings are motor abnormalities. Most of these are likely to be related to side effects from treatment with antipsychotic medications. Motor abnormalities that are secondary to neuroleptic treatment include Neuroleptic-Induced Tardive Dyskinesia (see 333.82 Neuroleptic-Induced Tardive Dyskinesia), Neuroleptic-Induced Parkinsonism (see 332.1 Neuroleptic-Induced Parkinsonism), Neuroleptic-Induced Acute Akathisia (see 333.99 Neuroleptic-Induced Acute Akathisia), Neuroleptic-Induced Acute Dystonia (see 333.7 Neuroleptic-Induced Acute Dystonia), and Neuroleptic Malignant Syndrome (see 333.92 Neuroleptic Malignant Syndrome). Spontaneous motor abnormalities resembling those that may be induced by neuroleptics (e.g., sniffing, tongue clucking, grunting) had been described in the preneuroleptic era and are also still observed, although they may be difficult to distinguish from neuroleptic effects. Other physical findings may be related to frequently associated disorders. For example, because Nicotine Dependence is so common in Schizophrenia, these individuals are more likely to develop cigarette-related pathology (e.g., emphysema and other pulmonary and cardiac problems).

Specific Culture, Age, and Gender Features
Clinicians assessing the symptoms of Schizophrenia in socioeconomic or cultural situations that are different from their own must take cultural differences into account.

Ideas that may appear to be delusional in one culture (e.g., sorcery and witchcraft) may be commonly held in another. In some cultures, visual or auditory hallucinations with a religious content may be a normal part of religious experience (e.g., seeing the Virgin Mary or hearing God's voice). In addition, the assessment of disorganized speech may be made difficult by linguistic variation in narrative styles across cultures that affects the logical form of verbal presentation. The assessment of affect requires sensitivity to differences in styles of emotional expression, eye contact, and body language, which vary across cultures. If the assessment is conducted in a language that is different from the individual's primary language, care must be taken to ensure that alogia is not related to linguistic barriers. Because the cultural meaning of self-initiated, goal-directed activity can be expected to vary across diverse settings, disturbances of volition must also be carefully assessed.

There is some evidence that clinicians may have a tendency to overdiagnose Schizophrenia in some ethnic groups. Studies conducted in the United Kingdom and the United States suggest that Schizophrenia may be diagnosed more often in individuals who are African American and Asian American than in other racial groups. It is not clear, however, whether these findings represent true differences among racial groups or whether they are the result of clinician bias or cultural insensitivity. Cultural differences have been noted in the presentation, course, and outcome of Schizophrenia. Catatonic behavior has been reported as relatively uncommon among individuals with Schizophrenia in the United States but is more common in non-Western countries. Individuals with Schizophrenia in developing nations tend to have a more acute course and a better outcome than do individuals in industrialized nations.

The onset of Schizophrenia typically occurs between the late teens and the mid-30s, with onset prior to adolescence rare (although cases with age at onset of 5 or 6 years have been reported). The essential features of the condition are the same in children, but it may be particularly difficult to make the diagnosis in this age group. In children, delusions and hallucinations may be less elaborated than those observed in adults, and visual hallucinations may be more common. Disorganized speech is observed in a number of disorders with childhood onset (e.g., Communication Disorders, Pervasive Developmental Disorders), as is disorganized behavior (e.g., Attention-Deficit/Hyperactivity Disorder, Stereotypic Movement Disorder). These symptoms should not be attributed to Schizophrenia without due consideration of these more common disorders of childhood. Schizophrenia can also begin later in life (e.g., after age 45 years). Late-onset cases tend to be similar to earlier-onset Schizophrenia, although a number of differences have been observed. For example, the proportion of affected women is greater, and individuals with late onset are more likely to have been married than individuals with an earlier age at onset, but they are nonetheless more socially isolated and impaired when contrasted to the general population. Clinical factors such as the postmenopausal state, human leukocyte antigen subtypes, and cerebrovascular disease are possible risk factors. The clinical presentation is more likely to include persecutory delusions and hallucinations, and less likely to include disorganized and negative symptoms. Often the course is characterized by a predominance of positive symptoms with preservation of affect and social functioning. The course is typically chronic, although individuals may be quite responsive to antipsychotic medications in lower doses. Among those with the oldest age at onset (i.e., over age 60 years), sensory deficits (e.g., auditory and visual loss) occur more commonly than in the general adult population, although their specific role in pathogenesis remains unknown. There is also evidence suggesting that cognitive impairment accompanies the clinical picture. However, the issue of whether identifiable brain pathology defines late-onset illness remains unclear.

Evidence from a large body of literature demonstrates that Schizophrenia is expressed differently in men and women. The modal age at onset for men is between 18 and 25 years, and that for women is between 25 and the mid-30s. The age-at-onset distribution is bimodal for women, with a second peak occurring later in life, but unimodal among men. Approximately 3%–10% of women have an age at onset after 40, whereas late onset is much less common in men. Women also have better premorbid functioning than men. Women with Schizophrenia tend to express more affective symptomatology, paranoid delusions, and hallucinations, whereas men tend to express more negative symptoms (flat affect, avolition, social withdrawal). Regarding the course of Schizophrenia, women have a better prognosis than men, as defined by number of rehospitalizations and lengths of hospital stay, overall duration of illness, time to relapse, response to neuroleptics, and social and work functioning. However, the gender advantage in these parameters appears to attenuate to some degree with age (i.e., short- to medium-term outcome is better in women, but long-term outcome for women, especially in the postmenopausal period, becomes more like that for men). A slightly higher incidence of Schizophrenia has been observed in men than in women. Further, a number of studies have demonstrated gender differences in the genetic transmission of Schizophrenia. Rates of Schizophrenia among family members of women with Schizophrenia are higher than those among family members of men with Schizophrenia, while relatives of men have a higher incidence of schizotypal and schizoid personality traits than do those of women.

Prevalence

Schizophrenia has been observed worldwide. Prevalences among adults are often reported to be in the range of 0.5% to 1.5%. Annual incidences are most often in the range of 0.5 to 5.0 per 10,000. Incidence estimates beyond this range have been reported for some population groups—for instance, a far higher incidence for second-generation African Caribbeans living in the United Kingdom.

Birth cohort studies suggest some geographic and historical variations in incidence. For example, an elevated risk has been reported among urban-born individuals compared with rural-born individuals, as well as a gradually declining incidence for later-born birth cohorts.

Course

The median age at onset for the first psychotic episode of Schizophrenia is in the early to mid-20s for men and in the late 20s for women. The onset may be abrupt or insidious, but the majority of individuals display some type of prodromal phase manifested by the slow and gradual development of a variety of signs and symptoms (e.g., social withdrawal, loss of interest in school or work, deterioration in hygiene and grooming, unusual behavior, outbursts of anger). Family members may find this behavior difficult to interpret and assume that the person is "going through a phase." Eventually, however, the appearance of some active-phase symptom marks the disturbance as Schizophrenia. The age at onset may have both pathophysiological and prognostic significance. Individuals with an early age at onset are more often male and have a poorer premorbid adjustment, lower educational achievement, more evidence of structural brain abnormalities, more prominent negative signs and symptoms, more evidence of cognitive impairment as assessed with neuropsychological testing, and a worse outcome. Conversely, individuals with a later onset are more often female, have less evidence of structural brain abnormalities or cognitive impairment, and display a better outcome.

Most studies of course and outcome in Schizophrenia suggest that the course may be variable, with some individuals displaying exacerbations and remissions, whereas others remain chronically ill. Because of variability in definition and ascertainment, an accurate summary of the long-term outcome of Schizophrenia is not possible. Complete remission (i.e., a return to full premorbid functioning) is probably not common in this disorder. Of those who remain ill, some appear to have a relatively stable course, whereas others show a progressive worsening associated with severe disability. Early in the illness, negative symptoms may be prominent, appearing primarily as prodromal features. Subsequently, positive symptoms appear. Because these positive symptoms are particularly responsive to treatment, they typically diminish, but in many individuals, negative symptoms persist between episodes of positive symptoms. There is some suggestion that negative symptoms may become steadily more prominent in some individuals during the course of the illness. Numerous studies have indicated a group of factors that are associated with a better prognosis. These include good premorbid adjustment, acute onset, later age at onset, absence of anosognosia (poor insight), being female, precipitating events, associated mood disturbance, treatment with antipsychotic medication soon after the onset of the illness, consistent medication compliance (i.e., early and consistent treatment predicts better response to later treatment with antipsychotic medication), brief duration of active-phase symptoms, good interepisode functioning, minimal residual symptoms, absence of structural brain abnormalities, normal neurological functioning, a family history of Mood Disorder, and no family history of Schizophrenia.

Familial Pattern

The first-degree biological relatives of individuals with Schizophrenia have a risk for Schizophrenia that is about 10 times greater than that of the general population. Concordance rates for Schizophrenia are higher in monozygotic twins than in dizygotic twins. Adoption studies have shown that biological relatives of individuals with Schizophrenia have a substantially increased risk for Schizophrenia, whereas adoptive relatives have no increased risk. Although much evidence suggests the importance of genetic factors in the etiology of Schizophrenia, the existence of a substantial discordance rate in monozygotic twins also indicates the importance of environmental factors. Some relatives of individuals with Schizophrenia may also have an increased risk for a group of mental disorders, termed the schizophrenia spectrum. Although the exact boundaries of the spectrum remain unclear, family and adoption studies suggest that it probably includes Schizoaffective Disorder and Schizotypal Personality Disorder. Other psychotic disorders and Paranoid, Schizoid, and Avoidant Personality Disorders may belong to the schizophrenia spectrum as well, but the evidence is more limited.

Differential Diagnosis

A wide variety of general medical conditions can present with psychotic symptoms. Psychotic Disorder Due to a General Medical Condition, a delirium, or a dementia is diagnosed when there is evidence from the history, physical examination, or laboratory tests that indicates that the delusions or hallucinations are the direct physiological consequence of a general medical condition (e.g., Cushing's syndrome, brain tumor) (see Psychotic Disorder Due to a General Medical Condition). Substance-Induced Psychotic Disorder, Substance-Induced Delirium, and Substance-Induced Persisting Dementia are distinguished from Schizophrenia by the fact that a substance (e.g., a drug of abuse, a medication, or exposure to a toxin) is judged to be etiologically related to the delusions or hallucinations (see Substance-Induced Psychotic Disorder). Many different types of Substance-Related Disorders may produce symptoms similar to those of Schizophrenia (e.g., sustained amphetamine or cocaine use may produce delusions or hallucinations; phencyclidine use may produce a mixture of positive and negative symptoms). Based on a variety of features that characterize the course of Schizophrenia and Substance-Related Disorders, the clinician must determine whether the psychotic symptoms have been initiated and maintained by the substance use. Ideally, the clinician should attempt to observe the individual during a sustained period (e.g., 4 weeks) of abstinence. However, because such prolonged periods of abstinence are often difficult to achieve, the clinician may need to consider other evidence, such as whether the psychotic symptoms appear to be exacerbated by the substance and to diminish when it has been discontinued, the relative severity of psychotic symptoms in relation to the amount and duration of substance use, and knowledge of the characteristic symptoms produced by a particular substance (e.g., amphetamines typically produce delusions and stereotypies, but not affective blunting or prominent negative symptoms).

Distinguishing Schizophrenia from Mood Disorder With Psychotic Features and Schizoaffective Disorder is made difficult by the fact that mood disturbance is common during the prodromal, active, and residual phases of Schizophrenia. If psychotic symptoms occur exclusively during periods of mood disturbance, the diagnosis is Mood Disorder With Psychotic Features. In Schizoaffective Disorder, there must be a mood episode that is concurrent with the active-phase symptoms of Schizophrenia, mood symptoms must be present for a substantial portion of the total duration of the disturbance, and delusions or hallucinations must be present for at least 2 weeks in the absence of prominent mood symptoms. In contrast, mood symptoms in Schizophrenia either have a duration that is brief in relation to the total duration of the disturbance, occur only during the prodromal or residual phases, or do not meet full criteria for a mood episode. When mood symptoms that meet full criteria for a mood episode are superimposed on Schizophrenia and are of particular clinical significance, an additional diagnosis of Depressive Disorder Not Otherwise Specified or Bipolar Disorder Not Otherwise Specified may be given. Schizophrenia, Catatonic Type, may be difficult to distinguish from a Mood Disorder With Catatonic Features.

By definition, Schizophrenia differs from Schizophreniform Disorder on the basis of duration. Schizophrenia involves the presence of symptoms (including prodromal or residual symptoms) for at least 6 months, whereas the total duration of symptoms in Schizophreniform Disorder must be at least 1 month but less than 6 months. Schizophreniform Disorder also does not require a decline in functioning. Brief Psychotic Disorder is defined by the presence of delusions, hallucinations, disorganized speech, or grossly disorganized or catatonic behavior lasting for at least 1 day but for less than 1 month.

The differential diagnosis between Schizophrenia and Delusional Disorder rests on the nature of the delusions (nonbizarre in Delusional Disorder) and the absence of other

381

characteristic symptoms of Schizophrenia (e.g., hallucinations, disorganized speech or behavior, or prominent negative symptoms). Delusional Disorder may be particularly difficult to differentiate from the Paranoid Type of Schizophrenia, because this subtype does not include prominent disorganized speech, disorganized behavior, or flat or inappropriate affect and is often associated with less decline in functioning than is characteristic of the other subtypes of Schizophrenia. When poor psychosocial functioning is present in Delusional Disorder, it arises directly from the delusional beliefs themselves.

A diagnosis of Psychotic Disorder Not Otherwise Specified may be made if insufficient information is available to choose between Schizophrenia and other Psychotic Disorders (e.g., Schizoaffective Disorder) or to determine whether the presenting symptoms are substance induced or are the result of a general medical condition. Such uncertainty is particularly likely to occur early in the course of the disorder.

Although Schizophrenia and Pervasive Developmental Disorders (e.g., Autistic Disorder) share disturbances in language, affect, and interpersonal relatedness, they can be distinguished in a number of ways. Pervasive Developmental Disorders are characteristically recognized during infancy or early childhood (usually before age 3 years), whereas such early onset is rare in Schizophrenia. Moreover, in Pervasive Developmental Disorders, there is an absence of prominent delusions and hallucinations; more pronounced abnormalities in affect; and speech that is absent or minimal and characterized by stereotypies and abnormalities in prosody. Schizophrenia may occasionally develop in individuals with a Pervasive Developmental Disorder; a diagnosis of Schizophrenia is warranted in individuals with a preexisting diagnosis of Autistic Disorder or another Pervasive Developmental Disorder only if prominent hallucinations or delusions have been present for at least a month. Childhood-onset Schizophrenia must be distinguished from childhood presentations combining disorganized speech (from a Communication Disorder) and disorganized behavior (from Attention-Deficit/Hyperactivity Disorder).

Schizophrenia shares features (e.g., paranoid ideation, magical thinking, social avoidance, and vague and digressive speech) with and may be preceded by Schizotypal, Schizoid, or Paranoid Personality Disorder. An additional diagnosis of Schizophrenia is appropriate when the symptoms are severe enough to satisfy Criterion

A of Schizophrenia. The preexisting Personality Disorder may be noted on Axis II followed by "Premorbid" in parentheses [e.g., Schizotypal Personality Disorder (Premorbid)].

Schizophrenia Subtypes

The subtypes of Schizophrenia are defined by the predominant symptomatology at the time of evaluation. Although the prognostic and treatment implications of the subtypes are variable, the Paranoid and Disorganized Types tend to be the least and most severe, respectively. The diagnosis of a particular subtype is based on the clinical picture that occasioned the most recent evaluation or admission to clinical care and may therefore change over time. Not infrequently, the presentation may include symptoms that are characteristic of more than one subtype. The choice among subtypes depends on the following algorithm: Catatonic Type is assigned whenever prominent catatonic symptoms are present (regardless of the presence of other symptoms); Disorganized Type is assigned whenever disorganized speech and behavior and flat or inappropriate affect are prominent (unless Catatonic Type is also present); Paranoid Type is assigned whenever there is a preoccupation with delusions or frequent hallucinations are prominent (unless the Catatonic or Disorganized Type is present). Undifferentiated Type is a residual category describing presentations that include prominent active-phase symptoms not meeting criteria for the Catatonic, Disorganized, or Paranoid Type; and Residual Type is for presentations in which there is continuing evidence of the disturbance, but the criteria for the active-phase symptoms are no longer met.

Because of the limited value of the schizophrenia subtypes in clinical and research settings (e.g., prediction of course, treatment response, correlates of illness), alternative subtyping schemes are being actively investigated. The alternative with the most empirical support to date proposes that three dimensions of psychopathology (psychotic, disorganized, and negative) may come together in different ways among individuals with Schizophrenia. This dimensional alternative is described in Appendix B (Alternative Dimensional Descriptors for Schizophrenia).

Appendix A-4: Obsessive-compulsive disorder

From the DSM-IV-TR [4th Ed.] Published by the American Psychiatric Association [APA]. Copyright APA. Used with Permission

300.3 Obsessive-Compulsive Disorder

Diagnostic criteria for

300.3

Obsessive-Compulsive Disorder

Either obsessions or compulsions: Obsessions as defined by (1), (2), (3), and (4): recurrent and persistent thoughts, impulses, or images that are experienced, at some time during the disturbance, as intrusive and inappropriate and that cause marked anxiety or distressthe thoughts, impulses, or images are not simply excessive worries about real-life problemsthe person attempts to ignore or suppress such thoughts, impulses, or images, or to neutralize them with some other thought or actionthe person recognizes that the obsessional thoughts, impulses, or images are a product of his or her own mind (not imposed from without as in thought insertion) Compulsions as defined by (1) and (2): repetitive behaviors (e.g., hand washing, ordering, checking) or mental acts (e.g., praying, counting, repeating words silently) that the person feels driven to perform in response to an obsession, or according to rules that must be applied rigidlythe behaviors or mental acts are aimed at preventing or reducing distress or preventing some dreaded event or situation; however, these behaviors or mental acts either are not connected in a realistic way with what they are designed to neutralize or prevent or are clearly excessiveAt some point during the course of the disorder, the person has recognized that the obsessions or compulsions are excessive or unreasonable. Note: This does not apply to children.The obsessions or compulsions cause marked distress, are time consuming (take more than 1 hour a day), or significantly interfere with the person's normal routine, occupational (or academic) functioning, or usual social activities or relationships.If another Axis I disorder is present, the content of the obsessions or compulsions is not restricted to it (e.g., preoccupation with food in the presence of an Eating Disorder; hair pulling in the presence of Trichotillomania; concern with appearance in the presence of Body Dysmorphic Disorder; preoccupation with drugs in the presence of a Substance Use Disorder; preoccupation with having a serious illness in the presence of Hypochondriasis; preoccupation with sexual urges or fantasies in the presence of a Paraphilia; or guilty ruminations in the presence of Major Depressive Disorder).The disturbance is not due to the direct physiological effects of a substance (e.g., a drug of abuse, a medication) or a general medical condition.

Specify if:

With Poor Insight: if, for most of the time during the current episode, the person does not recognize that the obsessions and compulsions are excessive or unreasonable

Diagnostic Features

The essential features of Obsessive-Compulsive Disorder are recurrent obsessions or compulsions (Criterion A) that are severe enough to be time consuming (i.e., they take more than 1 hour a day) or cause marked distress or significant impairment (Criterion C). At some point during the course of the disorder, the person has recognized that the obsessions or compulsions are excessive or unreasonable (Criterion B). If another Axis I disorder is present, the content of the obsessions or compulsions is not restricted to it (Criterion D). The disturbance is not due to the direct physiological effects of a substance (e.g., a drug of abuse, a medication) or a general medical condition (Criterion E).

Obsessions are persistent ideas, thoughts, impulses, or images that are experienced as intrusive and inappropriate and that cause marked anxiety or distress. The intrusive and inappropriate quality of the obsessions has been referred to as "ego-dystonic." This refers to the individual's sense that the content of the obsession is alien, not within his or her own control, and not the kind of thought that he or she would expect to have. However, the individual is able to recognize that the obsessions are the product of his or her own mind and are not imposed from without (as in thought insertion).

The most common obsessions are repeated thoughts about contamination (e.g., becoming contaminated by shaking hands), repeated doubts (e.g., wondering whether one has performed some act such as having hurt someone in a traffic accident or having left a door unlocked), a need to have things in a particular order (e.g., intense distress when objects are disordered or asymmetrical), aggressive or horrific impulses (e.g., to hurt one's child or to shout an obscenity in church), and sexual imagery (e.g., a recurrent pornographic image). The thoughts, impulses, or images are not simply excessive worries about real-life problems (e.g., concerns about current ongoing difficulties in life, such as financial, work, or school problems) and are unlikely to be related to a real-life problem.

The individual with obsessions usually attempts to ignore or suppress such thoughts or impulses or to neutralize them with some other thought or action (i.e., a compulsion). For example, an individual plagued by doubts about having turned off the stove attempts to neutralize them by repeatedly checking to ensure that it is off.

Compulsions are repetitive behaviors (e.g., hand washing, ordering, checking) or mental acts (e.g., praying, counting, repeating words silently) the goal of which is to prevent or reduce anxiety or distress, not to provide pleasure or gratification. In most cases, the person feels driven to perform the compulsion to reduce the distress that accompanies an obsession or to prevent some dreaded event or situation. For example, individuals with obsessions about being contaminated may reduce their mental distress by washing their hands until their skin is raw; individuals distressed by obsessions about having left a door unlocked may be driven to check the lock every few minutes; individuals distressed by unwanted blasphemous thoughts may find relief in counting to 10 backward and forward 100 times for each thought. In some cases, individuals perform rigid or stereotyped acts according to idiosyncratically elaborated rules without being able to indicate why they are doing them. By definition, compulsions are either clearly excessive or are not connected in a realistic way with what they are designed to neutralize or prevent. The most common compulsions involve washing and cleaning, counting, checking, requesting or demanding assurances, repeating actions, and ordering.

By definition, adults with Obsessive-Compulsive Disorder have at some point recognized that the obsessions or compulsions are excessive or unreasonable. This requirement does not apply to children because they may lack sufficient cognitive awareness to make this judgment. However, even in adults there is a broad range of insight into the reasonableness of the obsessions or compulsions. Some individuals are uncertain about the reasonableness of their obsessions or compulsions, and any given individual's insight may vary across times and situations. For example, the person may recognize a contamination compulsion as unreasonable when discussing it in a "safe situation" (e.g., in the therapist's office), but not when forced to handle money. At those times when the individual recognizes that the obsessions and compulsions are unreasonable, he or she may desire or attempt to resist them. When attempting to resist a compulsion, the individual may have a sense of mounting anxiety or tension that is often relieved by yielding to the compulsion. In the course of the disorder, after repeated failure to resist the obsessions or compulsions, the individual may give in to them, no longer experience a desire to resist them, and may incorporate the compulsions into his or her daily routines.

The obsessions or compulsions must cause marked distress, be time consuming (take more than 1 hour per day), or significantly interfere with the individual's normal routine, occupational functioning, or usual social activities or relationships with others. Obsessions or compulsions can displace useful and satisfying behavior and can be highly disruptive to overall functioning. Because obsessive intrusions can be distracting, they frequently result in inefficient performance of cognitive tasks that require concentration, such as reading or computation. In addition, many individuals avoid objects or situations that provoke obsessions or compulsions. Such avoidance can become extensive and can severely restrict general functioning.

Specifier

With Poor Insight. This specifier can be applied when, for most of the time during the current episode, the individual does not recognize that the obsessions or compulsions are excessive or unreasonable.

Associated Features and Disorders

Associated descriptive features and mental disorders.

Frequently there is avoidance of situations that involve the content of the obsessions, such as dirt or contamination. For example, a person with obsessions about dirt may avoid public restrooms or shaking hands with strangers. Hypochondriacal concerns are common, with repeated visits to physicians to seek reassurance. Guilt, a pathological sense of responsibility, and sleep disturbances may be present. There may be excessive use of alcohol or of sedative, hypnotic, or anxiolytic medications. Performing compulsions may become a major life activity, leading to serious marital, occupational, or social disability. Pervasive avoidance may leave an individual housebound.

In adults, Obsessive-Compulsive Disorder may be associated with Major Depressive Disorder, some other Anxiety Disorders (i.e., Specific Phobia, Social Phobia, Panic Disorder, Generalized Anxiety Disorder), Eating Disorders, and some Personality Disorders (i.e., Obsessive-Compulsive Personality Disorder, Avoidant Personality Disorder, Dependent Personality Disorder). In children, it may also be associated with Learning Disorders and Disruptive Behavior Disorders. There is a high incidence of Obsessive-Compulsive Disorder in children and adults with Tourette's Disorder, with estimates ranging from approximately 35% to 50%. The incidence of Tourette's Disorder in Obsessive-Compulsive Disorder is lower, with estimates ranging between 5% and 7%. Between 20% and 30% of individuals with Obsessive-Compulsive Disorder have reported current or past tics.

Associated laboratory findings.

No laboratory findings have been identified that are diagnostic of Obsessive-Compulsive Disorder. However, a variety of laboratory findings have been noted to be abnormal in groups of individuals with Obsessive-Compulsive Disorder relative to control subjects. There is some evidence that some serotonin agonists given acutely cause increased symptoms in some individuals with the disorder. Individuals with the disorder may exhibit increased autonomic activity when confronted in the laboratory with circumstances that trigger an obsession. Physiological reactivity decreases after the performance of compulsions.

Associated physical examination findings and general medical conditions.

Dermatological problems caused by excessive washing with water or caustic cleaning agents may be observed.

Specific Culture, Age, and Gender Features

Culturally prescribed ritual behavior is not in itself indicative of Obsessive-Compulsive Disorder unless it exceeds cultural norms, occurs at times and places judged inappropriate by others of the same culture, and interferes with social role functioning. Although cultural factors may not lead to Obsessive-Compulsive Disorder per se, religious and cultural beliefs may influence the themes of obsessions and compulsions (e.g., Orthodox Jews with religious compulsions may have symptoms focusing on dietary practices). Important life transitions and mourning may lead to an intensification of ritual behavior that may appear to be an obsession to a clinician who is not familiar with the cultural context.

Presentations of Obsessive-Compulsive Disorder in children are generally similar to those in adulthood. Washing, checking, and ordering rituals are particularly common in children. Children generally do not request help, and the symptoms may not be ego-dystonic. More often the problem is identified by parents, who bring the child in for treatment. Gradual declines in schoolwork secondary to impaired ability to concentrate have been reported. Like adults, children are more prone to engage in rituals at home than in front of peers, teachers, or strangers. For a small subset of children, Obsessive-Compulsive Disorder may be associated with Group A beta-hemolytic streptococcal infection (e.g., scarlet fever and "strep throat"). This form of Obsessive-Compulsive Disorder is characterized by prepubertal onset, associated neurological abnormalities (e.g., choreiform movements and motoric hyperactivity) and an abrupt onset of symptoms or an episodic course in which exacerbations are temporally related to the streptococcal infections. Older adults tend to show more obsessions concerning morality and washing rituals compared with other types of symptoms.

In adults, this disorder is equally common in males and females. However, in childhood-onset Obsessive-Compulsive Disorder, the disorder is more common in boys than in girls.

Prevalence

Community studies have estimated a lifetime prevalence of 2.5% and a 1-year prevalence of 0.5%–2.1% in adults. However, methodological problems with the assessment tool used raise the possibility that the true prevalence rates are much lower. Community studies of children and adolescents have estimated a lifetime prevalence of 1%–2.3% and a 1-year prevalence of 0.7%. Research indicates that prevalence rates of Obsessive-Compulsive Disorder are similar in many different cultures around the world.

Course

Although Obsessive-Compulsive Disorder usually begins in adolescence or early adulthood, it may begin in childhood. Modal age at onset is earlier in males than in females: between ages 6 and 15 years for males and between ages 20 and 29 years for females. For the most part, onset is gradual, but acute onset has been noted in some cases. The majority of individuals have a chronic waxing and waning course, with exacerbation of symptoms that may be related to stress. About 15% show progressive deterioration in occupational and social functioning. About 5% have an episodic course with minimal or no symptoms between episodes.

Familial Pattern

The concordance rate for Obsessive-Compulsive Disorder is higher for monozygotic twins than it is for dizygotic twins. The rate of Obsessive-Compulsive Disorder in first-degree biological relatives of individuals with Obsessive-Compulsive Disorder and in first-degree biological relatives of individuals with Tourette's Disorder is higher than that in the general population.

Differential Diagnosis

Obsessive-Compulsive Disorder must be distinguished from Anxiety Disorder Due to a General Medical Condition. The diagnosis is Anxiety Disorder Due to a General Medical Condition when the obsessions or compulsions are judged to be a direct physiological consequence of a specific general medical condition (see 293.84 Anxiety Disorder Due to a General Medical Condition). This determination is based on history, laboratory findings, or physical examination. A Substance-Induced Anxiety Disorder is distinguished from Obsessive-Compulsive Disorder by the fact that a substance (i.e., a drug of abuse, a medication, or exposure to a toxin) is judged to be etiologically related to the obsessions or compulsions (see Substance-Induced Anxiety Disorder).

Recurrent or intrusive thoughts, impulses, images, or behaviors may occur in the context of many other mental disorders. Obsessive-Compulsive Disorder is not diagnosed if the content of the thoughts or the activities is exclusively related to another mental disorder (e.g., preoccupation with appearance in Body Dysmorphic Disorder, preoccupation with a feared object or situation in Specific or Social Phobia, hair pulling in Trichotillomania). An additional diagnosis of Obsessive-Compulsive Disorder may still be warranted if there are obsessions or compulsions whose content is unrelated to the other mental disorder.

In a Major Depressive Episode, persistent brooding about potentially unpleasant circumstances or about possible alternative actions is common and is considered a mood-congruent aspect of depression rather than an obsession. For example, a depressed individual who ruminates that he is worthless would not be considered to have obsessions because such brooding is not ego-dystonic.

Generalized Anxiety Disorder is characterized by excessive worry, but such worries are distinguished from obsessions by the fact that the person experiences them as excessive concerns about real-life circumstances. For example, an excessive concern that one may lose one's job would constitute a worry, not an obsession. In contrast, the content of obsessions does not typically involve real-life problems, and the obsessions are experienced as inappropriate by the individual (e.g., the intrusive distressing idea that "God" is "dog" spelled backward).

If recurrent distressing thoughts are exclusively related to fears of having, or the idea that one has, a serious disease based on misinterpretation of bodily symptoms, then Hypochondriasis should be diagnosed instead of Obsessive-Compulsive Disorder. However, if the concern about having an illness is accompanied by rituals such as excessive washing or checking behavior related to concerns about the illness or about spreading it to other people, then an additional diagnosis of Obsessive-Compulsive Disorder may be indicated. If the major concern is about contracting an illness (rather than having an illness) and no rituals are involved, then a Specific Phobia of illness may be the more appropriate diagnosis.

The ability of individuals to recognize that the obsessions or compulsions are excessive or unreasonable occurs on a continuum. In some individuals with Obsessive-Compulsive Disorder, reality testing may be lost, and the obsession may reach delusional proportions (e.g., the belief that one has caused the death of another person by having willed it). In such cases, the presence of psychotic features may be indicated by an additional diagnosis of Delusional Disorder or Psychotic Disorder Not Otherwise Specified. The specifier With Poor Insight may be useful in those situations that are on the boundary between obsession and delusion (e.g., an individual whose extreme preoccupation with contamination, although exaggerated, is less intense than in a Delusional Disorder and is justified by the fact that germs are indeed ubiquitous).

The ruminative delusional thoughts and bizarre stereotyped behaviors that occur in Schizophrenia are distinguished from obsessions and compulsions by the fact that they are not ego-dystonic and not subject to reality testing. However, some individuals manifest symptoms of both Obsessive-Compulsive Disorder and Schizophrenia and warrant both diagnoses.

Tics (in Tic Disorder) and stereotyped movements (in Stereotypic Movement Disorder) must be distinguished from compulsions. A tic is a sudden, rapid, recurrent, nonrhythmic stereotyped motor movement or vocalization (e.g., eye blinking, tongue protrusion, throat clearing). A stereotyped movement is a repetitive, seemingly driven nonfunctional motor behavior (e.g., head banging, body rocking, self-biting). In contrast to a compulsion, tics and stereotyped movements are typically less complex and are not aimed at neutralizing an obsession. Some individuals manifest symptoms of both Obsessive-Compulsive Disorder and a Tic Disorder (especially Tourette's Disorder), and both diagnoses may be warranted.

Some activities, such as eating (e.g., Eating Disorders), sexual behavior (e.g., Paraphilias), gambling (e.g., Pathological Gambling), or substance use (e.g., Alcohol Dependence or Abuse), when engaged in excessively, have been referred to as "compulsive." However, these activities are not considered to be compulsions as defined in this manual because the person usually derives pleasure from the activity and may wish to resist it only because of its deleterious consequences.

Although Obsessive-Compulsive Personality Disorder and Obsessive-Compulsive Disorder have similar names, the clinical manifestations of these disorders are quite different. Obsessive-Compulsive Personality Disorder is not characterized by the presence of obsessions or compulsions and instead involves a pervasive pattern of preoccupation with orderliness, perfectionism, and control and must begin by early adulthood. If an individual manifests symptoms of both Obsessive-Compulsive Disorder and Obsessive-Compulsive Personality Disorder, both diagnoses can be given.

Superstitions and repetitive checking behaviors are commonly encountered in everyday life. A diagnosis of Obsessive-Compulsive Disorder should be considered only if they are particularly time consuming or result in clinically significant impairment or distress.

Appendix A-5: Narcissistic personality disorder

From the DSM-IV-TR [4th Ed.] Published by the American Psychiatric Association [APA]. Copyright APA. Used with Permission

301.81

Narcissistic Personality Disorder

Diagnostic criteria for

301.81

Narcissistic Personality Disorder

A pervasive pattern of grandiosity (in fantasy or behavior), need for admiration, and lack of empathy, beginning by early adulthood and present in a variety of contexts, as indicated by five (or more) of the following:has a grandiose sense of self-importance (e.g., exaggerates achievements and talents, expects to be recognized as superior without commensurate achievements) is preoccupied with fantasies of unlimited success, power, brilliance, beauty, or ideal lovebelieves that he or she is "special" and unique and can only be understood by, or should associate with, other special or high-status people (or institutions)requires excessive admirationhas a sense of entitlement, i.e., unreasonable expectations of especially favorable treatment or automatic compliance with his or her expectationsis interpersonally exploitative, i.e., takes advantage of others to achieve his or her own endslacks empathy: is unwilling to recognize or identify with the feelings and needs of othersis often envious of others or believes that others are envious of him or her shows arrogant, haughty behaviors or attitudes

Diagnostic Features

The essential feature of Narcissistic Personality Disorder is a pervasive pattern of grandiosity, need for admiration, and lack of empathy that begins by early adulthood and is present in a variety of contexts.

Individuals with this disorder have a grandiose sense of self-importance (Criterion 1). They routinely overestimate their abilities and inflate their accomplishments, often appearing boastful and pretentious. They may blithely assume that others attribute the same value to their efforts and may be surprised when the praise they expect and feel they deserve is not forthcoming. Often implicit in the inflated judgments of their own accomplishments is an underestimation (devaluation) of the contributions of others. They are often preoccupied with fantasies of unlimited success, power, brilliance, beauty, or ideal love (Criterion 2). They may ruminate about "long overdue" admiration and privilege and compare themselves favorably with famous or privileged people.

Individuals with Narcissistic Personality Disorder believe that they are superior, special, or unique and expect others to recognize them as such (Criterion 3). They may feel that they can only be understood by, and should only associate with, other people who are special or of high status and may attribute "unique,""perfect," or "gifted" qualities to those with whom they associate. Individuals with this disorder believe that their needs are special and beyond the ken of ordinary people. Their own self-esteem is enhanced (i.e., "mirrored") by the idealized value that they assign to those with whom they associate. They are likely to insist on having only the "top" person (doctor, lawyer, hairdresser, instructor) or being affiliated with the "best" institutions, but may devalue the credentials of those who disappoint them.

Individuals with this disorder generally require excessive admiration (Criterion 4). Their self-esteem is almost invariably very fragile. They may be preoccupied with how well they are doing and how favorably they are regarded by others. This often takes the form of a need for constant attention and admiration. They may expect their arrival to be greeted with great fanfare and are astonished if others do not covet their possessions. They may constantly fish for compliments, often with great charm. A sense of entitlement is evident in these individuals' unreasonable expectation of especially favorable treatment (Criterion 5). They expect to be catered to and are puzzled or furious when this does not happen. For example, they may assume that they do not have to wait in line and that their priorities are so important that others should defer to them, and then get irritated when others fail to assist "in their very important work." This sense of entitlement combined with a lack of sensitivity to the wants and needs of others may result in the conscious or unwitting exploitation of others (Criterion 6). They expect to be given whatever they want or feel they need, no matter what it might mean to others. For example, these individuals may expect great dedication from others and may overwork them without regard for the impact on their lives. They tend to form friendships or romantic relationships only if the other person seems likely to advance their purposes or otherwise enhance their self-esteem. They often usurp special privileges and extra resources that they believe they deserve because they are so special.

Individuals with Narcissistic Personality Disorder generally have a lack of empathy and have difficulty recognizing the desires, subjective experiences, and feelings of others (Criterion 7). They may assume that others are totally concerned about their welfare. They tend to discuss their own concerns in inappropriate and lengthy detail, while failing to recognize that others also have feelings and needs. They are often contemptuous and impatient with others who talk about their own problems and concerns. These individuals may be oblivious to the hurt their remarks may inflict (e.g., exuberantly telling a former lover that "I am now in the relationship of a lifetime!"; boasting of health in front of someone who is sick). When recognized, the needs, desires, or feelings of others are likely to be viewed disparagingly as signs of weakness or vulnerability. Those who relate to individuals with Narcissistic Personality Disorder typically find an emotional coldness and lack of reciprocal interest.

These individuals are often envious of others or believe that others are envious of them (Criterion 8). They may begrudge others their successes or possessions, feeling that they better deserve those achievements, admiration, or privileges. They may harshly devalue the contributions of others, particularly when those individuals have received acknowledgment or praise for their accomplishments. Arrogant, haughty behaviors characterize these individuals. They often display snobbish, disdainful, or patronizing attitudes (Criterion 9). For example, an individual with this disorder may complain about a clumsy waiter's "rudeness" or "stupidity" or conclude a medical evaluation with a condescending evaluation of the physician.

Associated Features and Disorders

Vulnerability in self-esteem makes individuals with Narcissistic Personality Disorder very sensitive to "injury" from criticism or defeat. Although they may not show it outwardly, criticism may haunt these individuals and may leave them feeling humiliated, degraded, hollow, and empty. They may react with disdain, rage, or defiant counterattack. Such experiences often lead to social withdrawal or an appearance of humility that may mask and protect the grandiosity. Interpersonal relations are typically impaired due to problems derived from entitlement, the need for admiration, and the relative disregard for the sensitivities of others. Though overweening ambition and confidence may lead to high achievement, performance may be disrupted due to intolerance of criticism or defeat. Sometimes vocational functioning can be very low, reflecting an unwillingness to take a risk in competitive or other situations in which defeat is possible. Sustained feelings of shame or humiliation and the attendant self-criticism may be associated with social withdrawal, depressed mood, and Dysthymic or Major Depressive Disorder. In contrast, sustained periods of grandiosity may be associated with a hypomanic mood. Narcissistic Personality Disorder is also associated with Anorexia Nervosa and Substance-Related Disorders (especially related to cocaine). Histrionic, Borderline, Antisocial, and Paranoid Personality Disorders may be associated with Narcissistic Personality Disorder.

Specific Age and Gender Features

Narcissistic traits may be particularly common in adolescents and do not necessarily indicate that the individual will go on to have Narcissistic Personality Disorder. Individuals with Narcissistic Personality Disorder may have special difficulties adjusting to the onset of physical and occupational limitations that are inherent in the aging process. Of those diagnosed with Narcissistic Personality Disorder, 50%–75% are male.

Prevalence

Estimates of prevalence of Narcissistic Personality Disorder range from 2% to 16% in the clinical population and are less than 1% in the general population.

Differential Diagnosis

Other Personality Disorders may be confused with Narcissistic Personality Disorder because they have certain features in common. It is, therefore, important to distinguish among these disorders based on differences in their characteristic features. However, if an individual has personality features that meet criteria for one or more Personality Disorders in addition to Narcissistic Personality Disorder, all can be diagnosed. The most useful feature in discriminating Narcissistic Personality Disorder from Histrionic, Antisocial, and Borderline Personality Disorders, whose interactive styles are respectively coquettish, callous, and needy, is the grandiosity characteristic of Narcissistic Personality Disorder. The relative stability of self-image as well as the relative lack of self-destructiveness, impulsivity, and abandonment concerns also help distinguish Narcissistic Personality Disorder from Borderline Personality Disorder. Excessive pride in achievements, a relative lack of emotional display, and disdain for others' sensitivities help distinguish Narcissistic Personality Disorder from Histrionic Personality Disorder. Although individuals with Borderline, Histrionic, and Narcissistic

Personality Disorders may require much attention, those with Narcissistic Personality Disorder specifically need that attention to be admiring. Individuals with Antisocial and Narcissistic Personality Disorders will share a tendency to be tough-minded, glib, superficial, exploitative, and unempathic. However, Narcissistic Personality Disorder does not necessarily include characteristics of impulsivity, aggression, and deceit. In addition, individuals with Antisocial Personality Disorder may not be as needy of the admiration and envy of others, and persons with Narcissistic Personality Disorder usually lack the history of Conduct Disorder in childhood or criminal behavior in adulthood. In both Narcissistic Personality Disorder and <u>Obsessive-Compulsive Personality Disorder</u>, the individual may profess a commitment to perfectionism and believe that others cannot do things as well. In contrast to the accompanying self-criticism of those with Obsessive-Compulsive Personality Disorder, individuals with Narcissistic Personality Disorder are more likely to believe that they have achieved perfection. Suspiciousness and social withdrawal usually distinguish those with <u>Schizotypal</u> or <u>Paranoid Personality Disorder</u> from those with Narcissistic Personality Disorder. When these qualities are present in individuals with Narcissistic Personality Disorder, they derive primarily from fears of having imperfections or flaws revealed. Grandiosity may emerge as part of <u>Manic</u> or <u>Hypomanic Episodes</u>, but the association with mood change or functional impairments helps distinguish these episodes from Narcissistic Personality Disorder. Narcissistic Personality Disorder must also be distinguished from symptoms that may develop in association with chronic substance use (e.g., Cocaine-Related Disorder Not Otherwise Specified).

Many highly successful individuals display personality traits that might be considered narcissistic. Only when these traits are inflexible, maladaptive, and persisting and cause significant functional impairment or subjective distress do they constitute Narcissistic Personality Disorder.

Appendix A-6: Dissociative identity disorder

[formerly known as Multiple Personality Disorder]

From the DSM-IV-TR [4th Ed.] Published by the American Psychiatric Association
[APA]. Copyright APA. Used with Permission

300.14 Dissociative Identity Disorder (formerly Multiple Personality Disorder)

Diagnostic criteria for

300.14

Dissociative Identity Disorder

The presence of two or more distinct identities or personality states (each with its own relatively enduring pattern of perceiving, relating to, and thinking about the environment and self).At least two of these identities or personality states recurrently take control of the person's behavior.Inability to recall important personal information that is too extensive to be explained by ordinary forgetfulness.The disturbance is not due to the direct physiological effects of a substance (e.g., blackouts or chaotic behavior during Alcohol Intoxication) or a general medical condition (e.g., complex partial seizures). Note: In children, the symptoms are not attributable to imaginary playmates or other fantasy play.

Diagnostic Features

The essential feature of Dissociative Identity Disorder is the presence of two or more distinct identities or personality states (Criterion A) that recurrently take control of behavior (Criterion B). There is an inability to recall important personal information, the extent of which is too great to be explained by ordinary forgetfulness (Criterion C). The disturbance is not due to the direct physiological effects of a substance or a general medical condition (Criterion D). In children, the symptoms cannot be attributed to imaginary playmates or other fantasy play.

Dissociative Identity Disorder reflects a failure to integrate various aspects of identity, memory, and consciousness. Each personality state may be experienced as if it has a distinct personal history, self-image, and identity, including a separate name. Usually there is a primary identity that carries the individual's given name and is passive, dependent, guilty, and depressed. The alternate identities frequently have different names and characteristics that contrast with the primary identity (e.g., are hostile, controlling, and self-destructive). Particular identities may emerge in specific circumstances and may differ in reported age and gender, vocabulary, general knowledge, or predominant affect. Alternate identities are experienced as taking control in sequence, one at the expense of the other, and may deny knowledge of one another, be critical of one another, or appear to be in open conflict. Occasionally, one or more powerful identities allocate time to the others. Aggressive or hostile identities may at times interrupt activities or place the others in uncomfortable situations.

Individuals with this disorder experience frequent gaps in memory for personal history, both remote and recent. The amnesia is frequently asymmetrical. The more passive identities tend to have more constricted memories, whereas the more hostile, controlling, or "protector" identities have more complete memories. An identity that is not in control may nonetheless gain access to consciousness by producing auditory or visual hallucinations (e.g., a voice giving instructions). Evidence of amnesia may be uncovered by reports from others who have witnessed behavior that is disavowed by the individual or by the individual's own discoveries (e.g., finding items of clothing at home that the individual cannot remember having bought). There may be loss of memory not only for recurrent periods of time, but also an overall loss of biographical memory for some extended period of childhood, adolescence, or even adulthood. Transitions among identities are often triggered by psychosocial stress. The time required to switch from one identity to another is usually a matter of seconds, but, less frequently, may be gradual. Behavior that may be frequently associated with identity switches include rapid blinking, facial changes, changes in voice or demeanor, or disruption in the individual's train of thoughts. The number of identities reported ranges from 2 to more than 100. Half of reported cases include individuals with 10 or fewer identities.

Associated Features and Disorders
Associated descriptive features and mental disorders.

Individuals with Dissociative Identity Disorder frequently report having experienced severe physical and sexual abuse, especially during childhood. Controversy surrounds the accuracy of such reports, because childhood memories may be subject to distortion and some individuals with this disorder are highly hypnotizable and especially vulnerable to suggestive influences. However, reports by individuals with Dissociative

Identity Disorder of a past history of sexual or physical abuse are often confirmed by objective evidence. Furthermore, persons responsible for acts of physical and sexual abuse may be prone to deny or distort their behavior. Individuals with Dissociative Identity Disorder may manifest posttraumatic symptoms (e.g., nightmares, flashbacks, and startle responses) or Posttraumatic Stress Disorder. Self-mutilation and suicidal and aggressive behavior may occur. Some individuals may have a repetitive pattern of relationships involving physical and sexual abuse. Certain identities may experience conversion symptoms (e.g., pseudoseizures) or have unusual abilities to control pain or other physical symptoms. Individuals with this disorder may also have symptoms that meet criteria for Mood, Substance-Related, Sexual, Eating, or Sleep Disorders. Self-mutilative behavior, impulsivity, and sudden and intense changes in relationships may warrant a concurrent diagnosis of Borderline Personality Disorder.

Associated laboratory findings.

Individuals with Dissociative Identity Disorder score toward the upper end of the distribution on measures of hypnotizability and dissociative capacity. There are reports of variation in physiological function across identity states (e.g., differences in visual acuity, pain tolerance, symptoms of asthma, sensitivity to allergens, and response of blood glucose to insulin).

Associated physical examination findings and general medical conditions.

There may be scars from self-inflicted injuries or physical abuse. Individuals with this disorder may have migraine and other types of headaches, irritable bowel syndrome, and asthma.

Specific Culture, Age, and Gender Features

Dissociative Identity Disorder has been found in individuals from a variety of cultures around the world. In preadolescent children, particular care is needed in making the diagnosis because the manifestations may be less distinctive than in adolescents and adults. Dissociative Identity Disorder is diagnosed three to nine times more frequently in adult females than in adult males; in childhood, the female-to-male ratio may be more even, but data are limited. Females tend to have more identities than do males, averaging 15 or more, whereas males average approximately 8 identities.

Prevalence

The sharp rise in reported cases of Dissociative Identity Disorder in the United States in recent years has been subject to very different interpretations. Some believe that the greater awareness of the diagnosis among mental health professionals has resulted in the identification of cases that were previously undiagnosed. In contrast, others believe that the syndrome has been overdiagnosed in individuals who are highly suggestible.

Course

Dissociative Identity Disorder appears to have a fluctuating clinical course that tends to be chronic and recurrent. The average time period from first symptom presentation to diagnosis is 6–7 years. Episodic and continuous courses have both been described. The disorder may become less manifest as individuals age beyond their late 40s, but may reemerge during episodes of stress or trauma or with Substance Abuse.

Familial Pattern

Several studies suggest that Dissociative Identity Disorder is more common among the first-degree biological relatives of persons with the disorder than in the general population.

Differential Diagnosis

Dissociative Identity Disorder must be distinguished from symptoms that are caused by the direct physiological effects of a general medical condition (e.g., seizure disorder) (see Mental Disorders Due to a General Medical Condition). This determination is based on history, laboratory findings, or physical examination. Dissociative Identity Disorder should be distinguished from dissociative symptoms due to complex partial seizures, although the two disorders may co-occur. Seizure episodes are generally brief (30 seconds to 5 minutes) and do not involve the complex and enduring structures of identity and behavior typically found in Dissociative Identity Disorder. Also, a history of physical and sexual abuse is less common in individuals with complex partial seizures. EEG studies, especially sleep deprived and with nasopharyngeal leads, may help clarify the differential diagnosis.

Symptoms caused by the direct physiological effects of a substance can be distinguished from Dissociative Identity Disorder by the fact that a substance (e.g., a drug of abuse or a medication) is judged to be etiologically related to the disturbance (see Substance-Induced Mental Disorders Included Elsewhere in the Manual).

The diagnosis of Dissociative Identity Disorder takes precedence over Dissociative Amnesia, Dissociative Fugue, and Depersonalization Disorder. Individuals with Dissociative Identity Disorder can be distinguished from those with trance and possession trance symptoms that would be diagnosed as Dissociative Disorder Not Otherwise Specified by the fact that those with pathological trance and possession trance symptoms typically describe external spirits or entities that have entered their bodies and taken control.

The differential diagnosis between Dissociative Identity Disorder and a variety of other mental disorders (including Schizophrenia and other Psychotic Disorders, Bipolar Disorder, With Rapid Cycling, Anxiety Disorders, Somatization Disorders, and Personality Disorders) is complicated by the apparently overlapping symptom presentations. For example, the presence of more than one dissociated personality state may be mistaken for a delusion or the communication from one identity to another may be mistaken for an auditory hallucination, leading to confusion with the Psychotic Disorders, and shifts between identity states may be confused with cyclical mood fluctuations leading to confusion with Bipolar Disorder). Factors that may support a diagnosis of Dissociative Identity Disorder are the presence of clear-cut dissociative symptomatology with sudden shifts in identity states, the persistence and consistency of identity-specific demeanors and behaviors over time, reversible amnesia, evidence of dissociative behavior that predates the clinical or forensic presentation (e.g., reports by family or co-workers), and high scores on measures of dissociation and hypnotizability in individuals who do not have the characteristic presentations of another mental disorder.

Dissociative Identity Disorder must be distinguished from Malingering in situations in which there may be financial or forensic gain and from Factitious Disorder in which there may be a pattern of help-seeking behavior.

Appendix A-7: See Specific phobias and post traumatic stress disorder, appendices A-2A and A-2B

From the DSM-IV-TR [4th Ed.] Published by the American Psychiatric Association [APA]. Copyright APA. Used with Permission

Appendix A-8: Bipolar Disorder

From the DSM-IV-TR [4th Ed.] Published by the American Psychiatric Association [APA]. Copyright APA. Used with Permission

Bipolar I Disorder, Most Recent Episode Unspecified

Bipolar II Disorder (Recurrent Major Depressive Episodes With Hypomanic Episodes)

Bipolar I Disorder, Most Recent Episode Unspecified

Criteria, except for duration, are currently (or most recently) met for a Manic (see Criteria for Manic Episode), a Hypomanic (see Criteria for Hypomanic Episode), a Mixed (see Criteria for Mixed Episode), or a Major Depressive Episode (see Criteria for Major Depressive Episode).There has previously been at least one Manic Episode (see Criteria for Manic Episode) or Mixed Episode (see Criteria for Mixed Episode).The mood symptoms cause clinically significant distress or impairment in social, occupational, or other important areas of functioning.The mood symptoms in Criteria A and B are not better accounted for by Schizoaffective Disorder and are not superimposed on Schizophrenia, Schizophreniform Disorder, Delusional Disorder, or Psychotic Disorder Not Otherwise Specified.The mood symptoms in Criteria A and B are not due to the direct physiological effects of a substance (e.g., a drug of abuse, a medication, or other treatment) or a general medical condition (e.g., hyperthyroidism).

Specify:

Longitudinal Course Specifiers (With and Without Interepisode Recovery) (see Longitudinal Course Specifiers (With and Without Full Interepisode Recovery))With Seasonal Pattern (applies only to the pattern of Major Depressive Episodes) (see Seasonal Pattern Specifier)With Rapid Cycling (see Rapid-Cycling Specifier)

Diagnostic Features

The essential feature of Bipolar I Disorder is a clinical course that is characterized by the occurrence of one or more Manic Episodes (see Manic Episode) or Mixed Episodes (see Mixed Episode). Often individuals have also had one or more Major Depressive Episodes (see Major Depressive Episode). Episodes of Substance-Induced Mood Disorder (due to the direct effects of a medication, other somatic treatments for depression, a drug of abuse, or toxin exposure) or of Mood Disorder Due to a General Medical Condition do not count toward a diagnosis of Bipolar I Disorder. In addition, the episodes are not better accounted for by Schizoaffective Disorder and are not superimposed on Schizophrenia, Schizophreniform Disorder, Delusional Disorder, or Psychotic Disorder Not Otherwise Specified. Bipolar I Disorder is subclassified in the fourth digit of the code according to whether the individual is experiencing a first episode (i.e., Single Manic Episode) or whether the disorder is recurrent. Recurrence is indicated by either a shift in the polarity of the episode or an interval between episodes of at least 2 months without manic symptoms. A shift in polarity is defined as a clinical course in which a Major Depressive Episode evolves into a Manic Episode or a Mixed Episode or in which a Manic Episode or a Mixed Episode evolves into a Major Depressive Episode. In contrast, a Hypomanic Episode that evolves into a Manic Episode or a Mixed Episode, or a Manic Episode that evolves into a Mixed Episode (or vice versa), is considered to be only a single episode. For recurrent Bipolar I Disorders, the nature of the current (or most recent) episode can be specified (Most Recent Episode Hypomanic, Most Recent Episode Manic, Most Recent Episode Mixed, Most Recent Episode Depressed, Most Recent Episode Unspecified).

Specifiers

If the full criteria are currently met for a Manic, Mixed, or Major Depressive Episode, the following specifiers may be used to describe the current clinical status of the episode and to describe features of the current episode:

Mild, Moderate, Severe Without Psychotic Features, Severe With Psychotic Features (see Severity/Psychotic/Remission Specifiers for Major Depressive Episode)With Catatonic Features (see Catatonic Features Specifier)With Postpartum Onset (see Postpartum Onset Specifier)

If the full criteria are not currently met for a Manic, Mixed or Major Depressive Episode, the following specifiers may be used to describe the current clinical status of the Bipolar I Disorder and to describe features of the most recent episode:

In Partial Remission, In Full Remission (see Severity/Psychotic/Remission Specifiers for Major Depressive Episode)With Catatonic Features (see Catatonic Features Specifier)With Postpartum Onset (see Postpartum Onset Specifier)

If criteria are currently met for a Major Depressive Episode, the following may be used to describe features of the current episode (or, if criteria are not currently met but the most recent episode of Bipolar I Disorder was a Major Depressive Episode, these specifiers apply to that episode):

Chronic (see Chronic Specifier for a Major Depressive Episode)With Melancholic Features (see Melancholic Features Specifier)With Atypical Features (see Atypical Features Specifier)

The following specifiers can be used to indicate the pattern of episodes:

Longitudinal Course Specifiers (With and Without Full Interepisode Recovery) (see Longitudinal Course Specifiers (With and Without Full Interepisode Recovery))With Seasonal Pattern (applies only to the pattern of Major Depressive Episodes) (see Seasonal Pattern Specifier)With Rapid Cycling (see Rapid-Cycling Specifier)

Recording Procedures

The diagnostic codes for Bipolar I Disorder are selected as follows:

The first three digits are 296. The fourth digit is 0 if there is a single Manic Episode. For recurrent episodes, the fourth digit indicates the nature of the current episode (or, if the Bipolar I Disorder is currently in partial or full remission, the nature of the most recent episode) as follows: 4 if the current or most recent episode is a Hypomanic Episode or a Manic Episode, 5 if it is a Major Depressive Episode, 6 if it is a Mixed Episode, and 7 if the current or most recent episode is Unspecified. The fifth digit (except for Bipolar I Disorder, Most Recent Episode Hypomanic, and Bipolar I Disorder, Most Recent Episode Unspecified) indicates the severity of the current episode if full criteria are met for a Manic, Mixed, or Major Depressive Episode as follows: 1 for Mild severity, 2 for Moderate severity, 3 for Severe Without Psychotic Features, 4 for Severe With Psychotic Features. If full criteria are not met for a Manic, Mixed, or Major Depressive Episode, the fifth digit indicates the current clinical status of the Bipolar I Disorder as follows: 5 for In Partial Remission, 6 for In Full Remission. If current severity or clinical status is unspecified, the fifth digit is 0. Other specifiers for Bipolar I Disorder cannot be coded. For Bipolar I Disorder, Most Recent Episode Hypomanic, the fifth digit is always 0. For Bipolar Disorder, Most Recent Episode Unspecified, there is no fifth digit.

In recording the name of a diagnosis, terms should be listed in the following order: Bipolar I Disorder, specifiers coded in the fourth digit (e.g., Most Recent Episode Manic), specifiers coded in the fifth digit (e.g., Mild, Severe With Psychotic Features, In

Partial Remission), as many specifiers (without codes) as apply to the current or most recent episode (e.g., With Melancholic Features, With Postpartum Onset), and as many specifiers (without codes) as apply to the course of episodes (e.g., With Rapid Cycling); for example, 296.54 Bipolar I Disorder, Most Recent Episode Depressed, Severe With Psychotic Features, With Melancholic Features, With Rapid Cycling.

Note that if the single episode of Bipolar I Disorder is a Mixed Episode, the diagnosis would be indicated as 296.0x Bipolar I Disorder, Single Manic Episode, Mixed.

Associated Features and Disorders

Associated descriptive features and mental disorders.

Completed suicide occurs in 10%—15% of individuals with Bipolar I Disorder. Suicidal ideation and attempts are more likely to occur when the individual is in a depressive or mixed state. Child abuse, spouse abuse, or other violent behavior may occur during severe Manic Episodes or during those with psychotic features. Other associated problems include school truancy, school failure, occupational failure, divorce, or episodic antisocial behavior. Bipolar Disorder is associated with Alcohol and other Substance Use Disorders in many individuals. Individuals with earlier onset of Bipolar I Disorder are more likely to have a history of current alcohol or other substance use problems. Concomitant alcohol and other substance use is associated with an increased number of hospitalizations and a worse course of illness. Other associated mental disorders include Anorexia Nervosa, Bulimia Nervosa, Attention-Deficit/Hyperactivity Disorder, Panic Disorder, and Social Phobia.

Associated laboratory findings.

There appear to be no laboratory features that are diagnostic of Bipolar I Disorder or that distinguish Major Depressive Episodes found in Bipolar I Disorder from those in Major Depressive Disorder or Bipolar II Disorder. Imaging studies comparing groups of individuals with Bipolar I Disorder with groups with Major Depressive Disorder or groups without any Mood Disorder tend to show increased rates of right-hemispheric lesions, or bilateral subcortical or periventricular lesions in those with Bipolar I Disorder.

Associated physical examination findings and general medical conditions.

An age at onset for a first Manic Episode after age 40 years should alert the clinician to the possibility that the symptoms may be due to a general medical condition or substance use. Current or past hypothyroidism or laboratory evidence of mild thyroid hypofunction may be associated with Rapid Cycling (see Rapid-Cycling Specifier). In addition, hyperthyroidism may precipitate or worsen manic symptoms in individuals with a preexisting Mood Disorder. However, hyperthyroidism in individuals without preexisting Mood Disorder does not typically cause manic symptoms.

Specific Culture, Age, and Gender Features

There are no reports of differential incidence of Bipolar I Disorder based on race or ethnicity. There is some evidence that clinicians may have a tendency to overdiagnose Schizophrenia (instead of Bipolar Disorder) in some ethnic groups and in younger individuals.

Approximately 10%—15% of adolescents with recurrent Major Depressive Episodes will go on to develop Bipolar I Disorder. Mixed Episodes appear to be more likely in adolescents and young adults than in older adults.

Recent epidemiological studies in the United States indicate that Bipolar I Disorder is approximately equally common in men and women (unlike Major Depressive Disorder, which is more common in women). Gender appears to be related to the number and type of Manic and Major Depressive Episodes. The first episode in males is more likely to be a Manic Episode. The first episode in females is more likely to be a Major Depressive Episode. In men the number of Manic Episodes equals or exceeds the number of Major Depressive Episodes, whereas in women Major Depressive Episodes predominate. In addition, Rapid Cycling (see Rapid-Cycling Specifier) is more common in women than in men. Some evidence suggests that mixed or depressive symptoms during Manic Episodes may be more common in women as well, although not all studies are in agreement. Thus, women may be at particular risk for depressive or intermixed mood symptoms. Women with Bipolar I Disorder have an increased risk of developing subsequent episodes in the immediate postpartum period. Some women have their first episode during the postpartum period. The specifier With Postpartum Onset may be used to indicate that the onset of the episode is within 4 weeks of delivery (see Postpartum Onset Specifier). The premenstrual period may be associated with worsening of an ongoing Major Depressive, Manic, Mixed, or Hypomanic Episode.

Prevalence

The lifetime prevalence of Bipolar I Disorder in community samples has varied from 0.4% to 1.6%.

413

Course

Average age at onset is 20 for both men and women. Bipolar I Disorder is a recurrent disorder—more than 90% of individuals who have a single Manic Episode go on to have future episodes. Roughly 60%—70% of Manic Episodes occur immediately before or after a Major Depressive Episode. Manic Episodes often precede or follow the Major Depressive Episodes in a characteristic pattern for a particular person. The number of lifetime episodes (both Manic and Major Depressive) tends to be higher for Bipolar I Disorder compared with Major Depressive Disorder, Recurrent. Studies of the course of Bipolar I Disorder prior to lithium maintenance treatment suggest that, on average, four episodes occur in 10 years. The interval between episodes tends to decrease as the individual ages. There is some evidence that changes in sleep-wake schedule such as occur during time zone changes or sleep deprivation may precipitate or exacerbate a Manic, Mixed, or Hypomanic Episode. Approximately 5%—15% of individuals with Bipolar I Disorder have multiple (four or more) mood episodes (Major Depressive, Manic, Mixed, or Hypomanic) that occur within a given year. If this pattern is present, it is noted by the specifier With Rapid Cycling (see Rapid-Cycling Specifier). A rapid-cycling pattern is associated with a poorer prognosis.

Although the majority of individuals with Bipolar I Disorder experience significant symptom reduction between episodes, some (20%—30%) continue to display mood lability and other residual mood symptoms. As many as 60% experience chronic interpersonal or occupational difficulties between acute episodes. Psychotic symptoms may develop after days or weeks in what was previously a nonpsychotic Manic or Mixed Episode. When an individual has Manic Episodes with psychotic features, subsequent Manic Episodes are more likely to have psychotic features. Incomplete interepisode recovery is more common when the current episode is accompanied by mood-incongruent psychotic features.

Familial Pattern

First-degree biological relatives of individuals with Bipolar I Disorder have elevated rates of Bipolar I Disorder (4%—24%), Bipolar II Disorder (1%—5%), and Major Depressive Disorder (4%—24%). Those individuals with Mood Disorder in their first-degree biological relatives are more likely to have an earlier age at onset. Twin and adoption studies provide strong evidence of a genetic influence for Bipolar I Disorder.

Differential Diagnosis

Major Depressive, Manic, Mixed, and Hypomanic Episodes in Bipolar I Disorder must be distinguished from episodes of a Mood Disorder Due to a General Medical Condition. The diagnosis is Mood Disorder Due to a General Medical Condition for episodes that are judged to be the direct physiological consequence of a specific general medical condition (e.g., multiple sclerosis, stroke, hypothyroidism) (see 293.83 Mood Disorder Due to a General Medical Condition). This determination is based on the history, laboratory findings, or physical examination.

A Substance-Induced Mood Disorder is distinguished from Major Depressive, Manic, or Mixed Episodes that occur in Bipolar I Disorder by the fact that a substance (e.g., a drug of abuse, a medication, or exposure to a toxin) is judged to be etiologically related to the mood disturbance (see Substance-Induced Mood Disorder). Symptoms like those seen in a Manic, Mixed, or Hypomanic Episode may be part of an intoxication with or withdrawal from a drug of abuse and should be diagnosed as a Substance-Induced Mood Disorder (e.g., euphoric mood that occurs only in the context of intoxication with cocaine would be diagnosed as Cocaine-Induced Mood Disorder, With Manic Features, With Onset During Intoxication). Symptoms like those seen in a Manic or Mixed Episode may also be precipitated by antidepressant treatment such as medication, electroconvulsive therapy, or light therapy. Such episodes may be diagnosed as a Substance-Induced Mood Disorder (e.g., Amitriptyline-Induced Mood Disorder, With Manic Features; Electroconvulsive Therapy—Induced Mood Disorder, With Manic Features) and would not count toward a diagnosis of Bipolar I Disorder. However, when the substance use or medication is judged not to fully account for the episode (e.g., the episode continues for a considerable period autonomously after the substance is discontinued), the episode would count toward a diagnosis of Bipolar I Disorder.

Bipolar I Disorder is distinguished from Major Depressive Disorder and Dysthymic Disorder by the lifetime history of at least one Manic or Mixed Episode. Bipolar I Disorder is distinguished from Bipolar II Disorder by the presence of one or more Manic or Mixed Episodes. When an individual previously diagnosed with Bipolar II Disorder develops a Manic or Mixed Episode, the diagnosis is changed to Bipolar I Disorder.

In Cyclothymic Disorder, there are numerous periods of hypomanic symptoms that do not meet criteria for a Manic Episode and periods of depressive symptoms that do not meet symptom or duration criteria for a Major Depressive Episode. Bipolar I Disorder is distinguished from Cyclothymic Disorder by the presence of one or more Manic or Mixed Episodes. If a Manic or Mixed Episode occurs after the first 2 years of Cyclothymic Disorder, then Cyclothymic Disorder and Bipolar I Disorder may both be diagnosed.

The differential diagnosis between Psychotic Disorders (e.g., Schizoaffective Disorder, Schizophrenia, and Delusional Disorder) and Bipolar I Disorder may be difficult (especially in adolescents) because these disorders may share a number of presenting symptoms (e.g., grandiose and persecutory delusions, irritability, agitation, and catatonic symptoms), particularly cross-sectionally and early in their course. In contrast to Bipolar I Disorder, Schizophrenia, Schizoaffective Disorder, and Delusional Disorder are all characterized by periods of psychotic symptoms that occur in the absence of prominent mood symptoms. Other helpful considerations include the accompanying symptoms, previous course, and family history. Manic and depressive symptoms may be present during Schizophrenia, Delusional Disorder, and Psychotic Disorder Not Otherwise Specified, but rarely with sufficient number, duration, and pervasiveness to meet criteria for a Manic Episode or a Major Depressive Episode. However, when full criteria are met (or the symptoms are of particular clinical significance), a diagnosis of Bipolar Disorder Not Otherwise Specified may be made in addition to the diagnosis of Schizophrenia, Delusional Disorder, or Psychotic Disorder Not Otherwise Specified.

If there is a very rapid alternation (over days) between manic symptoms and depressive symptoms (e.g., several days of purely manic symptoms followed by several days of purely depressive symptoms) that do not meet minimal duration criteria for a Manic Episode or Major Depressive Episode, the diagnosis is Bipolar Disorder Not Otherwise Specified.

296.89

Bipolar II Disorder (Recurrent Major Depressive Episodes With Hypomanic Episodes)
Diagnostic criteria for

296.89

Bipolar II Disorder

Presence (or history) of one or more Major Depressive Episodes (see Criteria for Major Depressive Episode).Presence (or history) of at least one Hypomanic Episode (see Criteria for Hypomanic Episode).There has never been a Manic Episode (see Criteria for Manic Episode) or a Mixed Episode (see Criteria for Mixed Episode).The mood symptoms in Criteria A and B are not better accounted for by Schizoaffective Disorder and are not superimposed on Schizophrenia, Schizophreniform Disorder, Delusional Disorder, or Psychotic Disorder Not Otherwise Specified.The symptoms cause clinically significant distress or impairment in social, occupational, or other important areas of functioning.

Specify current or most recent episode:

Hypomanic: if currently (or most recently) in a Hypomanic Episode (see Criteria for Hypomanic Episode)Depressed: if currently (or most recently) in a Major Depressive Episode (see Criteria for Major Depressive Episode)

If the full criteria are currently met for a Major Depressive Episode, specify its current clinical status and/or features:

Mild, Moderate, Severe Without Psychotic Features/Severe With Psychotic Features (see Severity/Psychotic/Remission Specifiers for Major Depressive Episode) Note: Fifth-digit codes specified on Criteria for Severity/Psychotic/Remission Specifiers for current (or most recent) Major Depressive Episode cannot be used here because the code for Bipolar II Disorder already uses the fifth digit.Chronic (see Chronic Specifier for a Major Depressive Episode)With Catatonic Features (see Catatonic Features Specifier)With Melancholic Features (see Melancholic Features Specifier)With Atypical Features (see Atypical Features Specifier)With Postpartum Onset (see Postpartum Onset Specifier)

If the full criteria are not currently met for a Hypomanic or Major Depressive Episode, specify the clinical status of the Bipolar II Disorder and/or features of the most recent Major Depressive Episode (only if it is the most recent type of mood episode):

In Partial Remission, In Full Remission (see Severity/Psychotic/Remission Specifiers for Major Depressive Episode) Note: Fifth-digit codes specified on Criteria for Severity/Psychotic/Remission Specifiers for current (or most recent) Major Depressive Episode cannot be used here because the code for Bipolar II Disorder already uses the fifth digit.Chronic (see Chronic Specifier for a Major Depressive Episode)With Catatonic Features (see Catatonic Features Specifier)With Melancholic Features (see Melancholic Features Specifier)With Atypical Features (see Atypical Features Specifier)With Postpartum Onset (see Postpartum Onset Specifier)

Specify:

Longitudinal Course Specifiers (With and Without Interepisode Recovery) (see Longitudinal Course Specifiers (With and Without Full Interepisode Recovery))With Seasonal Pattern (applies only to the pattern of Major Depressive Episodes) (see Seasonal Pattern Specifier)With Rapid Cycling (see Rapid-Cycling Specifier)

Diagnostic Features

The essential feature of Bipolar II Disorder is a clinical course that is characterized by the occurrence of one or more Major Depressive Episodes (Criterion A) accompanied by at least one Hypomanic Episode (Criterion B). Hypomanic Episodes should not be confused with the several days of euthymia that may follow remission of a Major Depressive Episode. The presence of a Manic or Mixed Episode precludes the diagnosis of Bipolar II Disorder (Criterion C). Episodes of Substance-Induced Mood Disorder (due to the direct physiological effects of a medication, other somatic treatments for depression, drugs of abuse, or toxin exposure) or of Mood Disorder Due to a General Medical Condition do not count toward a diagnosis of Bipolar II Disorder. In addition, the episodes must not be better accounted for by Schizoaffective Disorder and are not superimposed on Schizophrenia, Schizophreniform Disorder, Delusional Disorder, or Psychotic Disorder Not Otherwise Specified (Criterion D). The symptoms must cause clinically significant distress or impairment in social, occupational, or other important areas of functioning (Criterion E). In some cases, the Hypomanic Episodes themselves do not cause impairment. Instead, the impairment may result from the Major Depressive Episodes or from a chronic pattern of unpredictable mood episodes and fluctuating unreliable interpersonal or occupational functioning.

Individuals with Bipolar II Disorder may not view the Hypomanic Episodes as pathological, although others may be troubled by the individual's erratic behavior. Often individuals, particularly when in the midst of a Major Depressive Episode, do not recall periods of hypomania without reminders from close friends or relatives. Information from other informants is often critical in establishing the diagnosis of Bipolar II Disorder.

Specifiers

The following specifiers for Bipolar II Disorder should be used to indicate the nature of the current episode or, if the full criteria are not currently met for a Hypomanic or Major Depressive Episode, the nature of the most recent episode:

Hypomanic. This specifier is used if the current (or most recent) episode is a Hypomanic Episode.Depressed. This specifier is used if the current (or most recent) episode is a Major Depressive Episode.

If the full criteria are currently met for a Major Depressive Episode, the following specifiers may be used to describe the current clinical status of the episode and to describe features of the current episode:

Mild, Moderate, Severe Without Psychotic Features, Severe With Psychotic Features (see Severity/Psychotic/Remission Specifiers for Major Depressive Episode)Chronic (see Chronic Specifier for a Major Depressive Episode)With Catatonic Features (see Catatonic Features Specifier)With Melancholic Features (see Melancholic Features Specifier)With Atypical Features (see Atypical Features Specifier)With Postpartum Onset (see Postpartum Onset Specifier)

If the full criteria are not currently met for a Hypomanic or Major Depressive Episode, the following specifiers may be used to describe the current clinical status of the Bipolar II Disorder and to describe features of the most recent Major Depressive Episode (only if it is the most recent type of mood episode):

419

In Partial Remission, In Full Remission (see Severity/Psychotic/Remission Specifiers for Major Depressive Episode)Chronic (see Chronic Specifier for a Major Depressive Episode)With Catatonic Features (see Catatonic Features Specifier)With Melancholic Features (see Melancholic Features Specifier)With Atypical Features (see Atypical Features Specifier)With Postpartum Onset (see Postpartum Onset Specifier)

The following specifiers may be used to indicate the pattern or frequency of episodes: Longitudinal Course Specifiers (With and Without Interepisode Recovery) (see Longitudinal Course Specifiers (With and Without Full Interepisode Recovery))With Seasonal Pattern (applies only to the pattern of Major Depressive Episodes) (see Seasonal Pattern Specifier)With Rapid Cycling (see Rapid-Cycling Specifier)

Recording Procedures

The diagnostic code for Bipolar II Disorder is 296.89; none of the specifiers are codable. In recording the name of the diagnosis, terms should be listed in the following order: Bipolar II Disorder, specifiers indicating current or most recent episode (e.g., Hypomanic, Depressed), severity specifiers that apply to the current Major Depressive Episode (e.g., Moderate), as many specifiers describing features as apply to the current or most recent Major Depressive Episode (e.g., With Melancholic Features, With Postpartum Onset), and as many specifiers as apply to the course of episodes (e.g., With Seasonal Pattern); for example, 296.89 Bipolar II Disorder, Depressed, Severe With Psychotic Features, With Melancholic Features, With Seasonal Pattern.

Associated Features and Disorders

Associated descriptive features and mental disorders.

Completed suicide (usually during Major Depressive Episodes) is a significant risk, occurring in 10%—15% of persons with Bipolar II Disorder. School truancy, school failure, occupational failure, or divorce may be associated with Bipolar II Disorder. Associated mental disorders include Substance Abuse or Dependence, Anorexia Nervosa, Bulimia Nervosa, Attention-Deficit/Hyperactivity Disorder, Panic Disorder, Social Phobia, and Borderline Personality Disorder.

Associated laboratory findings.

There appear to be no laboratory features that are diagnostic of Bipolar II Disorder or that distinguish Major Depressive Episodes found in Bipolar II Disorder from those in Major Depressive Disorder or Bipolar I Disorder.

Associated physical examination findings and general medical conditions.

An age at onset for a first Hypomanic Episode after age 40 years should alert the clinician to the possibility that the symptoms may be due to a general medical condition or substance use. Current or past hypothyroidism or laboratory evidence of mild thyroid hypofunction may be associated with Rapid Cycling (see Rapid-Cycling Specifier). In addition, hyperthyroidism may precipitate or worsen hypomanic symptoms in individuals with a preexisting Mood Disorder. However, hyperthyroidism in other individuals does not typically cause hypomanic symptoms.

Specific Gender Features

Bipolar II Disorder may be more common in women than in men. Gender appears to be related to the number and type of Hypomanic and Major Depressive Episodes. In men the number of Hypomanic Episodes equals or exceeds the number of Major Depressive Episodes, whereas in women Major Depressive Episodes predominate. In addition, Rapid Cycling (see Rapid-Cycling Specifier) is more common in women than in men. Some evidence suggests that mixed or depressive symptoms during Hypomanic Episodes may be more common in women as well, although not all studies are in agreement. Thus, women may be at particular risk for depressive or intermixed mood symptoms. Women with Bipolar II Disorder may be at increased risk of developing subsequent episodes in the immediate postpartum period.

Prevalence

Community studies suggest a lifetime prevalence of Bipolar II Disorder of approximately 0.5%.

Course

Roughly 60%—70% of the Hypomanic Episodes in Bipolar II Disorder occur immediately before or after a Major Depressive Episode. Hypomanic Episodes often precede or follow the Major Depressive Episodes in a characteristic pattern for a particular person. The number of lifetime episodes (both Hypomanic Episodes and Major Depressive Episodes) tends to be higher for Bipolar II Disorder compared with Major Depressive Disorder, Recurrent. The interval between episodes tends to decrease as the individual ages. Approximately 5%—15% of individuals with Bipolar II Disorder have multiple (four or more) mood episodes (Hypomanic or Major Depressive) that occur within a given year. If this pattern is present, it is noted by the specifier With Rapid Cycling (see Rapid-Cycling Specifier). A rapid-cycling pattern is associated with a poorer prognosis.

Although the majority of individuals with Bipolar II Disorder return to a fully functional level between episodes, approximately 15% continue to display mood lability and interpersonal or occupational difficulties. Psychotic symptoms do not occur in Hypomanic Episodes, and they appear to be less frequent in the Major Depressive Episodes in Bipolar II Disorder than is the case for Bipolar I Disorder. Some evidence is consistent with the notion that marked changes in sleep-wake schedule such as occur during time zone changes or sleep deprivation may precipitate or exacerbate Hypomanic or Major Depressive Episodes. If a Manic or Mixed Episode develops in the course of Bipolar II Disorder, the diagnosis is changed to Bipolar I Disorder. Over 5 years, about 5%—15% of individuals with Bipolar II Disorder will develop a Manic Episode.

Familial Pattern

Some studies have indicated that first-degree biological relatives of individuals with Bipolar II Disorder have elevated rates of Bipolar II Disorder, Bipolar I Disorder, and Major Depressive Disorder compared with the general population.

Differential Diagnosis

Hypomanic and Major Depressive Episodes in Bipolar II Disorder must be distinguished from episodes of a Mood Disorder Due to a General Medical Condition. The diagnosis is Mood Disorder Due to a General Medical Condition for episodes that are judged to be the direct physiological consequence of a specific general medical condition (e.g., multiple sclerosis, stroke, hypothyroidism) (see 293.83 Mood Disorder Due to a General Medical Condition). This determination is based on the history, laboratory findings, or physical examination.

A Substance-Induced Mood Disorder is distinguished from Hypomanic or Major Depressive Episodes that occur in Bipolar II Disorder by the fact that a substance (e.g., a drug of abuse, a medication, or exposure to a toxin) is judged to be etiologically related to the mood disturbance (see Substance-Induced Mood Disorder). Symptoms like those seen in a Hypomanic Episode may be part of an intoxication with or withdrawal from a drug of abuse and should be diagnosed as a Substance-Induced Mood Disorder (e.g., a major depressive—like episode occurring only in the context of withdrawal from cocaine would be diagnosed as Cocaine-Induced Mood Disorder, With Depressive Features, With Onset During Withdrawal). Symptoms like those seen in a Hypomanic Episode may also be precipitated by antidepressant treatment such as medication, electroconvulsive therapy, or light therapy. Such episodes may be diagnosed as a Substance-Induced Mood Disorder (e.g., Amitriptyline-Induced Mood Disorder, With Manic Features; Electroconvulsive Therapy—Induced Mood Disorder, With Manic Features) and would not count toward a diagnosis of Bipolar II Disorder. However, when the substance use or medication is judged not to fully account for the episode (e.g., the episode continues for a considerable period autonomously after the substance is discontinued), the episode would count toward a diagnosis of Bipolar II Disorder.

Bipolar II Disorder is distinguished from Major Depressive Disorder by the lifetime history of at least one Hypomanic Episode. Attention during the interview to whether there is a history of euphoric or dysphoric hypomania is important in making a differential diagnosis. Bipolar II Disorder is distinguished from Bipolar I Disorder by the presence of one or more Manic or Mixed Episodes in the latter. When an individual previously diagnosed with Bipolar II Disorder develops a Manic or Mixed Episode, the diagnosis is changed to Bipolar I disorder.

In Cyclothymic Disorder, there are numerous periods of hypomanic symptoms and numerous periods of depressive symptoms that do not meet symptom or duration criteria for a Major Depressive Episode. Bipolar II Disorder is distinguished from Cyclothymic Disorder by the presence of one or more Major Depressive Episodes. If a Major Depressive Episode occurs after the first 2 years of Cyclothymic Disorder, the additional diagnosis of Bipolar II Disorder is given.

Bipolar II Disorder must be distinguished from Psychotic Disorders (e.g., Schizoaffective Disorder, Schizophrenia, and Delusional Disorder). Schizophrenia, Schizoaffective Disorder, and Delusional Disorder are all characterized by periods of psychotic symptoms that occur in the absence of prominent mood symptoms. Other helpful considerations include the accompanying symptoms, previous course, and family history.

Appendix A-9: See dissociative identity disorder, formerly known as multiple personality disorder, A-6

From the DSM-IV-TR [4th Ed.] Published by the American Psychiatric Association [APA]. Copyright APA. Used with Permission

Appendix A-10: Antisocial personality disorder, also known as psychopathic disorder

From the DSM-IV-TR [4th Ed.] Published by the American Psychiatric Association [APA]. Copyright APA. Used with Permission

301.7

Antisocial Personality Disorder

Diagnostic criteria for

301.7

Antisocial Personality Disorder

There is a pervasive pattern of disregard for and violation of the rights of others occurring since age 15 years, as indicated by three (or more) of the following:failure to conform to social norms with respect to lawful behaviors as indicated by repeatedly performing acts that are grounds for arrestdeceitfulness, as indicated by repeated lying, use of aliases, or conning others for personal profit or pleasureimpulsivity or failure to plan ahead irritability and aggressiveness, as indicated by repeated physical fights or assaultsreckless disregard for safety of self or othersconsistent irresponsibility, as indicated by repeated failure to sustain consistent work behavior or honor financial obligationslack of remorse, as indicated by being indifferent to or rationalizing having hurt, mistreated, or stolen from anotherThe individual is at least age 18 years.There is evidence of Conduct Disorder (see Diagnostic criteria for Conduct Disorder) with onset before age 15 years.The occurrence of antisocial behavior is not exclusively during the course of Schizophrenia or a Manic Episode.

Diagnostic Features

The essential feature of Antisocial Personality Disorder is a pervasive pattern of disregard for, and violation of, the rights of others that begins in childhood or early adolescence and continues into adulthood.

This pattern has also been referred to as psychopathy, sociopathy, or dyssocial personality disorder. Because deceit and manipulation are central features of Antisocial Personality Disorder, it may be especially helpful to integrate information acquired from systematic clinical assessment with information collected from collateral sources.

For this diagnosis to be given, the individual must be at least age 18 years (Criterion B) and must have had a history of some symptoms of Conduct Disorder before age 15 years (Criterion C). Conduct Disorder involves a repetitive and persistent pattern of behavior in which the basic rights of others or major age-appropriate societal norms or rules are violated. The specific behaviors characteristic of Conduct Disorder fall into one of four categories: aggression to people and animals, destruction of property, deceitfulness or theft, or serious violation of rules. These are described in more detail in Conduct Disorder.

The pattern of antisocial behavior continues into adulthood. Individuals with Antisocial Personality Disorder fail to conform to social norms with respect to lawful behavior (Criterion A1). They may repeatedly perform acts that are grounds for arrest (whether they are arrested or not), such as destroying property, harassing others, stealing, or pursuing illegal occupations. Persons with this disorder disregard the wishes, rights, or feelings of others. They are frequently deceitful and manipulative in order to gain personal profit or pleasure (e.g., to obtain money, sex, or power) (Criterion A2). They may repeatedly lie, use an alias, con others, or malinger. A pattern of impulsivity may be manifested by a failure to plan ahead (Criterion A3). Decisions are made on the spur of the moment, without forethought, and without consideration for the consequences to self or others; this may lead to sudden changes of jobs, residences, or relationships. Individuals with Antisocial Personality Disorder tend to be irritable and aggressive and may repeatedly get into physical fights or commit acts of physical assault (including spouse beating or child beating) (Criterion A4). Aggressive acts that are required to defend oneself or someone else are not considered to be evidence for this item. These individuals also display a reckless disregard for the safety of themselves or others (Criterion A5). This may be evidenced in their driving behavior (recurrent speeding, driving while intoxicated, multiple accidents). They may engage in sexual behavior or substance use that has a high risk for harmful consequences. They may neglect or fail to care for a child in a way that puts the child in danger.

Individuals with Antisocial Personality Disorder also tend to be consistently and extremely irresponsible (Criterion A6). Irresponsible work behavior may be indicated by significant periods of unemployment despite available job opportunities, or by abandonment of several jobs without a realistic plan for getting another job. There may also be a pattern of repeated absences from work that are not explained by illness either in themselves or in their family. Financial irresponsibility is indicated by acts such

428

as defaulting on debts, failing to provide child support, or failing to support other dependents on a regular basis. Individuals with Antisocial Personality Disorder show little remorse for the consequences of their acts (Criterion A7). They may be indifferent to, or provide a superficial rationalization for, having hurt, mistreated, or stolen from someone (e.g., "life's unfair,""losers deserve to lose," or "he had it coming anyway"). These individuals may blame the victims for being foolish, helpless, or deserving their fate; they may minimize the harmful consequences of their actions; or they may simply indicate complete indifference. They generally fail to compensate or make amends for their behavior. They may believe that everyone is out to "help number one" and that one should stop at nothing to avoid being pushed around.

The antisocial behavior must not occur exclusively during the course of Schizophrenia or a Manic Episode (Criterion D).

Associated Features and Disorders

Individuals with Antisocial Personality Disorder frequently lack empathy and tend to be callous, cynical, and contemptuous of the feelings, rights, and sufferings of others. They may have an inflated and arrogant self-appraisal (e.g., feel that ordinary work is beneath them or lack a realistic concern about their current problems or their future) and may be excessively opinionated, self-assured, or cocky. They may display a glib, superficial charm and can be quite voluble and verbally facile (e.g., using technical terms or jargon that might impress someone who is unfamiliar with the topic). Lack of empathy, inflated self-appraisal, and superficial charm are features that have been commonly included in traditional conceptions of psychopathy that may be particularly distinguishing of the disorder and more predictive of recidivism in prison or forensic settings where criminal, delinquent, or aggressive acts are likely to be nonspecific. These individuals may also be irresponsible and exploitative in their sexual relationships. They may have a history of many sexual partners and may never have sustained a monogamous relationship. They may be irresponsible as parents, as evidenced by malnutrition of a child, an illness in the child resulting from a lack of minimal hygiene, a child's dependence on neighbors or nonresident relatives for food or shelter, a failure to arrange for a caretaker for a young child when the individual is away from home, or repeated squandering of money required for household necessities. These individuals may receive dishonorable discharges from the armed services, may fail to be self-supporting, may become impoverished or even homeless, or may spend many years in penal institutions. Individuals with Antisocial Personality Disorder are more likely than people in the general population to die prematurely by violent means (e.g., suicide, accidents, and homicides).

Individuals with this disorder may also experience dysphoria, including complaints of tension, inability to tolerate boredom, and depressed mood. They may have associated Anxiety Disorders, Depressive Disorders, Substance-Related Disorders, Somatization Disorder, Pathological Gambling, and other disorders of impulse control. Individuals with Antisocial Personality Disorder also often have personality features that meet criteria for other Personality Disorders, particularly Borderline, Histrionic, and Narcissistic Personality Disorders. The likelihood of developing Antisocial Personality Disorder in adult life is increased if the individual experienced an early onset of Conduct Disorder (before age 10 years) and accompanying Attention-Deficit/Hyperactivity Disorder. Child abuse or neglect, unstable or erratic parenting, or inconsistent parental discipline may increase the likelihood that Conduct Disorder will evolve into Antisocial Personality Disorder.

Specific Culture, Age, and Gender Features

Antisocial Personality Disorder appears to be associated with low socioeconomic status and urban settings. Concerns have been raised that the diagnosis may at times be misapplied to individuals in settings in which seemingly antisocial behavior may be part of a protective survival strategy. In assessing antisocial traits, it is helpful for the clinician to consider the social and economic context in which the behaviors occur.

By definition, Antisocial Personality cannot be diagnosed before age 18 years. Antisocial Personality Disorder is much more common in males than in females. There has been some concern that Antisocial Personality Disorder may be underdiagnosed in females, particularly because of the emphasis on aggressive items in the definition of Conduct Disorder.

Prevalence

The overall prevalence of Antisocial Personality Disorder in community samples is about 3% in males and about 1% in females. Prevalence estimates within clinical settings have varied from 3% to 30%, depending on the predominant characteristics of the populations being sampled. Even higher prevalence rates are associated with substance abuse treatment settings and prison or forensic settings.

Course

Antisocial Personality Disorder has a chronic course but may become less evident or remit as the individual grows older, particularly by the fourth decade of life. Although this remission tends to be particularly evident with respect to engaging in criminal behavior, there is likely to be a decrease in the full spectrum of antisocial behaviors and substance use.

Familial Pattern

Antisocial Personality Disorder is more common among the first-degree biological relatives of those with the disorder than among the general population. The risk to biological relatives of females with the disorder tends to be higher than the risk to biological relatives of males with the disorder. Biological relatives of persons with this disorder are also at increased risk for Somatization Disorder and Substance-Related Disorders. Within a family that has a member with Antisocial Personality Disorder, males more often have Antisocial Personality Disorder and Substance-Related Disorders, whereas females more often have Somatization Disorder. However, in such families, there is an increase in prevalence of all of these disorders in both males and females compared with the general population. Adoption studies indicate that both genetic and environmental factors contribute to the risk of this group of disorders. Both adopted and biological children of parents with Antisocial Personality Disorder have an increased risk of developing Antisocial Personality Disorder, Somatization Disorder, and Substance-Related Disorders. Adopted-away children resemble their biological parents more than their adoptive parents, but the adoptive family environment influences the risk of developing a Personality Disorder and related psychopathology.

Differential Diagnosis

The diagnosis of Antisocial Personality Disorder is not given to individuals under age 18 years and is given only if there is a history of some symptoms of Conduct Disorder before age 15 years. For individuals over age 18 years, a diagnosis of Conduct Disorder is given only if the criteria for Antisocial Personality Disorder are not met.

When antisocial behavior in an adult is associated with a Substance-Related Disorder, the diagnosis of Antisocial Personality Disorder is not made unless the signs of

Antisocial Personality Disorder were also present in childhood and have continued into adulthood. When substance use and antisocial behavior both began in childhood and continued into adulthood, both a Substance-Related Disorder and Antisocial Personality Disorder should be diagnosed if the criteria for both are met, even though some antisocial acts may be a consequence of the Substance-Related Disorder (e.g., illegal selling of drugs or thefts to obtain money for drugs). Antisocial behavior that occurs exclusively during the course of Schizophrenia or a Manic Episode should not be diagnosed as Antisocial Personality Disorder.

Other Personality Disorders may be confused with Antisocial Personality Disorder because they have certain features in common. It is, therefore, important to distinguish among these disorders based on differences in their characteristic features. However, if an individual has personality features that meet criteria for one or more Personality Disorders in addition to Antisocial Personality Disorder, all can be diagnosed. Individuals with Antisocial Personality Disorder and Narcissistic Personality Disorder share a tendency to be tough-minded, glib, superficial, exploitative, and unempathic. However, Narcissistic Personality Disorder does not include characteristics of impulsivity, aggression, and deceit. In addition, individuals with Antisocial Personality Disorder may not be as needy of the admiration and envy of others, and persons with Narcissistic Personality Disorder usually lack the history of Conduct Disorder in childhood or criminal behavior in adulthood. Individuals with Antisocial Personality Disorder and Histrionic Personality Disorder share a tendency to be impulsive, superficial, excitement seeking, reckless, seductive, and manipulative, but persons with Histrionic Personality Disorder tend to be more exaggerated in their emotions and do not characteristically engage in antisocial behaviors. Individuals with Histrionic and Borderline Personality Disorders are manipulative to gain nurturance, whereas those with Antisocial Personality Disorder are manipulative to gain profit, power, or some other material gratification. Individuals with Antisocial Personality Disorder tend to be less emotionally unstable and more aggressive than those with Borderline Personality Disorder. Although antisocial behavior may be present in some individuals with Paranoid Personality Disorder, it is not usually motivated by a desire for personal gain or to exploit others as in Antisocial Personality Disorder, but rather is more often due to a desire for revenge.

Antisocial Personality Disorder must be distinguished from criminal behavior undertaken for gain that is not accompanied by the personality features characteristic of this disorder. Adult Antisocial Behavior (listed in the "Other Conditions That May Be a Focus of Clinical Attention" section, V71.01 Adult Antisocial Behavior) can be used to describe criminal, aggressive, or other antisocial behavior that comes to clinical attention but that does not meet the full criteria for Antisocial Personality Disorder. Only when antisocial personality traits are inflexible, maladaptive, and persistent and cause significant functional impairment or subjective distress do they constitute Antisocial Personality Disorder.

301.83

Appendix A-11A: Borderline personality disorder

From the DSM-IV-TR [4th Ed.] Published by the American Psychiatric Association [APA]. Copyright APA. Used with Permission

301.83

Borderline Personality Disorder

Diagnostic criteria for

301.83

Borderline Personality Disorder

A pervasive pattern of instability of interpersonal relationships, self-image, and affects, and marked impulsivity beginning by early adulthood and present in a variety of contexts, as indicated by five (or more) of the following:frantic efforts to avoid real or imagined abandonment. Note: Do not include suicidal or self-mutilating behavior covered in Criterion 5.a pattern of unstable and intense interpersonal relationships characterized by alternating between extremes of idealization and devaluationidentity disturbance: markedly and persistently unstable self-image or sense of selfimpulsivity in at least two areas that are potentially self-damaging (e.g., spending, sex, substance abuse, reckless driving, binge eating). Note: Do not include suicidal or self-mutilating behavior covered in Criterion 5.recurrent suicidal behavior, gestures, or threats, or self-mutilating behavioraffective instability due to a marked reactivity of mood (e.g., intense episodic dysphoria, irritability, or anxiety usually lasting a few hours and only rarely more than a few days)chronic feelings of emptinessinappropriate, intense anger or difficulty controlling anger (e.g., frequent displays of temper, constant anger, recurrent physical fights)transient, stress-related paranoid ideation or severe dissociative symptoms

Diagnostic Features

The essential feature of Borderline Personality Disorder is a pervasive pattern of instability of interpersonal relationships, self-image, and affects, and marked impulsivity that begins by early adulthood and is present in a variety of contexts.

Individuals with Borderline Personality Disorder make frantic efforts to avoid real or imagined abandonment (Criterion 1). The perception of impending separation or rejection, or the loss of external structure, can lead to profound changes in self-image, affect, cognition, and behavior. These individuals are very sensitive to environmental circumstances. They experience intense abandonment fears and inappropriate anger even when faced with a realistic time-limited separation or when there are unavoidable changes in plans (e.g., sudden despair in reaction to a clinician's announcing the end of the hour; panic or fury when someone important to them is just a few minutes late or must cancel an appointment). They may believe that this "abandonment" implies they are "bad." These abandonment fears are related to an intolerance of being alone and a need to have other people with them. Their frantic efforts to avoid abandonment may include impulsive actions such as self-mutilating or suicidal behaviors, which are described separately in Criterion 5.

Individuals with Borderline Personality Disorder have a pattern of unstable and intense relationships (Criterion 2). They may idealize potential caregivers or lovers at the first or second meeting, demand to spend a lot of time together, and share the most intimate details early in a relationship. However, they may switch quickly from idealizing other people to devaluing them, feeling that the other person does not care enough, does not give enough, is not "there" enough. These individuals can empathize with and nurture other people, but only with the expectation that the other person will "be there" in return to meet their own needs on demand. These individuals are prone to sudden and dramatic shifts in their view of others, who may alternately be seen as beneficent supports or as cruelly punitive. Such shifts often reflect disillusionment with a caregiver whose nurturing qualities had been idealized or whose rejection or abandonment is expected.

There may be an identity disturbance characterized by markedly and persistently unstable self-image or sense of self (Criterion 3). There are sudden and dramatic shifts in self-image, characterized by shifting goals, values, and vocational aspirations. There may be sudden changes in opinions and plans about career, sexual identity, values, and types of friends. These individuals may suddenly change from the role of a needy supplicant for help to a righteous avenger of past mistreatment. Although they usually have a self-image that is based on being bad or evil, individuals with this disorder may at times have feelings that they do not exist at all. Such experiences usually occur in situations in which the individual feels a lack of a meaningful relationship, nurturing, and support. These individuals may show worse performance in unstructured work or school situations.

Individuals with this disorder display impulsivity in at least two areas that are potentially self-damaging (Criterion 4). They may gamble, spend money irresponsibly, binge eat, abuse substances, engage in unsafe sex, or drive recklessly. Individuals with Borderline Personality Disorder display recurrent suicidal behavior, gestures, or threats, or self-mutilating behavior (Criterion 5). Completed suicide occurs in 8%–10% of such individuals, and self-mutilative acts (e.g., cutting or burning) and suicide threats and attempts are very common. Recurrent suicidality is often the reason that these individuals present for help. These self-destructive acts are usually precipitated by threats of separation or rejection or by expectations that they assume increased responsibility. Self-mutilation may occur during dissociative experiences and often brings relief by reaffirming the ability to feel or by expiating the individual's sense of being evil.

Individuals with Borderline Personality Disorder may display affective instability that is due to a marked reactivity of mood (e.g., intense episodic dysphoria, irritability, or anxiety usually lasting a few hours and only rarely more than a few days) (Criterion 6). The basic dysphoric mood of those with Borderline Personality Disorder is often disrupted by periods of anger, panic, or despair and is rarely relieved by periods of well-being or satisfaction. These episodes may reflect the individual's extreme reactivity to interpersonal stresses. Individuals with Borderline Personality Disorder may be troubled by chronic feelings of emptiness (Criterion 7). Easily bored, they may constantly seek something to do. Individuals with Borderline Personality Disorder frequently express inappropriate, intense anger or have difficulty controlling their anger (Criterion 8). They may display extreme sarcasm, enduring bitterness, or verbal outbursts. The anger is often elicited when a caregiver or lover is seen as neglectful, withholding, uncaring, or abandoning. Such expressions of anger are often followed by shame and guilt and contribute to the feeling they have of being evil. During periods of extreme stress, transient paranoid ideation or dissociative symptoms (e.g., depersonalization) may occur (Criterion 9), but these are generally of insufficient severity or duration to warrant an additional diagnosis. These episodes occur most frequently in response to a real or imagined abandonment. Symptoms tend to be transient, lasting minutes or hours. The real or perceived return of the caregiver's nurturance may result in a remission of symptoms.

Associated Features and Disorders

Individuals with Borderline Personality Disorder may have a pattern of undermining themselves at the moment a goal is about to be realized (e.g., dropping out of school just before graduation; regressing severely after a discussion of how well therapy is going; destroying a good relationship just when it is clear that the relationship could last). Some individuals develop psychotic-like symptoms (e.g., hallucinations, body-image distortions, ideas of reference, and hypnagogic phenomena) during times of stress. Individuals with this disorder may feel more secure with transitional objects (i.e., a pet or inanimate possession) than in interpersonal relationships. Premature death from suicide may occur in individuals with this disorder, especially in those with co-occurring Mood Disorders or Substance-Related Disorders. Physical handicaps may result from self-inflicted abuse behaviors or failed suicide attempts. Recurrent job losses, interrupted education, and broken marriages are common. Physical and sexual abuse, neglect, hostile conflict, and early parental loss or separation are more common in the childhood histories of those with Borderline Personality Disorder. Common co-occurring Axis I disorders include Mood Disorders, Substance-Related Disorders, Eating Disorders (notably Bulimia), Posttraumatic Stress Disorder, and Attention-Deficit/Hyperactivity Disorder. Borderline Personality Disorder also frequently co-occurs with the other Personality Disorders.

Specific Culture, Age, and Gender Features

The pattern of behavior seen in Borderline Personality Disorder has been identified in many settings around the world. Adolescents and young adults with identity problems (especially when accompanied by substance use) may transiently display behaviors that misleadingly give the impression of Borderline Personality Disorder. Such situations are characterized by emotional instability, "existential" dilemmas, uncertainty, anxiety-provoking choices, conflicts about sexual orientation, and competing social pressures to decide on careers. Borderline Personality Disorder is diagnosed predominantly (about 75%) in females.

Prevalence

The prevalence of Borderline Personality Disorder is estimated to be about 2% of the general population, about 10% among individuals seen in outpatient mental health clinics, and about 20% among psychiatric inpatients. It ranges from 30% to 60% among clinical populations with Personality Disorders.

Course

There is considerable variability in the course of Borderline Personality Disorder. The most common pattern is one of chronic instability in early adulthood, with episodes of serious affective and impulsive dyscontrol and high levels of use of health and mental health resources. The impairment from the disorder and the risk of suicide are greatest in the young-adult years and gradually wane with advancing age. Although the tendency toward intense emotions, impulsivity, and intensity in relationships is often lifelong, individuals who engage in therapeutic intervention often show improvement beginning sometime during the first year. During their 30s and 40s, the majority of individuals with this disorder attain greater stability in their relationships and vocational functioning. Follow-up studies of individuals identified through outpatient mental health clinics indicate that after about 10 years, as many as half of the individuals no longer have a pattern of behavior that meets full criteria for Borderline Personality Disorder.

Familial Pattern

Borderline Personality Disorder is about five times more common among first-degree biological relatives of those with the disorder than in the general population. There is also an increased familial risk for Substance-Related Disorders, Antisocial Personality Disorder, and Mood Disorders.

Differential Diagnosis

Borderline Personality Disorder often co-occurs with Mood Disorders, and when criteria for both are met, both may be diagnosed. Because the cross-sectional presentation of Borderline Personality Disorder can be mimicked by an episode of Mood Disorder, the clinician should avoid giving an additional diagnosis of Borderline Personality Disorder based only on cross-sectional presentation without having documented that the pattern of behavior has an early onset and a long-standing course.

Other Personality Disorders may be confused with Borderline Personality Disorder because they have certain features in common. It is, therefore, important to distinguish among these disorders based on differences in their characteristic features. However, if an individual has personality features that meet criteria for one or more Personality Disorders in addition to Borderline Personality Disorder, all can be diagnosed. Although Histrionic Personality Disorder can also be characterized by attention seeking, manipulative behavior, and rapidly shifting emotions, Borderline Personality Disorder is distinguished by self-destructiveness, angry disruptions in close relationships, and chronic feelings of deep emptiness and loneliness. Paranoid ideas or illusions may be present in both Borderline Personality Disorder and Schizotypal Personality Disorder, but these symptoms are more transient, interpersonally reactive, and responsive to external structuring in Borderline Personality Disorder. Although Paranoid Personality Disorder and Narcissistic Personality Disorder may also be characterized by an angry reaction to minor stimuli, the relative stability of self-image as well as the relative lack of self-destructiveness, impulsivity, and abandonment concerns distinguish these disorders from Borderline Personality Disorder. Although Antisocial Personality Disorder and Borderline Personality Disorder are both characterized by manipulative behavior, individuals with Antisocial Personality Disorder are manipulative to gain profit, power, or some other material gratification, whereas the goal in Borderline Personality Disorder is directed more toward gaining the concern of caretakers. Both Dependent Personality Disorder and Borderline Personality Disorder are characterized by fear of abandonment; however, the individual with Borderline Personality Disorder reacts to abandonment with feelings of emotional emptiness, rage, and demands, whereas the individual with Dependent Personality Disorder reacts with increasing appeasement and submissiveness and urgently seeks a replacement relationship to provide caregiving and support. Borderline Personality Disorder can further be distinguished from Dependent Personality Disorder by the typical pattern of unstable and intense relationships.

Borderline Personality Disorder must be distinguished from Personality Change Due to a General Medical Condition, in which the traits emerge due to the direct effects of a general medical condition on the central nervous system. It must also be distinguished from symptoms that may develop in association with chronic substance use (e.g., Cocaine-Related Disorder Not Otherwise Specified).

Borderline Personality Disorder should be distinguished from Identity Problem (see 313.82 Identity Problem), which is reserved for identity concerns related to a developmental phase (e.g., adolescence) and does not qualify as a mental disorder.

Appendix A-11B: Intermittent explosive disorder

From the DSM-IV-TR [4th Ed.] Published by the American Psychiatric Association [APA]. Copyright APA. Used with Permission

Diagnostic criteria for

312.34

Intermittent Explosive Disorder

Several discrete episodes of failure to resist aggressive impulses that result in serious assaultive acts or destruction of property.The degree of aggressiveness expressed during the episodes is grossly out of proportion to any precipitating psychosocial stressors.The aggressive episodes are not better accounted for by another mental disorder (e.g., Antisocial Personality Disorder, Borderline Personality Disorder, a Psychotic Disorder, a Manic Episode, Conduct Disorder, or Attention-Deficit/Hyperactivity Disorder) and are not due to the direct physiological effects of a substance (e.g., a drug of abuse, a medication) or a general medical condition (e.g., head trauma, Alzheimer's disease).

Diagnostic Features

The essential feature of Intermittent Explosive Disorder is the occurrence of discrete episodes of failure to resist aggressive impulses that result in serious assaultive acts or destruction of property (Criterion A). Examples of serious assaultive acts include striking or otherwise hurting another person or verbally threatening to physically assault another individual. Destruction of property entails purposeful breaking of an object of value; minor or unintentional damage is not of sufficient severity to meet this criterion. The degree of aggressiveness expressed during an episode is grossly out of proportion to any provocation or precipitating psychosocial stressor (Criterion B). A diagnosis of Intermittent Explosive Disorder is made only after other mental disorders that might account for episodes of aggressive behavior have been ruled out (e.g., Antisocial Personality Disorder, Borderline Personality Disorder, a Psychotic Disorder, a Manic Episode, Conduct Disorder, or Attention-Deficit/Hyperactivity Disorder) (Criterion C). The aggressive episodes are not due to the direct physiological effects of a substance (e.g., a drug of abuse, a medication) or a general medical condition (e.g., head trauma,

Alzheimer's disease) (Criterion C). The individual may describe the aggressive episodes as "spells" or "attacks" in which the explosive behavior is preceded by a sense of tension or arousal and is followed immediately by a sense of relief. Later the individual may feel upset, remorseful, regretful, or embarrassed about the aggressive behavior.

Associated Features and Disorders

Associated descriptive features and mental disorders.

Individuals with Intermittent Explosive Disorder sometimes describe intense impulses to be aggressive prior to their aggressive acts. Explosive episodes may be associated with affective symptoms (irritability or rage, increased energy, racing thoughts) during the aggressive impulses and acts, and rapid onset of depressed mood and fatigue after the acts. Some individuals may also report that their aggressive episodes are often preceded or accompanied by symptoms such as tingling, tremor, palpitations, chest tightness, head pressure, or hearing an echo. Individuals may describe their aggressive impulses as extremely distressing. The disorder may result in job loss, school suspension, divorce, difficulties with interpersonal relationships or other impairment in social or occupational spheres, accidents (e.g., in vehicles), hospitalization (e.g., because of injuries incurred in fights or accidents), financial problems, incarcerations, or other legal problems.

Signs of generalized impulsivity or aggressiveness may be present between explosive episodes. Individuals with Intermittent Explosive Disorder may report problems with chronic anger and frequent "subthreshold" episodes, in which they experience aggressive impulses but either manage to resist acting on them or engage in less destructive aggressive behaviors (e.g., screaming, punching a wall without damaging it). Individuals with narcissistic, obsessive, paranoid, or schizoid traits may be especially prone to having explosive outbursts of anger when under stress. Preliminary data suggest that Mood Disorders, Anxiety Disorders, Eating Disorders, Substance Use Disorders, and other Impulse-Control Disorders may be associated with Intermittent Explosive Disorder. Childhood histories may show severe temper tantrums, impaired attention, hyperactivity, and other behavioral difficulties, such as stealing and fire setting.

Associated laboratory findings.

There may be nonspecific EEG findings (e.g., slowing) or evidence of abnormalities on neuropsychological testing (e.g., difficulty with letter reversal). Signs of altered serotonin metabolism (e.g., low mean 5-hydroxyindoleacetic acid [5-HIAA] concentrations) have been found in the cerebrospinal fluid of some impulsive and temper-prone individuals, but the specific relationship of these findings to Intermittent Explosive Disorder is unclear.

Associated physical examination findings and general medical conditions.

There may be nonspecific or "soft" findings on neurological examinations (e.g., reflex asymmetries or mirror movements). Developmental difficulties indicative of cerebral dysfunction may be present (e.g., delayed speech or poor coordination). A history of neurological conditions (e.g., migraine headaches, head injury, episodes of unconsciousness, or febrile seizures in childhood) may be present. However, if the clinician judges that the aggressive behavior is a consequence of the direct physiological effects of a diagnosable general medical condition, the appropriate Mental Disorder Due to a General Medical Condition should be diagnosed instead (e.g., Personality Change Due to Head Trauma, Aggressive Type; Dementia of the Alzheimer's Type, Early Onset, Uncomplicated, With Behavioral Disturbance).

Specific Culture and Gender Features

Amok is characterized by an episode of acute, unrestrained violent behavior for which the person claims amnesia. Although traditionally seen in southeastern Asian countries, cases of amok have been reported in Canada and the United States. Unlike Intermittent Explosive Disorder, amok typically occurs as a single episode rather than as a pattern of aggressive behavior and is often associated with prominent dissociative features. Episodic violent behavior is more common in males than in females.

Prevalence

Reliable information is lacking, but Intermittent Explosive Disorder is apparently rare.

Course

Limited data are available on the age at onset of Intermittent Explosive Disorder, but it appears to be from childhood to the early 20s. Mode of onset may be abrupt and without a prodromal period. The course of Intermittent Explosive Disorder is variable, with the disorder having a chronic course in some individuals and a more episodic course in other individuals.

Familial Pattern

Mood Disorders, Substance Use Disorders, Intermittent Explosive Disorder, and other Impulse-Control Disorders may be more common among the first-degree relatives of individuals with Intermittent Explosive Disorder than among the general population.

Differential Diagnosis

Aggressive behavior can occur in the context of many other mental disorders. A diagnosis of Intermittent Explosive Disorder should be considered only after all other disorders that are associated with aggressive impulses or behavior have been ruled out. If the aggressive behavior occurs exclusively during the course of a delirium, a diagnosis of Intermittent Explosive Disorder is not given. Similarly, when the behavior develops as part of a dementia, a diagnosis of Intermittent Explosive Disorder is not made and the appropriate diagnosis is dementia with the specifier With Behavioral Disturbance. Intermittent Explosive Disorder should be distinguished from Personality Change Due to a General Medical Condition, Aggressive Type, which is diagnosed when the pattern of aggressive episodes is judged to be due to the direct physiological effects of a diagnosable general medical condition (e.g., an individual who has suffered brain injury from an automobile accident and subsequently manifests a change in personality characterized by aggressive outbursts). In rare cases, episodic violence may occur in individuals with epilepsy, especially of frontal and temporal origin (partial complex epilepsy).

A careful history and a thorough neurological evaluation are helpful in making the determination. Note that nonspecific abnormalities on neurological examination (e.g., "soft signs") and nonspecific EEG changes are compatible with a diagnosis of Intermittent Explosive Disorder and only preempt the diagnosis if they are indicative of a diagnosable general medical condition.

Aggressive outbursts may also occur in association with Substance Intoxication or Substance Withdrawal, particularly associated with alcohol, phencyclidine, cocaine and other stimulants, barbiturates, and inhalants. The clinician should inquire carefully about the nature and extent of substance use, and a blood or urine drug screen may be informative.

Intermittent Explosive Disorder should be distinguished from the aggressive or erratic behavior that can occur in <u>Oppositional Defiant Disorder</u>, <u>Conduct Disorder</u>, <u>Antisocial Personality Disorder</u>, <u>Borderline Personality Disorder</u>, a <u>Manic Episode</u>, and <u>Schizophrenia</u>. If the aggressive behavior is better accounted for as a diagnostic or associated feature of another mental disorder, a separate diagnosis of Intermittent Explosive Disorder is not given. However, impulsive aggression in individuals with Antisocial Personality Disorder and Borderline Personality Disorder can have specific clinical relevance, in which case both diagnoses may be made. For example, if an individual with an established diagnosis of Borderline Personality Disorder develops discrete episodes of failure to resist aggressive impulses resulting in serious physical or verbal assaultive acts or destruction of property, an additional diagnosis of Intermittent Explosive Disorder may be warranted.

"Anger attacks"—sudden spells of anger associated with autonomic arousal (tachycardia, sweating, flushing) and feelings of being out of control—have been described in individuals with <u>Major Depressive Disorder</u> and <u>Panic Disorder</u>. If these attacks occur only in the setting of a Major Depressive Episode or a Panic Attack, they should not count toward a diagnosis of Intermittent Explosive Disorder. However, if these anger attacks also occur at times other than during Major Depressive Episodes or Panic Attacks, and meet the Intermittent Explosive Disorder criterion for serious assaultive acts, then both diagnoses may be given.

Aggressive behavior may, of course, occur when no mental disorder is present. Purposeful behavior is distinguished from Intermittent Explosive Disorder by the presence of motivation and gain in the aggressive act. In forensic settings, individuals may malinger Intermittent Explosive Disorder to avoid responsibility for their behavior. Anger as a normal reaction to specific life events or environmental situations also needs to be distinguished from the anger that may occur as part of an aggressive episode in Intermittent Explosive Disorder, which occurs with little or no provocation.

Appendix B

Specie Enhancement Aspects of Psychiatric Disorders

by Herman Franck, Esq.

I. Introduction

It has come to my attention that the prevalence of so called psychiatric disorders is at a fairly substantial level within the human species. I am mindful of Professor Charles Darwin's theory that mother nature has a design for all species that generally help the species to survive.

With this in mind, I present the following theory:

Psychiatric disorders are part of the natural design of humans that enhance our species. They make us better, not worse.

II. Natural Selection

Consider what Professor Charles Darwin said about evolution. The following is from the introduction to Prof. Darwin's mastepiece, Darwin, Charles (1859) _On the Origin of Species by Means of Natural Selection, or the Preservation of Favoured Races in the Struggle for Life_ (1st ed.). London: John Murray. ISBN 1-4353-9386-4 [page 5]

> As many more individuals of each species are born than can possibly survive; and as, consequently, there is a frequently recurring struggle for existence, it follows that any being, if it vary however slightly in any manner profitable to itself, under the complex and sometimes varying conditions of life, will have a better chance of surviving, and thus be

447

naturally selected. From the strong principle of inheritance, any selected variety will tend to propagate its new and modified form.

This is from the conclusion of his book, at page 492:

> There is grandeur in this view of life, with its several powers, having been originally breathed into a few forms or into one; and that, whilst this planet has gone cycling on according to the fixed law of gravity, from so simple a beginning endless forms most beautiful and most wonderful have been, and are being, evolved.

III. Incidence of Psychiatric Disorders

Next, lets consider the incidence of psychiatric disorders in humans. The National Institute of Mental Health [http://www.nimh.nih.gov/statistics/1ANYDIS_ADULT.shtml] publishes data on the percentage of the USA population that is afflicted with some type of psychiatric disorder:

> Mental disorders are common in the United States, and in a given year approximately one quarter of adults are diagnosable for one or more disorders. While mental disorders are widespread in the population, the main burden of illness is concentrated among a much smaller proportion (about 6 percent, or 1 in 17) who suffer from a seriously debilitating mental illness.

According to one study cited by the NIMH, 46.4 percent of adults have some lifetime incidence of a psychiatric disorder. Kessler RC, Berglund PA, Demler O, Jin R, Walters EE. Lifetime prevalence and age-of-onset distributions of DSM-IV disorders in the National Comorbidity Survey Replication (NCS-R). Archives of General Psychiatry. 2005 Jun; 62(6):593-602.

A more recent report by the Substance Abuse and Mental Health Services Administration concludes that 20% of Americans suffer from some form of psyche disorder. SAMHSA, Mental Health, United States, 2010 [available online: http://www.samhsa.gov/data/2k12/MHUS2010/MHUS2010.pdf]

The following excerpts are from SAMHSA Mental Health, United States, 2010 at pages 5-6:

2.1.2 U.S. Population: Adults

(Exhibits 1 through 3 and Tables 1 through 7)

Estimates relevant to the U.S. adult population include the prevalence of mental disorders, serious mental illness (SMI), and serious psychological distress (SPD). The first estimates presented are of any mental illness (AMI) and SMI, which refers to diagnosable mental disorders that result in serious functional impairment (Tables 1 and 2). Other estimates describe the prevalence of major depressive episode (MDE) (Tables 3 and 4) and past 30-day SPD (Tables 5 through 7). SPD does not represent a diagnosis; rather, it reflects the presence of mental health symptoms that may negatively affect a person's ability to participate in family, community, and work life. This construct is measured by a symptom scale designed to assess recent psychological distress (within the past 30 days).

Whereas the concept of and term SMI is widely used by providers and policy makers, SPD is not as well known.

In 2009, 19.9 percent of the U.S. adult population experienced AMI (excluding substance use disorders) in the past year (Table 1). Prevalence of AMI was higher for females (23.8 percent) than males (15.6 percent). AMI also was higher for persons with Medicaid or Children's Health Insurance Program (CHIP) coverage (33.4 percent) or who are uninsured (24.9 percent) than for persons with private insurance (17.3 percent) or other coverage (16.1 percent). Exhibit 1 and Table 1 also indicate that 4.8 percent of adults had SMI, which equates to approximately 11 million U.S. adults annually. Table 2 shows the prevalence of specific types of mental disorder, including anxiety, mood, impulse control, and substance use disorders.

Major depressive disorder (MDD) is a serious mental disorder that can result in impairment and societal costs, including work disability and lost

450

productivity (Katon, 2009). MDE indicates the presence of a 2-week period in the past year when a person experienced depressed mood, which is one of the components of the diagnostic criteria for MDD. In 2009, 6.5 percent of U.S. adults experienced MDE in the past year (Table 3). Table 4 shows annual prevalence estimates of MDE from 2005 to 2009.

In 2009, 3.2 percent of U.S. adults experienced SPD in the past 30 days (Table 5). Exhibit 2 and Table 6 show annual prevalence estimates for SPD over time. The estimates demonstrate that national levels of recent psychological distress in adults have remained relatively stable for more than a decade. Table 7 displays rates of past 30-day SPD for persons with selected physical health disorders (e.g., asthma, diabetes, cancer).

2.1.3 U.S. Population: Children

(Exhibit 4 and Tables 8 through 12)

Children experience emotional and behavioral problems that are specific to childhood (e.g., separation anxiety, enuresis). Furthermore, the prevalence of mental disorders seen in adulthood, such as major depression, is different in children. Prevalence data for children in the United States include estimates of emotional and behavioral difficulties (Table 8), mental disorders (Table 9), attention deficit hyperactivity disorder (ADHD) (Table 10), and MDE (Tables 11 and 12).

It is estimated that one out of eight U.S. children has had some form of an emotional or behavioral health disorder in the past year (Merikangas et al., 2010). Based on combined data from 2001 through 2004, prevalence of diagnosable mental disorders with severe impairment was 11.3 percent for children aged 8 to 15, and ADHD was the most common specific disorder (Exhibit 4 and Table 9). In 2009, ADHD was more than twice as prevalent among males as   females (Table   10).   Table   11   presents   MDE prevalence rates for youth aged 12 to 17, broken out by demographic characteristics. In 2009, MDE was more prevalent among female youth (11.7 percent) than male youth (4.7 percent).

With these high incidence rates, let's agree that these so called disorders are actually part of our core human make up. They are too prevalent to be considered outliers or aberrations. They are so common that we have to ask, what was mother nature thinking of when she distributed these afflictions to us?

Or to put it another way, what would Professor Darwin say about natural selection and the reality of high levels of incidence of psychiatric disorders in people? Ironically, Professor Darwin himself has been said to have obsessive compulsive disorder. See Disabled World, Towards Tomorrow, Famous People with Obsessive Compulsive Disorder [http://www.disabled-world.com/artman/publish/famous-ocd.shtml] Disabled World, Towards Tomorrow, Famous People with Obsessive Compulsive Disorder, which has the following entry:

Charles Darwin - 1809-1882 Naturalist, author; OCD and stutterer.

Darwin's many lifelong and serious illnesses have been the subject of much speculation and study for over a century. Darwin stated that his health problems began as early as 1825 when he was only sixteen years old, and became incapacitating around age 28. The exact nature of Darwin's illness or illnesses remain mysterious at this time. Unless sophisticated molecular probing of his biological remains is allowed, no definitive diagnosis can be reached. It has been speculated that one of Darwin's conditions may have been Obsessive Compulsive Disorder.

With this OCD condition he was of course the perfect man to catalogue the species of the world.

IV. Natural Selection and Psychiatric Disorders

Would Professor Darwin have been able to catalogue the many species of the world if he hadn't been developed obsessive compulsive disorder?

Whatever the answer to this question, it shows the general concept that sometimes psyche disorders assist the human species by giving us powers and abilities that propel our understanding of our world upwards into new leagues. Professor Darwin's work in examining and cataloguing the many species of the world generated his theory of evolution, natural selection and survival of the fittest.

This is but one of many examples that can be laid out where the human specie has advanced its base of knowledge due to a psyche disorder. And while one or two or three of these can be dismissed as being mere coincidence, the shear numbers of them cannot.

Lets consider then the various psyche disorders, and some concepts of how these so called disorders could help promote the human species.

1.   Attention Deficit Disorder.

Picture a clan of cavemen long ago inside a fire warmed cave. There is an outdoor area teaming with various dangerous beasts hungry to eat a human. They need a few guards out there to protect themselves from being eaten. A good guard isn't fixated on a single tree or rock, he scans all over. A focused individual may make a wonderful engineer and designer of a bridge. But if you are worried about wild dogs, bears, tigers or lions you may want an ADD guard scanning every tree, every rock, every crevice, to see if he sees a pair of angry eyes.

2. Bi Polar Disorder.

The highs of Bi Polar disorder produce some very serious advances in the human quantum of knowledge. Do a google of "famous people with bipolar disorder." The list is rather impressive. Here are excerpts from http://en.wikipedia.org/wiki/List_of_people_with_bipolar_disorder:

Ernest Hemingway, **American author**

Jack London, American author

Friedrich Nietzsche, philosopher.[96]

Florence Nightingale, nurse and health campaigner.

Edgar Allan Poe, American Author

Vincent Van Gogh, Dutch Painter

Could these people have generated the contributions they made to human knowledge if they didn't have bipolar disorder?

3. Depressive Disorder.

According to Disabled World, Abraham Lincoln had bouts with depression. See, http://www.disabled-world.com/artman/publish/mooddisorders-famous.shtml

The downside of Bipolar also produces some extreme examples of new thought and mental capabilities.

Consider the words of Abraham Lincoln's Gettysburg Address, which is inscribed on the walls at the Lincoln Memorail in Washington DC:

FOUR SCORE AND SEVEN YEARS AGO OUR FATHERS
BROUGHT FORTH ON THIS CONTINENT A NEW NATION

CONCEIVED IN LIBERTY AND DEDICATED TO THE
PROPOSITION THAT ALL MEN ARE CREATED EQUAL •
NOW WE ARE ENGAGED IN A GREAT CIVIL WAR TESTING
WHETHER THAT NATION OR ANY NATION SO CONCEIVED AND
SO DEDICATED CAN LONG ENDURE • WE ARE MET ON A
GREAT BATTLEFIELD OF THAT WAR • WE HAVE COME TO
DEDICATE A PORTION OF THAT FIELD AS A FINAL RESTING
PLACE FOR THOSE WHO HERE GAVE THEIR LIVES THAT THAT
NATION MIGHT LIVE • IT IS ALTOGETHER FITTING AND
PROPER THAT WE SHOULD DO THIS • BUT IN A LARGER
SENSE WE CAN NOT DEDICATE~WE CAN NOT
CONSECRATE~WE CAN NOT HALLOW~THIS GROUND •
THE BRAVE MEN LIVING AND DEAD WHO STRUGGLED HERE HAVE
ONSECRATED IT FAR ABOVE OUR POOR POWER TO ADD OR
DETRACT • THE WORLD WILL LITTLE NOTE NOR LONG REMEMBER
WHAT WE SAY HERE BUT IT CAN NEVER FORGET WHAT THEY DID
HERE • IT IS FOR US THE LIVING RATHER TO BE DEDICATED HERE
TO THE UNFINISHED WORK WHICH THEY WHO FOUGHT HERE
HAVE THUS FAR SO NOBLY ADVANCED • IT IS RATHER FOR US TO
BE HERE DEDICATED TO THE GREAT TASK REMAINING BEFORE
US~THAT FROM THESE HONORED DEAD WE TAKE INCREASED
DEVOTION TO THAT CAUSE FOR WHICH THEY GAVE THE LAST
FULL MEASURE OF DEVOTION~THAT WE HERE HIGHLY RESOLVE
THAT THESE DEAD SHALL NOT HAVE DIED IN VAIN~THAT THIS
NATION UNDER GOD SHALL HAVE A NEW BIRTH OF
FREEDOM~AND THAT GOVERNMENT OF THE PEOPLE BY THE
PEOPLE FOR THE PEOPLE SHALL NOT PERISH FROM THE EARTH •

A recent example is Adele and her two songs *Rolling in the Deep* and *Someone Like You*.

Consider the opening lyrics to *Rolling in the Deep*, which are known by over 250 million fans:

Rolling in the Deep, by Adele

> There's a fire starting in my heart.
> Reaching a fever pitch and it's bring me out the dark
> Finally I can see you crystal clear.
> Go ahead and sell me out and I'll lay your ship bare.
> See how I'll leave, with every piece of you
> Don't underestimate the things that I will do
> There's a fire starting in my heart
> Reaching a fever pitch and its bring me out the dark.

Widespread press reports describe Adele's songs as being the results of her breakup with a love, which sent her into a shut in depression where she didn't want to see or speak with anyone. She was drinking quite a bit of wine, and came up with two songs that became part of her 21 CD. This CD was the highest grossing CD for 2011. It did better than Lady Gaga and Justin Beiber combined.

Her song *Rolling in the Deep* won best song for 2011 and a grammy. Her song Someone Like You won a grammy for best solo.

Could she have written these songs if she wasn't in the throes of depression? Would Lincoln have written the Emancipation Proclamation if he hadn't experienced the throes of depression?

4. Anti Social Disorder [Psychopath].

Long ago there was a need or one clan to eliminate another. Sadly this need still seems to persist today. The folks you want to gather together to go eliminate a neighboring clan are not the arts and craft group, you need the psychopaths. There is one example that comes to mind: a native american group in Colorado long ago eliminated a rival clan and ate them.

Consider this excerpt from *The Washington Post*, available on line at: http://www.trussel.com/prehist/news211.htm

Evidence of Cannibalism Found at Colorado Site

WASHINGTON - Archeologists have found the most conclusive evidence yet that the Anasazi people of North America's pre-Columbian southwest practiced cannibalism.

Three "pit houses" excavated in what is now southwest Colorado contained more than a thousand bones and bone fragments with marks showing that the bodies of at least four adults, two adolescents and a child had been dismembered and systematically butchered.

Moreover, the archaeological team at the so-called Cowboy Wash site also recovered ancient human feces, known as copralite, that contained human myoglobin, a protein found only in skeletal and heart muscles: "Consumption of human flesh did occur," the researchers concluded in Thursday's issue of the Journal Nature, because myoglobin would not be in the desiccated feces unless someone had eaten human muscle tissue.

I don't think this group of killer cannibals had any remorse for what they did.

For more on this topic, see Nassier Ghaemi MD, A First Rate Madness. Uncovering the Links Between Leadership and Mental Illness (Penguin Press 2011). Dr. Ghaemi opines that the best leaders during wartime are the psychopaths.

7.   Borderline Personality Disorder and Intermittent Explosive Disorder

The folks with these explosive personalities are often found at very high levels of life, including medical doctors, CEOs, lawyers, professors, etc. Princess Diana is reported to have been afflicted. There is some linkage to producing greatness and having a personality that will go "off" over some fairly trivial triggers. Not sure what that linkage is, but it is more than a coincidence that the high level people that have this disorder have achieved some pretty impressive accomplishments.

8.   Schizophrenia.

It may not surprise you to know some of the great geniuses that have been diagnosed with Schizoprenia [From: Disabled World - Disability News for all the Family: http://www.disabled-world.com/artman/publish/famous-schizophrenia.shtml#ixzz1s3D35Xok

John Nash - (born June 13, 1928) John Nash is an American mathematician working in differential geometry, game theory and partial differential equations. A hollywood movie has been made representing Nash, the movie itself name "A beautiful Mind" which was later nominated for 8 Oscars. The movie was based on his mathematical genius and his struggle with Schizophrenia. Nash would conduct scientific experiments in his room at a young age and would prefer to work alone. He was often rejected by his classmates and would most of the time laugh it off with practical jokes and intellectual superiority. He would see everyone elses daily activities as a distraction to his scientific work. Nash was awarded the John von Neumann Theory Prize for his invention of non-cooperative equilibria, now called Nash equilibria. Between 1945 and 1996 he had published a total of 23 scientific studies.

Eduard Einstein - (28 July 1910 - 25 October 1965) Eduard Einstein was extremely intelligent and always surpassed other students in school. Throughout his youth Eduard wanted to be a psychoanalyst but was afflicted with schizophrenia by the age of 20 which leaded him to be institutionalized several times. He died in an asylum at age 55 and his family lineage has been used to raise public awareness of schizophrenia.

Syd Barrett - (6 January 1946 - 7 July 2006) Syd was an English artist, songwriter, guitarist and artist being in the renowned rock band of Pink Floyd. He left the band in 1968 while many told stories of him having mental illnesses during his hard drug abuse. He eventually suffered a severe burnout and cut out all social aspects of his life while remaining in constant isolation. With time Barrett stopped contributing to music and would not like people mentioning his past with Pink Floyd.

Mary Todd Lincoln - (December 13, 1818 - July 16, 1882) Mary Todd was the wife of America's 16th President Abraham Lincoln and was the first lady of the United States. Abraham Lincoln always pursued his increasingly successful career and Mary Todd Lincoln was well educated and she shared the same fierce ambitions. In February 1862 her son Willie died at the age of 11 years old. After his death Mary spent a considerable amount of money to pay for mediums and spiritualists to try and contact her dead son, spending a lot of money the family did not have. She was known to suffer fro Schizophrenia.

Vaclav Nijinsky - Vaslav Fomich Nijinsky (March 12, 1889 - April 8, 1950) was a Polish ballet dancer and choreographer. Nijinsky was one of the most gifted male dancers in history, and he became celebrated for his virtuosity and for the depth and intensity of his characterizations. He could perform en pointe, a rare skill among male dancers at the time (Albright, 2004) and his ability to perform seemingly gravity-defying leaps was also legendary. Nijinsky had a nervous breakdown in 1919 and his career effectively ended.

He was diagnosed with schizophrenia and taken to Switzerland by his wife where he was treated by psychiatrist Eugene Bleuler. He spent the rest of his life in and out of psychiatric hospitals and asylums.

9.   Specific Phobias.

An irrational fear may seem odd. A fear of an elevator for example. Many of us go into them without thinking a second about a danger. Then there are those that are deathly afraid of them. How could this be? I have a concept that people may have suffered a past life experience with a danger, and are deathly afraid in this life of the same danger due to what happened to them in a past life. This may be a type of post-traumatic stress disorder involving past lives.

10.   Dissociative Personality Disorder [Multiple Personality Disorder]

Rita Carter wrote Multiplicity, The New Science of Personality, Identity, and The Self. (Little, Brown 2008). She opines that we all have different personalities within us. She gives the example of when we step back and say "I don't know what got into me" or "I just wasn't myself."

Thus the so called disorder is something that can be described as a common feature of humans. She refers to the other personality traits as "inner helpers" that come to bear when we ned them. For example the most delicate female in the world can become Xena warrior princess is someone threatens her child.

11.   Post Traumatic Stress Disorder.

This disorder is nature's way of helping us to deal with tragic events. Our minds may be numbed to them. And we become hyper vigilant, a bit like phobias, to avoid the harm ever again.

V. Conclusion

This theory of a pro-evolutionary natural selection purpose behind psychiatric disorders should be told. Perhaps telling it here will spawn further debate, examples and counter-examples.

More Beasts with Issues coming.

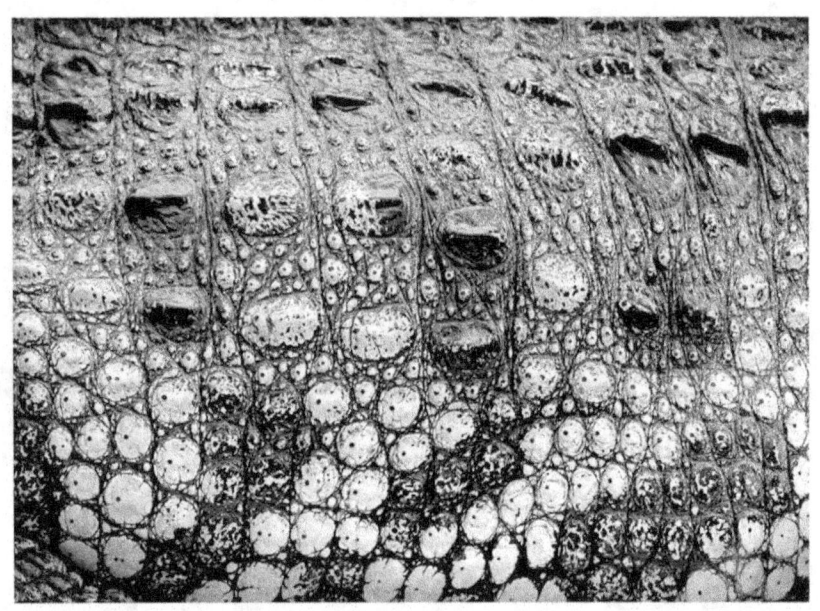

www.ingramcontent.com/pod-product-compliance
Lightning Source LLC
Chambersburg PA
CBHW082128290526
45794CB00008B/2968